PARALLEL PROGRAMMING WITH INTEL® PARALLEL STUDIO

MW00845031

Parallel Programming
with Intel® Parallel Studio XE

Parallel Programming
with Intel® Parallel Studio XE

Stephen Blair-Chappell
Andrew Stokes

John Wiley & Sons, Inc.

Parallel Programming with Intel® Parallel Studio XE

Published by
John Wiley & Sons, Inc.
10475 Crosspoint Boulevard
Indianapolis, IN 46256
www.wiley.com

Copyright © 2012 by John Wiley & Sons, Inc., Indianapolis, Indiana

Published simultaneously in Canada

ISBN: 978-0-470-89165-0
ISBN: 978-1-118-22113-6 (ebk)
ISBN: 978-1-118-23488-4 (ebk)
ISBN: 978-1-118-25954-2 (ebk)

Manufactured in the United States of America

10 9 8 7 6 5 4 3 2 1

For general information on our other products and services please contact our Customer Care Department within the United States at (877) 762-2974, outside the United States at (317) 572-3993 or fax (317) 572-4002.

Wiley publishes in a variety of print and electronic formats and by print-on-demand. Some material included with standard print versions of this book may not be included in e-books or in print-on-demand. If this book refers to media such as a CD or DVD that is not included in the version you purchased, you may download this material at http://booksupport.wiley.com. For more information about Wiley products, visit www.wiley.com.

Library of Congress Control Number: 2011945570

ABOUT THE AUTHORS

STEPHEN BLAIR-CHAPPELL has been working for Intel in the Software and Services Group (SSG) for the past 15 years. During his time with Intel, Stephen has worked on the compiler team as a developer and, more recently, as a technical consulting engineer helping users make the best use of the Intel software tools. Prior to working with Intel, Stephen was managing director of the UK office of CAD-UL, a German-based compiler and debugger company. During his time at CAD-UL Stephen was primarily responsible for technical support in the UK. Projects he worked on during that time included the design and specification of a graphical linker; the development and teaching of protected mode programming courses to programmers; and support to many varied companies in the telecoms, automotive, and embedded industries.

Stephen first studied electronics as a technician at Matthew Boulton Technical College, and later studied Applied Software Engineering at Birmingham City University (BCU), where he also eventually taught. Outside work, Stephen is a regular contributor to the life of his local church, St Martin in the Bull Ring, Birmingham, where he plays the organ, preaches, and leads the occasional service.

ANDREW STOKES is a retired lecturer in software and electronics at Birmingham City University (BCU), UK. Prior to lecturing, Andrew was a software developer in the research and commercial fields. He first started software development in the 1980s at Cambridge University Engineering Laboratory, where he worked on software for scanning electron microscopes. These software developments continued in the commercial field, where he worked on graphical programs in support of a Finite Element Analysis package.

During his time at BCU, Andrew developed many software simulation tools, including programs for artificial neural network simulation, CPU simulation, processor design, code development tools, and a PROLOG expert system. Andrew continues these software interests during retirement, with a healthy interest in games programming, such as 3-D chess, where parallel programming is paramount. Away from computing, Andrew is a keen gardener and particularly likes the vibrant colors of the typical English garden.

ABOUT THE TECHNICAL EDITORS

KITTUR GANESH is a Senior Technical Consulting Engineer at Intel, providing consulting, support, and training for more than 7 years on various software products targeting Intel architecture. Previously, for more than 6 years at Intel, Kittur designed and developed software primarily used for fracturing design data of Intel chips. Prior to joining Intel more than 13 years ago, Kittur was involved in developing commercial software in the EDA industry for more than 10 years. Kittur has a M.S. (Computer Science), M.S. (Industrial Engineering) and a B.S. (Mechanical Engineering).

PABLO HALPERN is a Senior Software Engineer at Intel Corporation, working in the parallel runtime libraries group. He is a member of the C++ Standards Committee and helped produce the recent C++11 revision of the standard. Pablo is the author of the well-received book, *The C++ Standard Library from Scratch* and a coauthor of the paper, *Reducers and Other Cilk++ Hyperobjects*, which was named best paper at ACM SPAA in 2009. He has more than three decades of experience in the software industry, with expertise in C++, language and compiler design, large-scale development and testing, and network management protocols. During this time, he has developed and taught both beginning and advanced courses on C++ programming. He currently lives in New Hampshire with his wife and two children.

CREDITS

ACQUISITIONS EDITOR
Paul Reese

PROJECT EDITOR
John Sleeva

TECHNICAL EDITORS
Kittur Ganesh
Pablo Halpern

PRODUCTION EDITOR
Daniel Scribner

COPY EDITOR
Kim Cofer

EDITORIAL MANAGER
Mary Beth Wakefield

FREELANCER EDITORIAL MANAGER
Rosemarie Graham

ASSOCIATE DIRECTOR OF MARKETING
David Mayhew

MARKETING MANAGER
Ashley Zurcher

BUSINESS MANAGER
Amy Knies

PRODUCTION MANAGER
Tim Tate

VICE PRESIDENT AND EXECUTIVE GROUP PUBLISHER
Richard Swadley

VICE PRESIDENT AND EXECUTIVE PUBLISHER
Neil Edde

ASSOCIATE PUBLISHER
Jim Minatel

PROJECT COORDINATOR, COVER
Katie Crocker

PROOFREADER
Mark Steven Long

INDEXER
Robert Swanson

COVER DESIGNER
LeAndra Young

COVER IMAGE
© Orlando Rosu / iStockPhoto

ACKNOWLEDGMENTS

FIRST, WE WOULD LIKE TO THANK our families and friends for being supportive and patient while we wrote this book.

We want to thank everyone at Wrox for giving us this opportunity. Thanks to Paul Reese, the acquisitions editor, who first asked us to write this book; to John Sleeva, the project editor, without whose help and guidance this book would not have made it to completion; to Kim Cofer, the copy editor; to Kittur Ganesh and Pablo Halpern, the technical editors, whose timely advice was a great help; to Gastón Hillar, who assisted by providing further technical reviews; and to the all the people in the graphics department, for your work on all the figures.

We'd like to say a special "thank you" to those who have contributed to the book, especially to Mark Davis, who wrote Chapter 10, "Parallel Advisor–Driven Design," and to Fred Tedeschi, who wrote Chapter 11, "Debugging Parallel Applications."

We also want to thank those who allowed us to write about their experiences in the case studies. Thanks to Lars Peters Endresen and Håvard Graff for their work in Chapter 13, "The World's First Sudoku 'Thirty-Niner'"; to Dr. Yann Golanski, for his input into Chapter 14, "Nine Tips to Parallel-Programming Heaven"; and to Hans Pabst, for his help with Chapter 15, "Parallel Track Fitting in the CERN Collider."

Our appreciation also goes to the many colleagues from Intel who tirelessly reviewed different chapters — in particular, Levent Akyil, Bernth Andersson, Julian Horn, Martyn Corden, Maxym Dmytrychenko, Max Domeika, Hubert Haberstock, Markus Metzger, Mark Sabahi, and Thomas Zipplies.

Finally, thanks to James Reinders, who encouraged the writing of this book and has been kind enough to provide the Foreword.

— STEPHEN BLAIR-CHAPPELL
ANDREW STOKES

CONTENTS

FOREWORD

Learning from real examples can filter theoretical distractions and inject less glamorous realities. Real experiences and examples help us to see what matters the most.

In this book, I am pleased that Stephen shares tips from his interviews to understand how to really use tools and develop parallel code. The result is a book with value that is not apparent from simply browsing the table of contents.

For instance, I know data layout critically affects the ability to process data in parallel, but I like to be convinced by real examples. The topic of data layouts, such as the need to use "structures of arrays" instead of "arrays of structures" (SOA vs. AOS), is brought to the forefront by Stephen asking the provocative question, "If you were doing the project again, is there anything you would do differently?" in the "Parallel Track Fitting in the CERN Collider" interview (Chapter 15). In response, the interviewed developer highlights the importance of data models to getting effective parallel programs. "The World's First Sudoku 'Thirty-Niner'" (Chapter 13) highlights that "much of the time taken was used in reworking the code so that there was less need to share data between the different running tasks."

The ubiquitous nature of parallelism affects every aspect of programming today. I'm encouraged by Stephen's work, which walks through each aspect instead of just coding. Covering the issues of discovery, debugging, and tuning is critical to understanding the challenges of parallel programming. I hope this book is an inspiration to all who read it.

"Think Parallel."

—James Reinders
Director, Parallel Evangelist, Intel
Portland, Oregon,
March 2012

INTRODUCTION

Nearly all the computers sold today have a multi-core processor, but only a small number of applications are written to take advantage of the extra cores. Most programmers are playing catch-up. A recent consultation with a group of senior programming engineers revealed the top three hurdles in adopting parallelism: the challenges of porting legacy code, the lack of education, and the lack of the right kinds of programming tools. This book helps to address some of these hurdles.

This book was written to help you use Intel Parallel Studio XE to write programs that use the latest features of multi-core CPUs. With the help of this book, you should be able to produce code that is fast, safe, and parallel. In addition to helping you write parallel code, some chapters cover other optimization topics that you can use in your code development, regardless of whether or not you are developing parallel code. Most of the chapters include hands-on activities that will help you apply the techniques being explained.

WHO THIS BOOK IS FOR

If you are writing parallel code or are interested in writing parallel code, this book is for you. The target audience includes:

➤ C and C++ developers who are adding parallelism to their code. The required technical skill is "average" to "experienced." Knowledge of C programming is a prerequisite.

➤ Students and academics who are looking to gain practical experience in making code parallel.

➤ Owners and users of Intel Parallel Studio XE.

WHAT THIS BOOK COVERS

This book, written using Parallel Studio XE 2011, shows how you can profile, optimize, and parallelize your code. By reading this book, you will learn how to:

➤ Analyze applications to determine the best place to implement parallelism.

➤ Implement parallelism using a number of language extensions/standards.

➤ Detect and correct difficult to find parallel errors.

➤ Tune parallel programs.

➤ Write code that is more secure.

➤ Use the compiler switches to create optimized code that takes advantage of the latest CPU extensions.

➤ Perform an architectural analysis to answer the question, "Is my program making the best use of the CPU?"

HOW THIS BOOK IS STRUCTURED

The book is comprised of the following parts:

➤ Part I: An Introduction to Parallelism

➤ Part II: Using Parallel Studio XE

➤ Part III: Case Studies

Every chapter in the book, with the exception of the first two chapters, offers hands-on activities. These activities are an important part of the book, although you can read the book without completing them.

Chapters 6–9 are intended to be used in sequence, showing how to add parallelism to your code using a well-tested, four-step methodology (analyze, implement, error-check, and tune). Examples of parallelism are provided using Cilk Plus, OpenMP, and Threading Building Blocks.

The case studies are based on larger projects and show how Parallel Studio XE was used to parallelize them.

WHAT YOU NEED TO USE THIS BOOK

You need the following to use this book:

➤ Intel Parallel Studio XE. You can download an evaluation version from the Intel Software Evaluation Center (http://software.intel.com/en-us/articles/intel-software-evaluation-center/).

➤ If you are using Windows:

➤ Visual Studio (not the Express edition) version 2005, 2008, or 2010

➤ Windows XP, Windows 2008, or Windows 7

➤ If you are using Linux:

➤ An installation of the GNU GCC compiler development tools

➤ Debian* 6.0; Red Hat Enterprise Linux* 4 (Deprecated), 5, 6; SUSE Linux Enterprise Server* 10, 11 SP1; or Ubuntu* 10.04

➤ A PC based on an IA-32 or Intel 64 architecture processor supporting the Intel Streaming SIMD Extensions 2 (Intel SSE2) instructions (Intel Pentium 4 processor or later), or compatible non-Intel processor. If you use a non-Intel processor, you will not be able to carry out the activities in Chapter 12, "Event-Based Analysis with VTune Amplifier XE."

CONVENTIONS

To help you get the most from the text and keep track of what's happening, we've used a number of conventions throughout the book.

 Boxes with a warning icon like this one hold important, not-to-be-forgotten information that is directly relevant to the surrounding text.

 The pencil icon indicates notes, tips, hints, tricks, and asides to the current discussion.

As for styles in the text:

➤ We *italicize* new terms and important words when we introduce them.

➤ We show keyboard strokes like this: Ctrl+A.

➤ We show filenames, URLs, and code within the text like so: `persistence.properties`.

➤ We present code in two different ways:

```
We use a monofont type with no highlighting for most code examples.
We use bold to emphasize code that is particularly important in the present context
or to show changes from a previous code snippet.
```

SOURCE CODE

As you work through the examples in this book, you may choose either to type in all the code manually, or to use the source code files that accompany the book. All the source code used in this book is available for download at www.wrox.com. When at the site, simply locate the book's title (use the Search box or one of the title lists) and click the Download Code link on the book's detail page to obtain all the source code for the book. Code that is included on the Web site is highlighted by the following icon:

**Available for
download on
Wrox.com**

Listings include the filename in the title. If it is just a code snippet, you'll find the filename in a code note such as this:

Code snippet filename

Because many books have similar titles, you may find it easiest to search by ISBN; this book's ISBN is 978-0-470-89165-0.

Once you download the code, just decompress it with your favorite compression tool. Alternately, you can go to the main Wrox code download page at www.wrox.com/dynamic/books/download .aspx to see the code available for this book and all other Wrox books.

ERRATA

We make every effort to ensure that there are no errors in the text or in the code. However, no one is perfect, and mistakes do occur. If you find an error in one of our books, like a spelling mistake or faulty piece of code, we would be very grateful for your feedback. By sending in errata, you may save another reader hours of frustration, and at the same time, you will be helping us provide even higher-quality information.

To find the errata page for this book, go to www.wrox.com and locate the title using the Search box or one of the title lists. Then, on the book details page, click the Book Errata link. On this page, you can view all errata that have been submitted for this book and posted by Wrox editors. A complete book list, including links to each book's errata, is also available at www.wrox.com/misc-pages /booklist.shtml.

If you don't spot "your" error on the Book Errata page, go to www.wrox.com/contact /techsupport.shtml and complete the form there to send us the error you have found. We'll check the information and, if appropriate, post a message to the book's errata page and fix the problem in subsequent editions of the book.

P2P.WROX.COM

For author and peer discussion, join the P2P forums at p2p.wrox.com. The forums are a web-based system for you to post messages relating to Wrox books and related technologies and interact with other readers and technology users. The forums offer a subscription feature to e-mail you topics of interest of your choosing when new posts are made to the forums. Wrox authors, editors, other industry experts, and your fellow readers are present on these forums.

At http://p2p.wrox.com, you will find a number of different forums that will help you, not only as you read this book, but also as you develop your own applications. To join the forums, just follow these steps:

1. Go to p2p.wrox.com and click the Register link.
2. Read the terms of use and click Agree.

3. Complete the required information to join, as well as any optional information you wish to provide, and click Submit.

4. You will receive an e-mail with information describing how to verify your account and complete the joining process.

 You can read messages in the forums without joining P2P, but in order to post your own messages, you must join.

Once you join, you can post new messages and respond to messages other users post. You can read messages at any time on the web. If you would like to have new messages from a particular forum e-mailed to you, click the Subscribe to this Forum icon by the forum name in the forum listing.

For more information about how to use the Wrox P2P, be sure to read the P2P FAQs for answers to questions about how the forum software works, as well as many common questions specific to P2P and Wrox books. To read the FAQs, click the FAQ link on any P2P page.

PART I
An Introduction to Parallelism

Parallelism Today

➤ How parallelism arrived and why parallel programming is feared

➤ Different parallel models that you can use, along with some potential pitfalls this new type of programming introduces

➤ How to predict the behavior of parallel programs

The introduction of multi-core processors brings a new set of challenges for the programmer. After a brief discussion on the power density race, this chapter looks at the top six parallel programming challenges. Finally, the chapter presents a number of different programming models that you can use to add parallelism to your code.

THE ARRIVAL OF PARALLELISM

Parallelism is not new; indeed, parallel computer architectures were available in the 1950s. What is new is that parallelism is ubiquitous, available to everyone, and now in every computer.

The Power Density Race

Over the recent decades, computer CPUs have become faster and more powerful; the clock speed of CPUs doubled almost every 18 months. This rise in speed led to a dramatic rise in the power density. Figure 1-1 shows the power density of different generations of processors. *Power density* is a measure of how much heat is generated by the CPU, and is usually dissipated by a heat sink and cooling system. If the trend of the 1990s were to continue into the twenty-first century, the heat needing to be dissipated would be comparable to that of the surface of the sun — we would be at meltdown! A tongue-in-cheek cartoon competition appeared on an x86 user-forum website in the early 1990s. The challenge was to design an alternative use of the Intel Pentium Processor. The winner suggested a high-tech oven hot plate design using four CPUs side-by-side.

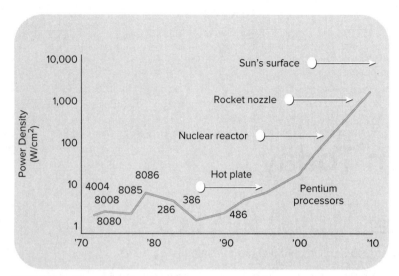

FIGURE 1-1: The power density race

Increasing CPU clock speed to get better software performance is well established. Computer game players use overclocking to get their games running faster. *Overclocking* involves increasing the CPU clock speed so that instructions are executed faster. Processors often are run at speeds above what the manufacturer specifies. One downside to overclocking is that it produces extra heat, which needs dissipating. Increasing the speed of a CPU by just a fraction can result in a chip that runs much hotter. So, for example, increasing a CPU clock speed by just over 20 percent causes the power consumption to be almost doubled.

Increasing clock speed was an important tool for the silicon manufacturer. Many of the performance claims and marketing messages were based purely on the clock speed. Intel and AMD typically were leapfrogging over each other to produce faster and faster chips — all of great benefit to the computer user. Eventually, as the physical limitations of the silicon were reached, further increases in CPU speed gave diminishing returns.

Even though the speed of the CPU is no longer growing rapidly, the number of transistors used in CPU design is still growing, with the new transistors used to supply added functionality and performance. Most of the recent performance gains in CPUs are because of improved connections to external memory, improved transistor design, extra parallel execution units, wider data registers and buses, and placing multiple cores on one die. The 3D-transistor, announced in May 2011, which exhibits reduced current leakage and improved switching times while lowering power consumption, will contribute to future microarchitecture improvements.

The Emergence of Multi-Core and Many-Core Computing

Hidden in the power density race is the secret to why multi-core CPUs have become today's solution to the limits on performance.

Rather than overclocking a CPU, if it were underclocked by 20 percent, the power consumption would be almost half the original value. By putting two of these underclocked CPUs on the same die, you get a total performance improvement of more than 70 percent, with a power consumption being about the same as the original single-core processor. The first multi-core devices consisted of two underclocked CPUs on the same chip. Reducing power consumption is one of the key ingredients to the successful design of multi-core devices.

Gordon E. Moore observed that the number of transistors that can be placed on integrated circuits doubles about every two years — famously referred to as *Moore's Law*. Today, those transistors are being used to add additional cores. The current trend is that the number of cores in a CPU is doubling about every 18 months. Future devices are likely to have dozens of cores and are referred to as being *many-core*.

It is already possible to buy a regular PC machine that supports many hardware threads. For example, the workstation used to test some of the example programs in this book can support 24 parallel execution paths by having:

➤   A two-socket motherboard

➤   Six-core XEON CPUs

➤   Hyper-threading, in which some of the internal electronics of the core are duplicated to double the amount of hardware threads that can be supported

One of Intel's first many-core devices was the Intel Teraflop Research Chip. The processor, which came out of the Intel research facilities, had 80 cores and could do one teraflop, which is one trillion floating-point calculations per second. In 2007, this device was demonstrated to the public. As shown in Figure 1-2, the heat sink is quite small — an indication that despite its huge processing capability, it is energy efficient.

FIGURE 1-2: The 80-core Teraflop Research Chip

There is the huge difference in power consumption between the lower and higher clock speeds; Table 1-1 provides sample values. With a one-teraflop performance (1×10^{12} floating-point calculations per second), 62 watts of power is used; to get 1.81 teraflops of performance, the power consumption is four times larger.

TABLE 1-1: Power-to-Performance Relationship of the Teraflop Research Chip

SPEED (GHZ)	POWER (WATTS)	PERFORMANCE (TERAFLOPS)
3.16	62	1.01
5.1	175	1.63
5.7	265	1.81

The Intel Many Integrated Core Architecture (MIC) captures the essentials of Intel's current many-core strategy (see Figure 1-3). Each of the cores is connected together on an internal network. A 32-core preproduction version of such devices is already available.

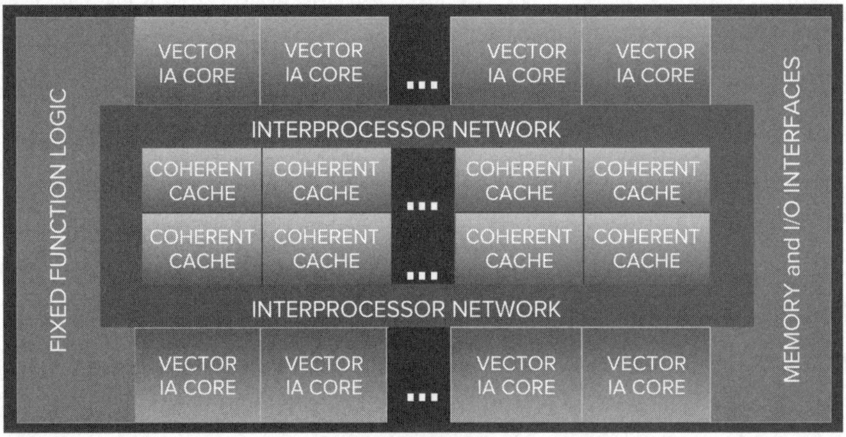

FIGURE 1-3: Intel's many-core architecture

Many programmers are still operating with a single-core computing mind-set and have not taken up the opportunities that multi-core programming brings.

For some programmers, the divide between what is available in hardware and what the software is doing is closing; for others, the gap is getting bigger.

Adding parallelism to programs requires new skills, knowledge, and the appropriate software development tools. This book introduces Intel Parallel Studio XE, a software suite that helps the C\C++ and Fortran programmer to transition from serial programmer to parallel programmer. Parallel Studio XE is designed to help the programmer in all phases of the development of parallel code.

The challenge (and opportunity) for the developer is knowing how to reap the rewards of improved performance through parallelism.

THE TOP SIX CHALLENGES

In a recent open forum in Nice, France, a group of software programmers and project managers were asked, "What's stopping you adopting parallelism?" Many reasons were cited, but when the comments were collated, a picture began to emerge of a number of commonly held reasons.

Those who took part in this exercise were from some of the key players in the software industry in Europe, representing both well-established software houses and newer high-tech startup companies. The views they expressed were founded on commercial and technical concerns — both rational and irrational.

This book aims to show some practical parallel programming techniques you can use to address some of these challenges.

Legacy Code

Adding parallelism to existing code does not sound that unusual. It is common for a programmer to start off with serial code and incrementally introduce parallelism. In fact, the method described in this book focuses on how to analyze serial programs, find out the best place for introducing parallelism, and then debug and tune the parallel application.

Some developers spoke of having several million lines of code to maintain. Some of the code was 30 or 40 years old, with the original designers no longer working with the company. With such a large code base, it is not always easy to understand how the code works. The style of old code does not always lend itself to easy partitioning for parallelization. Concepts of information hiding, modularization, and other standard software engineering practices are not always present in legacy code.

Several years ago, while visiting a large telecom company, I found the following comment in some C code: "If anyone knows what this code does, ring me on extension 1234." The code was startup code for a hand-rolled operating system and was part of a large monolithic code base, written 20 or so years earlier. Understanding legacy code is not a new problem that has just reared its head. When adding parallelism to legacy code, it is important that the legacy code is well understood.

 Chapter 16, "Parallelizing Legacy Code," shows you how to parallelize legacy C code.

Tools

Almost all the developers at the Nice conference expressed a desire to have better tools for creating and debugging parallel code. An ideal scenario was to have tools that just did all the parallelism automatically, but most of those present at the forum recognized that this sort of solution was not on the near horizon.

Tools should make implementing parallelism easier, not harder. They should integrate seamlessly into the current developer's environment to support both interactive and script-driven development.

Programmers need good thread-aware tools for debugging parallel applications. Using `printf()` to debug a serial application is fairly common; indeed, some developers do all their debugging using `printf()`, claiming it is much easier than using a debugger. However, when debugging a parallel program, using just `printf()` is impractical. At times it is necessary to be able to debug each thread in a program, to examine the contents of each stack, and to single-step or break in specific threads.

Education

The conference delegates were concerned about educating two different groups of people: programmers and customers.

Several of those present said that their companies had one parallel specialist. Whenever any parallelism was to be introduced into the code, the job was passed to the specialist. This kind of programming is perceived as a niche topic and difficult for the general programmer to achieve.

Some participants felt that customers needed to be educated about parallelism. The purpose was to set expectations. Developers feared that end users would expect unachievable performance improvements when moving to multi-core machines.

Fear of Many-Core Computing

Programming for two or four cores seems within the scope of most projects, but programming for 80 cores looks daunting. Making sure that programs written for today's multi-core machines will run on the many-core machines of the future is perceived to be a difficult task.

This concern has two aspects. First, being concerned about the number of cores probably indicates that there needs to be a change in the thinking of the developers. As in object-oriented programming, the concepts of information hiding and data encapsulation are central; so, in today's parallel programming practices, programmers should not be concerned with how many cores are available. When programming in parallel, the question "How many cores are there?" should not be asked.

The second aspect of this fear is the question of scalability. If a program runs well on 4 cores, is it possible to check if it will also run well on a 24-core machine? Will there be a corresponding speedup when moving to an architecture that has more cores?

Maintainability

Programmers want code that is easy to maintain. For some, the first thing they want is to avoid putting low-level, machine-specific code in their programs. The parallelism should be expressed with high-level abstractions that remain relevant across different generations of the project. Other developers look for help in tracking correctness and debugging applications.

Parallel Studio provides high-level parallel language support that makes code easier to understand and debug. Amplifier, Inspector, and the Parallel Debugger Extension help to maintain the code under development. The command-line versions of Amplifier and Inspector are ideal tools to add to regression testing. The ability to compare the results of different runs of these tools helps to spot potential problems.

Return on Investment

Some of the programmers were afraid the effort spent parallelizing a program would not pay off. Would the effort result in code that performs better? Would a parallelized program lead to increased sales of the product? Would it not be better just buying a faster machine?

You can use Parallel Studio to find which part of the code is the best place to optimize. You can then use this information to work out whether the likely effort will be considerable or easy.

Parallel Studio can help determine the performance benefit of adding parallelism. With Parallel Advisor, you can model parallelism in your code before implementing it, asking questions such as "What speedup will I achieve?" and "How scalable is my program?"

PARALLELISM AND THE PROGRAMMER

Today there is no "silver bullet" that will automatically make a serial program parallel. As a programmer, you have to make choices about what kind of parallelism you will use and in which programming language models you will implement the parallelism.

Types of Parallelism

You can achieve parallelism in a number of ways, including:

➤ **Distributed parallelism** — Complete applications are farmed out to different nodes in a cluster of computers. The Message Passing Interface (MPI), a send/receive message-passing protocol, is used to distribute and manage the applications.

➤ **Virtualization** — This technique involves running several operating systems on one CPU. Virtualization is often supported directly by the CPU. For example, a 2-core machine could host two virtual machines, one on each core. Each virtual machine hosts its own operating system with dedicated resources such as I/O and memory. Some resources are shared. A hypervisor helps manage the virtual machines and resources.

➤ **Task-level parallelism** — The focus is on work or tasks rather than threads. There may be many more tasks than there are threads, with each task being scheduled by a runtime scheduler.

➤ **Thread-level parallelism** — This parallelism is implemented within a program, with each of the parallel parts running on separate threads. In a multi-core environment, each thread runs on a separate core.

➤ **Instruction-level parallelism** — Most CPUs have several execution units; instruction-level parallelism is achieved by execution units executing in parallel. This is normally done automatically by the CPU, but it can be influenced by the layout of a program's code.

➤ **Data-level parallelism** — This parallelism relies on the CPU supporting single instruction, multiple data (SIMD) operations, such as can be found in the various Streaming SIMD

Extensions (SSE). In this mode, one instruction operates on wide registers that could hold several variables. So, for example, it is possible to compute four 32-bit additions with one instruction, the results being held in a single 128-bit-wide register. The 2nd Generation Intel Core architecture supports Intel Advanced Vector Extensions (AVX), increases the register size to 256-bit wide registers, and introduces three operand instructions rather than the two operand instructions found in SSE2.

You can use all these types of parallelism together. In this book we use examples of task-, thread-, data-, and instruction-level parallelism.

Intel's Family of Parallel Models

Intel's family of parallel models consists of Cilk Plus, Threading Building Blocks (TBB), domain-specific libraries, established standards, and some research and development products (see Figure 1-4).

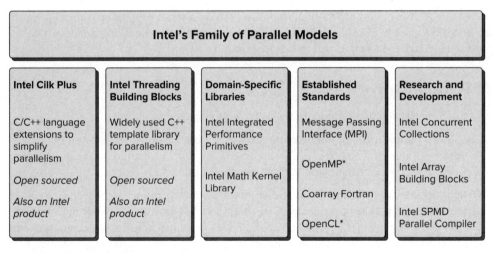

FIGURE 1-4: Intel's family of parallel models

Cilk Plus and Threading Building Blocks

Cilk Plus and TBB are designed to work seamlessly together.

➤ **Intel Cilk Plus** is a C/C++ language extension that provides new keywords for describing parallelism and a new notation for performing parallel computations on arrays. The language extensions simplify task and vector parallelism and consist of keywords/reducers, array notations, elemental functions, and a new pragma, `#pragma simd`, which can be used to force the compiler to vectorize code. Using Cilk Plus is one of the easiest ways to make a program parallel.

➤ **Intel Threading Building Blocks** (TBB) is a C++ template library that provides tasks, parallel algorithms, and containers.

TBB is a library, whereas Cilk Plus is a set of C/C++ language extensions implemented in the Intel compiler.

Domain-Specific Libraries

All the functions in fixed-function libraries are thread-safe and can be used in parallel programs. Some functions are already threaded and can be used to add parallelism to a program.

➤ **Intel Integrated Performance Primitives (IPP)** is a large collection of functions spread across multiple domains, including cryptography, compression, signal processing, and multimedia.

➤ **Intel Math Kernel Library (MKL)** is a collection of math functions used by the high-performance computing (HPC) community. The library includes BLAS, LAPACK, ScalaPACK1, sparse solvers, fast Fourier transforms, and vector math functionality.

Established Standards

The following standards can be used to make programs parallel:

➤ **Intel Message Passing Interface (MPI)** is a well-established standard that uses a send/receive protocol for running programs in parallel on a cluster of workstations.

➤ **Open Multi-Processing (OpenMP)** is a pragma-based language extension for incrementally adding parallelism to C, C++, and Fortran code.

➤ **Coarray Fortran** is part of the Fortran 2008 standard and provides a standardized way of doing parallel processing in Fortran.

➤ **Open Computing Language (OpenCL)** is a standard for use on heterogeneous computing environments. The language is based on C99.

Research and Development

The following parallel models are experimental and to be used for research only — that is, not for producing a commercial product. They reside on the `whatif.intel.com` website.

➤ **Intel Concurrent Collections (CnC)** is a parallel programming model that enables programmers to write parallel programs without being concerned about the low-level detail. Based on C++, CnC is also available for use with Haskell.

➤ **Intel Array Building Blocks (ArBB)** is a library that provides data-centric parallelization for use on arrays. The run time involves a just-in-time (JIT) compiler.

➤ **Intel SPMD Parallel Compiler** is an open-source compiler for single program multiple data (SPMD) programs. At run time, multiple program instances execute in parallel on the CPU's SIMD execution units.

Choosing the Right Parallel Constructs

When writing parallel programs, it is not necessary to stick to one particular set of constructs; you can mix and match constructs. This is not a new phenomenon, but the idea of mixing and matching may be new to those who are not experienced in parallel programming. For some years the HPC community has been mixing OpenMP and MPI constructs; and Windows programmers quite often use the Win32 API `InterlockedIncrement` function rather than the `#pragma omp critical` construct within their OpenMP programs.

Parallel constructs have different levels of abstraction. Some constructs are concerned mainly with the manipulation of data, whereas other constructs are task-oriented (see Figure 1-5).

Abstract Data Parallelism	Abstract Task Parallelism
Low-Level Data Parallelism	Low-Level Task Parallelism

FIGURE 1-5: Different levels of abstraction

High-Level vs. Low-Level Constructs

The higher levels of abstractions are used to express intent and indicate to the parallel run time, or the compiler, the desire that some code should be parallelized. Using the highest levels of abstraction does not guarantee that code will operate in parallel; that decision is delegated to the run time.

The lower-level constructs exert more direct control over the parallelism. Using the lowest-level constructs can sometimes break the parallelism and require expert knowledge. For example, the careless use of locks in parallel code can lead to a situation in which the whole execution environment is stalled, unable to progress toward the completion of any task. Low-level constructs are often tied to specific core count and do not scale automatically in a many-core architecture.

Data Parallelism vs. General Parallelism

Data parallelism is concerned mainly with operations on arrays of data. Some types of data parallelism, such as SIMD, are supported directly in CPU hardware. Other techniques, such as the manipulation of arrays, are supported by library and language extensions. Data parallelism has a special significance in the era of the many-core computing, where huge numbers of cores are available on single-chip devices. Writing data-parallel code leads to code that is scalable and capable of benefiting on the trend toward increasing numbers of cores.

General parallelism is the execution of separate tasks in parallel. Nonnumeric code is usually implemented with task-parallel rather than data-parallel algorithms.

Examples of Mixing and Matching Parallel Constructs

The following two sections describe examples of mixing and matching parallel constructs. Intel's family of parallel models is intended to be used together, so mixing and matching the constructs is anticipated and supported in Parallel Studio.

Cilk Plus and TBB

The code in Listing 1-1 uses a TBB-scalable allocator in a `cilk_for` loop. Each iteration of the `cilk_for` loop dynamically allocates memory to the array of `char` pointers. The loop iterations are balanced among available workers and run in parallel.

LISTING 1-1: An example of using Cilk Plus and TBB

```
#include <stdio.h>
#include <time.h>
#include <cilk/cilk.h>
#include <stdlib.h>
```

```
#define MALLOC_SIZE 1
#define ARRAY_SIZE 10000000
#include "tbb/scalable_allocator.h"

char * array[ARRAY_SIZE];

int main(int argc, char* argv[])
{
  clock_t start, stop;

  // get the start time
  start = clock();

  // load balance scalable malloc between available workers
  cilk_for(int i = 0; i < ARRAY_SIZE; i++)
  {
    array[i] = (char *)scalable_malloc(MALLOC_SIZE);
  }

  // free the blocks of memory
  cilk_for(int i = 0; i < ARRAY_SIZE; i++)
  {
    scalable_free(array[i]);
  }

  // get the stop time
  stop = clock();

  // display the time taken
  printf("The time was %f seconds\n",((double)(stop - start)/1000.0));
  return 0;
}
```

code snippet Chapter1\1-1.cpp

Using a scalable memory allocator on a two-core PC (Intel Mobile Core 2 Duo T7300), the code took 1.8 seconds to complete. When the normal `malloc` and `free` memory allocation functions were used, the code took 12.6 seconds to complete. The speedup was achieved by combining the Cilk Plus parallelism with the TBB scalable allocators *together*. The normal `malloc` function ensures thread-safeness by putting locks around some of its internal code. Locks make the code thread safe, but also slow down the code. The `scalable_malloc` function does not have locks, which means the parallel code runs much faster.

Cilk Keywords and Array Notations

Listing 1-2 shows an example of using different features of Cilk Plus. The code takes advantage of the parallelism provided by the CPU cores and the vector unit. The function declared in Lines 2 and 3 adds the two parameters x and y together and returns the new value. The __declspec (vector) keyword causes the compiler to generate short vector versions of the function ef_add. This elemental function is then applied to each element of the array in Lines 12, 18, and 24.

LISTING 1-2: An example of using Cilk keywords and array notations

```
1: include <cilk/cilk.h>
2: __declspec (vector) double ef_add (double x, double y) {
3:   return x + y;
4: }
5: int main()
6: {
7:   double a[5];
8:   double b[] = {1,2,3,4,5};
9:   double c[] = {6,7,8,9,10};
10:
11:   // apply function to whole array
12:   a[:] = ef_add(b[:],c[:]);
13:
14:   a[:] = 0;
15:   int n = 2;
16:   int s = 1;
17:   // apply function to a sub range
18:   a[0:n:s] = ef_add(b[0:n:s],c[0:n:s]);
19:
20:   a[:] = 0;
21:   // apply function in parallel
22:   cilk_for (int j = 0; j < n; ++j)
23:   {
24:     a[j] = ef_add(b[j],c[j]);
25:   }
26:}
```

code snippet Chapter1\1-2.cpp

Three arrays (a, b, and c), which are declared outside this code snippet, are arrays of doubles. The ef_add function is applied to array a in three different ways:

➤ **To a whole array** — Line 12 is an example of applying the function ef_add to complete arrays. Each element of array b is added to each element of array c, with the results written into each element of array a.

```
a[:] = ef_add(b[:],c[:]);
```

➤ **To part of an array** — Line 18 is an example of applying the function ef_add on part of an array. The calculation is applied on a subrange of the arrays, with n being the length of operation and s being the stride value:

```
a[0:n:s] = ef_add(b[0:n:s],c[0:n:s]);
```

➤ **In parallel** — Lines 22 to 25 present an example of loop-based parallelism. The cilk_for construct load-balances the loop iterations between the numbers of workers available. Lines 14 and 20 set all the values in the array a to zero.

```
cilk_for (int j = 0; j < n; ++j)
{
  a[j] = ef_add(b[j],c[j]);
}
```

The code at Lines 12 and 18 results in the compiler generating serial code that calls the vector function. The example at Lines 22 to 25 produces parallel code that calls the vector function.

 For more details of the array-notation syntax, see Chapter 2, "An Overview of Parallel Studio XE," and Chapter 4, "Producing Optimized Code."

Parallel Programming Errors

Adding parallelism to code exposes developers to new categories of programming errors. Some errors can be spotted by doing a code inspection or by running the code through a static analysis tool, such as lint. Other errors are much more difficult to find and can be detected only at run time using a dynamic analysis tool. The following threading problems are the most prevalent.

Data Races

Data races are caused when two or more threads running in parallel access the same memory location, and at least one of them tries to write to that memory location without using any kind of synchronization mechanism.

You can avoid data races by:

➤ Making global data local to each task or thread.

➤ Demoting the scope of variables by using stack or automatic variables.

➤ Using atomic operations.

➤ As a last resort, using locks and mutexes to protect shared resources. Locks and mutexes are low-level synchronization primitives that effectively serialize the access to a shared resource.

The easiest way to detect data races is to use a correctness tool, such as Intel Parallel Inspector XE (see Chapter 8, "Checking for Errors").

Determinacy Races

A determinacy race occurs when a program produces the right result only when the parallel parts execute in a particular order.

Imagine that you have a program that monitors the rise of temperature in a gas furnace:

1. It takes the current temperature.

2. It waits four seconds.

3. It takes the new temperature.

4. If the new temperature is 10 or more degrees greater than the first temperature, the program reduces the gas flow.

Each step must be made in the right sequence; otherwise, the logic of the program will be broken. Making steps 1–3 run in parallel would be a mistake, because there would be no guarantee which step would run first.

A program can have a determinacy race even though it doesn't have a data race. Almost every data race is a determinacy race, but not vice versa.

Deadlocks

Deadlocks are caused when two threads are endlessly waiting for each other, neither progressing to completion. Consider the following two code examples. At first they seem to be identical; in fact, they are supposed to be identical. However, on closer inspection, you can see that the critical sections, L1 and L2, are used in a different order in the two code excerpts. The critical sections use Win32 synchronization objects that control access to the lines of code and act as gatekeepers.

The Win32 API calls EnterCriticalSection and LeaveCriticalSection to act as gatekeepers for the enclosed code. The code between these calls can execute only on one thread.

Walking through both sets of code shows the problem. Imagine a thread is executing this code:

```
DWORD WINAPI threadA(LPVOID arg)
{
    EnterCriticalSection(&L1);
        EnterCriticalSection(&L2);
            processA(data1, data2);
        LeaveCriticalSection(&L2);
    LeaveCriticalSection(&L1);
    return(0);
}
```

And at the same time a second thread is executing this code:

```
DWORD WINAPI threadB(LPVOID arg)
{
    EnterCriticalSection(&L2);
        EnterCriticalSection(&L1);
            processB(data2, data1) ;
        LeaveCriticalSection(&L1);
    LeaveCriticalSection(&L2);
    return(0);
}
```

When the first thread hits the line EnterCriticalSection(&L1), it claims the exclusive use of the code for itself, protected by the critical section object L1.

At the same time, when the second thread hits the line EnterCriticalSection(&L2), it claims the exclusive use of the code for itself, protected by the critical section object L2.

Now back to the first thread. It tries to execute the next line, EnterCriticalSection(&L2), but it has to wait because the critical section object L2 is already being used by the second thread.

Likewise, the second thread cannot execute the next line, EnterCriticalSection(&L1), because the critical section L1 is already being used by the first thread.

So, we have deadlock — the first thread is waiting for the second thread to release L2, and the second thread is waiting for the first thread to release L1.

Most deadlocks can be avoided by using a consistent order for acquiring locks. As with data races, the easiest way to detect deadlocks is to use a correctness tool, such as Intel Parallel Inspector XE.

Poor Load Balancing

Load balancing is the act of making sure all threads are working equally hard utilizing all available cores on the CPU. Ideally, all threads in a parallel program should do equal amounts of work — that is, the load is well balanced. Poor load balancing leads to some threads being idle and constitutes a wasted resource.

The most common cause of poor load balancing is having too coarse a granularity of work assigned to each task. This can be fixed by reducing the amount of work each task can do, along with making each chunk of work be of similar size. The easiest way to detect poor load balancing is to use a thread-aware profiling tool, such as Intel Parallel Amplifier XE.

Threading/Tasking Overhead

Launching threads consumes some processor time, so it is important that threads have a decent amount of work to do so that this overhead is insignificant compared to the work being done by the thread. If the amount of work that a thread does is low, the threading overhead can dominate the application. This overhead usually is caused by having too fine a granularity of work. This can be fixed by increasing the amount of work each chunk does.

There is a trade-off between the amount of work a thread does, its impact on threading overhead, and the load balancing that can be achieved. Getting the right amount of work per thread may need some experimentation before the best results are achieved.

Synchronization Overhead

Synchronization overhead comes from using too many locks, barriers, mutexes, or other synchronization primitives. If you are not careful, you can inadvertently use too many primitives by using them in oft-repeated code, such as loops or recursive code. In this case, you should try to use less expensive synchronization constructs or restructure the code so that the constructs are used fewer times. Some programmers try to avoid using locks altogether by designing their software to use just atomic operations. Most lock-free programming relies on atomic operations that compare-and-swap, or read-modify-write using atomic instructions provided by the CPU.

The easiest way to detect synchronization overhead is to use a synchronization-aware profiling tool. For example, Intel Parallel Amplifier XE is capable of profiling locks and waits.

Memory Errors

When a serial program is made parallel, any memory allocation errors that already exist could result in a program that no longer works. Parallel programming also brings two new types of memory errors: false sharing and real sharing.

Memory Allocation Errors

A memory leak — that is, the dynamic allocation of memory without returning the memory to the memory manager — can result in excessive consumption of memory. Symptoms will include out-of-memory messages and excessive disk-thrashing as virtual memory is swapped in and out by the memory manager.

Memory managers that rely on the C runtime library to allocate memory from the heap are poor parallel performers. An example is the function `malloc`, which uses a single block of memory known as the *heap*. To make sure that threaded calls to `malloc` do not corrupt the heap pointers, `malloc` uses a lock. This lock has the effect of serializing any parallel use of `malloc`, making the parallel program run slow.

Scalable and lockless allocation functions are available to overcome this problem — for example, `scalable_malloc` provided with TBB.

Some memory allocation problems can be detected by static analysis of the code, whereas others can be detected only at run time.

False Sharing

False sharing is quite a low-level concept, but it is worth being aware of because it can seriously impact a running program.

Reading and writing from memory is slow, so CPUs have local on-chip memory called *caches* that are used to store copies of code and data from external memory. Each cache is organized into cache lines of contiguous memory.

Most CPUs have two or three cache levels. For example, my laptop (Intel Mobile Core 2 Duo) has an L1 and an L2 cache, with the L2 cache being shared between the CPU cores. The L2 cache is nearest the external memory; the L1 cache is nearest the CPU. The cache nearest external memory is referred to as the *last level cache*. Sharing the last level cache can introduce false sharing.

Figure 1-6 shows an example of false sharing. Variables Var A and Var B have already been loaded from external memory into the L2 cache line; in turn, each core also holds its own copy in its L1 cache.

The variables are not shared between the two cores; Var A is only ever accessed by Core 1, and Var B by Core 2. Because of the close proximity in memory of the two variables, they end up sitting in the same cache line.

When Core 2 changes the value of Var B, the processor will see that Core 1 also has a copy of the cache line and mark Core 1's cache line as invalid.

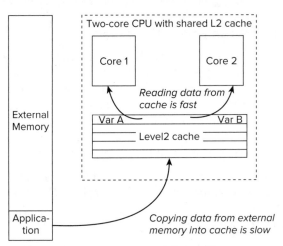

FIGURE 1-6: A 2-core CPU with shared caches

When Core 1 then modifies the value of Var A, the CPU will first flush its invalid L1 cache line and then reload the cache line from L2. If Core 1 alters Var A and then Core 2 alters Var B in a repeated sequence, this will result in the cache lines being continually flushed and updated. The flushing and updating of the cache line adds extra cycles to the time it takes to read the variables.

Although the variables are not logically shared between the two cores, because the two variables sit on the same cache line, they are effectively being shared by the mechanism the CPU employs to keep the cache line values correct.

Detecting false sharing is difficult, but it can be made easier with a tool such as VTune Amplifier XE, which enables you to carry out an architectural analysis of the running program. Chapter 12, "Event-Based Analysis with VTune Amplifier XE," describes how to do this.

Real Sharing

Real sharing is a variation on false sharing. The difference is that two threads share the same variable. Two cores that are constantly reading and writing to the same memory location will result in a similar cache-thrashing and will hurt performance.

Speedup and Scalability

One of the challenges of parallel programming is to write programs that perform better as you run them on processors with an additional number of cores. Well-written parallel software should display improved performance as you increase the number of cores, and should be agnostic as to how many cores are available.

Calculating Speedup

It is useful to be able to work out how fast a program will speed up if made parallel. The process is not difficult to understand but still worth spelling out.

Speedup

The following code snippet contains three calls to the function work(). At run time the function will be called six times, four of the calls coming from within the for loop. If the for loop is made parallel — for example, by using Cilk Plus or OpenMP — the projected speedup and scalability can be worked out.

```
1: work(1);
2: for(int i = 0; i < 4; i++)
3: {
4:     work(i+2);
5: }
6: work(6);
```

Figure 1-7 shows the parallelism that might be achieved on a different number of cores.

If each call to work() consumes 500 steps, the serial execution of the code would take 3,000 steps — see row (p), column (a).

Column (b) of Figure 1-7 shows what would happen if the for loop were parallelized and run on a 2-core machine. The speedup would be 1.5, which is calculated by dividing the original number of steps by the new number.

$$\text{Speedup} = \text{Original number of steps} / \text{new number of steps}$$

$$3000 / 2000 = 1.5$$

In column (c), the number of cores is increased to 4, so the new speedup is 2.

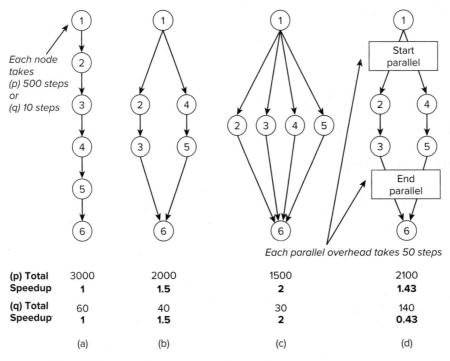

Each node takes (p) 500 steps or (q) 10 steps

Each parallel overhead takes 50 steps

	(a)	(b)	(c)	(d)
(p) Total	3000	2000	1500	2100
Speedup	1	1.5	2	1.43
(q) Total	60	40	30	140
Speedup	1	1.5	2	0.43

FIGURE 1-7: Calculating speedup

Parallel Overhead

In practice, an overhead is associated with implementing parallelism. The two squares in column (d) of Figure 1-7 represent this overhead. If we assume that the overhead in this example introduces 50 extra steps at the start and end of the parallel code, the total number of steps executed is 2,100, with the speedup becoming 1.43. In this example the overhead has had a slight negative impact on the speedup.

When making code parallel, it is important that there is sufficient work done in the parallel part of the code; otherwise, the overhead of the threading would dominate the performance. In row (q) of Figure 1-7, the same calculations are performed as in row (p), but the function `work()` now changes to consume only 10 steps. In this situation the speedup of the code, including the threading overhead, is only 0.43 — that is, the code will run at half the speed of the original serial code.

Amdahl's Law and Gustafson's Observation

Two laws are often cited when working out an expected speedup: Amdahl's Law and Gustafson's comments on Amdahl's Law (see Figure 1-8).

Amdahl says "…the effort on achieving high parallel processing rates is wasted unless it is accompanied by achievements in sequential processing rates of very nearly the main magnitude." [Amdahl, Gene M., "Validity of the single processor approach to achieving large scale computing capabilities." AFIPS Spring Joint Computer Conference, 1967]

$$S = \frac{1}{(1 - P) + P/N}$$

S *is the speedup*
P *is the fraction of code that*
   will be made parallel
N *is the number of processors*

Amdahl's Law

$$S(P) = P - \alpha.(p - 1)$$

S *is the speedup*
P *is the number of processors*
α *is the non-parallelized*
   part of the program

Gustafson's Law

FIGURE 1-8: Two laws for calculating speedup

Gustafson says "…speedup should be measured by scaling the problem to the number of processors not by fixing the problem size." [Gustafson, John L., "Reevaluating Amdahl's Law." Communications of the ACM; Volume 31, 1988]

Amdahl focused on the best speedup that could be obtained on a given problem size. Gustafson, on the other hand, contended that the problem size grows to match the resources available.

Amdahl's Law is sometimes used to paint a pessimistic picture of parallelism. Gustafson is far more optimistic, recognizing that programs grow to take up all resources available to them. Whether you use Gustafson's or Amdahl's Law, two things are true:

➤ The more code you remove from the serial part and make parallel, the better speedup you will achieve when executing code on modern multi-core architecture.

➤ The best parallel methods scale by solving bigger problems.

Predicting Scalability

Scalability is an observation of the speedup of a program as the number of cores is increased. A scalable program is one that responds well to an increased number of cores. A perfectly scalable program runs twice as fast on a 4-core machine than on a 2-core machine, and runs four times faster on an 8-core machine. In practice, it is rare to achieve perfect scalability.

You can forecast the scalability of the code by increasing the number of cores in the speedup calculation and plotting the trend. Figure 1-9 shows the same code as in the previous section, with calculations for 1 to 6 cores. The reading at zero cores represents the original serial code.

The *Work with no overhead* line represents the speedup values without the overhead element being added to the equation.

The *Large work with overhead* and the *Small work with overhead* lines represent the speedup values taking into account the synchronization overhead.

As shown in the *Work with no overhead* line, the speedup flattens when there are four or more cores. The reason for this is that when the `for` loop is parallelized, the number of loops is shared among the available cores. Because the code has only four loops, a maximum of four `work()` functions can be called in parallel.

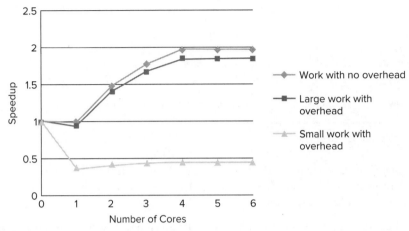

FIGURE 1-9: Calculating speedup

The key point to note here is that the design of the parallel code has introduced an upper bound into the parallelism that can be achieved.

When the parallel overhead is added to the graph, you can see that with a large amount of work, the speedup is only slightly impacted.

When the work() consumes only ten steps, two things happen: the parallel version of the code runs slower than the original serial code, and the speedup does not improve as additional cores are added.

Using language models such as Cilk Plus or TBB, you should be able to write programs that scale well as silicon moves from multi-core to many-core. The work-stealing schedulers in these models will help you produce software that is automatically load-balanced, with the correct ratio of work-load-to-overhead software that can be regarded as "future-proof."

Parallelism and Real-Time Systems

Parallelism introduces some exciting opportunities for those working with real-time or embedded systems. One of the challenges is keeping as much of the program as possible at a high level of abstraction without losing the determinacy your program requires. Partitioning your real-time requirements between hard and soft real-time may help you.

Hard and Soft Real-Time

Timing requirements for real-time systems can be divided between *soft real-time* and *hard real-time*. In hard real-time, response rates to some events, such as external interrupts and timer events, need to happen within a guaranteed time, usually in the order of microseconds or within in a certain number of CPU clock cycles. In soft real-time, the requirements are less deterministic, with response rates being measured in the order of milliseconds.

The higher-level parallel implementations described in this book are not validated in a hard real-time environment. Some of the requirements of hard real-time, such as deterministic behavior, preemptive scheduling, and guaranteed execution times, are not designed into the underlying runtime libraries.

A Hard Real-Time Example using RTX

IntervalZeros's RTX is one example of how to use the higher-level parallel models in a real-time system. RTX is a runtime extension to Windows that provides the missing hard real-time behavior. As shown in Figure 1-10, the number of cores available on a system is divided between the Win32 side (which is running Windows) and the RTX side (the real-time extension). Any parallelism on the RTX side is programmed using low-level threading constructs provided by the Windows API. The parallelism on the Win32 side is programmed using higher-level constructs, such as Cilk Plus or OpenMP. Any threaded code that requires a hard real-time response is run in the RTX space. Communication between the two domains is via interprocess communication (IPC) or using shared memory.

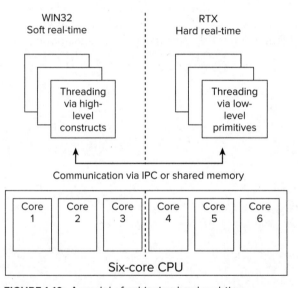

FIGURE 1-10: A model of achieving hard real-time

Advice for Real-Time Programmers

Everything in this chapter about parallelism is just as relevant to real-time programming as it is to non-real-time programming.

If your programs have a real-time aspect, you should:

➤ Keep to a higher level of abstraction as much as possible. This will help you produce scalable, well-balanced applications.

➤ Look out for data races. Use static and dynamic analysis to detect them.

➤ Not be afraid to "borrow" bits from different parallel models.

➤ Be very conservative with hard real-time requirements. Most general-purpose parallelism libraries are not validated for real-time.

SUMMARY

Multiple cores available on the latest generation of CPUs bring new opportunities for programmers to optimize their code. You can use a variety of different parallel programming models to add parallelism to your programs.

When writing your code, take special care to avoid introducing parallel programming errors into your newly parallelized programs. Aim to write parallel programs that exhibit good speedup, have good load balancing, and are scalable.

The next two chapters introduce Intel Parallel Studio XE, which is designed to help in all stages of the development of parallel code. Chapter 2, "An Overview of Parallel Studio XE," gives an overview of Parallel Studio; Chapter 3, "Parallel Studio XE for the Impatient," is a hands-on session to familiarize you with the different tools.

2

An Overview of Parallel Studio XE

WHAT'S IN THIS CHAPTER?

➤ An overview of Parallel Studio XE

➤ An overview of Advisor XE

➤ An overview of Composer XE

➤ An overview of Amplifier XE

➤ An overview of Inspector XE

This chapter gives an overview of Intel Parallel Studio XE, highlighting the main features of each tool.

Parallel Studio XE enables you to develop, debug, optimize, and tune both threaded and non-threaded applications on Linux and Windows. On Windows, Parallel Studio XE plugs into Visual Studio; on Linux, it works alongside the GNU Compiler Collection (GCC).

Developers use Parallel Studio XE in a number of different ways. The chapter concludes with a discussion on three different ways that you might want to use Parallel Studio XE.

WHY PARALLEL STUDIO XE?

In Chapter 1, "Parallelism Today," high on the list of the top six challenges was tools. Programmers need tools that work well together and help productivity. Intel Parallel Studio XE is a comprehensive tool suite that is designed to help you develop parallel applications.

Programmers and developers like to follow their own way of doing things. Not everyone follows the same methodology — some like top-down, others like bottom-up, and others mix and match methodologies. Some developers prefer to use tools with a graphical user interface, whereas others find using the command line much more productive. Some experienced programmers dive straight into adding parallelism to their code with a minimum of guidance, whereas others look for as much help as possible. Parallel Studio XE is designed to help developers add parallelism to their existing code and to develop completely fresh code, regardless of their approach and experience.

WHAT'S IN PARALLEL STUDIO XE?

Parallel Studio is available in two versions:

> **Intel Parallel Studio XE** — Available on both Windows and Linux

> **Intel Parallel Studio** — A Windows-only product

This book is based on Parallel Studio XE, although you can use most of the concepts in the non-XE version, as well.

INTEL PARALLEL STUDIO XE

Parallel Studio XE is a suite of software tools that contains the following:

> **Intel Parallel Advisor** — Parallel Advisor gives advice on how to add parallelism to a program. Advisor enables you to model the effect of parallelism before committing to the final implementation.

> **Intel Parallel Composer XE** — Composer XE contains a compiler and libraries used to create optimized and parallel code. Within Composer there is also the Parallel Debugger Extension (PDE), which is used to debug threaded code. A standalone debugger — the Intel Debugger (IDB) — is available with the Linux version of the tools.

> **Intel Parallel Inspector XE** — Inspector XE is used to check a running program for common parallel-type errors, such as deadlocks and data races, and memory errors, such as memory and resource leaks in both parallel and serial programs.

> **Intel VTune Amplifier XE** — Amplifier XE is used to profile an application to identify program hotspots and bottlenecks. It also analyzes parallel programs to show how parallel and how efficient they are. You can also use Amplifier XE to show how well the CPU is being used in an application, helping you identify any underlying problems.

On Windows, Parallel Studio XE is installed alongside Microsoft Visual Studio and is compatible with the Microsoft tools. The C/C++ compiler in Composer XE is a plug-and-play replacement for the Microsoft compiler.

On Linux, Parallel Studio XE is installed alongside the GNU software development tools and is compatible with GCC. The C/C++ compiler in Composer XE is a plug-and-play replacement for GCC on Linux.

Parallel Studio XE supports program development in C/C++ and Fortran. Table 2-1 lists the features that are in Parallel Studio XE along with the non-XE version.

TABLE 2-1: Key Features of Parallel Studio XE

COMPOSER	NON-XE	XE
C/C++ compiler	X	X
Fortran compiler		X
Profile-guided optimization		X
Parallel Debugger Extension	X	X
Intel Debugger (Linux only)		X
Threaded performance libraries	X	X
Threaded math library		X
INSPECTOR		
Memory and Thread analyses	X	X
Advanced Memory and Thread analyses	X	X
Static Security analysis		X
AMPLIFIER		
Hotspot, Concurrency, and Locks and Waits analyses	X	X
Timeline		X
Frame analysis		X
Event-based sampling		X
Source view	X	X
Assembly view		X
ADVISOR		
Threading advice for serial applications	X	X
USER INTERFACE		
Visual Studio integration	X	X
Standalone graphical interface		X
Command line	Basic	Advanced
OPERATING SYSTEM		
Windows	X	X
Linux		X

INTEL PARALLEL ADVISOR

Intel Parallel Advisor provides a methodology for modeling parallelism in code. The five-step model provides an implementation-neutral means of modeling parallelism in an application under development. Advisor guides the programmer through each step of the model without the need to commit to a particular parallel program implementation until the last step of the modeling.

The Advisor Workflow

Intel Parallel Advisor guides you through a series of steps to help you experiment with adding parallelism to your code (see Figure 2-1). In practice, programmers usually step back and forth between some of the steps until they have achieved good results. You can launch each step from the Advisor Workflow tab (in the Solution Explorer) or from the Advisor toolbar/menus.

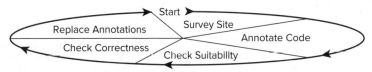

FIGURE 2-1: The five-step Advisor workflow

Surveying the Site

The first step in the Advisor workflow is surveying the site to find any hotspots — that is, code with significant CPU activity within the application. Once the survey is run, Advisor reports on screen how much time has been spent executing each part of the program. The amount of time of each function call and loop is displayed in the *Survey Report*. In Figure 2-2 the recursive call to setQueen is identified as the main hotspot.

Function Call Sites and Loops	Total Time %	Total Time	Self Time	Source Location
setQueen [loop]	100.0%	3.0685s	0s	nqueens_serial.cpp:65
setQueen [loop]	100.0%	3.0685s	0s	nqueens_serial.cpp:85
setQueen	100.0%	3.0685s	0s	nqueens_serial.cpp:88
setQueen [loop]	100.0%	3.0685s	0s	nqueens_serial.cpp:65
setQueen [loop]	99.7%	3.0585s	0s	nqueens_serial.cpp:85
setQueen	99.7%	3.0585s	0s	nqueens_serial.cpp:88
setQueen [loop]	99.3%	3.0485s	0s	nqueens_serial.cpp:65
setQueen [loop]	98.7%	3.0284s	0s	nqueens_serial.cpp:85
setQueen	98.7%	3.0284s	0s	nqueens_serial.cpp:88
setQueen [loop]	98.4%	3.0184s	0s	nqueens_serial.cpp:65
setQueen [loop]	93.8%	2.8785s	0s	nqueens_serial.cpp:85
setQueen	93.8%	2.8785s	0.0500s	nqueens_serial.cpp:88
setQueen [loop]	88.6%	2.7185s	0s	nqueens_serial.cpp:65
setQueen [loop]	76.4%	2.3449s	0s	nqueens_serial.cpp:85
setQueen	76.4%	2.3449s	0.0599s	nqueens_serial.cpp:88
setQueen [loop]	72.8%	2.2348s	0s	nqueens_serial.cpp:65
setQueen [loop]	55.2%	1.6941s	0s	nqueens_serial.cpp:85
setQueen	55.2%	1.6941s	0.0700s	nqueens_serial.cpp:88
setQueen [loop]	49.3%	1.5143s	0s	nqueens_serial.cpp:85
setQueen [loop]	28.3%	0.8689s	0s	nqueens_serial.cpp:85
setQueen [loop]	20.7%	0.6353s	0s	nqueens_serial.cpp:67
setQueen	0.3%	0.0101s	0.0101s	nqueens_serial.cpp:85
setQueen	3.6%	0.1099s	0.1099s	nqueens_serial.cpp:91
setQueen [loop]	17.6%	0.5407s	0s	nqueens_serial.cpp:67
setQueen	1.6%	0.0502s	0.0502s	nqueens_serial.cpp:91

FIGURE 2-2: A Survey Report in Advisor

Annotating Code

After identifying hotspots in the code, the next step is to add *annotations* to mark areas of parallelism. You can insert the annotations into the code by hand, or you can insert them via the context-sensitive menu. The Advisor modeling engine uses these markers to predict the effect of adding parallelism. Following is an example of code annotation:

```
#include <advisor-annotate.h>
void solve()
{
   int * queens = new int[size];

 ANNOTATE_SITE_BEGIN(solve)
   for(int i=0; i<size; i++) {
     // try all positions in first row
     ANNOTATE_TASK_BEGIN(setQueen)
       setQueen(queens, 0, i);
     ANNOTATE_TASK_END(setQueen)
   }
 ANNOTATE_SITE_END(solve)
}
```

You need to include the header file `advisor-annotate.h` before using the annotation macros.

The macros `ANNOTATE_SITE_BEGIN` and `ANNOTATE_SITE_END` mark the area of code that will contain one or more tasks. The task itself — that is, the block of code that will be run in parallel — is marked with the macros `ANNOTATE_TASK_BEGIN` and `ANNOTATE_TASK_END`.

Note that the code has one error purposefully included. Each task accesses the dynamically allocated array `queens`. This will cause a data race, but it will be detected when Advisor does the correctness modeling.

The annotations do not actually implement parallelism; rather, they help you answer the question, "What would happen if I inserted parallelism here?" When Advisor runs the code, the code is still run in serial, with Advisor using the annotations to predict what the parallel behavior will be.

The annotations `ANNOTATE_LOCK_ACQUIRE` and `ANNOTATE_LOCK_RELEASE` are used to protect a shared variable. Manipulation of the shared variable is performed within these two annotations:

```
ANNOTATE_LOCK_ACQUIRE(0);
   shared_variable ++;
ANNOTATE_LOCK_RELEASE(0);
```

Typically, you should add the lock annotations only after you have run the correctness tool and have found cases of unprotected data sharing.

Checking Suitability

After adding the annotations to the code, you can use Advisor to generate a *Suitability Report*. The Suitability Report shows the effect of parallelism and the likely scaling that will be achieved.

The All Sites pane of the Suitability Report displays the speedup of each site in a table (see Figure 2-3). You can model the number of CPUs to see how each site responds to different CPU counts.

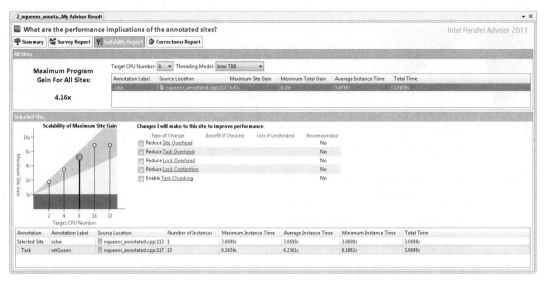

FIGURE 2-3: Modeling speedup in the Suitability Report

The Selected Site pane shows a graphical summary of the speedup. Advisor knows the impact the parallelism overhead has on the running program. You can use this pane to speculate on the benefit of reducing the overhead.

Checking Correctness

After creating the Suitability Report, you can use Advisor to check for any potential data-sharing problems. You can launch correctness checking by selecting the Correction analysis button on the Advisor toolbar. Advisor lists all detected errors in the Correctness Report (see Figure 2-4).

FIGURE 2-4: A Correctness Report in Advisor

Replacing Annotations

Once you are satisfied with the results of the Suitability and Correctness Reports, the final step is to change the annotations in the source code to real parallel programming constructs. You can choose these from the family of parallel models that are supported by Parallel Composer, as discussed in Chapter 7, "Implementing Parallelism." The process is not automatic; you are responsible for making the changes by hand and fixing the potential correctness issues identified in the report.

 You can find more details about Advisor in Chapter 10, "Parallel Advisor-Driven Design."

INTEL PARALLEL COMPOSER XE

Intel Parallel Composer XE contains the following:

- ➤ An optimizing C/C++ and Fortran compiler
- ➤ A collection of threading and optimization libraries
    - ➤ Threading Building Blocks (TBB)
    - ➤ Integrated Performance Primitives (IPP)
    - ➤ Math Kernel Library (MKL)
- ➤ Debugging tools
    - ➤ Parallel Debugger Extension (PDE) for Windows
    - ➤ Intel Debugger (IDB) for Linux

Intel C/C++ Optimizing Compiler

The compiler is a direct replacement for the Microsoft compiler and the GNU GCC compiler, and is used to create optimized code. Together, the compiler and libraries support Intel's family of parallel models, as mentioned in Chapter 1.

Table 2-2 lists some of the key features of the compiler (discussed in more detail in Chapter 4, "Producing Optimized Code," Chapter 5, "Writing Secure Code," and Chapter 7, "Implementing Parallelism").

TABLE 2-2: Key Features of Intel C/C++ Compiler

OPTIMIZATION	DESCRIPTION
Automatic optimization	Optimizes an application for speed or size. Use the /O1 option to optimize for size, /O2 to optimize for speed, and /O3 for a more aggressive speed optimization.
Interprocedural optimization (IPO)	Performs cross-file optimization (sometimes referred to as *global optimization*).

continues

TABLE 2-2 *(continued)*

OPTIMIZATION	DESCRIPTION
Profile-guided optimization (PGO)	Initial run of the application drives compiler options.
Automatic vectorization	Converts calculations within loops to use SSE instructions. You often can achieve significant performance improvements with this option.
Floating-point performance	Controls the precision and speed of floating-point operations. For some applications, you can reduce the accuracy of the floating-point calculations (with compiler switches) to get faster results.
Intrinsic functions	Inserts SSE, data pre-fetching, and other optimized routines.
PARALLELIZATION	
Cilk Plus	Provides the easiest way to parallelize a program.
OpenMP	Provides support for OpenMP 3.0.
Automatic parallelization	Provides loop-centric automatic parallelism.
TOOLS AND REPORTING	
Guided auto-parallelizaton (GAP)	Advises on code changes required to satisfy auto-parallelization and auto-vectorization.
Optimization reports	Provides detailed reports on all stages of optimization.
Static Security analysis (SSA)	Checks for security issues that could compromise the application being developed.

Profile-Guided Optimization

In PGO, you create a set of statistics, or profiles, by running the actual application being developed, and then feeding this information back into the compilation stage of the program, using the profile to automatically influence the behavior of the compiler. You conduct PGO in three stages (see Figure 2-5):

1. Use the compiler option /Qprof-gen to build an instrumented version of an application. You use the instrumentation to capture runtime information about your application's behavior.

2. Execute the instrumented application my.exe. As the program runs, the instrumentation produces a .dyn file that contains information on how the program executes.

   It is important to use appropriate test data in stage 2. If the application behaves quite differently with different types of test data, it may be worth doing multiple runs of stage 2.

3. Use the compiler option /Qprof-use, which causes the compiler to use the .dyn file(s) to produce an optimized application.

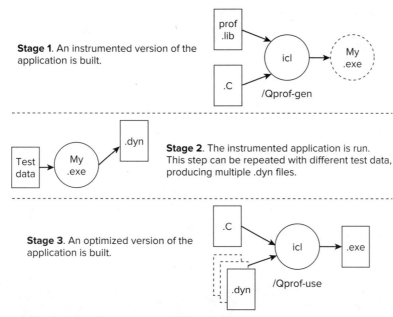

Stage 1. An instrumented version of the application is built.

prof .lib

.C

icl

My .exe

/Qprof-gen

Stage 2. The instrumented application is run. This step can be repeated with different test data, producing multiple .dyn files.

Test data

My .exe

.dyn

Stage 3. An optimized version of the application is built.

.C

.dyn

icl

.exe

/Qprof-use

FIGURE 2-5: The three stages of PGO

PGO improves application performance by:

➤ Reorganizing code layout

➤ Reducing instruction-cache problems

➤ Shrinking code size

➤ Reducing branch mispredictions

Cilk Plus

Cilk Plus is an extension to C/C++ to support parallelism. Using just three new keywords, Cilk Plus is one of the easiest ways to add parallelism to a program. With Cilk Plus you express parallel *intent*, rather than parallel *control*.

Cilk Plus has the following key features:

➤ Keywords

➤ Reducers

➤ Array notations

➤ Elemental functions

➤ SIMD pragma

The Cilk Plus scheduler decides at run time whether to run the code in parallel. The scheduler automatically takes care of load balancing. You can influence the Cilk Plus program with the following keywords, environmental variable, and APIs:

➤ Keywords

    ➤ `cilk_spawn`

    ➤ `cilk_sync`

    ➤ `cilk_for`

➤ Environment variable

    ➤ `CILK_NWORKERS`

➤ APIs

    ➤ `__cilkrts_set_param("nworkers","4")`

    ➤ `__cilk_get_nworkers()`

    ➤ `__cilkrts_get_total_workers()`

    ➤ `__cilkrts_getworker_number()`

When you run a Cilk Plus program, a number of workers are created — usually the same number as the number of cores on the host system. You can override the default number of workers by using the Cilk Plus API. You can also set the number of workers by using the environment variable `CILK_NWORKERS`.

Listing 2-1 shows an example of using `cilk_spawn` and `cilk_sync`. The program calculates the 40th value of the Fibonacci series.

LISTING 2-1: A simple Cilk program

```
#include <stdio.h>
#include <cilk/cilk.h>

long fibonacci(long n)
{
  long x, y;
  if (n < 2) return n;

  // find the n-1 number
  x = cilk_spawn fibonacci(n-1);

  // find the n-2 number
  y = fibonacci(n-2);

  // workers wait here until all have finished
  cilk_sync;
```

```
    return (x+y);
}

int main()
{
    // work out the 40th value in fibonacci series
    long fib = fibonacci(40);
    // display the results
    printf("Fibonacci 50: %d\n",fib);
}
```

code snippet Chapter2\2-1.cpp

The lines following the `cilk_spawn` statement (that is, starting with `y = …`) up to the `cilk_sync` statement are known as the *continuation*. The `cilk_spawn` keyword gives permission to the run time to run `fibonacci(n-1)` in parallel with the continuation code. At run time, if a spare worker is available, the scheduler steals the *continuation code* from the first worker and assigns it to a second worker. At the same time, the first worker continues executing the call to `fibonacci(n-2)`.

Cilk Plus *reducers* are used to prevent data races by using them in place of nonlocal variables, In Listing 2-2, the variable `j`, which was originally an integer, has been changed into a reducer. This change prevents a data race from occurring. At run time, each worker is given its own *view* of the reducer.

LISTING 2-2: An example of using a Cilk Plus reducer

Available for download on Wrox.com

```
#include <cilk/cilk.h>
#include <cilk/reducer_opadd.h>
#include <stdio.h>

int main()
{
    cilk::reducer_opadd<int> j;

    cilk_for(int i = 0; i < 100; i++)
    {
        j += i;
    }
    printf("J is %d",j.get_value());
}
```

code snippet Chapter2\2-2.cpp

The values of the individual views are combined back together when the parallel strands come back together. You retrieve the combined value in the `printf` statement by calling the reducer function `get_value()`. The operation used to combine the values is specific to the type of reducer that is being used. In this example the reducer type is a `reducer_opadd`, so the views are combined by adding the values together. Table 2-3 lists other available Cilk Plus reducers. You can also write your own reducers.

TABLE 2-3: Cilk Plus Reducers

REDUCER	DESCRIPTION
reducer_list_append	Adds items to the end of a list
reducer_list_prepend	Adds items to the beginning of a list
reducer_max	Finds the maximum value from a set of values
reducer_max_index	Finds the index of maximum values from a set of values
reducer_min	Finds the minimum value from a set of values
reducer_min_index	Finds the index of minimum values from a set of values
reducer_opadd	Performs a sum
reducer_ostream	Provides an output stream that can be written in parallel
reducer_basic_string	Creates a string using append or += operations

 Cilk Plus is one of the easiest ways to add parallelism to a program.

Array notations provide data parallelism for arrays. *Elemental functions* are functions that can be applied to arrays and scalars to enable data parallelism. The *SIMD pragma* is used to enforce vectorization. The compiler issues a warning if it fails to vectorize the code.

Listing 2-3 is an example of using array notation and elemental functions. Each array element in a[] and b[] is added together, putting the results in c[]. The following lines perform the same calculations:

```
int sum = __sec_reduce_add(c[:])

for(int i=0; i<4; i++){c[i] = a[i] + b[i];}.
```

The call to __sec_reduce_add adds together all the elements of the array c. You can perform the addition in parallel if you have sufficient CPU resources available at runtime.

LISTING 2-3: A simple array notation example

```
int main()
{
    int a[] = {1,2,3,4};
    int b[] = {2,4,6,8};
    int c[] = {0,0,0,0};
```

```
    c[:]=a[0:4] + b[0:4]; // 3,6,9,12
    int sum = __sec_reduce_add(c[:]);  // 30

    return sum;
}
```

OpenMP

OpenMP is a well-established standard for parallel programming. Intel Parallel Composer supports OpenMP version 3.0. OpenMP consists of pragmas, APIs, and environment variables that you can use to add parallelism to code incrementally.

The OpenMP task example in Listing 2-4 shows how tasks are used. To successfully build the code with the Intel compiler, you must use the /Qopenmp option.

Available for download on Wrox.com

LISTING 2-4: A simple OpenMP task example

```
#include <stdio.h>
#include <omp.h>
int main()
{
  int j = 0;
  // create a parallel region
  #pragma omp parallel
  {
    // this task will run on just one thread
    #pragma omp single nowait
      {
        for (int i = 0; i < 10; i++)
        {
          // every time loop iteration hits this next line
          // an omp task will be created and will
          // be run the moment a thread is available
          #pragma omp task firstprivate(i)
          {
            #pragma omp atomic
            j++;
            printf("i: %d thread:%d\n",i,omp_get_thread_num());
          } // end #pragma omp task
        } // end for …
      } //end #pragma omp single nowait
  } // end #pragma omp parallel
  return 0;
}
```

At the start of the `#pragma omp parallel`, a pool of threads is made available. The `#pragma omp single` statement ensures that the following block of code is run by only one thread.

Within the single running thread is a loop that causes the `#pragma omp task` statement to create ten tasks. Once a task is created, it is free to be executed by the first available free thread.

Once the single thread has created all the tasks, the thread on which it was running becomes available to the OpenMP runtime — the `nowait` clause makes sure the thread is released immediately.

There is an implicit barrier at the end of the `#pragma omp parallel` block: no thread can go beyond this point until all threads have completed their work.

The variable j has the potential to cause a data race, so it is incremented in an atomic operation.

Intel Threading Building Blocks

Intel Threading Building Blocks (TBB) is a C++ template library for parallelizing C++ programs. Using TBB to add parallelism to your program makes sense only if you wrote your program in C++ and you are comfortable with such concepts as templates, overloading, and inheritance.

TBB has had wide adoption, with a number of commercial software products having their parallelism provided under the hood by TBB.

The library is available under the GNU Public License (GPL) and non-GPL development. The version shipped with Parallel Studio is the non-GPL version.

TBB consists of the following components:

- ➤ Parallel algorithms
- ➤ Task scheduler
- ➤ Concurrent containers
- ➤ Thread local storage and scalable memory allocators
- ➤ Low-level synchronization primitives

The main unit of work is the *task*, which is scheduled by a work-stealing scheduler. Tasks are allocated to threads by the scheduler and are held in queues. When a thread's task queue is empty, the scheduler will steal a task from another thread's queue, thereby keeping all the threads busy.

You can mix TBB with other parallel language constructs. For example, you can write a parallel program using Cilk Plus and use TBB to supply memory allocation and synchronization. Table 2-4 lists some of the templates that are available in TBB.

TABLE 2-4: Some TBB Templates

ALGORITHMS	DESCRIPTION
parallel_for	Performs parallel iteration over a range of values
parallel_reduce	Computes reduction over a range
parallel_scan	Computes parallel prefix

parallel_do	Processes work items in parallel
parallel_for_each	Provides parallel variant of std::for_each
parallel_pipeline	Performs pipelined execution
parallel_sort	Sorts a sequence
parallel_invoke	Evaluates several functions in parallel
CONTAINERS	
concurrent_hash_map	Provides associative container with concurrent access
concurrent_queue	Provides queue with concurrent operations
concurrent_bounded_queue	Provides bounded dual queue with concurrent operations
concurrent_vector	Provides class for vectors that can be concurrently grown and accessed
concurrent_unordered_map	Provides container that supports concurrent insertion and traversal
PRIMITIVES	
mutex	Provides mutual exclusion of threads from sections of code
atomic	Used for atomic operations
ALLOCATORS	
tbb_allocator	Allocates memory (may not be scalable)
scalable_allocator	Provides scalable memory allocation
zero_allocator	Allocates zeroed memory space
aligned_space	Allocates uninitialized memory space

Listing 2-5 shows an example of using the parallel_for algorithm to print the value of a loop variable.

Available for download on Wrox.com

LISTING 2-5: A simple example of the TBB parallel_for algorithm

```
1: #include "tbb/tbb.h"
2: #include <stdio.h>
3: using namespace tbb;
4:
5: int main()
6: {
7:   parallel_for( size_t(0),size_t(20),size_t(1),
```

continues

LISTING 2-5 *(continued)*

```
8:      [=](size_t n) {
9:        std::printf("%d ",n);
10:     }
11:   );
12:   return 0;
13:}
```

code snippet Chapter2\2-5.cpp

The first three parameters of `parallel_for` are the loop start, loop end, and loop increment values.

Lines 8 to 10 define a lambda function, which is supported by the C++0x standard. You have to use the option `/Qstd=c++0x` with the Intel compiler to successfully build the code shown in Listing 2-5. This parameter does not need to be a lambda function; you could use a normal C function instead.

Parameter n in line 8 is the current loop counter. The scheduler passes in the current loop count via this variable.

Lines 9 to 10 are the body of the lambda function, which gets executed once every iteration.

The TBB scheduler load-balances the loop iterations between separate TBB tasks, the order of execution being indeterminate.

Intel Integrated Performance Primitives

The Intel Integrated Performance Primitives (IPP) library is a vast collection of functions covering audio, video, speech, data compression, signal processing, and cryptography (see Table 2-5). Before writing your own libraries and algorithms, you should consider using IPP instead. This library might stop you from "reinventing the wheel" and significantly shorten your development time.

TABLE 2-5: IPP Libraries and Domains

LIBRARY	DOMAIN
ippAC	Audio coding
ippCC	Color conversion
ippCH	String operations
ippCP	Cryptography
ippCV	Computer vision
ippDC	Data compression
ippDI	Data integrity
ippGEN	Generated functions

ippIP	Image processing
ippJP	Image compression
ippMX	Small matrix operations
ippRR	Rendering and 3D
ippSC	Speech coding
ippSP	Signal processing
ippSR	Speech recognition
ippVC	Video coding
ippVM	Vector math

The functions in IPP are optimized for different architectures. A top-level, architectural-neutral function determines at runtime which instruction set the host supports, and then calls the appropriate architectural-specific, low-level function. This technique, known as *software dispatching*, is done automatically at run time. Where dispatching is not required, it is possible to link directly to the lower-level optimized libraries. You can link applications with the IPP library either statically or dynamically.

An Application Example

Figure 2-6 gives an example of where the Fast Fourier Transform (FFT) functions of the IPP library are the real-time manipulation of a sound stream.

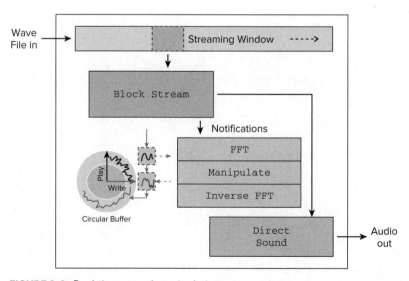

FIGURE 2-6: Real-time sound manipulation

The design was part of a program that changes the characteristics of a wave file as it is being played. The reading and playing of the sound uses Windows DirectSound, with an FFT being applied in real time.

A block of data `Block Stream` is read from a wave file. As each block is read, the play and write pointers are maintained as a circular buffer.

The address of the circular buffer is passed to the FFT function, after which the sound is modified using the manipulate block; finally, the modified sound data is inverse FFT'd and written back to the circular buffer.

Listing 2-6 shows how the IPP FFT function is called. The code is not complete, but it shows how FFT is achieved using IPP. The FFT function `ippsFFTFwd_RToPerm_32f` does the actual FFT. Initialization is performed with the `ippsFFTInitAlloc_R_32f` and `ippsZero_32fc` functions.

LISTING 2-6: Using the IPP FFT functions

```cpp
// Function that will call IPP FFT
int FFT(float in[], const float out[], int len)
{
    int power = 12;
    Ipp32fc* pFilterCCS;
    IppsFFTSpec_R_32f *pFFTSpec;

    // allocate space for FFT
    pFilterCCS = (Ipp32fc*)ippsMalloc_32f(len+2);

    // FFT configure
    Ipp32fc one = {1.0, 0.0};

    // zero initialize the FFT space
    ippsZero_32fc( pFilterCCS, len/2+1 );

    //initialize the FFT
    ippsFFTInitAlloc_R_32f( &pFFTSpec,
                 power, IPP_FFT_DIV_BY_SQRTN, ippAlgHintFast );

    // do the FFT
    ippsFFTFwd_RToPerm_32f(in, (Ipp32f*)out, pFFTSpec, 0 );

    // free up the FFT space
    ippsFree(pFFTSpec);

    return 0;
}
```

code snippet Chapter2\2-6.cpp

IPP and Threading

Some library functions are already parallelized. A nonparallelized version of the library is also provided. You can find the list of threaded functions by looking at the file `ThreadedFunctionsLists.txt` in the documentation directory of your IPP installation.

All the functions in IPP are *thread-safe*, which means you can safely use them in your parallel code, knowing that the functions will be race-free.

The IPP library provides a series of performance tests for each application domain.

 When using any library in a threaded or parallel application, it is important that you use thread-safe libraries. All IPP libraries are thread-safe.

Intel Parallel Debugger Extension

The Intel Parallel Debugger Extension (PDE) provides:

➤ Thread Data-Sharing analysis

➤ Cilk Plus and OpenMP awareness

➤ SSE register viewing/debugging

The PDE works alongside the standard Visual Studio debugger and provides additional functionality to help debug parallel applications. Figure 2-7 shows an example of some of the PDE windows.

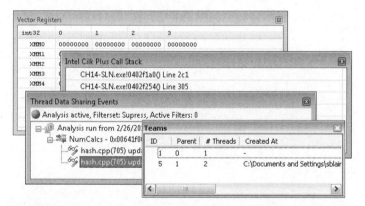

FIGURE 2-7: Some of the windows in the Parallel Debugger Extension

 You can find more details about PDE in Chapter 11, "Debugging Parallel Applications."

Intel Debugger

The Intel Debugger (IDB) is a standalone debugger available on the Linux platform. It has all the features you would expect of a debugger, including breakpoints, watchpoints, single-stepping, source code, and disassembler views.

IDB has its own graphical user interface as well as a command-line interface. All the parallel debugging features mentioned in the previous section are available in IDB.

Math Kernel Library

The Math Kernel Library (MKL) is a collection of math routines for use in science, engineering, and financial applications. The library is well optimized and often gives superior results over hand-crafted code or other comparable libraries. The libraries and functions in MKL are well known in the HPC community, so they are not described further here.

MKL offers the following functionality:

➤ Dense linear algebra

  ➤ Basic Linear Algebra Subprograms (BLAS)

  ➤ Linear Algebra PACKage (LAPACK)

  ➤ Trust Region Solver

➤ Sparse linear algebra

  ➤ Sparse BLAS

  ➤ Sparse format converters

➤ Sparse solvers

  ➤ PARDISO direct sparse solver

  ➤ Iterative sparse solvers

  ➤ Preconditioners

➤ Fast Fourier transforms

➤ Optimized LINPACK benchmark

➤ Vector math library

➤ Vector random number generators

➤ Cluster support

  ➤ Scalable LAPACK (ScaLAPACK)

  ➤ Cluster FFT

You can use the library functions in either Fortran or C/C++ code. Some of the functions have variants that have parallelism implemented internally. All the functions are thread-safe.

Listing 2-7 shows how to perform a matrix multiplication using the MKL. Two matrices, A and B, and are filled with random numbers. The function `cblas_sgemm` is used to multiply A and B and write the results in C.

Available for download on Wrox.com

LISTING 2-7: Using the MKL to perform a matrix multiplication

```
#include <stdlib.h>
#include <time.h>
#include "mkl_cblas.h"
```

```cpp
#define MATRIX_SIZE 100
#define BUFFER_SIZE MATRIX_SIZE * MATRIX_SIZE
int main(void)
{
  float A[BUFFER_SIZE];
  float B[BUFFER_SIZE];
  float C[BUFFER_SIZE];

  // seed the random number generator
  srand( (unsigned)time( NULL ) );

  // initialize the matrices with random values
  for (int i = 0; i < BUFFER_SIZE; i++)
  {
    A[i] = rand();
    B[i] = rand();
    C[i] = 0;
  }

  // matrix multiply using MKL
  cblas_sgemm(
      CblasRowMajor,
      CblasNoTrans,
      CblasNoTrans,
      MATRIX_SIZE,  MATRIX_SIZE,  MATRIX_SIZE, 1.0,
      A, MATRIX_SIZE,
      B, MATRIX_SIZE, 0.0,
      C, MATRIX_SIZE
  );
}
```

code snippet Chapter2\2-7.cpp

Because the MKL is designed to work with a number of different combinations of compilers and operating systems, several variants of the libraries ship with Parallel Studio XE. You can use the online wizard at `http://software.intel.com/en-us/articles/intel-mkl-link-line-advisor/` to help decide which MLK library to use.

VTUNE AMPLIFIER XE

VTune Amplifier XE is a profiling tool to find bottlenecks in your application. You can conduct the analysis at the algorithm level, where the focus is on the code, or at a more advanced level, where the performance of code on the processor microarchitecture is considered:

➤ Algorithm analysis

  ➤ Hotspots

  ➤ Concurrency

  ➤ Locks and Waits

➤ Advanced analysis

  ➤ General Exploration

  ➤ Memory Access

  ➤ Bandwidth

  ➤ Cycles and uOps

  ➤ Front-End Investigation

The profiling results are displayed graphically. A comparison of several results can be displayed side by side.

Advanced-level analysis relies on *event-based sampling*, which uses counters in the processor to measure how well your code performs. Read more in Chapter 12, "Event-Based Analysis with VTune Amplifier XE."

The first stage of the four-step tuning methodology (see Chapter 3) uses Amplifier to find code hotspots. In the final tuning step, Amplifier detects any parallel overhead and determines how parallel the code is.

All analyses should be carried out on the optimized version of your application.

 Use Amplifier on the optimized version of your application.

Hotspot Analysis

Hotspot analysis is used to find parts of the code that consume the most CPU activity. Hotspots are prime candidates for running in parallel (see Figure 2-8). The top part of the window gives a summary of the hotspots, the biggest being at the top of the list. To the far right is the call stack of the highlighted hotspot. The bottom of the window is a timeline view.

Concurrency Analysis

The Concurrency analysis gives a summary of how parallel an application runs. *Concurrency* is a measure of how many threads were running in parallel. The colored bars are a summary of how much time each function took, and the color of the bars indicates how much concurrency there is. You can filter the information in the graph by module, thread, processor, and utilization (see Figure 2-9).

Locks and Waits Analysis

The Locks and Waits analysis shows where a program is waiting for synchronization. Two groups of synchronization objects are supported: objects used for synchronization between threads, and objects used with waits on I/O operations.

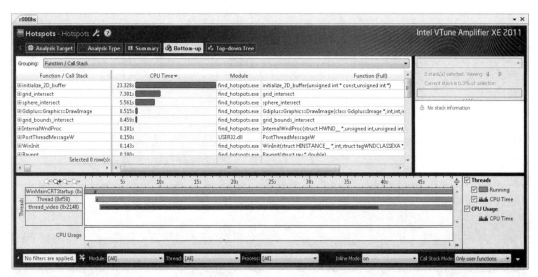

FIGURE 2-8: Hotspot analysis using Amplifier

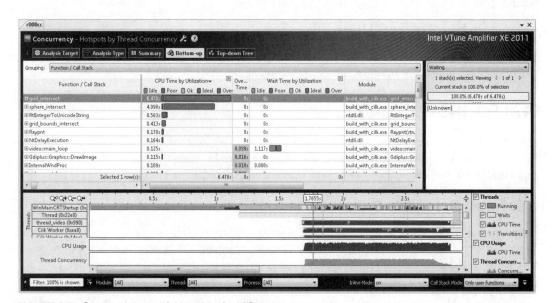

FIGURE 2-9: Concurrency analysis using Amplifier

In Figure 2-10, the longest red bars indicate the synchronization objects that are causing the longest wait time. You should try to fix these first.

You can also launch Amplifier XE from the command line. When you perform the profiling from the command line, the results are displayed as text. You can also view the results generated from the command line in the graphical version of Amplifier XE.

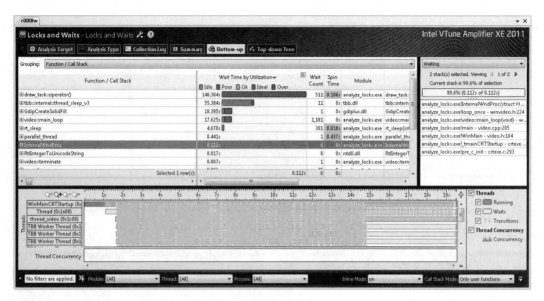

FIGURE 2-10: Locks and Waits analysis using Amplifier

Dissassembly Source View

You can drill down to the disassembly view of your code with Amplifier XE. You can choose to display assembler, source, or interleaved assembler and source.

PARALLEL INSPECTOR XE

Intel Parallel Inspector XE checks for threading and memory allocation errors. Inspector XE detects these errors at run time, usually working on an unoptimized version of the program under test. Data races and deadlocks are detected and their location pinpointed.

Predefined Analysis Types

Inspector XE is a dynamic analysis tool that observes the application under test while it is running. When Inspector XE launches an application, it first instruments the binary and then begins to capture runtime information. Several predefined analysis types are available (see Figure 2-11).

When Inspector XE executes code, it flags errors even if they did not actually cause a problem at run time. For example, if you run code that has a potential deadlock but the deadlock did not actually happen, Inspector XE still recognizes the potential problem and reports it.

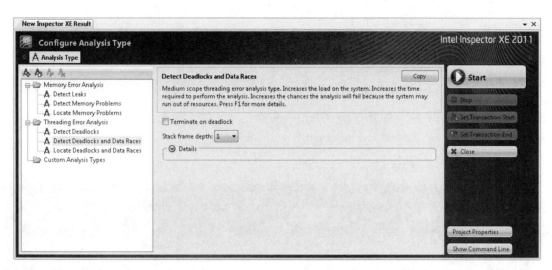

FIGURE 2-11: Controlling the analysis depth

Errors and Warnings

Inspector XE reports for the following types of errors and warnings:

➤ Threading errors

   ➤ Data races

   ➤ Deadlocks

   ➤ Lock hierarchy violations

   ➤ Potential privacy infringements

   ➤ Other threading information

➤ Memory errors

   ➤ GDI resource leaks

   ➤ Incorrect memcpy calls

   ➤ Invalid deallocations

   ➤ Invalid memory access

➤ Invalid partial memory access

➤ Kernel resource leaks

➤ Memory leaks

➤ Uninitialized memory access

➤ Uninitialized partial memory access

Figures 2-12 and 2-13 show how the results are displayed.

FIGURE 2-12: A threading error report in Inspector XE

Some errors that Inspector XE reports may be false positives — that is, they are not really errors but the tool thinks they are. Such errors can be added to a suppression file, and these errors are ignored in subsequent runs.

In addition to the GUI version of Inspector XE, a command-line version of Inspector is available, with the results displayed as text. You can also view the results generated from the command line in the graphical version of the tool.

 You can read more about Inspector XE in Chapter 8, "Checking for Errors."

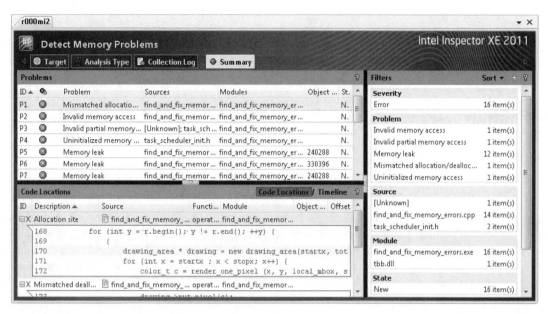

FIGURE 2-13: A memory error report in Inspector XE

STATIC SECURITY ANALYSIS

The primary goal of SSA is to harden applications against security attacks; it is also useful as a way to detect some programming errors. SSA relies on Composer XE and Inspector XE. The compiler performs the analysis, and Inspector XE displays the results.

The analysis checks for the following:

➤ Buffer overflows

➤ Misuse of pointers and heap storage

➤ Unsafe or incorrect use of C/C++ language and libraries

➤ Unsafe or incorrect use of Fortran language and libraries

➤ Misuse of OpenMP

➤ Misuse of Cilk Plus

When the compiler performs an SSA, it does not produce a working executable; however, it does produce intermediate object files, which contain extra information that is analyzed at the link stage.

Various scripts are available to help in preparing an analysis. For a more detailed description, see Chapter 5, "Writing Secure Code."

DIFFERENT APPROACHES TO USING PARALLEL STUDIO XE

Parallel Studio XE contains many different components to help you write parallel code and supports more than one model of use. Not all developers stick to one particular way of doing things. When using Parallel Studio XE, take a moment to consider which approach to using Parallel Studio might suit you. Here are some suggestions that might help:

➤ **If you are looking for as much guidance as possible** — Use Parallel Advisor, which offers a high-level methodology of developing parallelism. Advisor uses the technology of the underlying tools but does not rely on you firing up individual tools. This methodology doesn't suit everyone. If you are looking for a technique that helps model parallelism before implementing it, and keeps an overarching view of what you are doing, this might be for you.

Chapters 10 and 18 are dedicated to developing code using the Advisor-driven methodology.

➤ **If you prefer to control individual analysis and development steps** — Use the individual tools from Parallel Studio XE, launching the tools directly from the toolbars (rather than relying on Advisor). You can use the tools in Parallel Studio XE (Amplifier XE, Composer XE, and Inspector XE) as part of the popular four-step development cycle.

Chapter 3 introduces the four-step development cycle: analysis, implementation, error checking, and tuning.

➤ **If you hate graphical user interfaces or prefer script-driven development** — Use a compiler-centric focus, with all development work being carried out from the heart of your code using just command-line tools. You can drive the compiler, libraries, Amplifier XE, and Inspector XE from the command line.

SUMMARY

Parallel Studio XE includes most of the tools you need to write and debug simple and complex parallel applications.

Composer XE, which includes a C/C++ and Fortran compiler along with a set of optimized thread-safe libraries, can be used to write optimized/parallelized code. Amplifier XE and Inspector XE are used to profile and error-check your applications. Parallel Advisor enables you to model the effect of introducing parallelism into your code before committing to a particular implementation.

The next chapter gives you the chance to try Parallel Studio by following hands-on examples.

3

Parallel Studio XE for the Impatient

WHAT'S IN THIS CHAPTER?

➤ An overview of the four-step methodology for adding parallelism

➤ Using Cilk Plus to add parallelism

➤ Using OpenMP to add parallelism

The previous chapter introduced three ways of using Intel Parallel Studio XE: Advisor-driven design, compiler-centric development, and a four-step methodology.

This chapter describes the four-step methodology for transforming a serial program into a parallel program. The chapter's hands-on content guides you through the steps to create a completely parallelized program.

In the examples in this chapter, you use two parallel models, Intel Cilk Plus and OpenMP, to add parallelism to the serial code. Cilk Plus is regarded as one of the easiest ways to add parallelism to a program. OpenMP is a well-established standard that many parallel programmers have traditionally used.

You use various key components of Intel Parallel Studio XE to achieve the parallelization. This chapter describes how to use Intel VTune Amplifier XE 2011, an easy-to-use yet powerful profiling tool, to identify hotspots in the serial application, as well as analyze the parallel program for synchronicity, efficiency, and load balancing.

You use Composer XE to build the newly parallelized application, and then use Intel Inspector XE 2011 to reveal threading and memory errors. Finally, you return to Amplifier XE to check for thread concurrency and fine-tuning.

THE FOUR-STEP METHODOLOGY

Initially, parallelizing a serial program may seem fairly simple, with the user following a set of simple rules and applying common sense. But this may not always achieve the most efficient parallel program running at the expected speeds. Indeed, it is possible that faulty attempts at parallelization will actually make a program run more slowly than the original serial version, even though all parallel cores are running.

The four-step methodology, as shown in Figure 3-1, is a tried and tested method of adding parallelism to a program.

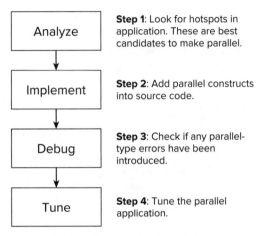

Step 1: Look for hotspots in application. These are best candidates to make parallel.

Step 2: Add parallel constructs into source code.

Step 3: Check if any parallel-type errors have been introduced.

Step 4: Tune the parallel application.

FIGURE 3-1: The four-step methodology

1. Analyze the serial program for opportunities to parallelize. This is probably the most important step; decisions made here will affect the final parallelized program.

2. Implement the parallelism using constructs from the parallel model you have chosen to use.

3. Debug or check if any parallel-type errors have been introduced. Is the program running correctly? Does it have threading or memory errors?

4. Tune the parallel application. Are all the threads doing equal amounts of work? Has an excessive overhead been introduced into the program as a result of adding parallelism?

With the exception of the debug step, you should carry out the steps on an optimized version of the application.

EXAMPLE 1: WORKING WITH CILK PLUS

In this example, you add parallelism to a serial program using Cilk Plus. Later, you parallelize the same serial code using OpenMP.

Obtaining a Suitable Serial Program

Not all serial programs are suitable for making parallel. Parallelization itself carries an overhead, which you must take into account when considering whether a program would benefit from being parallelized. You must test parallel programs extensively both by running them and by using analytical tools to ensure their results are the same as their serial versions.

Listing 3-1 shows the simple serial program that you'll make parallel using the four-step methodology. This is a contrived program, put together to show parallelization problems.

The program incorporates two loops: an outer loop and an inner work loop. The outer loop is designed to run the timed inner work loop several times; this reveals variations in timings caused by other background tasks being carried out by the computer. The time taken for the work loop to run is captured and reported back. The work loop itself iterates many times, with each iteration containing two further nested loops that calculate the sums of arithmetic series. The number of terms in the two series is determined by the loop count of the work loop. That is, as the work loop iteration count increases, the number of terms in the series increases, meaning that more work is required to calculate each series.

Then the inverse of the square root of each series is added to a running total; this is output at the end of the work loop. This stops the compiler from optimizing all the calculated values out of existence. Also, the output after each work loop has finished reveals the number of times the work loop has iterated, and the time taken for it to run.

LISTING 3-1: The starting serial program

```c
// Example Chapter 3 Serial Program
#include <stdio.h>
#include <windows.h>
#include <mmsystem.h>
#include <math.h>

const long int VERYBIG = 100000;
// ********************************************************************
int main( void )
{
    int i;
    long int j, k, sum;
    double sumx, sumy, total;
    DWORD starttime, elapsedtime;
// -------------------------------------------------------------------
    // Output a start message
    printf( "None Parallel Timings for %d iterations\n\n", VERYBIG );

    // repeat experiment several times
    for( i=0; i<6; i++ )
    {
        // get starting time
```

```
        starttime = timeGetTime();

        // reset check sum & running total
        sum = 0;
        total = 0.0;
        // Work Loop, do some work by looping VERYBIG times
        for( j=0; j<VERYBIG; j++ )
        {
            // increment check sum
            sum += 1;

            // Calculate first arithmetic series
            sumx = 0.0;
            for( k=0; k<j; k++ )
                sumx = sumx + (double)k;

            // Calculate second arithmetic series
            sumy = 0.0;
            for( k=j; k>0; k-- )
                sumy = sumy + (double)k;

            if( sumx > 0.0 )total = total + 1.0 / sqrt( sumx );
            if( sumy > 0.0 )total = total + 1.0 / sqrt( sumy );
        }

        // get ending time and use it to determine elapsed time
        elapsedtime = timeGetTime() - starttime;

        // report elapsed time
        printf("Time Elapsed %10d mSecs  Total=%lf   Check Sum = %ld\n",
                    (int)elapsedtime, total, sum );
    }

    // return integer as required by function header
    return 0;
}
// ********************************************************************
```

code snippet Chapter3\3-1.cpp

Even novice C programmers should have no problem understanding most of this program; however, it does contain a few lines of code that merit explanation. The program uses calls to the Windows API function `timeGetTime()`, which returns the current system time in milliseconds. By calling this function before and after the main work loop, you can determine the time involved in executing the loop. The time is returned by the function in a DWORD type variable. Looking at the start of the program code, you can see that a number of declarations are made:

➤   `#include <stdio.h>`, to enable input and output to and from the program in the usual manner.

➤   `#include <windows.h>`, to enable DWORD variable types to be declared.

➤ `#include <mmsystem.h>`, because it holds the prototype of the library function `timeGetTime()`.

➤ `const long int VERYBIG 100000`, which sets a constant that is used to control the number of times the main work loop will repeat. This is the controlling variable, which you can alter to vary the amount of work to be carried out, and therefore the length of time taken. This is shown as 100000.

Running the Serial Example Program

Before you undertake any parallelism, it is a good idea to build and run the existing serial version of the program. This gives a benchmark for the application and also shows what the output should look like. After parallelization, you should always check that the output of the program remains the same as for the serial version.

Creating the Project

To create a new project in Microsoft Visual Studio, perform the following steps:

1. Create a new project in Microsoft Visual Studio; it should be an empty console application project with no precompiled headers. Add a new C++ code file and paste the code from Listing 3-1.

2. Select the Release version of the project in the drop-down box at the top of the screen (Figure 3-2).

3. Add an additional library so that `timeGetTime()` can be used. Select Project ➪ Properties and add the library name `winmm.lib` to the Additional Dependencies fields of the Linker Input category (Figure 3-3).

4. Select Project ➪ Properties and make sure Optimization is set to Maximum Speed (Figure 3-4).

> *To avoid compilation errors from being produced when Cilk Plus reducers are used later in this chapter, it is important that the file extension is* `.cpp`, *not* `.c`.

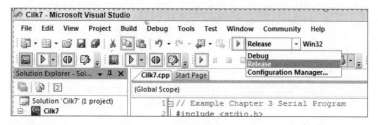

FIGURE 3-2: Selecting the Release configuration

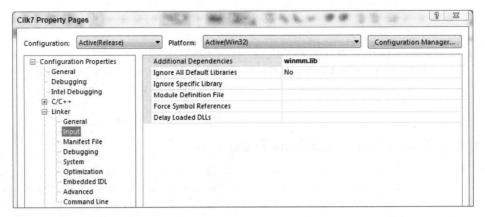

FIGURE 3-3: Adding winmm.lib to the linker options

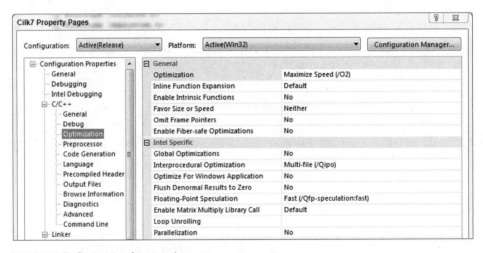

FIGURE 3-4: Optimizing for speed

Running the Serial Version of the Code

You will be building two serial versions of the application; the first version uses the Microsoft compiler, and then the second version uses the Intel compiler.

Using the Microsoft Compiler

You are now ready to build and run the serial example. The example program can be built using the Microsoft compiler in the usual manner. You can launch the program from within Visual Studio by pressing Ctrl+F5. Figure 3-5 shows the output, using the initial controlling constant VERYBIG set as 100000. Your output timings may be different due to differences between computer systems.

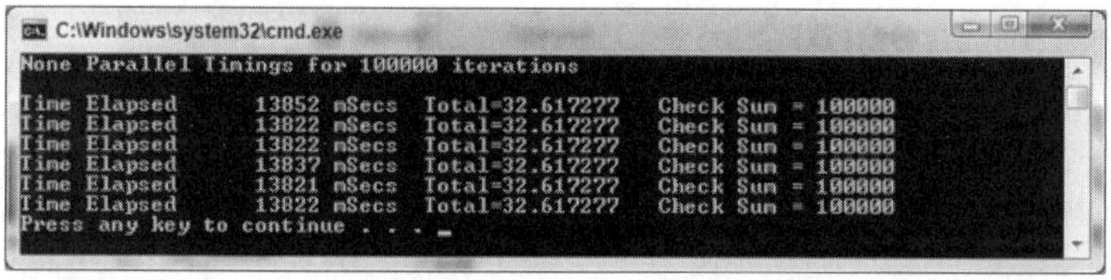

FIGURE 3-5: Serial timings for 100,000 iterations using the Microsoft compiler

Using the Intel Compiler

The first version of the program was built using the Microsoft compiler. To change to use the Intel compiler, follow these steps within the Microsoft Visual Studio environment:

1. Select Project ➪ Intel C++ Composer XE ➪ Use Intel C++.

A pop-up box asks if you want your project to be reconfigured for using the Intel C++ compiler. Click OK. It is prudent to just check that the project properties remain the same.

2. Build and run the program and compare the results. Remember to use Ctrl+F5 to run.

You should find that the executable runs a lot faster, as shown in Figure 3-6. This is because the Intel compiler optimizer is smarter about removing and refactoring redundant or expensive computations.

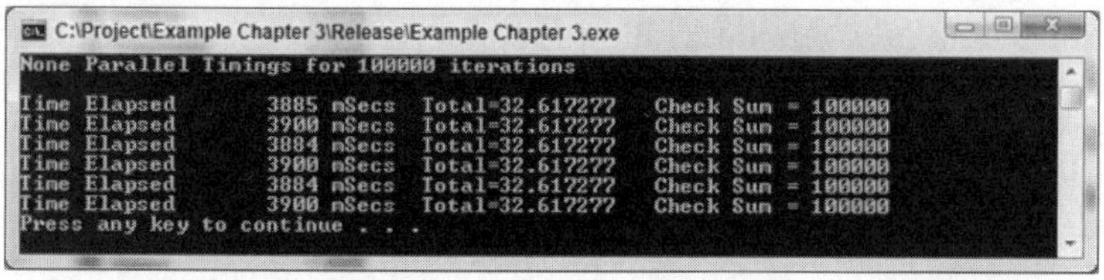

FIGURE 3-6: Serial timings for 100,000 iterations built with Intel compiler

The check sum value is a consistent 100000, which is the same as the number of iterations of the inner or working loop. The Total value is the result of the arithmetic calculations involved within the inner loop. If you want to reduce the time taken to run the program, make the value of VERYBIG smaller. Figure 3-7 shows the output run for a value of 10000.

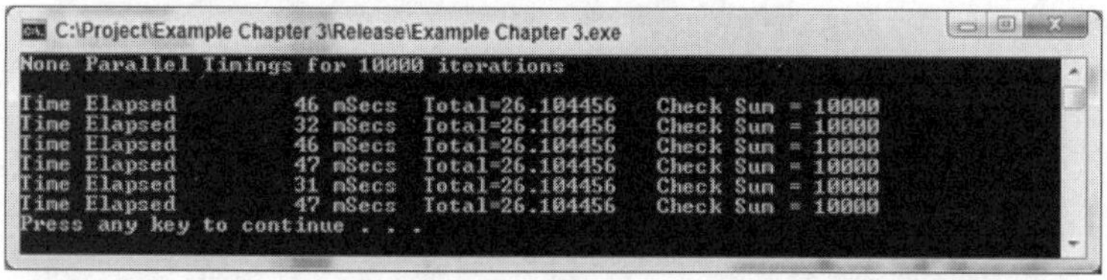

FIGURE 3-7: Serial timings for 10,000 iterations

Step 1: Analyze the Serial Program

The purpose of this step is to find the best place to add parallelism to the program. In simple programs you should be able to spot obvious places where parallelization might be applied. However, for any program of even just moderate complexity, it is essential that you use an analysis tool, such as Intel Parallel Amplifier XE. Although this is a rather trivial programming example, you can use the steps on more complex programs.

Using Intel Parallel Amplifier XE for Hotspot Analysis

When Intel Parallel Studio XE was installed into Microsoft Visual Studio, it set up a number of additional toolbars, one of which is for Intel Parallel Amplifier XE (introduced in Chapter 2). Amplifier is a profiling tool that collects and analyzes data as the program runs.

This example uses Amplifier XE to look for parts of the code that are using the most CPU time; referred to as *hotspots*, they are prime candidates for parallelization.

Because Amplifier XE does slow down the execution of the program considerably, it is recommended that you run an application with reduced data. Provide data input and reduce loop iterations, where possible, to reduce the run time.

For this example, the outer loop is reduced to 1. This will not prevent Amplifier from finding the hotspots, because the outer loop merely runs through the same work loop several times. Hotspots found in the first iteration of the work loop will be the same in any further iterations of it. Also, leave VERYBIG set as 10000. You will need to rebuild with these new settings before using Amplifier.

 Amplifier XE is described in more detail in Chapter 6, "Where to Parallelize."

Starting the Analysis

To start the analysis, follow these steps:

1. Select New Analysis from the Amplifier XE part of the toolbar, as shown in Figure 3-8. This brings up the start-up page.

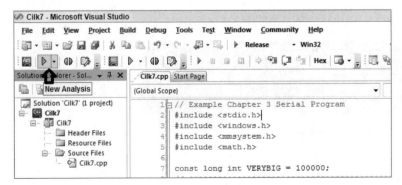

FIGURE 3-8: Selecting a new Amplifier analysis

2. Select the analysis type Hotspots, as shown in Figure 3-9. Hotspot analysis looks for code that is consuming the most CPU activity.

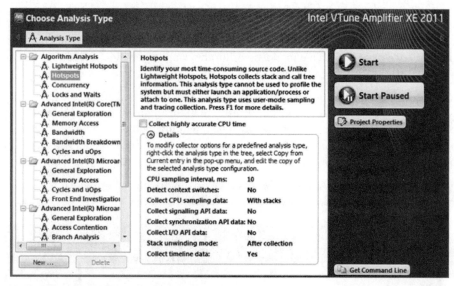

FIGURE 3-9: Start-up page of the Amplifier XE

3. Click the Start button. Amplifier runs a hotspot analysis on your program. Because there is no pause at the end of your program, Amplifier will both start and finish your program itself.

Figure 3-10 shows the results.

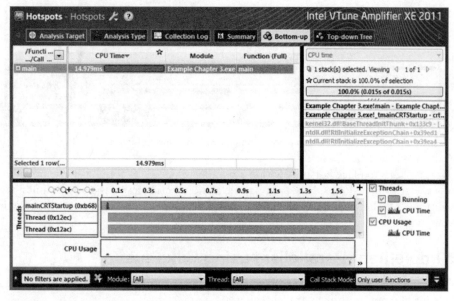

FIGURE 3-10: Hotspot analysis using Amplifier XE

Drilling Down into the Source Code

Figure 3-10 shows how much CPU time was spent in each function. In this example, because there is only a single function, main, only this one entry is present. To examine the source code of the hotspot, double-click the entry for function main. This reveals the program code, with the hotspots shown as bars to their right with lengths proportional to CPU time spent on each line (Figure 3-11). Note that the code pane has been expanded within the Amplifier window, and that line numbers within Parallel Studio have been turned on.

In the code shown, Amplifier automatically centers on the line of code that consumes the most CPU time — in this case, line 43. Two groups of three lines are using most of the CPU time; these involve the loops calculating the two arithmetic series. The remaining code lines consume little CPU time in comparison and so show nothing. These arithmetic loops are the hotspots within your program. Your own computer system may give different times, but it should follow a similar pattern.

You should also note that the Amplifier results for this run are placed in the Amplifier XE folder under the project solution. You can see this to the left of the screen.

FIGURE 3-11: Hotspot analysis using Amplifier XE, showing hotspots

Parallelization aims to place hotspots within a parallel region. You could just attempt a parallelism of each of the arithmetic loops. However, parallelization works best if the largest amount of code can be within a parallel region. Parallelizing the work loop places both sets of hotspots within the same loop.

Step 2: Implement Parallelism using Cilk Plus

After identifying the hotspots in the code, your next step is to parallelize the code in such a way as to include the hotspots within a parallel region.

To make the code parallel, follow these steps:

1. Add the following `include` to the top of the program:

```
#include <cilk/cilk.h>
```

2. Add a `cilk_for` loop by changing the C++ `for` loop to a `cilk_for` loop. Notice that you must declare the loop counter within the loop control bracket:

```
// Work Loop, do some work by looping VERYBIG times
cilk_for( int j=0; j<VERYBIG; j++ )
```

3. Change the output start message, for completeness:

```
// Output a start message
printf( "Cilk Plus Parallel Timings for %d iterations \n\n",VERYBIG );
```

And that's it! Simple, isn't it?

Well, not quite. You have a few problems to overcome. You should rebuild a Release version of your program with VERYBIG set as 10000, but change your outer loop count back to the original 6.

When your program now runs, it creates a pool of threads, where the number of threads is usually the same as the number of cores. These threads are made ready to be available within the parallel regions. When a parallel region is reached, such as the `cilk_for` loop, the threads distribute the work of executing the loop among themselves dynamically. This should, in theory, speed up the execution time.

In fact, when you now run your program, you will find that instead of reducing the execution time, it has actually increased it enormously. Figure 3-12 shows the new timings, using a 4-core installation. Compare these timings with the serial version shown in Figure 3-7; the parallelized version is much slower. And remember that all 4 cores were running, so it is actually four times slower than the numbers suggest. Also, notice the values of Total and Check Sum are incorrect.

FIGURE 3-12: Timings for the initial Cilk Plus parallelized program

Obviously, something is wrong. The problem is, by introducing parallelism, you also introduced problems caused by concurrent execution. In the next few steps you investigate how to fix these problems by enhancing both the speed and performance of the application.

Step 3: Debug and Check for Errors

With the introduction of parallelism into the program, the program no longer runs correctly. This step checks the program to see if any parallel-type errors exist, such as deadlocks and data races, which are responsible for slowing down the program. These errors are caused by multiple threads reading and writing the same data variables simultaneously — always a potential cause of trouble.

Checking for Errors

You can find data races and deadlocks by using Intel Parallel Inspector XE. It is recommended that you perform any error checking on the debug version of the program, not the Release version. Building in the Release version will carry out optimizations, including in-lining, which may accidentally hide an error. Using the debug build also means that the information reported by Inspector is more precise and more aligned with the actual code written.

Running an Inspector analysis is a lot slower than just running the program normally. As with Amplifier, you should reduce the running time by reducing loop counts and using small data sets.

To check for errors, follow these steps:

1. Change the solution configuration to be a debug version, but don't rebuild just yet.

2. Because Inspector is slow, reset VERYBIG to just 1000, and reduce the outer loop to be just 1:

```
// repeat experiment several times
for( i=0; i<1; i++ )
```

Errors found in the first iteration of the loop will just be repeated in further loops, so there is no point in having more loops.

3. Add the dependency winmm.lib to the linker, as in the Release version, and set it for no optimization. Of course, for a debug build any optimizations will be ignored, even if their options are set.

4. Rebuild the application.

5. Launch Inspector XE from the toolbar, and select New Analysis (Figure 3-13).

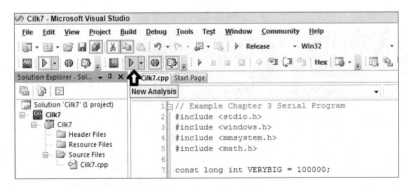

FIGURE 3-13: Selecting a new Inspector analysis

6. In Inspector's configuration window, select the analysis type Locate Deadlocks and Data Races (Figure 3-14).

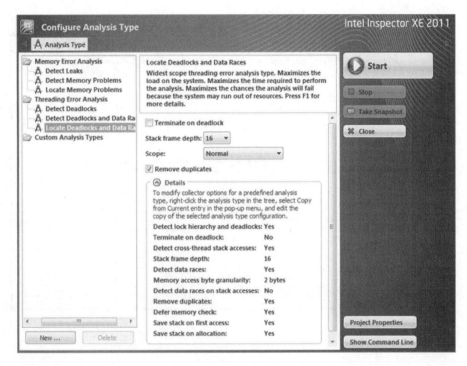

FIGURE 3-14: Selecting for locating deadlocks and data races

7. Click the Start button. Inspector runs your program, carrying out an analysis as it does so. Inspector targets the analysis to find deadlocks and data races, with the results as shown in Figure 3-15.

The top-left pane of the Inspector window summarizes the problems. The bottom-left pane shows the events associated with any selected problem. Try clicking on the various problems. In Figure 3-15 problem P3, a data race, is selected; its associated events are listed in the lower pane. Altogether, five problems, P2 to P6, are shown as data races. These are marked with an x in a red circle. The other problem, "Cross-thread stack access," is actually just information, as indicated by its associated yellow triangle, and can be ignored.

8. Double-click the P3 problem to reveal the code associated with it (Figure 3-16).

Two code snippets are shown, with the location of one of the events in each. The top code pane, Focus Code Location, shows where the data race was detected during a write event. The lower of the two code snippets, Related Code Location, shows the read event that was involved in the data race.

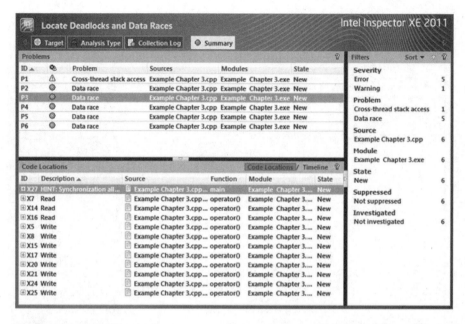

FIGURE 3-15: Summary of threading errors detected by the Inspector XE analysis

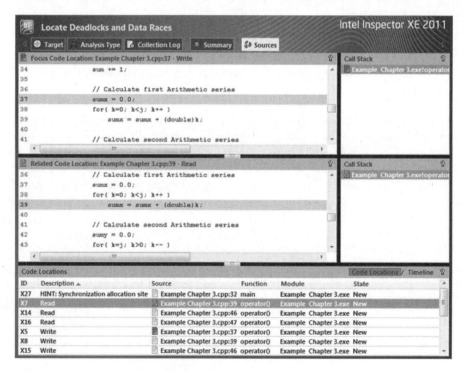

FIGURE 3-16: A data race exposed in the source code

From these two code snippets you can determine that variable sumx is the problem. The Focus Code Location pane shows the variable being changed (write), at line 37 of the code. The Related Code Location pane shows the variable being read, at line 39 of the code. When multiple threads are running there arises the danger of one thread changing the value of sumx (resetting to 0), while a second concurrently running thread is still using it, thereby making the second thread have an incorrect value. This is referred to as a *data race*.

Examining the other data race problems, you should be able to determine which variables they involve. The full list of variables causing data races is sum, total, sumx, sumy, and k. All five of these variables were created at the start of the function, and their scope is that of the function. However, the arguments that follow would be the same regardless of whether these variables are global or static. During parallel execution all the threads are competing to read from and write to these function-scoped variables. These are referred to as *shared variables*, and they are all shared by the concurrently executing threads. For future reference, they will be referred to as *nonlocal variables*.

 Inspector XE is described in more detail in Chapter 8, "Checking for Errors."

Narrowing the Scope of the Shared Variables

Looking at the variables k, sumx, and sumy, you can see that they are set and used wholly within the parallel region; they are not used outside it. One solution for this is to declare them within the parallel region. As each thread independently runs through the code of the parallel region, it creates its own private versions of these variables. They will be local variables to each thread.

Indeed, this is exactly what happened when the Cilk Plus version of the for loop was declared: its loop variable j was declared within the loop control bracket. It is a local variable that will be private for each thread.

You can modify the first few lines of the work loop, as shown in Listing 3-2. You can remove the original declarations of these variables from the top of the program if you wish. Removing them cleans up the program and makes it easier for other programmers to understand; however, if you don't remove the variables from the top of the program, the compiler simply creates locally scoped variables that overlay the variables at the top of the program. This also applies to loop counter j, which was redeclared within the loop control bracket.

 LISTING 3-2: Amendments to beginning of the work loop for Cilk Plus implementation

```
// Work loop, do some work by looping VERYBIG times
cilk_for( int j=0; j<VERYBIG; j++ )
{
   long int k;
   double sumx, sumy;

   // increment check sum
   sum += 1;
```

code snippet Chapter3\3-2.cpp

Set the work loop controlling variable VERYBIG to 100000, and the outer loop iteration value back to 6. Then rebuild a Release version of the application and rerun. Figure 3-17 shows the timings for this new run on a 4-core machine. Remember, your actual values may be different for your computer.

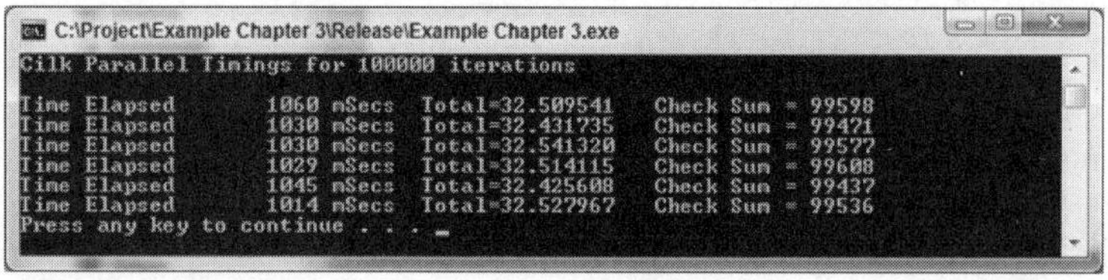

FIGURE 3-17: Timings for the Cilk Plus parallelized program using loop local variables

Notice that the Total and Check Sum values are incorrect and inconsistent between the runs. These errors are also caused by data races, but making thread-private copies of the offending variables total and sum locally within the loop will not help in this case, because these variables must be shared between all the threads.

Figure 3-18 illustrates what happens when more than one thread attempts to increment the check sum in the code line:

```
sum += 1;
```

As you can see from Figure 3-18, if sum starts with a value of 12, after both threads have incremented the result is 13, instead of the expected 14.

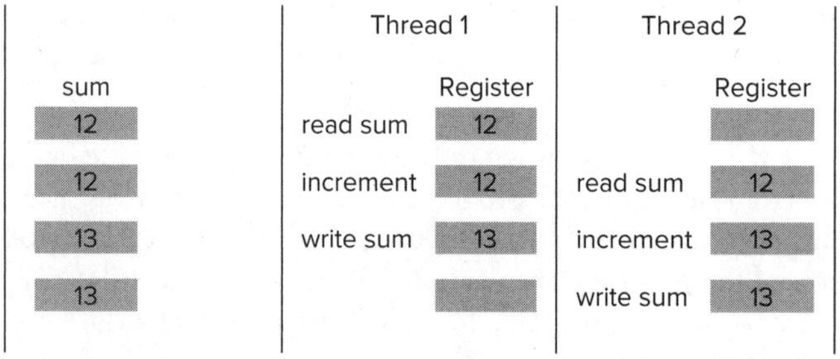

FIGURE 3-18: Problematic access to global variables

One solution for a variable of this type is to use a synchronization object or primitive, such as a lock. This ensures that only a single thread at a time has access to it. Other threads requiring access at the same time must wait for the variable to become free. However, this solution has the drawback of slowing down the execution time. Alternatively, Cilk Plus offers a special variable form called a *reduction* variable, which is discussed in the next section.

Adding Cilk Plus Reducers

Cilk Plus reducers are objects that address the need to use shared variables in parallel code. Conceptually, a reducer can be considered to be a shared variable. However, during run time each thread has access to its own private copy, or *view*, of the variable, and works on this copy only. As the parallel strands finish, the results of their views of the variable are combined asynchronously into the single shared variable. This eliminates the possibility of data races without requiring time-consuming locks.

A Cilk Plus reducer is defined in place of the normal nonlocal shared variable definition. Remember that here, *nonlocal* refers to automatic and static function variables as well as program global variables. The Cilk Plus reducer has to be defined outside the scope of the parallel section of code in which it is to be used.

To add Cilk Plus reducers to the code, follow these steps:

1. Add an extra header declaration:

   ```
   #include <cilk/reducer_opadd.h>
   ```

2. Delete the declaration for sum and total at the top of the program.

3. Redeclare the variables sum and total to be Cilk Plus reducers. The reducer implicitly resets the variable to 0, but it is always a good idea to explicitly say what you want. This gives you more control.

   ```
   cilk::reducer_opadd<long int> sum(0);
   cilk::reducer_opadd<double> total(0.0);
   ```

   Place these within the outer loop, in place of the statements:

   ```
   sum = 0;
   total = 0.0;
   ```

   This ensures that for every iteration of the outer loop, sum and total will be reset to zero.

4. Change the printf statement to use the reducer function get_value(), which gives the combined value of a reducer variable:

   ```
   printf("Time Elapsed %10d mSecs  Total=%lf   Check Sum = %ld\n",
           (int)elapsedtime, total.get_value(), sum.get_value() );
   ```

5. Build and rerun the program to make sure the results are correct.

Listing 3-3 gives the final Cilk Plus program.

LISTING 3-3: The final version of the Cilk Plus parallelized program

```
// Example Chapter 3 Cilk Plus Program
#include <stdio.h>
#include <windows.h>
#include <mmsystem.h>
#include <math.h>
#include <cilk/cilk.h>
#include <cilk/reducer_opadd.h>
```

```
const long int VERYBIG = 100000;
// ********************************************************************
int main( void )
{
  int i;
  DWORD starttime, elapsedtime;
// --------------------------------------------------------------------
  // Output a start message
  printf( "Cilk Plus Parallel Timings \n\n" );

  // repeat experiment several times
  for( i=0; i<6; i++ )
  {
    // get starting time
    starttime = timeGetTime();

    // define check sum and total as reduction variables
    cilk::reducer_opadd<long int> sum(0);
    cilk::reducer_opadd<double> total(0.0);

    // Work Loop, do some work by looping VERYBIG times
    cilk_for( int j=0; j<VERYBIG; j++ )
    {
      // define loop local variables
      long int k;
      double sumx, sumy;

      // increment check sum
      sum += 1;

      sumx = 0.0;
      for( k=0; k<j; k++ )
        sumx = sumx + (double)k;

      sumy = 0.0;
      for( k=j; k>0; k-- )
        sumy = sumy + (double)k;

      if( sumx > 0.0 )total = total + 1.0 / sqrt( sumx );
      if( sumy > 0.0 )total = total + 1.0 / sqrt( sumy );
    }

    // get ending time and use it to determine elapsed time
    elapsedtime = timeGetTime() - starttime;

    // report elapsed time
    printf("Time Elapsed %10d mSecs  Total=%lf   Check Sum = %ld\n",
           (int)elapsedtime, total.get_value(), sum.get_value() );
  }

  // return integer as required by function header
  return 0;
}
// ********************************************************************
```

code snippet Chapter3\3-3.cpp

Running the Corrected Application

Figure 3-19 shows the application's new timings on a 4-core machine after you have fixed all the errors and rebuilt a new Release version. Again, these timings were generated on a 4-core computer system and may differ from your timings, depending on what system you are running.

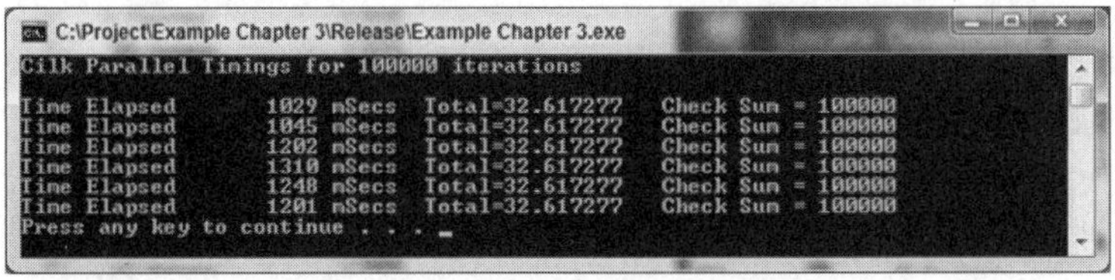

FIGURE 3-19: Timings for the Cilk Plus parallelized program with reducers added

A speedup ratio of about 3.74 was achieved compared to the speeds shown in Figure 3-6. The Check Sum and Total values are now correct, being the same as in the serial version of the program. Running the Intel Parallel Inspector again shows that the data race problems have been resolved.

It is important to note that using the Intel C++ compiler with Cilk Plus parallelization has sped up the process approximately 13 times over the timings obtained using the default Microsoft C++ compiler shown in Figure 3-5.

Step 4: Tune the Cilk Plus Program

Cilk Plus works by allowing the various parallel threads to distribute work among themselves dynamically. In most cases this leads to a well-balanced solution; that is, each thread is doing an equal amount of work overall. To use Intel Parallel Amplifier XE to check for this concurrency and efficiency, follow these steps:

1. Start a new analysis from the Parallel Studio menu bar, as before.

2. Select Concurrency from the list of analysis types.

3. Run Amplifier for concurrency analysis by clicking its Start button. Amplifier will now run your program and generate a new output of results.

4. Click the drop-down button (Figure 3-20) to obtain a list of alternative ways to display the information, and select /Thread/Function/Call Stack. Figure 3-21 shows the result. Your actual results may look different to that shown, depending on the number of cores your machine has.

   The top pane of Figure 3-21 shows the threads and their utilization, in order of usage. The highlighted thread, mainCRTStartup, is the management thread, which executes the serial part of the program and creates the four Cilk Plus worker threads (for a 4-core machine). These threads are run on the 4 cores concurrently during parallel execution. The two other threads were created by the operating system and are not Cilk Plus worker threads; they do no work and can be ignored.

   The CPU Time by Utilization column shows how well each thread was used by means of a bar. The bars are color-coded to indicate how efficiently their time was utilized; the aim is to get as large a portion showing Ideal as possible. All the threads are shown as being ideally utilized for most of their time. Also note that the lengths of the bars indicate how much time each thread was used; they are nearly the same, showing a well-balanced execution. As before, note that the times shown may be different on your computer system.

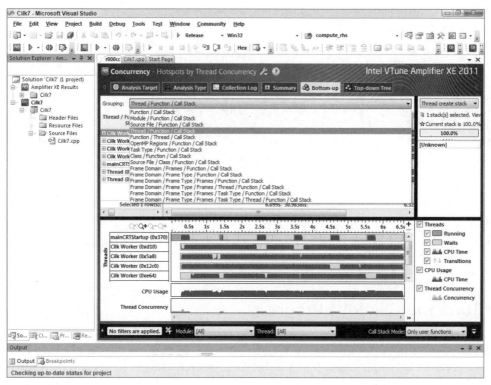

FIGURE 3-20: Selecting for viewing concurrency information

FIGURE 3-21: Concurrency analysis from Amplifier for Cilk Plus program

The bottom pane of Figure 3-21 shows how these threads were used during execution. It shows a profile analysis timeline of the threads. You may need to move the boundaries between upper and lower panes, and move parts of your display around to get the same view, or just use the scroll buttons to view.

The top five timelines show the activity of the main (serial) thread, `mainCRTStartup,` and the four Cilk Plus worker threads. Notice the main thread does six spurts of work, which correspond to the outer loop of the program being iterated, doing some work, and then entering the parallel regions. Try changing the iteration count of the outer loop to 4 and see what happens.

The next timeline, CPU Usage, shows that usage was very nearly consistently 100 percent. The final timeline, Thread Concurrency, shows a nearly 100 percent thread concurrency usage. Indeed, when the percentage of concurrency usage dropped, it coincided with the main thread doing its work in serial.

5. Finally, for now, select the Summary tab along the top of the Amplifier to obtain summary information. Scroll down until you get to the view shown in Figure 3-22. This shows the time spent when 0, 1, 2, 3, and 4 threads were running concurrently. For most of the time four threads were running in concurrent operation, which led to an overall average of concurrency of 3.74 — the speedup achieved by parallelizing the serial program.

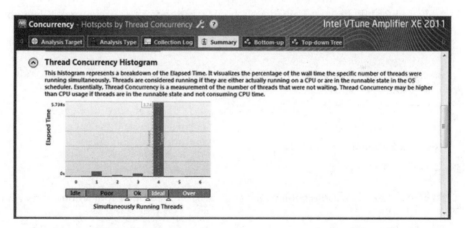

FIGURE 3-22: Amplifier information showing thread concurrency for the Cilk Plus program

All this Amplifier information shows that the Cilk Plus program is highly efficient and concurrent. As such, no further tuning is required.

EXAMPLE 2: WORKING WITH OPENMP

The following sections assume that you are using the Intel C++ compiler. However, note that Microsoft Visual C++ compiler also supports OpenMP, should you want to use it.

Step 1: Analyze the Serial Program

The analysis step is identical to the one you already did for the Cilk Plus example, so there is no need to do anything else. If you didn't run the first analysis, go to Example 1 and, starting from Listing 3-1, complete the steps outlined in the following sections:

1. Obtaining a Suitable Serial Program

2. Running the Serial Example Program

3. Step 1. Analyze the Serial Program

Once you have done these you are ready to start the next section.

Step 2: Implement Parallelism using OpenMP

OpenMP uses `pragma` directives within existing C++ code to set up parallelism. You can modify the directives using clauses.

To add parallelism to the original serial program of Listing 3-1, follow these steps:

1. Enable OpenMP on the project property pages (Figure 3-23).

2. Add an OpenMP directive immediately before the loop to be parallelized. Remember that after the Amplifier analysis toward the beginning of this chapter, it was decided to apply parallelism to the work loop:

```
// Work loop, do some work by looping VERYBIG times
#pragma omp parallel for
for( int j=0; j<VERYBIG; j++ )
{
```

3. Add an additional `include` file:

```
#include <omp.h>
```

4. Build and run a Release version of the program, with an outer loop count of 6 and `VERYBIG` set as 100000.

When the OpenMP directive is encountered, a parallel region is entered and a pool of threads is created. The number of threads in the pool usually matches the number of cores. Execution of the `for` loop that follows is parallelized, with its execution being shared between the threads.

Figure 3-24 shows the timings for a 4-core processor. The timings are not very encouraging when compared against the serial timings given in Figure 3-6. And, once again, the `Total` and `Check Sum` values are incorrect. As in the Cilk Plus case, the problem is with data races. Remember, your times may be different from those shown here.

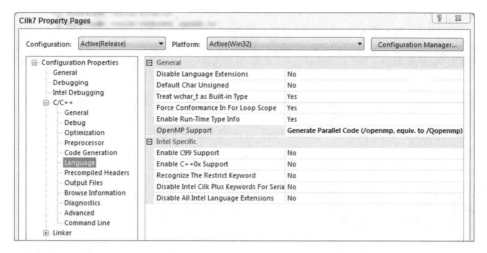

FIGURE 3-23: Enabling OpenMP in the compiler

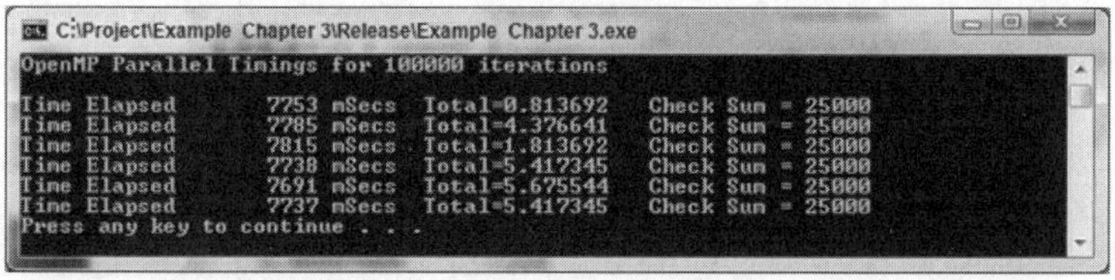

FIGURE 3-24: Timings for the OpenMP parallelized program, initial stage

Step 3: Debug and Check for Errors

An inspection of the threading errors using Intel Parallel Inspector shows the same data race problems occurring as revealed in the Cilk Plus example (refer to Figure 3-15). Remember to limit the activity of the program and build a debug version. The solutions applied to eliminate the data races revealed are similar but work subtly differently from those applied under Cilk Plus. As before, the data races break down into two types: those that can be solved by using private variables, and those that need to use reduction variables. OpenMP can handle both types, but it does so in a different way from Cilk Plus, by using clauses on its directives.

Making the Shared Variables Private

You can fix the data races caused by variables `sumx`, `sumy`, and `k` by creating private variables for each thread by adding a `private` clause to the parallel `pragma` directive, as follows:

```
#pragma omp parallel for \
private( sumx, sumy, k )
```

The backslash (\) is used as a continuation marker and its use after the first line is merely to indicate that the directive continues onto the next line. In an OpenMP parallelized `for` loop, its loop counter is, by default, always made private, which is why it did not show up in the inspection as an extra data race. The variables in the list must already exist as declared nonlocal variables — that is, as automatic, static, or global variables.

When the worker threads are created, they automatically make private versions of all the variables in the private list. During execution each thread uses its own private copy of variables, so no conflicts occur and the data races associated with these variables are resolved.

Adding a Reduction Clause

As with the Cilk Plus solution, a different approach is required for variables within the loop that must be shared by the threads; they cannot be made private. This is handled in OpenMP by adding a `reduction` clause to the OpenMP directive:

```
#pragma omp parallel for       \
    private( sumx, sumy, k )   \
    reduction( +: sum, total )
```

When the parallel section is reached, each participating thread creates and uses private copies, or versions, of the listed reduction variables. When the parallel section ends, the private thread versions of the variables are operated on according to the operator within the reduction brackets — in this case, they are added together. The resultant value is then merged back into the original nonlocal variable for future use. Other operators, such as multiply and subtract (but not divide), are also allowed. Note that it is up to the programmer to ensure that the operation on the variables within the loop body matches the operator of the `reduction` clause. In this case, both `sum` and `total` are added to each iteration of the work loop, which matches the `reduction` operator of +.

After rebuilding and running the Release version, you should see the times obtained for a 4-core machine (Figure 3-25). This corrects the `Check Sum` and `Total` values, but with an average time increase of only 2.28 times that of Figure 3-6. Further tuning is required. Remember, your times may be different, depending on the system you are running.

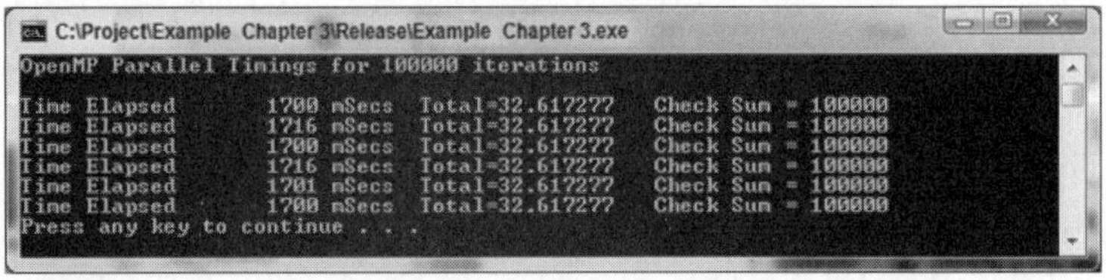

FIGURE 3-25: Timings for the OpenMP parallelized program, with private and reduction variables

Step 4: Tune the OpenMP Program

To use Intel Parallel Amplifier XE to check for concurrency and efficiency within the OpenMP program, follow these steps:

1. Start a new analysis from the Parallel Studio menu bar, as before.

2. Select Concurrency from the list of analysis types.

3. Run the Amplifier for concurrency analysis by clicking its Start button. Amplifier will now run your program and generate a new output of results.

4. Click the drop-down button to obtain a list of alternative ways to display the information, and select /Thread/Function/Call Stack. The result should be as shown in Figure 3-26. As with the Cilk Plus concurrency analysis (refer to Figure 3-21), the various panes have had their borders moved to produce the display shown. Your actual results may look different to that shown, depending on the number of cores your machine has.

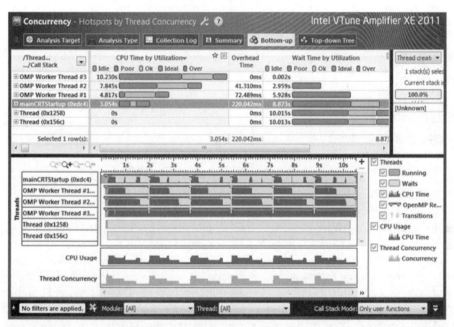

FIGURE 3-26: Concurrency information showing unbalanced loads

The results are very different from those shown for Cilk Plus. The top pane shows the `mainCRT-Startup` thread, as with the Cilk Plus model, but now there are only three other OMP Worker Threads, numbered 1 to 3 — because the main (serial) thread is also used as one of the parallel threads. This is different from Cilk Plus. Two other threads, created by the operating system, do not take part in the parallel operations and do no work, so you can ignore them.

The top pane, which shows CPU utilization time for each thread, clearly indicates an imbalance between the threads, with the `mainCRTStartup` thread doing less than a third of the work of OMP Worker Thread 3.

This imbalance is reflected in the lower pane, where the timelines of each of the parallel threads are given. Brown shows when a thread is doing work, and green shows when it is idle. You can clearly see that the `mainCRTStartup` thread is doing little work compared to the OMP Worker Thread 3. Also notice the same sixfold pattern to the work caused by the outer loop running six times.

The CPU Usage and Thread Concurrency timelines both show poor performance. This is demonstrated in Figure 3-27, which can be obtained by clicking the Summary button. This shows the amount of time spent with 0, 1, 2, 3, and 4 threads running concurrently. Only a small part of the time are four threads running together, with more than a quarter of the time spent running only a single thread. Overall, an average of 2.26 threads were running concurrently, which agrees almost exactly with the increase in speed.

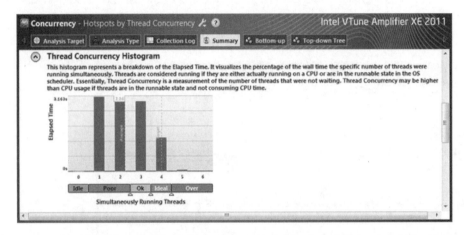

FIGURE 3-27: Amplifier showing thread concurrency for the OpenMP program before tuning

The problem occurs because the arithmetic series required more terms as the iteration count of the work loop grew larger. As the work loop counter increases, so too does the amount of work required to calculate the arithmetic series. However, unlike Cilk Plus, the default scheduling operation of OpenMP is to simply divide the execution of the work loop between the available threads in a straightforward fashion. Each thread is given the task of iterating the work loop a fixed number of times, referred to as the *chunk size*. For example, on a 4-core machine, with an iterative count of 100,000, OpenMP simply divides the iterations of the loop by four equal ranges:

➤ One thread is given iterations for loop counter 0 to 24,999.

➤ The next thread is given iterations for loop counter 25,000 to 49,999.

➤ The next thread is given iterations for loop counter 50,000 to 74,999.

➤ The final thread is given iterations for loop counter 75,000 to 99,999.

For most purposes, this would be a balanced workload, with each thread doing an equal amount of work. But not in this case. Threads working through higher-value iterations encounter arithmetic series with greater numbers of terms, the number of terms being dependent on the iteration value. This means that the threads working on the higher iterations have to do more work, creating unbalanced loading of the threads.

Figure 3-28 demonstrates a simplified problem with unbalanced loads. In this example a serial program enters a loop with a count of 12, where each iteration of the loop carries out work whose execution takes longer. This is indicated by the blocks marked 1 through 12 on the top bar, labeled

Single Thread (78 time units). This bar represents the running of the serial program, where the width of each block is the time taken to execute each of the 12 loops. In this example the first loop takes 1 time unit, the second loop takes 2 time units, and so on, with the final loop taking 12 time units — making a total time of 78 time units to run the serial program.

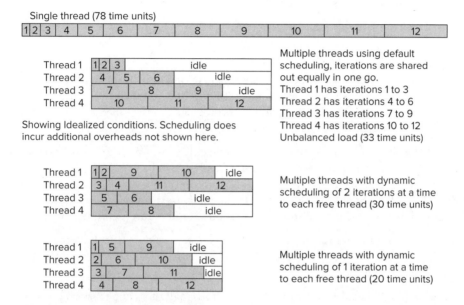

FIGURE 3-28: Example demonstrating unbalanced loading

Ideally, the parallelized time to run the same loop on a 4-core machine should be 78/4 = 19.5 time units; however, this is not the full story.

The default scheduling behavior for OpenMP is to distribute the loops equally to all the available threads — in this case, as follows:

➤ Thread 1 is allocated iterations 1 to 3.

➤ Thread 2 is allocated iterations 4 to 6.

➤ Thread 3 is allocated iterations 7 to 9.

➤ Thread 4 is allocated iterations 10 to 12.

When you run the parallel program under these default conditions, the result is shown by the second block of Figure 3-28. Thread 4 has all the high iterations, which take more time. Thread 4's running time is 10+11+12=33 time units, which is clearly shown in the diagram. Concurrently running thread 3 takes only 7+8+9=24 time units to execute its allocated work. Thread 2 takes 15 time units, and thread 1 takes only 6 time units. Since all threads must synchronize at the end of the parallelized loop before continuing, it means that threads 1 to 3 must wait for thread 4 to complete. A lot of time that could be otherwise used is wasted.

You can alter the scheduling preferences of OpenMP by using the scheduling clause. This clause enables you to set how many iterations each thread will be allocated — referred to as the *chunk size*. Each thread will execute its allocated iteration of the loop before coming back to the scheduler for more.

The third block of Figure 3-28 shows what happens when a new scheduling preference of 2 is used. At the start of the loop each available thread receives two iterations, as follows:

➤   Thread 1 is allocated iterations 1 and 2.

➤   Thread 2 is allocated iterations 3 and 4.

➤   Thread 3 is allocated iterations 5 and 6.

➤   Thread 4 is allocated iterations 7 and 8.

In this case thread 1 quickly executes its 2 allocated iterations, taking only 3 time units to do so. It then returns to the scheduler for more, and is given iterations 9 and 10 to execute. Thread 2 also finishes its allocated work, taking 7 time units, before returning back to the scheduler to be given iterations 11 and 12 to execute.

When threads 3 and 4 finish, they also return back to the scheduler, but since there is no more iterations to be executed they are given no more work. These threads must idle until the other threads finish their work. The first thread must also idle for a time since the execution of its allocated iterations finishes before the second thread. All this is clearly shown by the third block of Figure 3-28, where the second thread dictates the overall time of execution — in this case, 30 time units.

The fourth block of Figure 3-28 demonstrates what happens if the chunk size for the scheduler is reduced to just 1. The overall time of execution, decided by the fourth thread, reduces to just 20 time units and minimal idle time.

There is an overhead because scheduling chunks takes time; too small of a chunk size could end up being detrimental to the operation. Only by trying various values can you find the correct chunk size for your particular program.

Improving the Load Balancing

To obtain a balanced load, you need to override the default scheduling behavior. In this case the loop iterates 100,000 times, so as a first attempt use a chunk size of, say, 2000. You can override the default scheduling algorithm for a `for` loop by using the `schedule` clause on the directive:

```
#pragma omp parallel for           \
    private( sumx, sumy, k )        \
    reduction( +: sum, total )  \
    schedule( dynamic, 2000 )
```

This causes the OpenMP directive to use the fixed chunk size given in parentheses — in this case, 2000. After each thread finishes its chunk of work (2,000 iterations), it comes back for more. This divides the work more evenly. Adjusting the size of the chunk fine-tunes the solution further. The problem of an unbalanced load does not arise with Cilk Plus, because its approach for dividing up the work is different.

After rebuilding the solution with these changes, run Parallel Amplifier again to check for concurrency. Again, select Thread/Function/Call Stack. Figure 3-29 shows the result.

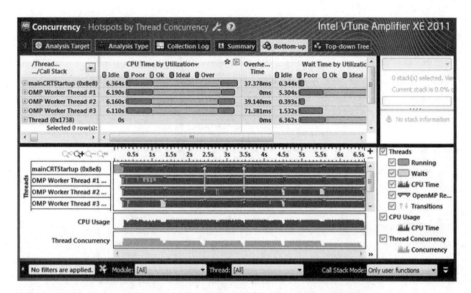

FIGURE 3-29: Concurrency showing balanced (but still not ideal) loads

The figure shows nicely balanced loads, but the load bars show mainly Ok (orange), not Ideal (green). Figure 3-30 shows the Thread Concurrency Histogram, with the average number of threads running concurrently still only 2.76.

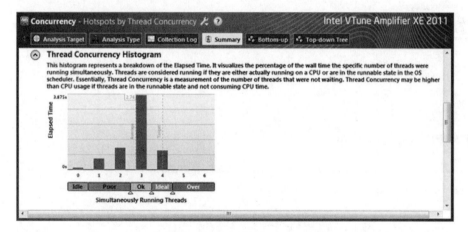

FIGURE 3-30: Concurrent information after first tuning attempt

You can try tuning further by changing the chunk size to 1000. Figure 3-31 shows the results of the concurrency; clearly, all four threads are running in an Ideal state (green). This is verified in the Thread Concurrency Histogram (Figure 3-32), which shows an average thread concurrency of 3.75 — in line with the speedup shown in Figure 3-33 compared to the serial times given in Figure 3-6.

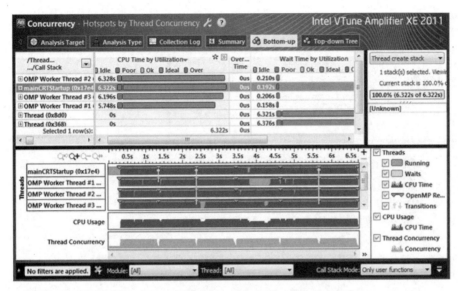

FIGURE 3-31: Concurrency showing balanced and ideal loads

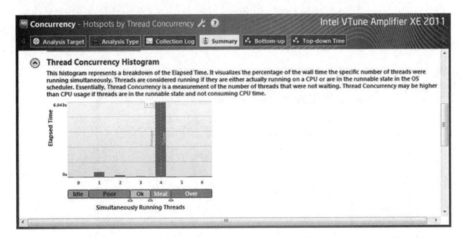

FIGURE 3-32: Concurrent thread information after final tuning

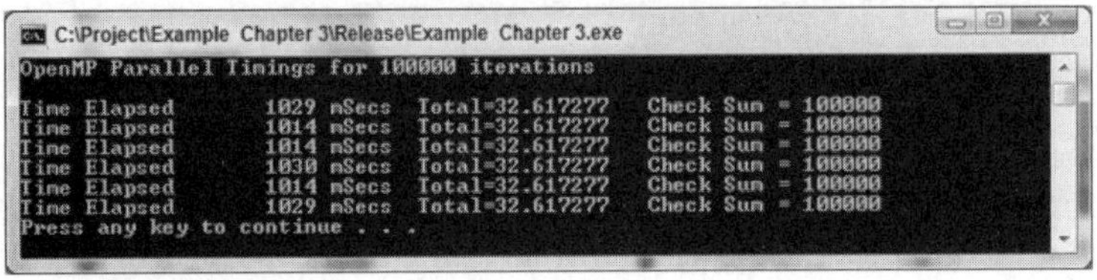

```
C:\Project\Example Chapter 3\Release\Example Chapter 3.exe
OpenMP Parallel Timings for 100000 iterations

Time Elapsed      1029 mSecs  Total=32.617277  Check Sum = 100000
Time Elapsed      1014 mSecs  Total=32.617277  Check Sum = 100000
Time Elapsed      1014 mSecs  Total=32.617277  Check Sum = 100000
Time Elapsed      1030 mSecs  Total=32.617277  Check Sum = 100000
Time Elapsed      1014 mSecs  Total=32.617277  Check Sum = 100000
Time Elapsed      1029 mSecs  Total=32.617277  Check Sum = 100000
Press any key to continue . . .
```

FIGURE 3-33: Final timings for the OpenMP parallelization

Listing 3-4 gives the final OpenMP program. Its performance compares very well with that achieved using the Cilk Plus method of parallelization.

LISTING 3-4: The final version of the OpenMP program

```c
// Example Chapter 3 OpenMP Program
#include <stdio.h>
#include <windows.h>
#include <mmsystem.h>
#include <math.h>
#include <omp.h>

const long int VERYBIG = 100000;
// ***********************************************************************
int main( void )
{
  int i;
  long int j, k, sum;
  double sumx, sumy, total, z;
  DWORD starttime, elapsedtime;
  // ------------------------------------------------------------------
  // Output a start message
  printf( "OpenMP Parallel Timings for %d iterations \n\n", VERYBIG );

  // repeat experiment several times
  for( i=0; i<6; i++ )
  {
    // get starting time
    starttime = timeGetTime();

    // reset check sum and total
    sum = 0;
    total = 0.0;

    // Work loop, do some work by looping VERYBIG times
    #pragma omp parallel for          \
      private( sumx, sumy, k )        \
      reduction( +: sum, total )      \
      schedule( dynamic, 1000 )
      for( int j=0; j<VERYBIG; j++ )
      {
        // increment check sum
        sum += 1;

        // Calculate first arithmetic series
        sumx = 0.0;
        for( k=0; k<j; k++ )
          sumx = sumx + (double)k;

        // Calculate second arithmetic series
        sumy = 0.0;
        for( k=j; k>0; k-- )
          sumy = sumy + (double)k;
```

```
        if( sumx > 0.0 )total = total + 1.0 / sqrt( sumx );
        if( sumy > 0.0 )total = total + 1.0 / sqrt( sumy );
    }

    // get ending time and use it to determine elapsed time
    elapsedtime = timeGetTime() - starttime;

    // report elapsed time
    printf("Time Elapsed %10d mSecs  Total=%lf   Check Sum = %ld\n",
           (int)elapsedtime, total, sum );
    }

  // return integer as required by function header
  return 0;
}
// *************************************************************************
```

code snippet Chapter3\3-4.cpp

SUMMARY

The four-step method (analyze, implement, debug, and tune) is used to transform a serial program into a parallel program using the tools of Intel Parallel Studio XE. The technique can be used for small or large programs.

This chapter described using both Intel Cilk Plus and OpenMP to make a serial program parallel. The use of Intel Parallel Studio XE makes the transformation from serial to parallel efficient and effective. The tools also detect both threading and memory errors, and enable you to check a program's concurrency.

Other parallel programming techniques are available and are introduced in subsequent chapters of the book. Which parallelizing methodology is best to use remains the choice of the programmer. That decision can be influenced by many things, including the type of problem being solved, the software tools available, or just what the programmer feels comfortable with.

Part II, "Using Parallel Studio XE," takes a more detailed look at the four steps. A greater understanding of the pitfalls that can occur when parallelizing will give you much more confidence to tackle large and complex programs, where you can reap the full benefit of using parallel computing. Part II covers each step in turn, revealing the detailed nuances that enable you to undertake efficient and, more important, safe parallelism.

PART II
Using Parallel Studio XE

4

Producing Optimized Code

WHAT'S IN THIS CHAPTER?

➤ A seven-step optimization process

➤ Using different compiler options to optimize your code

➤ Using auto-vectorization to tune your application to different CPUs

This chapter discusses how to use the Intel C/C++ compiler to produce optimized code. You start by building an application using the /O2 compiler option (optimized for speed) and then add additional compiler flags, resulting in a speedup of more than 300 percent.

The different compiler options you use are the course-grained general options, followed by auto-vectorization, interprocedural optimization (IPO), and profile-guided optimization (PGO). The chapter concludes with a brief look at how you can use the guided auto-parallelization (GAP) feature to get additional advice on tuning auto-vectorization.

The steps in this chapter will help you to maximize the performance you get from the Intel compiler.

Most of the text of this chapter uses the Windows version of the compiler options. You can use the option-mapping tool to find the equivalent Linux option. The following example is used to find the Linux equivalent of /Oy-:

```
map_opts -tl -lc -opts /Oy-
Intel(R) Compiler option mapping tool

mapping Windows options to Linux for C++

'-Oy-' Windows option maps to
  --> '-fomit-frame-pointer-' option on Linux
  --> '-fno-omit-frame-pointer' option on Linux
  --> '-fp' option on Linux
```

continues

(continued)

The -t *option is used to set the target OS, which can be* l *(or* linux*) and* w *(or* windows*).*

The -l *option sets the language, and can be either* c *or* f *(or* fortran*). All text after the* -opts *option is treated as options that should be converted. The option-mapping tool does not compile any code; it only prints out the mapped options.*

To use the option-mapping tool, make sure that the Intel compiler is in your path.

INTRODUCTION

When buying a new product — a must-have kitchen gadget, a new PC, or the latest-and-greatest release of your favorite software — it's likely that you will not look at the user manual. Most of us just power up the new gizmo to see what it can do, referring to the manual only when the thing doesn't work.

Product manufacturers spend huge amounts of effort in making sure this first out-of-the-box experience is a good one. Software developers, and in particular compiler vendors, are no different; they, too, want their customers to have a good first experience.

When you first try out the Intel compiler, it should seamlessly integrate into your current development environment and produce code that has impressive performance. Many developers, however, simply use the compiler out of the box, without considering other compiler options. The following story illustrates the point.

A company that specializes in providing analysis software to the oil exploration industry is an enthusiastic user of the Intel compiler. Just before it was about to release a new version of its software, the developers decided to experiment with a new version of the Intel compiler. To their amazement, the new compiler gave a 40 percent speedup of its application. Normally, they would not consider swapping compilers so close to the software release dates, but with such a significant speedup, they thought the upgrade was worth doing. So, what was the reason for the speedup? The answer was the auto-vectorizer in the compiler.

In earlier versions of the Intel compiler, users had to turn on auto-vectorization explicitly; it was not enabled by default. As a result, many developers failed to reap the benefits of this great feature. A newer version of the compiler changed that behavior so that auto-vectorization was enabled out of the box. When the company built its code with the newer compiler, the code was auto-vectorized by default, resulting in the 40 percent speedup.

Once the developers realized that the performance improvements delivered by the new compiler were also available in the old compiler, they added the extra options to the current build environment and got the speedup. They also scheduled an upgrade of the compiler once the current software release had been completed.

The moral of the story is this: Don't rely on the compiler's default options, because you may inadvertently miss out on a performance benefit.

THE EXAMPLE APPLICATION

This chapter's example application reuses some of the code from Chapter 2, but it also includes an additional matrix multiplication. The full source code, which is divided into several smaller files, is in Listing 4-5 at the end of this chapter. Table 4-1 lists the files involved.

TABLE 4-1: The Example Application Files

FILE	DESCRIPTION
chapter4.c	Dynamically creates three matrices, and then initializes two of them with a numeric series and multiplies them together. This is done six times, with the timing printed to screen each time.
work.c	Contains the work() function that is used to initialize one of the matrices. Called from main(), it contains a large loop that calls series1() and series2().
series.c	Contains the functions series1() and series2(), which calculate two numeric series.
addy.c	Contains AddY(), which is called from Series2() and adds two values.
wtime.c	Contains code to measure how long the parts of the program run.
chapter4.h	Has the function prototypes and defines.
Makefile	This is the makefile used to build the application.

The example application is quite contrived and doesn't solve any particular problem. Its only purpose is to provide some code that you can optimize and see an improvement in performance as you perform each optimization step. Figure 4-1 shows the output of the program. As you can see, the output is very similar to the application used in Chapter 3 — the main difference being that the Total and Check sum displayed are different values from that chapter.

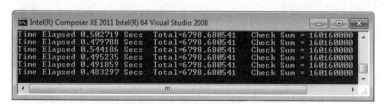

FIGURE 4-1: Output of the example application

In addition to using the code example in Listing 4-5, you might like to try applying the seven optimization steps to your own code or from code in one of the case studies (Chapters 13 through 18). You may find that some optimization steps deliver significant performance improvements, whereas other steps may actually slow down your application.

The results shown in this chapter were from three different machines:

➤ **Core 2 laptop** — Lenovo T66, Intel Core 2 Duo CPU, T7300 @ 2.00 GHz, 2GB RAM.

➤ **Sandy Bridge laptop** — Lenovo W520, Intel Core i7-2820QM @ 2.30 GHz, 8GB RAM. This machine is used to give two sets of results, one with Intel Turbo Boost Technology 2.0 enabled, and one without.

➤ **Xeon workstation** — OEM, Intel Xeon CPU, X5680 @ 3.33 GHz (2 processors, 12GB RAM).

> *"Intel Turbo Boost Technology 2.0 automatically allows processor cores to run faster than the base operating frequency if it's operating below power, current and temperature specification limits."*
>
> — `www.intel.com/content/www/us/en/architecture-and-technology/`
> `turbo-boost/turbo-boost-technology.html`

OPTIMIZING CODE IN SEVEN STEPS

Figure 4-2 shows the steps followed in this chapter, which are based on the *Quick-Reference Guide to Optimization* (which you can find at `http://software.intel.com/sites/products/collateral/hpc/compilers/compiler_qrg12.pdf`).

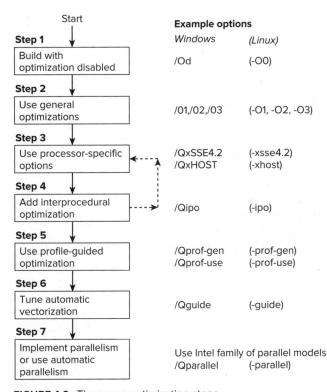

FIGURE 4-2: The seven optimization steps

In the first step you build the application with no optimization. You do this to make sure that your program works as expected. Sometimes an optimization step can break the application, so it's prudent to start with an unoptimized application. Once you are confident that no errors exist in your program, it's okay to go to the next step.

Figure 4-2 shows the Windows and Linux versions of the options used in this chapter. In most of the text of this chapter the Windows version of the options is used, but they can be substituted with the Linux options.

 This chapter doesn't cover step 7, implementing parallelism; that's covered by Chapters 6–9.

Using the Compiler's Reporting Features

For each optimization step, the Intel compiler can generate a report that is useful for gleaning what optimizations the compiler has carried out:

➤ **Optimization report** — Use the `/Qopt-report` option, as described in the section "Step 2: Use General Optimizations."

➤ **Auto-Vectorization report** — Use the `/Qvec-report` option, as described in the section "Step 3: Use Processor-Specific Optimizations."

➤ **Auto-Parallelism report** — Use the `/Qpar-report` option, as described in Chapter 6, "Where to Parallelize."

➤ **Guided Auto-Parallelism report** — Use the `/Qguide` option, as described in the section "Step 6: Tune Auto-Vectorization."

Step 1: Build with Optimizations Disabled

Before doing any optimization you should ensure that the unoptimized version of your code works. On very rare occasions optimizing can change the intended behavior of your applications, so it is always best to start from a program you know builds and works correctly.

The `/Od` (`-O0`) option actively stops any optimizations from taking place. It generally is used while the application is being developed and inspected for errors. Single-stepping through code with a debugger is much easier with programs built at `/Od`. If you ever end up having to look at the assembler code the compiler generates, it is much easier to understand the output from `/Od` than from some of the other options.

Table 4-2 shows the results of building the application with optimizations disabled using the `/Od` option as well as the default build (`/O2`). The program has a loop that executes six times, printing the time each iteration took. The table records the lowest value.

TABLE 4-2: Results of Running the /Od and /O2 Builds

BUILD MACHINE	/OD	/O2
Core 2 laptop	3.041	0.474
Sandy Bridge	2.164	0.293
Sandy Bridge (with Turbo Boost)	1.588	0.211
Xeon workstation	1.325	0.238

If you are benchmarking on a machine that supports Turbo Boost Technology, it is better that you disable it in the computer's BIOS before proceeding. When Turbo Boost Technology is turned on, the clock speed of the CPU can dynamically change, depending on how busy the CPU is, which can distort the results. Of course, you should turn it back on again at the end.

Another technology that can lead to an inconsistent set of benchmarks is Intel Hyper-Threading Technology. When hyper-threading is enabled, the processor looks as though it has twice as many cores as it really has. This is done by sharing the execution units and using extra electronics that save the state of the various CPU registers. One side effect of using hyper-threading is that the results of your benchmarks can be distorted as the different hyper-threads contend for resources from the execution units.

Many optimization practitioners choose to turn off both Turbo Boost Technology and Hyper-Threading Technology so that they get more consistent results in the different stages of tuning. You should be able to disable both technologies in the BIOS of your PC. See your PC's handbook for instructions.

The Intel compiler assumes that you are building code for a computer that can support SSE2 instructions. If you are building for a very old PC (for example, a Pentium 3), you will need to add the option /arch32 (Windows) or -mia32 (Linux) for your code to run successfully. Architecture-specific options are discussed more in the section "Step 3: Use Processor-Specific Optimizations."

You can try out this first step for yourself in Activity 4-1.

ACTIVITY 4-1: BUILDING AN UNOPTIMIZED VERSION OF THE EXAMPLE APPLICATION

In this activity you build an unoptimized version of the example application.

Setting Up the Build Environment

1. Copy the contents of Listing 4-5 into the separate source files.

2. Copy the Makefile from Listing 4-6. If you are using Linux, you will need to comment out the Windows-specific variables at the beginning of the Makefile and uncomment the Linux variables.

3. Open a command prompt or shell:

   ➤ On Windows, open an Intel compiler command prompt. The path to the command prompt will be similar to the following. (The exact names and menu items will vary, depending on which version of Parallel Studio and Visual Studio you have installed.)

   Start ⇨ All Programs ⇨ Intel Parallel Studio XE 2011 ⇨ Command Prompt ⇨ Intel64 Visual Studio Mode

   ➤ On Linux, make sure the compiler variables have been sourced:

   ```
   $ source /opt/intel/bin/compilervars.sh intel64
   ```

   If you are running a 32-bit operating system, the parameter passed to the `compilervars.sh` file should be `ia32`.

Building and Running the Program

4. Build the application `intel.noopt.exe` using the Intel compiler:

   ➤ Linux

   ```
   make clean
   make TARGET=intel.noopt CFLAGS= -O0 (Note : this is a capital 'O'
   followed by zero)
   ```

   ➤ Windows

   ```
   nmake clean
   nmake TARGET=intel.noopt CFLAGS=/Od
   ```

5. Run the program `intel.noopt.exe` and record the results. Use the lowest time as the benchmark figure.

Note that if your CPU supports Turbo Boost Technology Mode, you may want to disable it in the BIOS. See your PC's handbook for instructions.

Step 2: Use General Optimizations

Table 4-3 describes four course-grained optimization switches: /O1, /O2, /O3, and /Ox. These switches are a good starting point for optimizing your code. Each option is progressively more aggressive at the optimizations it applies. The option /O1 generates smaller code than the other options. When you call the compiler without any switches, the compiler defaults to using /O2.

 It's always worth trying all the general options. Sometimes /O2 produces faster code than /O3, and occasionally even /O1 produces the fastest code.

TABLE 4-3: The General Optimization Switches

OPTION	DESCRIPTION
/O1 (-O1)	Optimizes for speed and size. This option is very similar to /O2 except that it omits optimizations that tend to increase object code size, such as the inlining of functions. The option is generally useful where memory paging due to large code size is a problem, such as server and database applications. Note that auto-vectorization is not turned on at /O1, even if it is invoked individually by its fine-grained switch /Qvec. However, at /O1 the vectorization associated with array notations is enabled.
/O2 (-O2)	Optimizes for maximum speed. This option creates faster code in most cases. Optimizations include scalar optimizations; inlining and some other interprocedural optimizations between functions/subroutines in the same source file; vectorization; and limited versions of a few other loop optimizations, such as loop versioning and unrolling that facilitate vectorization.
/O3 (-O3)	Optimizes for further speed increases. This includes all the /O2 optimizations, as well as other high-level optimizations, including more aggressive strategies such as scalar replacement, data pre-fetching, and loop optimization, among others.
/Ox (Windows only)	Full optimization. This option generates fast code without some of the fine-grained option strategies adopted by /O2.

Using the General Options on the Example Application

Figure 4-3 shows the results of running the example application on the four target platforms.

➤ The option /O1, an option designed to produce smaller code, runs slower than the other options.

➤ There is no difference between the performance of the /O2 option and the more aggressive /O3 or /Ox options.

There is no guarantee that the more aggressive optimization options will result in your application running faster. In the case of the example application, /O2 seems the best choice.

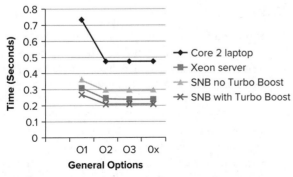

FIGURE 4-3: The results of running the example application

Generating Optimization Reports Using /Qopt-report

The compiler can produce reports on what optimizations were carried out. By default, these reports are disabled. Enabling the reports can sometimes help you identify whether a piece of code has been optimized. Note that the coarse- and fine-grained options you use determine which optimizations are applied, including auto-vectorization. If auto-parallelization is also turned on by /Qparallel, messages about auto-parallelizing of loops are also included. You can read more about auto-parallelism and the /Qparallel option in Chapter 6, "Where to Parallelize."

Reducing the Size of the Report

Using /Qopt-report on its own can result in a fairly large report. To reduce the size of the report, you can:

➤ Control the level of detail by using /Qopt-report: *n*, where *n* is a number between 0 and 3.

  ➤ 0 — No reports.

  ➤ 1 — Tells the compiler to generate reports with minimum level of detail.

  ➤ 2 — Tells the compiler to generate reports with medium level of detail. This is the default level of reporting when this option is not included on the command line.

  ➤ 3 — Tells the compiler to generate reports with maximum level of detail.

➤ Select which phases to have a report on by using the /Qopt-report-phase option.

➤ Limit the report to specific functions by using the /Qopt-report-routine:<string> option.

Table 4-4 shows the different phases used with the /Qopt-report-phase option.

TABLE 4-4: Phase Names Used in Report Generation

PHASE	DESCRIPTION
ipo_inl	Gives an inlining report from the interprocedural optimizer
hlo	Reports on high-level optimization (HLO), including loop and memory optimizations
hpo	Reports on high-performance optimization (HPO), including auto-vectorization and auto-parallelization optimizations
pgo	Reports on profile-guided optimizations

Creating Focused Reports

Each phase in Table 4-4 is a collection of even smaller reports — too many to describe here. If you are interested in just one specific phase, you can generate one of these smaller reports using the option /Qopt-report-phase. Running the option /Qopt-report-help as follows brings up a list of all the phases available:

```
icl /Qopt-report-help
Intel(R) C++ Intel(R) 64 Compiler XE for applications running on Intel(R) 64,
```

```
Version 12.0.3.175 Build 20110309
Copyright (C) 1985-2011 Intel Corporation. All rights reserved.


Intel(R) Compiler Optimization Report Phases
usage:  -Qopt_report_phase <phase>

ipo, ipo_inl, ipo_cp, ipo_align, ipo_modref, ipo_lpt, ipo_subst, ipo_ratt, ipo_vaddr,
ipo_pdce, ipo_dp, ipo_gprel, ipo_pmerge, ipo_dstat, ipo_fps, ipo_ppi, ipo_unref, ipo_wp,
ipo_dl, ipo_psplit, ilo, ilo_arg_prefetching, ilo_lowering, ilo_strength_reduction,
ilo_reassociation, ilo_copy_propagation, ilo_convert_insertion, ilo_convert_removal,
ilo_tail_recursion, hlo, hlo_fusion, hlo_distribution, hlo_scalar_replacement,
hlo_unroll, hlo_prefetch, hlo_loadpair, hlo_linear_trans, hlo_opt_pred, hlo_data_trans,
hlo_string_shift_replace, hlo_ftae, hlo_reroll, hlo_array_contraction,
hlo_scalar_expansion, hlo_gen_matmul, hlo_loop_collapsing, hpo, hpo_analysis,
hpo_openmp, hpo_threadization, hpo_vectorization, pgo, tcollect, offload, all
```

After using the general optimizations, the next step is to experiment with processor-specific optimization. Before doing that, however, try out the general optimizations by completing Activity 4-2.

ACTIVITY 4-2: BUILDING THE EXAMPLE APPLICATION USING THE GENERAL OPTIMIZATION OPTIONS

In this activity you use the general optimization options to build the code from Listing 4-5.

1. Build the application from Activity 4-1 using the Intel compiler:

> Linux

```
make clean
make CFLAGS="-O1" TARGET="intel.O1"
```

> Windows

```
nmake clean
nmake CFLAGS="/O1" TARGET="intel.O1"
```

2. Run the program `intel.O1.exe` and record the results.

3. Repeat steps 1 and 2 using the options O2, O3, and Ox (Windows only).

To spot which optimizations have been carried out, turn on the optimization reports using the `/Qopt-report` (Windows) or `-opt-report` (Linux) option.

Step 3: Use Processor-Specific Optimizations

Auto-vectorization is one of the most significant contributions the Intel compiler makes to getting really fast code. Four points need to be made straight away:

> When you use the compiler out of the box (that is, the default behavior), auto-vectorization is enabled, supporting SSE2 instructions. This is safe to use on all but the very oldest Intel and non-Intel devices.

➤ You can enhance the optimization of auto-vectorization beyond the default behavior by explicitly using some additional options. In the following example, the example application is rebuilt to support AVX instructions, leading to a 10 percent improvement when the application is run on the Sandy Bridge laptop.

➤ If you run an application on a CPU that does not support the level of auto-vectorization you chose when it was built, the program will fail to start. The following error message will be displayed: `This program was not built to run on the processor in your system`.

➤ You can get the compiler to add multiple paths in your code so that your code can run on both lower- and higher-spec CPUs, thus avoiding the risk of getting an error message or program abort. This topic is covered later in this chapter in "Building Applications to Run on More Than One Type of CPU."

What Is Auto-Vectorization?

Auto-vectorization makes use of the SIMD (Single Instruction Multiple Data) instructions within the processor to speed up execution times. The original SIMD instructions, MMX (MultiMedia eXtensions), were written for special 64-bit registers resident within the processor. This has been superseded by the SSE (Streaming SIMD Extension), which was first introduced in 1999 and operated on 128-bit floating-point registers. Figure 4-4 shows the innovations in SIMD from then until the present date.

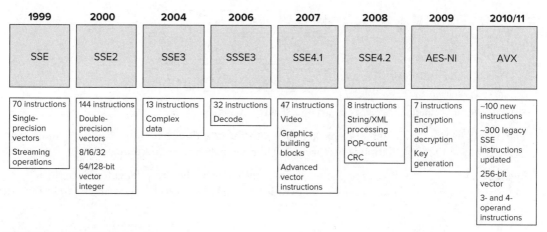

FIGURE 4-4: The SIMD timeline

SIMD instructions operate on multiple data elements in one instruction using the extrawide SIMD registers. The Intel compiler uses these SIMD instructions to apply auto-vectorization to loopy code. Consider the following code snippet:

```
#define MAX 1024
float x[MAX];
float y[MAX];
float z[MAX];
for(i = 0; i <= MAX; i++)
  z[i] = x[i] + y[i];
```

Without auto-vectorization, the compiler produces a separate set of instructions that does the following for each iteration of the loop:

➤ Reads x[i] and y[i] for the current loop iteration

➤ Adds them together

➤ Writes the results in z[i] for the current loop iteration

Array z would be updated 1,024 times. The compiler might even use SSE *scalar instructions* — that is, instructions that operate on one data item at a time.

If auto-vectorization is enabled, the compiler will use SSE *packed instructions* rather than scalar instructions. Figure 4-5 shows a scalar and a packed instruction. The first instruction, addss, is a scalar instruction that adds x1 to y1. One calculation is performed on one data item.

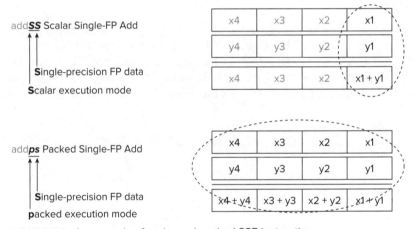

FIGURE 4-5: An example of scalar and packed SSE instructions

The second instruction, addps, is a packed (or vector) instruction that adds x1, x2, x3, and x4 to y1, y2, y3, and y4. One calculation is performed simultaneously on four data items.

By applying the auto-vectorizer to the preceding code snippet, the compiler can reduce the loop count MAX by a factor of four, so only 256 iterations of the loop need be performed, rather than the original 1,024.

Auto-Vectorization Guidelines

To be amenable to auto-vectorization, any loops must follow the following guidelines:

➤ The loop trip count must be known runtime at loop entry and remain the same for the duration of the loop.

➤ The loop counter may be a variable as long as that variable is set before the loop starts and remains unchanged during the loop run.

➤ The loop cannot be terminated within itself or by some data dependency within the loop, because this would imply an inconstant loop count. By the same considerations, the loop must be a single entry-and-exit loop.

➤ There must be no backward dependencies between iterations of the loop. If the compiler cannot determine that there are no dependencies, it will assume there are and subsequently not vectorize the loop.

➤ Loops involving overlapping arrays cannot be vectorized because loop dependencies may occur. Usually the compiler can easily determine if declared arrays overlap, because their addresses are constants. The compiler will assume overlapping arrays have loop dependencies unless told otherwise by the programmer. In simple cases, the compiler can test for overlapping arrays at run time.

➤ There must be no function calls in a loop. However, inlined functions and elemental functions (as used in array notation) will not cause a problem.

Turning On Auto-Vectorization

Auto-vectorization is included implicitly within some of the general optimization options, and implicitly switched off by others. It can be further controlled by the auto-vectorization option /Qvec. Normally, the only reason you would use the /Qvec option would be to disable auto-vectorization (that is, /Qvec-) for the purposes of testing.

Here's the default behavior of the general options:

➤ The general options /O2, /O3, and /Ox turn on auto-vectorization. You can override these options by placing the negative option /Qvec- directly on the compiler's command line.

➤ The general options /Od and /O1 turn off auto-vectorization, even if it is specifically set on the compiler's command line by using the /Qvec option.

Enhancing Auto-Vectorization

When auto-vectorization is enabled, the compiler uses the SSE2 instructions, which were introduced in 2000. If your target CPU is more recent, you can get better performance by using the /Qx<architecture> option, where <architecture> can be one of SSE2, SSE3, SSSE3, SSE4.1, SSE4.2, or AVX.

Table 4-5 shows the speed of the example application on the Sandy Bridge laptop with Turbo Boost Technology disabled. Turning on AVX gives a performance boost of a further 9 percent, compared to using the default auto-vectorization.

TABLE 4-5: Auto-Vectorization Speedup

SETTING	TIME	SPEEDUP
SSE2	0.293	1
AVX	0.270	1.09

Using the /Qx option to enhance auto-vectorization causes two potential problems. The moment you build an application using the /Qx option, it will not run on a non-Intel CPU. For example, any application built with /Qx will not run on an AMD device. To solve this, you should use the /arch options rather than the /Qx options, described in the following section.

If you run the optimized application on a generation of Intel CPU that does not support the option you used, the application will fail to run. For example, an application built with /QxAVX will not run on a first-generation Intel Core 2 CPU.

Figure 4-6 shows an example of a message you will get if you run an application on hardware that does not support the level of auto-vectorization you have chosen.

FIGURE 4-6: Running a mismatched application

Building for Non-Intel CPUs

If you intend to run code on Intel and non-Intel devices, you should use the /arch:<architecture> option, where architecture can be ia32, SSE2, SSE3, SSSE3, or SSE4.1.

For example, using the option /arch:SSE4.1 produces an application that will run on any CPU that supports SSE4.1, whether it is an Intel CPU or not.

If you intend your code to run on a non-Intel processor, do not use the /Qx *option; instead, use the* /arch: *option.*

Determining That Auto-Vectorization Has Happened

You can get a detailed report from the vectorizer by using the /Qvec-report option. The /Qvec-report *n* option reports on auto-vectorization, where *n* can be set from 0 to 5 to specify the level of detail required in the report, as follows:

➤ *n* = 0 — No diagnostic information (default if *n* omitted).

➤ *n* = 1 — Reports only loops successfully vectorized.

➤ *n* = 2 — Reports which loops were vectorized and which were not (and why not).

➤ *n* = 3 — Same as 2 but adds the dependency information that caused the failure to vectorize.

➤ *n* = 4 — Reports only loops not vectorized.

➤ *n* = 5 — Reports only loops not vectorized and adds dependency information.

When you build the example application with the /Qvec-report1 option, the compiler reports the following:

```
chapter4.c(64): (col. 5) remark: PERMUTED LOOP WAS VECTORIZED.
series.c(7): (col. 5) remark: LOOP WAS VECTORIZED.
```

Building with the /Qvec-report4 option gives a list of loops that are not vectorized. Here's a cut-down version of the output:

```
chapter4.c(54): (col. 5) remark: loop was not vectorized: not inner loop.
... lots more like this

chapter4.c(45): (col. 3) remark: loop was not vectorized: nonstandard loop is not a
vectorization candidate.

chapter4.c(11): (col. 7) remark: loop was not vectorized: existence of
vector dependence.
```

For a further discussion on these types of failures to vectorize, see the next section, "When Auto-Vectorization Fails." There's a further development of the auto-vectorized code after IPO has been applied — see the section "The Impact of Interprocedural Optimization on Auto-Vectorization."

When Auto-Vectorization Fails

The auto-vectorizer has a number of rules that must be fulfilled before vectorization can happen. When the compiler is unable to vectorize a piece of code, the vectorization report will tell you which rules were broken (provided you have turned on the right level of reporting detail — refer to the section "Determining That Auto-Vectorization Has Happened" earlier in this chapter).

Error Messages

Following are some of the main report messages associated with non-vectorization of a loop:

➤ **Low trip count** — The loop does not have sufficient iterations for vectorization to be worthwhile.

➤ **Not an inner loop** — Only the inner loop of a nested loop may be vectorized, unless some previous optimization has produced a reduced nest level. On some occasions the compiler can vectorize an outer loop, but obviously this message will not then be generated.

➤ **Nonstandard loop is not a vectorization candidate** — The loop has an incorrect structure. For example, it may have a trip count that is modified within the loop, or it may contain one or more breakouts.

➤ **Vector dependency** — The compiler discovers, or suspects, a dependency between successive iterations of the loop. You can invite the compiler to ignore its suspicions by using the #pragma ivdep directive, provided you know that any vectorization would be safe.

➤ **Vectorization possible but seems inefficient** — The compiler has concluded that vectorizing the loop would not improve performance. You can override this by placing #pragma vector always before the loop in question.

➤ **Statement cannot be vectorized** — Certain statements, such as those involving switch and printf, cannot be vectorized.

➤ **Subscript too complex** — An array subscript may be too complicated for the compiler to handle. You should always try to use simplified subscript expressions.

Organizing Data to Aid Auto-Vectorization

Sometimes auto-vectorization will fail because access to data is not performed consecutively within the vectorizable loop.

You can load four consecutive 32-bit data items directly from memory in a single 128-bit SSE instruction. If access is not consecutive, you need to reorder the code to achieve auto-vectorization.

When working on legacy code that has a lot of nonsequential data items, some programmers write wrapper functions and use intermediate data structures to make auto-vectorization possible.

Non-Unit Strides

Consider the following matrix multiplication example. The nested loop results in access to array c being nonconsecutive (that is, a non-unit stride):

```
double a[4][4], b[4][4], c[4][4];
for (int j = 0; j < 4; j++)
  for (int i = 0; i <= j; i++)
    c[i][j] = a[i][j]+b[i][j];
```

The example loops through the rows, which means that the data items in a vector instruction will not be adjacent. The compiler reports the following:

```
elem2.cpp(15): (col. 3) remark: loop was not vectorized: not inner loop.
elem2.cpp(16): (col. 4) remark: loop was not vectorized: vectorization possible but
seems inefficient.
```

However, the code can be made to be vectorizable by changing the order in which the data is stored and, therefore, changing the order of the loop:

```
double a[4][4], b[4][4], c[4][4];
for (int j = 0; j < 4; j++)
  for (int i = 0; i <= j; i++)
    c[j][i] = a[i][j]+b[i][j];
```

The compiler will now report success:

```
elem2.cpp(15): (col. 1) remark: loop was not vectorized: not inner loop.
elem2.cpp(16): (col. 2) remark: LOOP WAS VECTORIZED.
```

Notice that arrays a and b are still accessed by row, and hence non-unit strides.

Figure 4-7 shows how a two-dimensional array has its columns stored consecutively in memory, but its row elements are stored in memory with a gap (or stride) between each. By iterating through such an array by columns, rather than by rows, vectorization becomes possible.

Structure of Arrays vs. Arrays of Structures

The simplest data structure in use is the array, which contains a contiguous collection of data items that can be accessed by an ordinal index, making it ideal for vectorizing. Data organized as a structure of arrays (SOA) are also ideal candidates for vectorizing because it is still being done at the array level. However, data organized as an array of structures (AOS), although an excellent format for encapsulating data, is a poor candidate for vector programming.

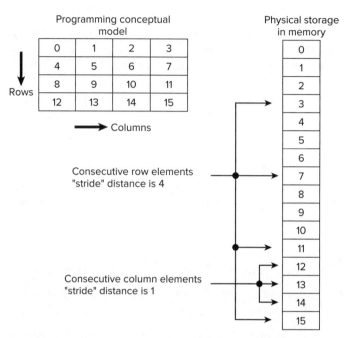

FIGURE 4-7: Stride values when accessing a two-dimensional array

Helping the Compiler to Vectorize

To ensure correct code generation, the compiler treats any assumed dependencies as though they were proven dependencies, which prevents vectorization. The compiler always assumes a dependency where it cannot prove that it is not a dependency. However, if you are certain that a loop can be safely vectorized and any dependencies ignored, the compiler can be informed in the following ways.

Using #pragma ivdep

One way of informing the compiler that there are no dependencies within a loop is to place #pragma ivdep just before the loop. The pragma applies only to the single following loop, not all the following loops. Note that the compiler will ignore only assumed dependencies; it won't ignore any that it can prove. Use #pragma ivdep only when you know that the assumed loop dependencies are safe to ignore.

The following example will not vectorize without the ivdep keyword if the value of k is unknown, because it may well be negative:

```
#pragma ivdep
for(int i = 0;i < m; i++)
    a[i] = a[i + k] * c;
```

Using the restrict Keyword

Another way to override assumptions concerning overlapping arrays is to use the restrict keyword on pointers when declaring them. The use of the restrict keyword in pointer declarations informs the compiler that it can assume that during the lifetime of the pointer only this single pointer has access to the data addressed by it — that is, no other pointers or arrays will use the same data space. Normally, it is adequate to just restrict pointers associated with the left-hand side of any assignment statement, as in the following code example. Without the restrict keyword, the code will not vectorize.

```
void f(int n, float *x, float *y, float *restrict z, float *d1, float *d2)
{
  for (int i = 0; i < n; i++)
    z[i] = x[i] + y[i]-(d1[i]*d2[i]);
}
```

The restrict keyword is part of the C99 standard, so you will have to either enable C99 in the compiler (using /Qstd:c99) or use the /Qrestrict option to force the compiler to recognize the restrict keyword.

Using #pragma vector always

The compiler will not vectorize if it thinks there is no advantage in doing so, issuing the message:

```
C:\Multiplicity.CPP(11): (col. 5) remark: loop was not vectorized: vectorization
possible but seems inefficient
```

If you want to force the compiler to vectorize a loop, place #pragma vector always immediately before the subsequent loop in the program, as in the following code:

```
void vec_always(int *a, int *b, int m)
{
  #pragma vector always
    for(int i = 0; i <= m; i++)
      a[32*i] = b[99*i];
}
```

Again, it applies only to the loop that follows; its use instructs the compiler to vectorize the following loop, provided it is safe to do so. You can use #pragma vector always to override any efficiency heuristics during the decision to vectorize or not, and to vectorize non-unit strides or unaligned memory accesses. The loop will be vectorized only if it is safe to do so. The outer loop of a nest of loops will not be vectorized, even if #pragma vector always is placed before it.

Using #pragma simd

You can use #pragma simd to tell the compiler to vectorize the single loop that follows. This option is more dangerous than the other vectorization pragmas because it forces the compiler to vectorize a loop, even when it is not safe to do so. This complements, but does not replace, the fully automatic approach. You can use #pragma simd with a selection of clauses, including:

➤ vectorlength (n1[,n2]...), where n is a vector length, which must be an integer of value 2, 4, 8, or 16. If more than one integer is specified, the compiler will choose from them.

➤ private (var1[,var2]...), where var must be a scalar variable. Private copies of each variable are used within each iteration of the loop. Each copy takes on any initial value the variable might have before entry to the loop. The value of the copy of the variable used in the last iteration of the loop gets copied back into the original variable. Multiple clauses get merged as a union.

➤ `linear (var1:step1[,var2:step2] … )`, where `var` is a scalar variable and `step` is a compile-time positive integer constant expression. For each iteration of a scalar loop, `var1` is incremented by `step1`, `var2` is incremented by `step2`, and so on. Multiple clauses get merged as a union.

➤ `reduction (oper:var1[,var2] … )`, where `oper` is a reduction operator, such as +, -, or *, and `var` is a scalar variable. The compiler applies the vector reduction indicated by `oper` to the variables listed in a similar manner to that of the OpenMP reduction clause.

➤ `[no]assert`, which directs the compiler to assert (or not to assert) when the vectorization fails. The default is `noassert`. Note that using `assert` turns failure to vectorize from being a warning to an error.

 See Chapter 8 for more information on OpenMP.

Following is an example using `#pragma simd`:

```
#pragma simd private(b)
for( i=0; i<MAXIMUS; i++ )
{
  if( a[i] > 0 )
  {
    b = a[i];
    a[i] = 1.0/a[i];
  }
  if( a[i] > 1 )a[i] += b;
}
```

The compiler will report success with the following message:

```
C:\Multiplicity.cpp(42): (col. 4) remark: SIMD LOOP WAS VECTORIZED.
```

Placing the negative option `/Qsimd-` on the compiler command line disables any `#pragma simd` statements in the code.

Using #pragma vector [un]aligned

The compiler can also write more efficient code if aligned data is used, starting either on 32-bit boundaries in the case of IA-32 processors, or 64-bit boundaries for 64-bit processors. If the compiler cannot decide if a data object is aligned, it will always assume it is unaligned. Coding for unaligned data is less efficient than coding for aligned data. You can always override the failsafe tendencies of the compiler by using the following two pragmas:

➤ `#pragma vector aligned` — Instructs the compiler to use aligned data movement instructions for all array references when vectorizing.

➤ `#pragma vector unaligned` — Instructs the compiler to use unaligned data movement instructions for all array references when vectorizing.

All code following the use of #pragma vector aligned is assumed to be aligned; likewise, all code following the use of #pragma vector unaligned is assumed to be unaligned. By using these pragmas, you can tell the compiler that different parts of your code can be assumed to use aligned or unaligned data. If you use the aligned pragma on an unaligned SSE data access, it is likely to result in failure. This is not the case for AVX.

You can align data by using __declespec(align) or the _mm_malloc() SSE-intrinsic function, as follows:

```
// align data to 32-byte address
__declepec(align(32)) double data[15];

// Allocate 100 bytes of memory; the start address is aligned to 16 bytes
double *pData = (double *)_mm_malloc(100,16);

// free the memory
_mm_free(pdata);
```

The call to _mm_malloc() results in the allocation of 100 bytes of memory that is aligned to a 16-byte address, which is later deallocated using the function _mm_free().

ACTIVITY 4-3: BUILDING THE EXAMPLE APPLICATION USING AUTO-VECTORIZATION OPTIONS

In this activity you build the example application from Listing 4-5 using the auto-vectorization options.

Controlling the Default Auto-Vectorization Options

1. Build and run the application from Listing 4-5 with no options, apart from the TARGET name:

   ➤ Linux

   ```
   make clean
   make TARGET=default
   .\default.exe
   ```

   ➤ Windows

   ```
   nmake clean
   nmake TARGET=default
   default.exe
   ```

2. Repeat step 1, adding the CFLAG option /Qvec- (Windows) or -vec- (Linux) to disable the auto-vectorization (notice the minus sign at the end of the option).

   ➤ Linux

   ```
   make clean
   make CFLAGS="-vec-" TARGET=novec
   .\novec.exe
   ```

➤ Windows

```
nmake clean
nmake CFLAGS="/Qvec-""TARGET=novec
novec.exe
```

The two executables from steps 1 and 2 should run at different speeds.

3. Investigate how vectorization differed by generating a vectorization report for both builds. To do this, add the option /Qvec-report2 (Linux: -vec-report2) to the CFLAGS.

Enhancing the Auto-Vectorization Options

4. Build and run the application several times using the different /Qx (Linux: -x) options (SSE2, SSE3, SSSE3, SSE4.1, SSE4.2, AVX). For example:

➤ Linux

```
make clean
make CFLAGS="-xSSE2" TARGET=intel.SSE2
.\intel.SSE2.exe
```

➤ Windows

```
nmake clean
nmake CFLAGS="-/QxSSE2" TARGET=intel.SSE2
intel.SSE2.exe
```

Note that if you don't have an Intel processor, use the /arch: (Linux: -m) options instead.

Creating a Portable Application

5. Rebuild using the /QaxAVX (Linux: -xAVX) option:

➤ Linux

```
make clean
make CFLAGS="-axAVX" TARGET=intel.axAVX
.\intel.axAVX.exe
```

➤ Windows

```
nmake clean
nmake CFLAGS="-/QaxAVX" TARGET=intel.axAVX
intel.axAVX.exe
```

6. Run the program. The program should run fine, even if your CPU does not support AVX.

Step 4: Add Interprocedural Optimization

Interprocedural optimization (IPO) performs a static, topological analysis of an application. With the option /Qip the analysis is limited to occur within each source file. With the option /Qipo the analysis spans across all the source files listed on the command line. IPO analyzes the entire program and is particularly successful for programs that contain many frequently used functions of small and medium length. IPO reduces or eliminates duplicate calculations and inefficient use of memory, and simplifies loops.

Other optimizations carried out include alias analysis, dead function elimination, unreferenced variable removal, and function inlining to be carried out across source files. IPO can reorder the functions for better memory layout and locality. In some cases, using IPO can significantly increase compile time and code size.

Figure 4-8 shows how the compiler performs IPO. First, each individual source file is compiled, and an object file is produced. The object files hold extra information that is used in a second compilation of the files. In this second compilation, all the objects are read together, and a cross-file optimization is performed. The output from this second pass is one or more regular objects. The linker is then used to combine the regular objects with any libraries that are needed, producing the final optimized application.

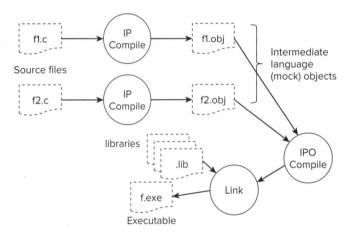

FIGURE 4-8: Interprocedural optimization

During build time you can control the number of object files created from the multiple source files by using the option /Qipo<n>, where n is the number of object files to be created. If n is zero or is omitted (the default), the compiler is left to decide how many objects are created. For large programs several object files may be created; otherwise, just one. The maximum number of object files that can be created is one for each source file.

Adding Interprocedural Optimization to the Example Application

The fourth column of Table 4-6 gives the results of using IPO on the example application. As you can see, there is more than a 60 percent speedup on three of the platforms when comparing an /O2 build with a /Qipo build.

TABLE 4-6: The Results of Using IPO with /O2 and /QhHost

PLATFORM	O2	IPO	QX	SPEEDUP O2 TO IPO	SPEEDUP O2 TO QX
Core 2 laptop	0.474	0.272	0.266	1.74	1.78
SNB without Turbo Boost	0.293	0.181	0.171	1.62	1.71
SNB with Turbo Boost	0.211	0.132	0.124	1.60	1.70
Xeon workstation	0.239	0.211	0.209	1.13	1.14

If you are using Microsoft Visual Studio, rather than the command line, you will find that /Qipo is already enabled in the release build of your project.

The Impact of Interprocedural Optimization on Auto-Vectorization

The *Quick-Reference Guide to Optimization* recommends that you carry out IPO after using any processor-specific options. The truth is that in many cases auto-vectorization will bring better results after IPO has been applied. However, experience shows that using IPO is sometimes difficult to achieve, so for pragmatic reasons IPO has been placed later in the optimization cycle. In this book we have the luxury of being able to spend a few more words explaining the issues — hence, the extra feedback arrow that was introduced in Figure 4-2.

IPO introduces extra time and complexity into the build process. Occasionally the compiler can run out of memory or slow down to such a pedestrian pace that the developer gets impatient and abandons IPO. On some large projects, it is impossible to successfully complete an IPO session. Because of these potential difficulties, IPO has been placed after some of the easier-to-handle optimizations in the optimization steps. One downside of doing this is that code presented to the auto-vectorizer will not have had the benefit of IPO, especially the cross-file function inlining.

If it's not practical to use the /Qipo option in your build environment, try using /Qip, which does IPO just within the single files.

IPO Improves Auto-Vectorization Results of the Example Application

If you find that your project will run IPO successfully, it is worthwhile to apply the auto-vectorization options again, especially if you have already ruled out one of the higher specification options because you saw no difference in performance. The sixth column of Table 4-6 shows the impact of using IPO on the example application when enhanced auto-vectorization has been used. For each build, the highest SIMD instruction set that the CPU could support was used.

IPO Brings New Auto-Vectorization Opportunities

It is also worth getting a fresh vectorization report to see what new things turn up. In the previous step, when the vectorization reports were generated, they were generated for each individual file at compilation time. Once /Qipo is used, the report generation is delayed until the final cross-file compilation.

Building with the /Qvec-report3 option gives a list of loops that were not vectorized. What is interesting is that both new failures and new successes are reported for line 51:

```
chapter4.c(51): (col. 11) remark: LOOP WAS VECTORIZED.
. . .
chapter4.c(51): (col. 11) remark: loop was not vectorized: not inner loop.
chapter4.c(51): (col. 11) remark: loop was not vectorized: not inner loop.
chapter4.c(51): (col. 11) remark: loop was not vectorized: existence of vector
dependence.
```

The reason for more than one vectorization activity being reported on a single line is that the use of /Qipo has resulted in several of the functions being inlined. You effectively have a triple-nested loop at line 51. This line has a call to the work() function. The following code snippet shows the nested loop within the work() function that calls the Series1() and Series2() functions:

```
for (i=0;i<N;i++){
    for (j=0;j<N;j++) {
        sum += 1;
        // Calculate first Arithmetic series
        sumx= Series1(j);

        // Calculate second Arithmetic series
        sumy= Series2(j);

        // initialize the array
        if( sumx > 0.0 )*total = *total + 1.0 / sqrt( sumx );
        if( sumy > 0.0 )*total = *total + 1.0 / sqrt( sumy );
        a[N*i+j] = *total;
    }
}
```

The effect of /Qipo inlining means that the most deeply nested loops associated with line 51 come from Series1() and Series2():

```
double Series1(int j)
{
    int k;
    double sumx = 0.0;
      for( k=0; k<j; k++ )
        sumx = sumx + (double)k;
    return sumx;
}

double Series2(int j)
{
    int k;
    double sumy = 0.0;
    for( k=j; k>0; k--,sumy++ )
      sumy = AddY(sumy, k);
    return sumy;
}
```

The two messages about the loop not being an inner loop refer to the two loops in work.c, which have become outer loops as a result of the inlining. The question is, what is the loop-dependency message referring to? One way to find out which message refers to which loop is to comment out the call to `Series1()` and `Series2()` in turn and see which messages disappear from the vectorization report. After experimenting, it is clear that the call to `Series2()` is the cause of the vector-dependency message. By commenting out the `sumy++` in the loop and the `sumy--` in the `AddY()` function, the dependency is removed, as shown in Listing 4-1.

Available for download on Wrox.com

LISTING 4-1: Modifications to the AddY function

series.c

```
double Series2(int j)
{
  int k;
  double sumy = 0.0;
  for( k=j; k>0; k--)
  {
    // sumy++;
    sumy = AddY(sumy, k);
  }
  return sumy;
}
```

addy.c

```
double AddY( double sumy, int k )
{
// sumy--;
sumy = sumy + (double)k;
  return sumy;
}
```

code snippet Chapter4\4-1\series.c and addy.c

Making the preceding changes has a positive impact on performance, improving it by an additional 20 percent.

You can try out IPO for yourself in Activity 4-4.

ACTIVITY 4-4: BUILDING THE EXAMPLE APPLICATION USING INTERPROCEDURAL OPTIMIZATION OPTIONS

In this activity you use the IPO options to build the code from Listing 4-5.

1. Build and run the application using the `/Qipo` option:

➤ Linux

```
make clean
make CFLAGS="-ipo" TARGET="intel.ipo.exe"
.\intel.ipo.exe
```

continues

continued

> Windows

```
nmake clean
nmake CFLAGS="/Qipo" TARGET="intel.ipo.exe"
intel.ipo.exe
```

2. Repeat step 1, adding the highest auto-vectorization that works on your platform (SSE2, SSE3, SSSE3, SSE4.1, SSE4.2, AVX). For example, a Sandy bridge would use the following options:

> Linux

```
make clean
make CFLAGS="-ipo -xAXV" TARGET="intel.ipo.xavx.exe"
.\intel.ipo.xavx.exe
```

> Windows

```
nmake clean
nmake CFLAGS="/Qipo /QxAVX" TARGET="intel.ipo.xavx.exe"
intel.ipo.xavx.exe
```

Step 5: Use Profile-Guided Optimization

So far, all the optimization methods described have been static — that is, they analyze the code without running it. Static analysis is good, but it leaves many questions open, including:

> How often is variable x greater than variable y?

> How many times does a loop iterate?

> Which part of the code is run, and how often?

Benefits of Profile-Guided Optimization

PGO uses a dynamic approach. One or more runs are made on unoptimized code with typical data, collecting profile information each time. This profile information is then used with optimizations set to create a final executable.

Some of the benefits of PGO include:

> More accurate branch prediction

> Basic code block movements to improve instruction cache behavior

> Better decision of functions to inline

> Can optimize function ordering

> Switch-statement optimizer

> Better vectorization decisions

The Profile-Guided Optimization Steps

Carrying out PGO involves three steps, as shown in Figure 4-9.

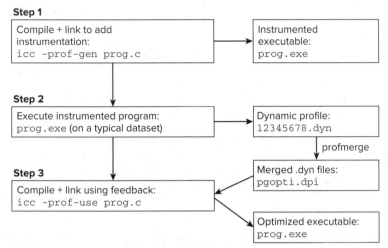

Step 1

| Compile + link to add instrumentation: `icc -prof-gen prog.c` | → | Instrumented executable: `prog.exe` |

Step 2

| Execute instrumented program: `prog.exe` (on a typical dataset) | → | Dynamic profile: `12345678.dyn` |

profmerge

Merged .dyn files: `pgopti.dpi`

Step 3

| Compile + link using feedback: `icc -prof-use prog.c` |

Optimized executable: `prog.exe`

FIGURE 4-9: The three steps to using PGO

1. Compile your unoptimized code with PGO:

    ➤ **Windows** — `icl /Qprof-gen prog.c`

    ➤ **Linux** — `icc -prof-gen prog.c`

    This instruments the code to collect profile information when run. This step automatically disables some optimizations if they are inadvertently left on.

2. Make multiple runs with different sets of typical data input; each run automatically produces a dynamic information (`.dyn`) file.

    Each `.dyn` file is given a different name and resides by default in the release directory of the project.

    The test data in the example runs must be representative of typical usage scenarios; otherwise, profile-guided feedback has the potential of harming the overall performance of the final executable. It is important that you directly remove unwanted files before the final build; otherwise, runs representing wrong data sets will be averaged and incorporated into the final feedback information used by the optimizations. For example, if you change your code during test runs, you need to remove any existing `.dyn` files before creating others with the new code.

3. Finally, switch on all your desired optimizations and do a feedback compile with PGO to produce a final PGO executable:

    ➤ **Windows** — `icl /Qprof-use prog.c`

    ➤ **Linux** — `icc -prof-use prog.c`

PGO uses the results of the test runs of the instrumented program to help apply the final optimizations when building the executable. For example, the compiler can decide whether a function is worth inlining by using the profile feedback information to establish how often the function is called.

The various `.dyn` files are averaged to produce a single version, which is then used. After step 3 has completed, the files are deleted.

Table 4-7 shows the different options that you can use in PGO.

TABLE 4-7: PGO Compiler Options

LINUX	WINDOWS	DESCRIPTION
`-prof-gen`	`/Qprof-gen`	Adds PGO instrumentation, which creates a new `.dyn` file every time the instrumented application is run
`-prof-use`	`/Qprof-use`	Uses collected feedback from all the `.dyn` files to create the final optimized application
`-prof-gen=srcpos`	`/Qprof-gen:srcpos`	Creates extra information for use with the Intel code coverage tool
`-opt-report-phase=pgo`	`/Qopt-report-phase:pgo`	Creates a PGO report

Table 4-8 shows the results of using PGO on four different platforms.

TABLE 4-8: The Results of Using PGO

PLATFORM	IPO	PGO	SPEEDUP
Core 2 laptop	0.370	0.261	1.42
SNB without Turbo Boost	0.264	0.198	1.33
SNB with Turbo Boost	0.189	0.141	1.34
Xeon workstation	0.211	0.131	1.61

ACTIVITY 4-5: BUILDING THE EXAMPLE APPLICATION USING PROFILE-GUIDED OPTIMIZATION OPTIONS

In this activity you use the general optimization options to build the code from Listing 4-5.

1. Build the application from Listing 4-5, enabling PGO generation:

➤ Linux

```
make reallyclean
make CFLAGS="-prof-gen" TARGET="intel.pgo.gen.exe"
```

➤ Windows

```
nmake reallyclean
nmake CFLAGS="/Qprof-gen" TARGET="intel.pgo.gen.exe"
```

Notice the `reallyclean` target, which deletes any intermediate PGO files that might be lying around.

2. Run the program `intel.pgo.gen.exe`.

Look in the directory where you ran the program. A `.dyn` file should have been created.

3. Rebuild the application, telling the compiler to use the dynamic information you just generated:

➤ Linux

```
make clean
make CFLAGS="-prof-use" TARGET="intel.pgo.exe"
```

➤ Windows

```
nmake clean
nmake CFLAGS="/Qprof-use" TARGET="intel.pgo.exe"
```

4. Run the program `intel.pgo.exe`. You should see a significant improvement in performance.

One of the main optimizations the PGO does on the example code is to change the instructions generated for the initialization of matrix b, especially where the variable `denominator` is used:

```
// initialize matrix b;
    for (i = 0; i < N; i++) {
        for (j=0; j<N; j++) {
            for (k=0;k<DENOM_LOOP;k++) {
                sum += m/denominator;
            }
            b[N*i + j] = sum;
        }
    }
```

Try to confirm that this is the case. Hint: generate an optimization report using `/Qopt-report-phase:pgo` (Linux: `-opt-report-phase=pgo`). Also, generate an assembler file using the `/S` (Linux: `-S`) option to see which different instructions are generated by the compiler. Be sure to delete or rename the assembler file afterward, because `make`'s default rules will try to build them into your application the next time you do a build.

The Results

Figure 4-10 shows the results from the various steps applied to the example application in Listing 4-5. The application was run on the Sandy Bridge laptop. In each step, new optimizations were incrementally added using the compiler options. The result labeled "Fix" is where the code in Series2.c was modified.

If the application had been built with just the default options, the application would have run at the /O2 setting, giving a run time of 0.211 seconds. At the PGO step, the final speed was 0.064 seconds, giving an impressive speedup of 3.3.

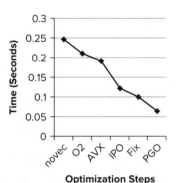

FIGURE 4-10: Applying all the optimization steps results in a speedup of more than 300 percent

Step 6: Tune Auto-Vectorization

The auto-vectorizer in the Intel compiler expects a certain standard of code. You can use the compiler's reporting features to tell you when the compiler was unable to auto-vectorize. The section "When Auto-Vectorization Fails" covers many of the rules and error messages that can help you understand what the compiler is doing. In addition to the compiler's reporting features, you can also use the GAP option to give you additional advice. Table 4-9 lists some of the differences between the GAP and vectorizer reports.

TABLE 4-9: Differences Between GAP and Vectorizer Reports

FEATURE	VECTORIZER REPORTS	GAP
Executable or usable object produced	Y	N
Performs application-wide analysis	N	Y
Detects breaking of vectorization rules	Y	Y
Gives advice on what to do	N	Y

It is best that you do not use both /Qguide and /Qvec-report at the same time, because this can lead to confusion; rather, use them sequentially after each other. Don't be tempted to skip one of these reports, because experience shows that there will be occasions when the vectorizer will emit a message but the GAP option will not give any specific advice.

GAP gives advice on auto-vectorization and auto-parallelization. This section considers only tuning auto-vectorization; Chapter 6, "Where to Parallelize," discusses using GAP for auto-parallelism.

Activating Guided Auto-Parallelization

You can activate GAP by using the following option switch:

```
/Qguide=n
```

where n can be set from 1 to 4, as follows:

> $n = 1$ — Simple diagnostics are generated.

> $n = 2$ — Moderate diagnostics are generated.

> $n = 3$ — Maximum diagnostics are generated.

> $n = 4$ — Extreme diagnostics are generated (the default if n is not set).

The higher the value of n, the deeper the analysis and the longer it takes.

While the GAP option is set, the compiler will not build an executable; it runs in advisor mode only, generating diagnostic messages telling you how you can improve the code. After making any changes you feel happy with, you need to recompile the application without the /Qguide option to produce an executable file.

 GAP requires a general optimization level of /O2 or higher; otherwise, the compiler will simply ignore the /Qguide option.

An Example Session

Listing 4-2 is an example session that uses both /Qguide and /Qvec-report options.

LISTING 4-2: Sample code suitable for vectorization

```
void f(int n, float *x, float *y, float *z, float *d1, float *d2)
{
  for (int i = 0; i < n; i++)
    z[i] = x[i] + y[i] - (d1[i]*d2[i]);
}
```

code snippet Chapter4\4-2.cpp

The following steps show what output the auto-vectorizer and GAP produces when you compile Listing 4-2:

1. Compile the code, asking for a report from the auto-vectorizer:

   ```
   icl /c test.cpp /Qvec-report2 /c
   ```

   C:\dv\guide\test.cpp(3): (col. 3) remark: loop was not vectorized: existence of vector dependence.

   Notice from the generated message that the loop was not vectorized, but no real hint is given about what to do next.

2. Use GAP to see if it can provide any other useful advice:

   ```
   icl /c test.cpp /Qguide /c
   ```

   test.cpp

```
GAP REPORT LOG OPENED ON Thu Aug 25 18:33:06 2011

remark #30761: Add -Qparallel option if you want the compiler to generate
recommendations for improving auto-parallelization.

C:\dv\guide\test.cpp(3): remark #30536: (LOOP) Add -Qno-alias-args option for better
type-based disambiguation analysis by the compiler, if appropriate (the option will
apply for the entire compilation). This will improve optimizations such as vectorization
for the loop at line 3. [VERIFY] Make sure that the semantics of this option is obeyed
for the entire compilation. [ALTERNATIVE] Another way to get the same effect is to add
the "restrict" keyword to each pointer-typed formal parameter of the routine "f".
This allows optimizations such as vectorization to be applied to the loop at line 3.
[VERIFY] Make sure that semantics of the "restrict" pointer qualifier is satisfied:
in the routine, all data accessed through the pointer must not be accessed through
any other pointer. Number of advice-messages emitted for this compilation session: 1.
END OF GAP REPORT LOG
```

The compiler does not know if any of the pointers overlap and advises you to use either `-Qno-alias-args` or the `restrict` keyword.

3. Help the compiler to successfully vectorize the code by using the command-line option `/Qno-alias-args`, per the advice from GAP:

```
icl /c test.cpp /Qguide /Qno-alias-args

test.cpp
GAP REPORT LOG OPENED ON Thu Aug 25 19:01:29 2011

remark #30761: Add -Qparallel option if you want the compiler to generate
recommendations for improving auto-parallelization.

Number of advice-messages emitted for this compilation session: 0.
END OF GAP REPORT LOG
```

Now the advice message has gone.

4. Compile the code, asking for a report:

```
icl /c test.cpp /Qvec-report2 /Qno-alias-args
test.cpp
C:\dv\guide\test.cpp(3): (col. 3) remark: LOOP WAS VECTORIZED.
```

Presto, you have a vectorized loop!

MORE ON AUTO-VECTORIZATION

Two additional vectorization-related topics are worth examining:

➤ Building applications that will safely run on different CPUs

➤ Other ways of inserting vectorization into your code

Building Applications to Run on More Than One Type of CPU

First, a gentle reminder: If you build an application and use just the general options, or no options at all, then any vectorized code will run on all CPUs that support SSE2. Default builds are safe!

Once you start enhancing auto-vectorization, the compiler adds CPU-specific code into your application — that is, code that will not run on every CPU.

CPU dispatch (sometimes called *multipath auto-vectorization*) is a means whereby you can add several coexisting specialized paths to your code. Figure 4-11 illustrates the concept. The compiler generates the specialized paths when you use the /Qax option, rather than the /Qx option. (Notice the extra *a*.)

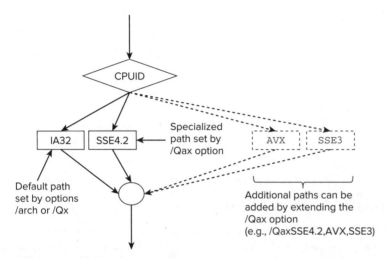

FIGURE 4-11: Multipath auto-vectorization

When the code is run, the CPU is first identified using the CPUID instruction. The most appropriate code path is then selected based on the instruction set your CPU can support. When you use the /Qax option, the compiler generates a default path and one or more specialized paths.

You can set the specification of the default path with either the /arch option or the /Qx option. If you think your code will ever be run on a non-Intel CPU, you must not use the /Qx option to create the default path, but rather use the /arch option. For non-Intel devices, the default path is always taken.

Table 4-10 gives some examples of how to use the /Qax option.

TABLE 4-10: Multipath Vectorization Example

	EXAMPLE	DEFAULT		SPECIALIZED	
		Intel	Non-Intel	Intel	Non-Intel
1	/QaxSSE2	SSE2	SSE2	SSE2	N/A
2	/QaxSSE3	SSE2	SSE2	SSE3	N/A
3	/QaxAVX /arch:SSE3	SSE3	SSE3	AVX	N/A
4	/QaxAVX,SSE4.1	SSE2	SSE2	AVX and SSE4.1	N/A
5	/QaxAVX /QxSSE3	SSE3	Error	AVX	Error

Examples 1 to 4 will run on Intel and non-Intel devices. Example 5 will run only on an Intel device, because the default path has been set up using the /Qx option.

Example 3 is a little more complicated. If the code runs on:

➤ An Intel device that supports AVX, it will use the AVX specialized path.

➤ An older Intel device that does not support AVX but still supports SSE3, it will use the default path.

➤ An older Intel device that supports only SSE2 (or lower), the program will fail to run.

➤ A non-Intel device that is capable of supporting SSE3 (or higher), it will run on the default path.

➤ An older non-Intel device that supports only SSE2 (or lower), the program will fail to run.

 For best portability and superior optimization, use the –/Qax (-ax) *option or one of its variants.*

Additional Ways to Insert Vectorization

In addition to using auto-vectorization, you can insert vectorization in your code by other means. The ways mentioned in Figure 4-12 range from the fully automatic vectorization to low-level assembler writing. The lower in the diagram, the more difficult it is to do.

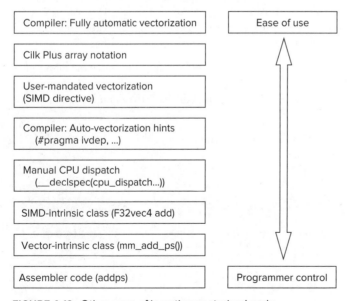

FIGURE 4-12: Other ways of inserting vectorized code

Note the following:

- ➤ The vector-intrinsic functions are supported by other compilers as well as the Intel compiler.

- ➤ The SIMD-intrinsic classes are C++ classes provided by the Intel compiler. You can see an example of SIMD-intrinsic classes in Chapter 13, "The World's First Sudoku 'Thirty-Niner.'"

- ➤ User-mandated vectorization and auto-vectorization hints are discussed in the section "When Auto-Vectorization Fails."

- ➤ Cilk Plus array notation and manual CPU dispatching are discussed in the following sections, respectively.

Using Cilk Plus Array Notation

Array extensions are a very convenient way of adding vectorized code to your application. When you build an application at optimization level /O1 or higher, the compiler replaces the array notation with vectorized code. If you build with no optimization (/Od), the compiler generates nonvectorized code.

The compiler uses exactly the same rules as for auto-vectorization with respect to which instruction set is used. By default, the compiler uses SSE2 instructions. You can override this behavior by using the /arch, /Qx, or /Qax options.

The Section Operator

Cilk Plus array notation is an extension to the normal C/C++ array notation and is supported by the Intel compiler. A section operator (:) is provided that enables you to express data-parallel operations over multiple elements in an array. The section operator has the format Array[lower bound : length : stride]. Here are some examples:

```
A[:] // All of array A
B[4:7] // Elements 4 to 10 of array B
C[:][3] // Column 3 of matrix C
D[0:3:2] // Elements 0,2,4 of array D
```

The first example accesses all the elements of array a[]. The other three examples access arrays B[], C[], and D[] portions as a range, a column, and a stride, respectively.

C/C++ Operators

Most C/C++ operators are available for use on array sections. Each operation is mapped implicitly to each element of the array. Here are two examples of using operators:

```
z[:] = x[:] * y[:] // element-wise multiplication
c[3:2][3:2] = a[3:2][3:2] + b[5:2][5:2] // 2x2 matrix addition
```

In the first example, each element of x[] is multiplied by its corresponding element in y[], and the results are written to the corresponding element in z[].

The second example shows that two submatrices are accessed and added and the results placed in another submatrix. The code is equivalent to the following:

```
c[3][3] = a[3][3] + b[5][5];
c[3][4] = a[3][4] + b[5][6];
```

```
c[4][3] = a[4][3] + b[6][5];
c[4][4] = a[4][4] + b[6][6];
```

The Assignment Operator

The assignment operator (=) applies in parallel every element of the right-hand side to every element of the left-hand side. For example:

```
a[:][:] = b[:][2][:] + c;
e[:] = d;
```

The equivalent code for the first example is as follows (assuming array declarations of a[3][3] and b[3][3][3]):

```
a[0][0] = b[0][2][0] + c;
a[0][1] = b[0][2][1] + c;
a[0][2] = b[0][2][2] + c;
a[1][0] = b[1][2][0] + c;
a[1][1] = b[1][2][1] + c;
a[1][2] = b[1][2][2] + c;
a[2][0] = b[2][2][0] + c;
a[2][1] = b[2][2][1] + c;
a[2][2] = b[2][2][2] + c;
```

In the second example, the value of d is assigned to every element of array e[].

Reducers

Reducers accumulate all the values in an array using one of nine reducer functions, or alternatively using your own user-defined function. The nine provided reducers are as follows:

➤ __sec_reduce_add — Adds values

➤ __sec_reduce_mul — Multiplies values

➤ __sec_reduce_all_zero — Tests that all elements are zero

➤ __sec_reduce_all_nonzero — Tests that all elements are nonzero

➤ __sec_reduce_any_nonzero — Tests that any element is nonzero

➤ __sec_reduce_max — Determines the maximum value

➤ __sec_reduce_min — Determines the minimum value

➤ __sec_reduce_max_ind — Determines index of element with maximum value

➤ __sec_reduce_min_ind — Determines index of element with minimum value

Here's an example of using the __sec_reduce_add reducer:

```
// add all elements using a reducer
int sum = __sec_reduce_add(c[:])

// add all elements using a loop
int sum = 0; for(int i = 0;i < sizeof(c);i++){sum += c[i]);
```

In the first line of code, every element of c[] is added together using the reducer __sec_reduce_add. In the second line, the same operation is performed using a loop.

Elemental Functions

Elemental functions are user-defined functions that can be used to operate on each element of an array. The three steps to writing a function are as follows:

1. Write the function using normal scalar operations. Restrictions exist on what kind of code can be included. Specifically, you must *not* include loops, switch statements, goto, setjmp, longjmp, function calls (except to other elemental functions or math library intrinsics), operations on a struct (other than selection), cilk_spawn, array notations, or C++ exceptions.

2. Decorate the function name with __declspec(vector). As an interesting aside, you can make the function CPU-specific by using the processor(cpuid) clause.

3. Call the function with vector arguments.

In the following code snippet, the multtwo function is applied to each element of array A. At optimization levels /O1 and above, the compiler generates vectorized code for the example.

```
int __declspec(vector) multtwo(int i){return i * 2;}

int main()
{
  int A[100];
  A[:] = 1;
  for (int i = 0 ; i < 100; i++)
    multtwo(A[i]);
}
```

Using Array Notations in the Example Application

The most obvious place to use the array notation is in the multiplication of the matrix in chapter4.c. Listing 4-3 first shows the original code and then the new version.

LISTING 4-3: Using array notation in the matrix multiplication

ORIGINAL VERSION

```
void MatrixMul(double a[N][N], double b[N][N], double c[N][N])
{
  int i,j,k;
  for (i=0; i<N; i++) {
    for (j=0; j<N; j++) {
      for (k=0; k<N; k++) {
        c[i][j] += a[i][k] * b[k][j];
      }
    }
  }
}
```

continues

LISTING 4-3 *(continued)*

VERSION USING ARRAY NOTATION

```
void MatrixMul(double a[N][N], double b[N][N], double c[N][N])
{
  int i,j;
  for (i=0; i<N; i++) {
    for (j=0; j<N; j++) {
      c[i][j] += a[j][:] * b[:][j];
    }
  }
}
```

code snippet Chapter4\4-3.c

By building the application with the /S option, you can examine the assembler code and confirm that the code has been vectorized. The highlighted lines in the following code snippet use a packed multiply double and a packed add double instruction (indicated by the *p* and *d* in the instruction's name). Remember that a packed instruction is performing a SIMD operation.

```
movsd     xmm1, QWORD PTR [r14+r13*8]                    ;14.31
movsd     xmm0, QWORD PTR [r8]                           ;14.10
movhpd    xmm0, QWORD PTR [8+r8]                         ;14.10
unpcklpd  xmm1, xmm1                                     ;14.31
mulpd     xmm1, xmm0                                     ;14.31
movsd     xmm2, QWORD PTR [rdi+r9*8]                     ;14.10
movhpd    xmm2, QWORD PTR [8+rdi+r9*8]                   ;14.10
addpd     xmm2, xmm1                                     ;14.10
```

Manual CPU Dispatch: Rolling Your Own CPU-Specific Code

Occasionally, developers want to write their own CPU-specific code that they can dispatch manually. The Intel compiler provides two functions to achieve this:

➤   `__declspec(cpu_dispatch(cpuid,cpuid…))`

➤   `__declspec(cpu_specific(cpuid))`

Listing 4-4 gives an example. First, you should declare an empty function (lines 3 and 4) that must list all the different CPUIDs to be used in the `__declspec` statement. Table 4-11 shows the valid CPUIDs.

TABLE 4-11: CPUID Parameters for Manual Dispatching

PARAMETER	ARCHITECTURE
core_2nd_gen_avx	Intel AVX
core_aes_pclmulqdq	AES
core_i7_sse4_2	SSE4.2

PARAMETER	ARCHITECTURE
atom	Intel Atom processors
core_2_duo_sse4_1	SSE4.1
core_2_duo_ssse3	SSSE3
pentium_4_sse3	SSE3
pentium_4	Pentium 4
pentium_m	Pentium M
pentium_iii	Pentium III
generic	Other IA-32 or Intel 64 (Intel and non-Intel)

Each CPUID declared in the empty function list then needs to have its own CPU-specific function, as shown at lines 7 and 10. The code will also work if the functions have return types rather than void functions. Note that all the CPUIDs, except the generic one, are Intel-specific.

Available for download on Wrox.com

LISTING 4-4: Example of manual dispatching

```
1:  #include <stdio.h>
2:  // need to create specific function versions
3:  __declspec(cpu_dispatch(generic, future_cpu_16))
4:  void dispatch_func() {};
5:
6:  __declspec(cpu_specific(generic))
7:  void dispatch_func() {  printf("Generic \n");}
8:
9:  __declspec(cpu_specific(future_cpu_16))
10: void dispatch_func(){ printf("AVX!\n");}
11:
12: int main()
13: {
14:    dispatch_func();
15:    return 0;
16: }
```

code snippet Chapter4\4-4.c

SOURCE CODE

Listing 4-5 contains the source coded for the example application used in this chapter. The code is written in such a way that the different compiler optimizations used in the chapter "make a difference." As mentioned previously, the code is not an example of writing good optimized code; in fact, some of the code is quite contrived and artificial.

LISTING 4-5: The example application

chapter4.c

```c
// Example Chapter 4 example program
#include <stdio.h>
#include <stdlib.h>
#include "chapter4.h"

void MatrixMul(double a[N][N], double b[N][N], double c[N][N])
{
  int i,j,k;
  for (i=0; i<N; i++) {
    for (j=0; j<N; j++) {
      for (k=0; k<N; k++) {
        c[i][j] += a[i][k] * b[k][j];
      }
    }
  }
}

// ********************************************************************
int main( int argc, char * argv[] )
{
  int i,j,k,l,m;
  long int sum;
  double ret, total;
  int denominator = 2;
  double starttime, elapsedtime;
  double *a,*b,*c;

// ----------------------------------------------------------------------
  m = 2;

  if(argc == 2)
    denominator = atoi(argv[1]);

  // allocate memory for the matrices
  a = (double *)malloc(sizeof (double) * N * N);
  if(!a) {printf("malloc a failed!\n");exit(999);}

  b = (double *)malloc(sizeof (double) * N * N);
  if(!b) {printf("malloc b failed!\n");exit(999);}

  c = (double *)malloc(sizeof (double) * N * N);
  if(!c) {printf("malloc c failed!\n");exit(999);}

  // repeat experiment six times
  for( l=0; l<6; l++ )
  {
    // get starting time
    starttime = wtime();

    // initialize matrix a
```

```
      sum = Work(&total,a);

      // initialize matrix b;
      for (i = 0; i < N; i++) {
        for (j=0; j<N; j++) {
          for (k=0;k<DENOM_LOOP;k++) {
            sum += m/denominator;
          }
          b[N*i + j] = sum;
        }
      }

      // do the matrix multiply
      MatrixMul( (double (*)[N])a, (double (*)[N])b, (double (*)[N])c);

       // get ending time and use it to determine elapsed time
      elapsedtime = wtime() - starttime;

      // report elapsed time
      printf("Time Elapsed %03f Secs  Total=%lf   Check Sum = %ld\n",
                  elapsedtime, total, sum );
    }
    // return a value from matrix c
    // just here to make sure matrix calc doesn't get optimized away.
    return (int)c[100];
}
// *********************************************************************
```

work.c

```
#include "chapter4.h"
#include <math.h>

long int Work(double *total,double a[])
{
  long int i,j,sum;
  double sumx, sumy;
  sum = 0;
  *total = 0.0;

  for (i=0;i<N;i++){
    for (j=0;j<N;j++) {
      sum += 1;
      // Calculate first Arithmetic series
      sumx= Series1(j);

      // Calculate second Arithmetic series
      sumy= Series2(j);

      // initialize the array
      if( sumx > 0.0 )*total = *total + 1.0 / sqrt( sumx );
      if( sumy > 0.0 )*total = *total + 1.0 / sqrt( sumy );
      a[N*i+j] = *total;
```

continues

LISTING 4-5 *(continued)*

```
    }
  }
  return sum;
}
```

series.c

```c
extern double AddY( double sumy, int k );

double Series1(int j)
{
  int k;
  double sumx = 0.0;
    for( k=0; k<j; k++ )
      sumx = sumx + (double)k;
  return sumx;
}

double Series2(int j)
{
  int k;
  double sumy = 0.0;
  for( k=j; k>0; k--,sumy++ )
    sumy = AddY(sumy, k);
  return sumy;
}
```

addy.c

```c
double AddY( double sumy, int k )
{
  sumy = sumy + (double)k -1;
  return sumy;
}
```

wtime.c

```c
#ifdef _WIN32
#include <windows.h>
double wtime()
{
  LARGE_INTEGER ticks;
  LARGE_INTEGER frequency;
  QueryPerformanceCounter(&ticks);
  QueryPerformanceFrequency(&frequency);
  return (double)(ticks.QuadPart/(double)frequency.QuadPart);
}
#else
#include <sys/time.h>
#include <sys/resource.h>
double wtime()
```

```
{
    struct timeval time;
    struct timezone zone;
    gettimeofday(&time, &zone);
    return time.tv_sec + time.tv_usec*1e-6;
}
#endif
```

chapter4.h

```
#pragma once
#define N 400
#define DENOM_LOOP 1000
// prototypes
double wtime();
long int Work(double *total,double a[]);
double Series1(int j);
double Series2(int j);
double AddX( double sumx, int k );
double AddY( double sumy, int k );
```

code snippet Chapter4\4-5\chapter4.c, work.c, series.c, addy.c, wtime.c, and chapter4.h

Listing 4-6 is the makefile used to build the application. If you are using Linux, then you will need to comment out the first three lines of the file (where CC, DEL and OBJ are set), and uncomment their equivalent lines that are just below.

LISTING 4-6: The makefile

```
## TODO: EDIT next set of lines according to OS

## WINDOWS OS specific vars.
CC=icl
DEL=del
OBJ=obj

# LINUX SPECIFIC, uncomment these for LINUX
# CC=icc
# DEL=rm -Rf
# OBJ=o


## -------------- DO NOT EDIT BELOW THIS LINE -------------
LD=$(CC)
CFLAGS =
LFLAGS =

OBJS = addy.$(OBJ) chapter4.$(OBJ) series.$(OBJ) work.$(OBJ) wtime.$(OBJ)
TARGET = main
.c.$(OBJ):
    $(CC) -c $(CFLAGS) $<
```

continues

LISTING 4-6 *(continued)*

```
$(TARGET).exe:$(OBJS) chapter4.h Makefile
    $(LD) $(LFLAGS) $(OBJS) $(LIBS) -o $@

clean:
    $(DEL) $(OBJS)
    $(DEL) $(TARGET).exe

reallyclean:
    $(DEL) $(OBJS)
    $(DEL) *.exe
    $(DEL) *.pdb
    $(DEL) *.dyn
    $(DEL) *.dpi
    $(DEL) *.lock
    $(DEL) *.asm
    $(DEL) *.s
```

code snippet Chapter4\4-6\Makefile

SUMMARY

You should use the seven optimization steps in this chapter as a starting point for all your optimization work. Most of the optimizations can be enabled by just adding an additional compiler option. Although the optimization switches seem to make no difference, you can use the reporting features of the compiler to help you understand what might be stopping the compiler from doing a better job.

Of all the optimization options available, auto-vectorization stands out as one of the great favorites among developers. When you combine this feature with some of the hand-tuning of the code that can be done, you can potentially get some astounding results.

Using the different optimization options of the Intel compiler can result in some great performance improvements. This chapter demonstrated that it is important not to just accept the out-of-the-box settings. The steps taken in this chapter are the foundation for further optimization work.

The next chapter looks at how to write safe code — code that is less vulnerable to hacking and malicious attacks.

5

Writing Secure Code

WHAT'S IN THIS CHAPTER?

➤ Running a Static Security analysis

➤ Tracking the status of security problems throughout the life of a project

➤ Understanding the programming practices that can leave your code vulnerable to attack

Many security threats take advantage of weaknesses introduced in programs written in C or C++. The weak type checking and the ability to write programs that directly access memory and hardware make it easy to write insecure programs. Most attacks fall into one of two categories:

➤ Threats that crash or overwhelm an application

➤ Threats that hijack the code path by inserting foreign code

The Intel compiler's Static Security analysis detects many of these code weaknesses, displaying the results in Intel Inspector XE. More than 250 different errors are detected in the following categories:

➤ Buffer overflows and boundary violations

➤ Uninitialized variables and objects

➤ Memory leaks

➤ Incorrect usage of pointers and dynamically allocated memory

➤ Dangerous use of unchecked input

➤ Arithmetic overflow and divide by zero

➤ Dead or redundant code

➤ Misuse of string, memory, and formatting library routines

➤ Inconsistent object declarations in different program units

➤ Incorrect use of OpenMP and Intel Cilk Plus

➤ Error-prone C++ and Fortran language usage

This chapter discusses how to use Intel Parallel Studio XE to perform Static Security analysis on your code. The primary goal of Static Security analysis is to harden applications against security attacks, but it is also useful for detecting some programming errors.

A SIMPLE SECURITY FLAW EXAMPLE

Listing 5-1 has security errors that could be used in an attack. An attacker could use the unchecked user input to create a buffer overflow.

LISTING 5-1: A program with several security errors

```c
#include <stdio.h>
#include <stdlib.h>
#include <string.h>
// user functions
int NotePad(){printf("    USER: here we launch notepad\n\n"); return 0;}
int Exit(){ exit(0);}

// system functions
int Dir(){printf("    SYSTEM: here we launch dir\n\n"); return 0;}
int Delete(){printf("    SYSTEM:  here we launch Del\n\n"); return 0;}
int ReturnToMain(){return -1;}

int SystemMenu();
int MainMenu();

int (*user_table[])(void) = {NotePad, SystemMenu,Exit};
int (*system_table[])(void) = {Dir, Delete, ReturnToMain};

int SystemMenu()
{
  char password[20];
  int id;
  int ret = 0;
  printf("System Menu\n");
  printf("Enter the Password before continuing!...\n");
  scanf("%s",password);
  if (strcmp(password, "PASSWORD") == 0)
  {
    while (ret != -1)
    {
```

```
        printf("Enter a number:\n");
        printf("1: dir\n");
        printf("2: delete everything\n");
        printf("3: back to main menu\n");
        scanf("%d",&id);
        ret = system_table[id-1]();
      }
    }
    else
    {
      printf("Invalid Password!\n");
      return 0;
    }
    return 0;
  }

int MainMenu()
{
  int id;
  printf("What would you like to do?\n");
  printf("Enter a number:\n");
  printf("1: run Notepad\n");
  printf("2: go to system menu\n");
  printf("3: quit\n");
  scanf("%d",&id);
  return user_table[id-1]();
}

int main ()
{
  int ret = 0;
  while( ret != -1)
    ret = MainMenu();
  return ret;
}
```

code snippet Chapter5\5-1.c

The program consists of two menus: a user menu and a system menu. When the program first starts, the MainMenu() function gives the user three choices:

```
What would you like to do?
Enter a number:
1: run Notepad
2: go to system menu ·
3: quit
```

The user input is captured using scanf(), which stores the result in id. The value in id (minus 1) is used as an index into the array user_table, which is an array of function pointers.

Choosing 1 calls the NotePad function; choosing 2 causes the SystemMenu() function to display the system menu; choosing 3 exits the program via the Exit() function.

The `SystemMenu()` function works in a similar way to `MainMenu()`, using the array `system_table` to jump to the `Dir()`, `Delete()`, and `ReturnToMain()` functions. Before the system menu is launched, the user is prompted for a password (`PASSWORD`). If the password is wrong, a message is displayed and control is returned to the `MainMenu()` calling function, which, in turn, returns zero to the `while` loop in `main()`.

Choosing 2 from the user menu displays the password-controlled system menu. The following shows the menu after the correct password has been entered:

```
System Menu
Enter the password before continuing!...
PASSWORD
Enter a number:
1: dir
2: delete everything
3: back to main menu
```

UNDERSTANDING STATIC SECURITY ANALYSIS

It is difficult to anticipate how an attacker will attack a program. Attackers are cunning and devious, taking advantage of any weakness in your code. Writing a series of runtime tests or debugging an application will not help find many weaknesses. At best, using such methods, you can test only what is actually executed, with some kinds of threats being impossible to test for.

Static Security analysis differs from standard debugging in that it analyzes the code without executing it. Every possible code path is examined, even those that are never executed by any of your tests.

Running a Static Security analysis on Listing 5-1 reports the following error messages. The problems could be used as a vehicle for a security attack.

➤ `main.c(28): error #12329` — specify field width in format specifier to avoid buffer overflow on argument 2 in call to `scanf`.

➤ `main.c(38): error #12305` — unvalidated value is received from call to an external function at (`file:main.c line:37`), which can be used in index expression of `system_table`.

➤ `main.c(59): error #12305` — unvalidated value is received from call to an external function at (`file:main.c line:58`), which can be used in index expression of `user_table`.

Someone could attack the code as follows:

➤ **By using invalid user input to bypass the system menu password** — If you enter a number higher than 3 in the user menu, the functions from the system menu are executed. A password is not even requested!

```
What would you like to do?
Enter a number:
1: run Notepad
2: go to system menu
3: quit
5
    SYSTEM:  here we would launch Del
```

This happens because the arrays `user_table` and `system_table` are next to each other in memory. The `user_table` array has three entries. Using an index of 4 means that a function pointer gets constructed from memory that is beyond the end of the array, reading the first entry in the `system_table` array.

➤ **By using invalid user or system input to cause the program to crash or to execute random code** — If you enter a very high number for the menu choice, the program will start executing code at an address not taken from either of the arrays. If you are lucky, the code will be harmless or will simply crash. In the worst case, you could start executing some valid and dangerous code.

➤ **By passing in a very long password to cause the application to crash** — The variable `password` can hold 20 characters. The following example uses a password that is much longer. When `scanf` is called, the extra characters corrupt the stack, causing the program to crash.

```
What would you like to do?
Enter a number:
1: run Notepad
2: go to system menu
3: quit
2
System Menu
Enter the Password before continuing!...
A_VERY_VERY_LONG_PASSWORD
Invalid Password!
    . . .                (program crashes after this)
```

False Positives

Not all the threats that Static Security analysis reports will be real problems — these are called *false positives*.

In the following code, the Static Security analyzer is not smart enough to know that the false part of the first `if` statement and the true part of the second `if` statement will never be executed together:

```
int y;
if ((x & 1) == 0) {
  y = 0;
}
if (x == ((x >> 1) << 1)) {
  z = y; // is y always zero here, or can it be uninitialized?
}
```

The first `if` statement checks if bit 0 in variable x is set to 1. If it is not, y gets initialized to zero.

The second `if` statement compares the variable x to the value of y, which has been shifted right by one and then shifted left by one. This shifting has the effect of clearing the lowest bit.

So, if x holds the value 0, the first test will evaluate to true and y will get initialized to 0; the second test will also evaluate to true, and the line z = y will be executed.

If x holds the value 1, both the first and second tests will evaluate to false, so the code y=0 and z=0 will not be executed.

Despite this, the analysis will report a "possible uninitialized variable," which is a false positive.

Static Security Analysis Workflow

The central activity when working with the results of Static Security analysis is to investigate the potential security problems that were reported and decide whether they need to be fixed. You record the results of your investigation as state information attached to the diagnostic. Typically, you would mark genuine errors as "Confirmed" and false positives as "Not a problem." You should log confirmed issues in whatever bug-tracking system you normally use for later correction.

Static Security analysis works on the whole program. This means that every file in the program is analyzed together. Because of the time it takes to run a whole program analysis, running the analysis each time you fix a problem is not a practical way forward, unless the program is small. Rather, it is better to run the Static Security analysis periodically.

Conducting a Static Security Analysis

The Intel compiler runs in a special mode to perform a Static Security analysis. In this mode, the compiler skips generating any instructions (see Figure 5-1). The compiler first processes the source files, generating a collection of pseudo-object files that contain analysis information. At link time these pseudo-object modules are combined and analysis is done. During this final analysis step, errors that span function and file boundaries are detected. The results are stored in XML format, which can be viewed and manipulated by Inspector XE. When the results are viewed in Inspector XE, its engine (represented by inspxe in the diagram) updates the states of the new results.

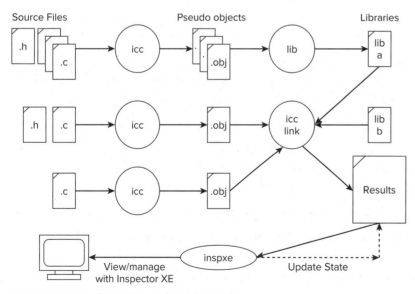

FIGURE 5-1: How Static Security analysis works

If you want the sources of a library to be part of the analysis, you must first perform the analysis on the library sources and build the library from the resulting pseudo-object modules. For example, in Figure 5-1, the contents of lib-a will participate fully in the error analysis, but lib-b, which might be a third-party library or some other library whose sources have not been analyzed, will not participate.

You can use either the GUI or the command-line version of Inspector XE to view or manage the results.

As you investigate the results using Inspector XE, record your conclusions by assigning state information to diagnostics. You can mark a problem as *Confirmed*, meaning it is a real issue that needs to be fixed, or as *Not a problem*, meaning the issue described in the diagnostic does not require fixing. This state information is carried forward from the previous result automatically when a new result is first loaded into Inspector XE.

When new results are loaded, Inspector XE constructs a problem-by-problem correspondence between the old and the new results. The correspondence engine is quite intelligent and is able to match problems between the old and new results, even if the sources have been moved around. Thanks to the correspondence engine, you should not have to reinvestigate old problems as your code grows and changes.

The steps for conducting a Static Security analysis are as follows:

➤ **If you are building inside Visual Studio**

   1. Select the projects or solution that you want to analyze.

   2. Invoke the menu item in the Build menu named Build Solution for Intel Static Security Analysis.

   The first time you do this, a new build configuration, Intel_SSA, is created. The analysis session then commences by building this configuration.

➤ **If you are *not* using Visual Studio**

   1. Create a new build configuration specifically for the analysis. This should be based on a debug build.

   2. Adjust the settings for the new configuration, adding the compiler and linker options that enable Static Security analysis (see Table 5-1).

TABLE 5-1: Options to Enable Static Security Analysis

OPTION	DESCRIPTION
/Qdiag-enable:sc{[1|2|3]} (linux -diag-enable:sc …)	Enables Static Security analysis. The number specifies the severity level of diagnostics reported, as follows: 1 — Only critical errors 2 — All errors 3 — All errors and warnings
/Qdiag-enable:sc-include (linux -diag-enable:sc-include)	Analyzes include files as well as source files. By default, apparent errors in include files are not reported.

3. Build the `Intel_SSA` configuration of the project. This causes the analysis to run.

You can view the results with the GUI version of Inspector XE with the command `inspxe-gui <directory where result is>`. If the analysis is run from Visual Studio, Inspector XE launches automatically. Figure 5-2 shows the summary screen.

Each problem is given a *weight*, a *state*, and a *category*, with the problems initially sorted in weight order. The errors with the highest weight are considered to be the most dangerous.

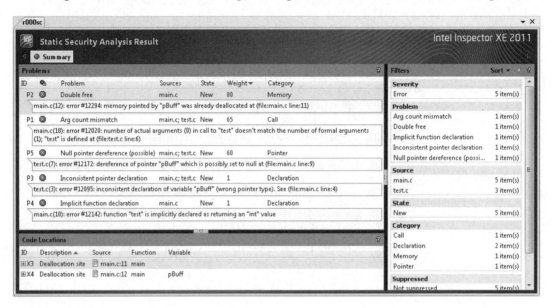

FIGURE 5-2: The summary screen

Investigating the Results of the Analysis

Once you have the list of problems, the next step is to investigate each issue and assign a state:

1. Choose a problem and investigate it. Examine the source locations associated with the problem. When you have understood the implications of the problem, change its state accordingly. You should handle confirmed problems using your normal bug-tracking process. You can manipulate the states via a context menu (see Figure 5-3). To display the menu, highlight a message and click the right mouse button.

The next section describes the significance of each state in more detail.

2. Keep working on the problems (that is, repeat step 1).

You can use filters to reduce the number of errors that are displayed or to focus in on a particular kind of problem. The problems can be filtered in or out, based on the Severity, Problem, Source, State, Category, and so on (see Figure 5-4). One particularly useful choice is to filter to "Not investigated" problems, which causes problems to disappear after you have investigated them.

The left-hand portion of Figure 5-4 shows the view without any filters applied, and the right-hand portion shows the content being filtered by source file. The set of problems shown in the summary window are reduced accordingly.

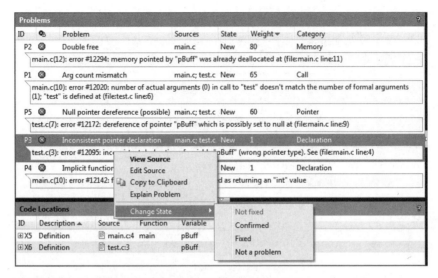

FIGURE 5-3: Changing the state of a problem

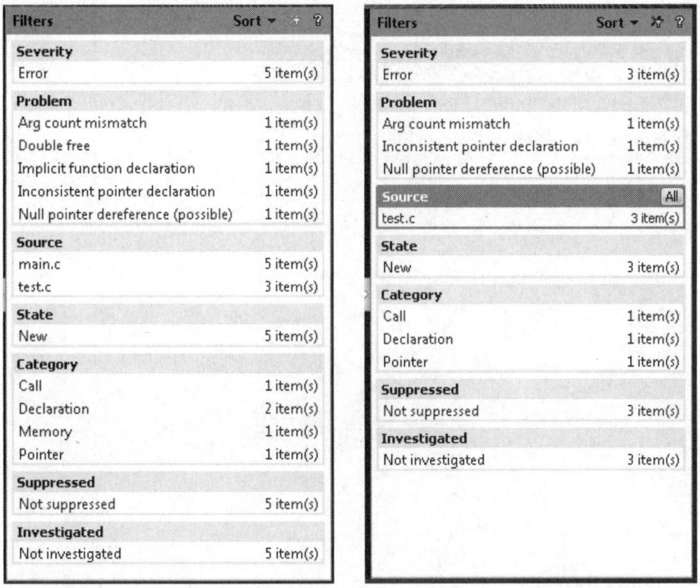

FIGURE 5-4: The one-click filters

3. If you don't understand the meaning of a problem, use the context menu to read an explanation (see Figures 5-5 and 5-6).

4. At some point you will want to stop analyzing the results and start modifying the application sources to fix the problems that were found (or to analyze a newer source version). Go back to step 3 and analyze the updated sources.

5. Repeat all the steps you have just done, starting at step 3 from the previous section, "Conducting a Static Security Analysis," until no problems remain to be investigated.

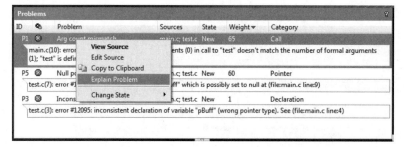

FIGURE 5-5: Choosing Explain Problem from the context menu

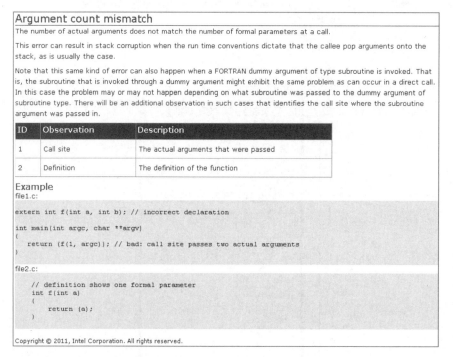

FIGURE 5-6: An example explanation

You can try these steps for yourself in Activity 5-1.

Working with Problem States

Problems will be in one of six states (see Figure 5-7).

A typical workflow would be as follows:

➤ The tool sets initial state = *New*

➤ You decide: does it need fixing?

- ➤ No: set state = *Not a problem*
- ➤ Yes: set state = *Confirmed*
- ➤ When you fix a *Confirmed* issue, set state = *Fixed*
  - ➤ If the tool sees a *New* issue again, state = *Not fixed*

  This means it's still uninvestigated, just not new.
- ➤ If the tool sees a *Fixed* issue again, state = *Regression*

  This means your fix didn't work.
- ➤ Each problem is either *Investigated* or *Not investigated*.
  - ➤ You will never come to a point where no problems exist. For example, there will always be false positives that you mark as *Not a problem*.
  - ➤ The goal is to have all problems *Investigated*.
  - ➤ When viewing the results in Inspector XE, it is good practice to filter the results so that only the *Not investigated* problems are displayed.

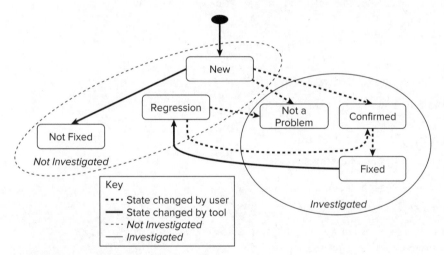

FIGURE 5-7: Tracking the investigation status

Table 5-2 describes each state.

TABLE 5-2: Problem States

STATE	DESCRIPTION	CLASSIFICATION
New	A new problem. This state is set by the analysis tool and not the user.	Not investigated
Not fixed	A problem from a previous analysis, either New or Not fixed. This state is set by the analysis tool, not the user.	Not investigated

continues

TABLE 5-2 *(continued)*

STATE	DESCRIPTION	CLASSIFICATION
Not a problem	A problem is not really a problem (for example, it might be a false positive). This state is set by the user.	Investigated
Fixed	The problem has been fixed. This state is set by the user.	Investigated
Confirmed	A problem is confirmed to be a problem. This state is set by the user.	Investigated
Regression	A problem previously marked as being Fixed still exists. This state is set by the analysis tool, not the user.	Not investigated

ACTIVITY 5-1: RUNNING A STATIC SECURITY ANALYSIS

In this activity you run a Static Security analysis session either from within Visual Studio or from the command line. The command-line version can be run on Windows or Linux.

Choose which environment you want to use, and then jump to the appropriate section:

➤　For Visual Studio IDE, start at step 1.

➤　For the command prompt, start at step 9.

Creating a Project (Visual Studio)

Begin by performing the following steps:

1.　Open Visual Studio.

2.　Create a new console application.

3.　Ensure the project is empty and does not use precompiled headers (just a personal preference of the author).

4.　Add two new files, `main.c` and `test.c`, to the project.

5.　Copy the source code from Listings 5-2 and 5-3 (at the end of the chapter) into the two empty files.

Creating a Dedicated Build and Running the Analysis (Visual Studio)

When performing Static Security analysis, you should always create a specific build configuration dedicated to the analysis activity. This will keep the pseudo-objects separate from your regular build objects.

6.　Highlight the project and select Build ➪ Build Solution for Intel Static Security Analysis.

The resulting dialog asks permission to prepare the project so that the Intel compiler can build a configuration. Note that this dialog will not appear if you are using Visual Studio 2010.

7. Click the Prepare project(s) and Continue button.

The resulting dialog shows the settings that will be used for Static Security analysis and offers to create a build configuration. Accept the default settings.

8. Select the Create Configuration and Build for SSA button.

A configuration file named `Intel_SSA` is created and built. When the analysis is complete, Inspector XE automatically opens the results of analysis.

Visual Studio users should now jump to step 14 to continue the activity.

Creating a Project (Command Prompt)

Begin by performing the following steps:

9. Copy the contents of Listing 5-2 and Listing 5-3 into the separate source files.

10. Copy the `Makefile` from Listing 5-4. If you are using Linux, you will need to comment out the Windows-specific variables at the beginning of the `Makefile` and uncomment the Linux variables.

11. Open a command prompt or shell:

➤ On Windows, open an Intel compiler command prompt. The path to the command prompt will be similar to the following. (The exact names and menu items will vary, depending on which version of Parallel Studio and Visual Studio you have installed.)

Start ➪ All Programs ➪ Intel Parallel Studio XE 2011 ➪ Command Prompt ➪ Intel64 Visual Studio Mode

➤ On Linux, make sure the compiler variables have been sourced:

```
$ source /opt/intel/bin/compilervars.sh intel64
```

If you are running a 32-bit operating system, the parameter passed to the `compilervars.sh` file should be `ia32`.

Creating a Dedicated Build and Running the Analysis (Command Prompt)

When performing Static Security analysis, you should always create a specific build configuration dedicated to the analysis activity. This will keep the pseudo-objects separate from your regular build objects.

continues

continued

12. Build the application enabling Static Security analysis:

> ➤ Linux

```
make clean
make CFLAGS="-diag-enable sc3" LFLAGS="-diag-enable sc3"
```

> ➤ Windows

```
nmake clean
nmake CFLAGS= /Qdiag-enable:sc3 LFLAGS=/Qdiag-enable:sc3
```

The results will be placed in a folder called `r000sc` in the current working directory.

13. Start the GUI version of inspector to view the results:

```
inspxe-gui r000sc
```

Remember that each time you run an analysis session, the compiler generates a folder named `rxxxsc` for the results, incrementing the `xxx` part of the name on each analysis. If you have run the analysis more than once, the folder name you use will be different.

Fixing the Errors

14. For each problem reported:

    a. Decide if the errors are genuine and not false positives.

    b. Mark any false positives as *Not a problem*.

    c. Mark those that are errors as *Confirmed*.

15. Set the filter to show only problems in the *Confirmed* state.

16. For each *Confirmed* problem:

    a. Implement a solution in the source.

    b. Mark each diagnostic as *Fixed*.

17. Run the analysis again using step 6 (Visual Studio) or step 12 (command prompt).

18. View the new results as before. This time the results folder will be `r0001sc`:

```
inspxe-gui r000sc
```

> This time the problems you fixed should not appear. If any of your fixes failed to repair the problem, those diagnostics will appear in a *Regression* state.

Activity 5-1 Summary

In this activity you ran a Static Security analysis twice — the first time to find any problems, and the second time to confirm that the problems had been fixed. Between the two runs you modified the state of each problem as it was being investigated and fixed.

You could have run the analysis after every fix, but the better way is to first investigate a number of problems, fix the problems, and then rerun the analysis.

Although the programming errors in the sample code are rather trivial and obvious, in a real program these kinds of errors could be easily missed and become a security risk.

Some errors are genuine programming errors, whereas others, from a programming point of view, are correct. Both kinds of errors pose a security risk.

Note for Visual Studio Users

You can also change the options for Static Security analysis by modifying the properties for the `Intel_SSA` configuration. To do this, you can use the following property pages:

> C/C++ ⇨ Diagnostics ⇨ Level of Static Security Analysis
>
> C/C++ ⇨ Diagnostics ⇨ Analyze Include Files
>
> C/C++ ⇨ Diagnostics ⇨ Analysis results container (The default location is My Inspector XE Results-*<product name>*directory in the project root directory.)

THE BUILD SPECIFICATION

The recommended first step in doing Static Security analysis is to create a new build configuration that is dedicated just to the analysis. If you do not build under Visual Studio and your build environment makes it difficult to create a new build configuration, you can create a *build specification file*.

A build specification file holds all the commands necessary for performing a Static Security analysis build, and can be launched from a command-line utility.

You can create a build specification file in two ways: by *injection* and by *wrapping*. Both methods are supported by utilities that come with the Intel compiler.

When using injection, the utility `inspxe-inject` launches your normal build and captures a history of the compilation, librarian, or linker steps. This information is stored in a build specification file.

Wrapping involves manually inserting a call to the utility `inpsxe-wrap` around every compilation, librarian, or linker step in your build scripts. When you run the instrumented build script, the wrap utility executes the wrapped commands and then adds them to the build specification file.

Creating a Build Specification File by Injection

The `inspxe-inject` utility automatically recognizes the Intel C++ compiler, Intel Fortran compiler, Microsoft C compiler, and the GNU GCC compiler. Figure 5-8 shows how the injection works.

The `inspxe-inject` utility launches a build. Each invocation of the compiler, linker, or librarian is recorded in a build specification file.

After creating the build specification file, you can use it to run an analysis. Start the analysis by calling the utility `inpxe-runsc`. This replays every action in the build specification file, but uses the Intel compiler and adds the options to enable Static Security analysis. This has the benefit that your main build

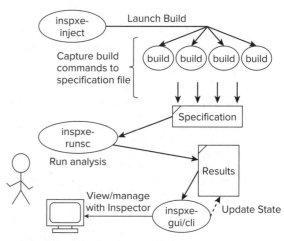

FIGURE 5-8: Command injection

could use another compiler, for example GCC, but the Intel compiler would still be used to perform the Static Security analysis. The results are placed in the folder specified on the command line (`test1` in this example).

You can either view the results from the GUI version of Inspector XE or query them from the command-line version of Inspector XE. When the results are first loaded into Inspector XE, each problem found is given a state.

Following is an example call to the `inspxe-inject` utility All the options after the `--` are the build commands. In this example, `make` is called to perform a build:

```
inspxe-inject -save-spec myfile.spec -- make
```

After creating the specification file, use `inpxe-runsc` to launch an analysis:

```
inspxe-runsc -spec-file myfile.spec  -r test1
```

Utility Options

Table 5-3 shows the command-line options available with the `inspxe-inject` utility.

TABLE 5-3: Injection and Wrapping Tool Options

OPTION	DESCRIPTION
`-?, -h, -help`	Displays brief tool description and usage
`-V, -version`	Displays version information
`-option-file=<string>`	Specifies the file that contains a list of tool options
`-tmp-dir=<string>`	Uses the specified directory to store temporary files

OPTION	DESCRIPTION
`-log-dir=<string>`	Uses the specified directory to store log files
`-v, -verbose`	Prints additional information
`-q, -quiet`	Suppresses nonessential messages
`-save-spec=<string>`	Specifies the file for storing the build specification

The Directory Structure of the Results

Figure 5-9 shows how the results are stored. Each time you run an analysis session, the compiler generates a folder named `rxxxsc` for the results, incrementing the *xxx* part of the name on each analysis.

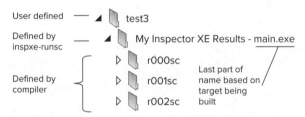

FIGURE 5-9: The directory structure of the results

The folder structure is the same whether you are running on Windows or Linux so that results generated on a Linux machine can be read on a Windows platform and vice versa.

As you load a new set of results into Inspector XE, Inspector looks at the previous set of results and assigns a state to all the problems found in the current set. The highest-level directory (`test3`) is user defined; the `My Inspector XE Results` folder is defined by the `inspxe-runsc` utility, which adds the name of the executable (`main.exe`) to the folder name.

ACTIVITY 5-2: USING BUILD CONFIGURATIONS

In this activity you use the `inspxe-inject` utility to create a build configuration file. The activity is intended to be run from the command prompt or shell.

Building the Program

To start:

1. Copy Listings 5-2 to 5-4 (from the end of the chapter) into a new directory.

2. Call `make` to ensure the program builds

   ➤ Linux

   ```
   make clean
   make
   ```

   continues

continued

> ➤   Windows

```
nmake clean
nmake
```

3.   Run the program. Even though the code built okay, it's quite likely that the program will abort at run time due to the programming errors.

On Linux, your run time errors message may look like this:

```
[sblairch@localhost ssa]$ ./main
Start of application
*** glibc detected *** ./main: double free or corruption (top):
    0x0000000007078010 ***
```

On Windows, the application will just run for an unduly long time.

Creating a Build Specification Using Injection

Do the following:

4.   Clean the build and call the `make` file using the `inspxe-inject` utility:

> ➤   Linux

```
make clean
inspxe-inject -save-spec myspec01.spec -v -- make
```

> ➤   Windows

```
nmake clean
inspxe-inject -save-spec myspec01.spec -v -- nmake
```

You add the `-v` (verbose) option so that you can see which actions are being carried out.

5.   Open the specification file `myspec01.spec` with a text editor and see if you can understand the contents.

6.   Use the specification file to run the Static Security analysis:

```
inspxe-runsc -spec-file myspec01.spec -r test1
```

The utility will report where the results have been stored. You should copy this for use in the next step.

7.   Open the results in the GUI version of Inspector XE:

```
inspxe-gui "<path to the results folder from step 7>"
```

8.   Explore the results, and then close Inspector XE.

Other Activities

If you want:

9. Correct all the errors reported.

10. Rerun the analysis.

Activity 5-2 Summary

You created a build specification file using injection. The injection method is fairly automatic, requiring few or no changes to the build environment. However, you do need to regenerate the build specification file each time the project changes (for example, if a new source file is added).

Occasionally, the injection method may capture commands that are not required to perform the analysis. When first running a Static Security analysis session, it is prudent to examine the contents of the specification file to make sure it has the expected contents. You can delete unwanted commands in the file using a text editor.

USING STATIC SECURITY ANALYSIS IN A QA ENVIRONMENT

Some developers and managers use Static Security analysis for regression testing and metrics tracking, often in an automatic or a scripted environment.

Regression Testing

The main goal of regression testing is to track the status of a project to ensure that no new problems are introduced when adding code changes to an application. The steps might be as follows:

1. Analyze the application (the base line).

2. Make some source changes/updates.

3. Reanalyze the application. This could be part of a nightly build.

4. Look for new problems that appear.

Steps 1 and 2 are carried out by the developer as part of his or her usual schedule; steps 3 and 4 are for regression testing using the command-line version of Inspector XE, and could be carried out by the developer or a quality assurance engineer. The output from step 3 (reanalyze, etc.) will look similar to this when new errors have been found:

```
inspxe-cl -user-data-dir "QA1/My Inspector XE Results - main" -report problems \
-filter-include state=New
```

The sample output:

```
Problem P1: New Error: Double free
main.cpp(14): error #12294: memory pointed by "pGlobal" was already deallocated at
   (file:main.cpp line:13)
X1: Deallocation site: main.cpp(13): Function main
X2: Deallocation site: main.cpp(14): Function main: Variable Name pGlobal
```

The command assumes that a set of results is already available from a previous analysis. The location of the results will change with each analysis, and take the form rxxxsc, where *xxx* is a number that is incremented each time the analysis is run. The –user-data-dir switch selects as input the highest-numbered (latest) result.

You can detect new problems by filtering the report so that only problems in a "new" state are reported. The results can then easily be mailed to the author of the most recent change.

Metrics Tracking

Project managers can use metrics to track a team's progress in investigating the results of analysis. For example, you can track the percentage of problems that have been investigated or fixed over a period of time.

1. Developer analyzes code using the GUI, changing the states of the problems detected as he investigates them (similar to Activity 5-1).

2. Developer makes source changes.

3. Developer repeats steps 1 and 2.

4. On a less frequent basis than the developer, the project manager runs the command-line version of Inspector XE to capture the status.

5. Over a period of time, the manager repeats step 4 and records the status. He might use the ratio of problems investigated versus problems not investigated as a "% investigated" metric.

You can find the status of each problem with the following command:

```
inspxe-cl -r "DEV1/My Inspector XE Results - main/r001sc" -report status
```

The results might look like this:

```
196 problem(s) found
2 Investigated
194 Not investigated
Breakdown by state:
1 Confirmed
1 Fixed
194 New
```

You can parse the results using either a Perl script or a shell script.

Activity 5-3 gives an example of how to use Static Security analysis in regression testing and metric tracking.

ACTIVITY 5-3: REGRESSION TESTING

In this activity you run a Static Security analysis session from the command line and track the results. This activity will be of special interest to those who want to incorporate Static Security analysis in their QA or regressions testing, where semiautomatic, batch-driven testing is the norm.

Building the Program and Running an Analysis

If you haven't already done so:

1. Do Activity 5-2.

2. Run the command-line version of Inspector, asking for a report on errors:

  ➤ Linux

```
inspxe-cl -r "test1/My Inspector/ XE/ Results/ - main/r000sc"
-report problems -filter-include state=New
```

  ➤ Windows

```
inspxe-cl -r "test1\My Inspector XE Results - main\r000sc"
-report problems -filter-include state=New
```

Changing the State Implicitly

3. Rerun the specification file:

```
inspxe-runsc -spec-file myspec03.spec -r test3
```

  This should result in all the new files becoming "Not fixed."

4. Look at the results again:

  ➤ Linux

```
inspxe-cl -r "test1/My Inspector/ XE/ Results/ - main/r001sc"
-report problems -filter-include state=New
```

  ➤ Windows

```
inspxe-cl -r "test1\My Inspector XE Results - main\r001sc"
-report problems -filter-include state=New
```

  No new problems should be reported.

Adding a New Error

5. Edit the test.c file to introduce a new error:

```
void test(int num)
{
  int i;
  pBuff[0] = num/i;
}
```

continues

continued

6. Clean the application and then run the specification file (Windows users use nmake):

```
make clean
inspxe-runsc -spec-file myspec03.spec -r test3
```

7. Run the command-line version of Inspector, asking for a report on the problems detected:

```
inspxe-cl -r "test1/My Inspector XE Results - main/r002sc"  \
-report problems -filter-include state=New
```

You will now see that there is a mixture of "new" problems and "Not fixed" problems.

Activity 5-3 Summary

The analysis carried out was run from the command line, with the results being filtered so that just new problems were reported. Each time a set of results is loaded into Inspector XE, the problems are assigned a state. In the first analysis, all the problems were reported as new. When the analysis was rerun and reloaded into Inspector XE, the previously found problems had their state changed to "Not fixed." In regression testing, it is the "new" problems that are of interest.

SOURCE CODE

Two files, `main.c` and `test.c`, are used in the hands-on activities. Each of the source files has some silly and obvious mistakes. The `Makefile` in Listing 5-4 is used for Activity 5-2 and Activity 5-3.

Available for download on Wrox.com

LISTING 5-2: main.c

```
#include <stdio.h>
#include <stdlib.h>
extern test();
char *pBuff;
int main()
{
    int not_used;
    printf("Start of application\n");
    pBuff = malloc(100);
    test();
    free (pBuff);
    free (pBuff);
```

```
    return (int)pBuff;
}
```

code snippet Chapter5\main.c

LISTING 5-3: test.c

```c
#include <stdlib.h>
void test(int num);
extern int *pBuff;

void test(int num)
{
    pBuff[0] = num;
}
```

code snippet Chapter5\test.c

LISTING 5-4: Makefile

```
## TODO: EDIT next set of lines according to OS

## WINDOWS OS specific vars.
CC=icl
DEL=del
OBJ=obj


# LINUX SPECIFIC, uncomment these for LINUX
# CC=icc
# DEL=rm -Rf
# OBJ=o


## -------------- DO NOT EDIT BELOW THIS LINE -------------
CFLAGS =
LFLAGS =

OBJS = main.$(OBJ) test.$(OBJ)
TARGET = main
.c.$(OBJ):
        $(CC) -c $(CFLAGS) $<

$(TARGET).exe:$(OBJS)  Makefile
        $(LD) $(LFLAGS) $(OBJS) $(LIBS) -o $@

clean:
        $(DEL) $(OBJS)
        $(DEL) $(TARGET).exe
```

code snippet Chapter5\Makefile

SUMMARY

Writing code that is secure and not vulnerable to attack is important. By performing a Static Security analysis on your source code, you can identify and fix many of the potential problems. Many of the vulnerabilities are caused by common programming errors or misuse of standard libraries. Using the Intel compiler and Inspector XE together is an effective method of identifying these vulnerabilities.

Chapter 6, "Where to Parallelize," introduces the first of a four-step process for making code parallel. The chapter shows how to spot regions of your code that are suitable for making parallel.

Where to Parallelize

➤   Hotspot analysis using the Intel compiler

➤   Hotspot analysis using the auto-parallelizer

➤   Hotspot analysis using Amplifier XE

The purpose of parallelization is to improve the performance of an application. Performance can be measured either by how much time a program takes to run or by how much work a program can do per second. Within a program, it is the busy sections, or *hotspots*, that should be made parallel. The more the hotspots contribute to the overall run time of the program, the better the performance improvement you will obtain by parallelizing them.

Hotspot analysis is an important first step in the parallelism process. This chapter shows three different ways to identify hotspots in your code using Parallel Studio XE. Without carrying out Hotspot analysis, there is a danger that you will end up making little or no difference to your program's performance. The section "Hotspot Analysis Using the Auto-Parallelizer" includes some tips on how to help the auto-parallelizer do its job better.

A NOTE FOR LINUX USERS

Most of the text of this chapter uses the Windows version of the compiler options. You can use the option-mapping tool to find the equivalent Linux option. The following example finds the Linux equivalent of /Oy-:

```
map_opts -tl -lc -opts /Oy-
Intel(R) Compiler option mapping tool

mapping Windows options to Linux for C++

'-Oy-' Windows option maps to
```

continues

continued

```
    --> '-fomit-frame-pointer-' option on Linux
    --> '-fno-omit-frame-pointer' option on Linux
    --> '-fp' option on Linux
```

The -t option sets the target OS and can be either l (or linux) or w (or windows).

The -l option sets the language and can be either c or f (or fortran). All the text after the -opts option is treated as options that should be converted. The option-mapping tool does not compile any code; it only prints the mapped options.

To use the option-mapping tool, make sure that the Intel compiler is in your path.

DIFFERENT WAYS OF PROFILING

You are already familiar with the four steps to parallelization (described in Chapter 3, "Parallel Studio XE for the Impatient"): analyze, implement, debug, and tune. It's now time to carry out the first of those steps, analyzing the hotspots in your code.

This book describes four ways of conducting a Hotspot analysis, the first three of which are covered in this chapter:

➤ Using the Intel compiler's loop profiler and associated profile viewer

➤ Letting the Intel compiler's auto-parallelizer help you find the hotspots

➤ Using Amplifier XE

➤ Performing a survey using Advisor (covered in Chapter 10, "Parallel Advisor Driven Design")

Each approach has its merits, and you will probably grow to like a particular one. What you shouldn't do is guess where the hotspots are! If you do, you could end up spending wasted effort making code parallel with little or no return on your invested time.

LOOPS ARE NOT THE ONLY PLACE TO PARALLELIZE

All the hotspot examples in this chapter use loop parallelism. Most of the time, you will find that you implement your parallelism effort at the loop level. However, other programming constructs also lend themselves to being made parallel, such as sequential code sections, recursive code, linked lists, and pipelines. These kinds of examples are explored in Chapter 7, "Implementing Parallelism."

In this chapter the focus is on loop parallelism, but the Hotspot analysis techniques can be used for other programming patterns, as well.

THE EXAMPLE APPLICATION

The code in Listing 6-1 (at the end of this chapter) produces a black-and-white picture of a Mandelbrot fractal. The picture is stored as a PPM file and can be viewed with any PPM viewer. If you don't have a viewer, try IrfanView (www.irfanview.com).

Listing 6-1 is split into the following files:

- ➤ `main.cpp` — The entry point to the program
- ➤ `mandelbrot.cpp` — Calculates the fractal
- ➤ `mandelbrot.h` — Contains a number of defines and prototypes
- ➤ `ppm.cpp` — Prints the fractal to a PPM file
- ➤ `wtime.c` — A utility for measuring the application run time

When you run the example application, it displays the following simple text on the screen:

```
calculating...
printing...
Time to calc :...3.707
Time to print :...7.548
Time (Total) :...11.25
```

Figure 6-1 shows the `default.ppm` file generated by running the application and viewed using IrfanView.

Table 6-1 shows the results of running the program built with the Intel compiler, using the options `/O2` (optimize for speed) and `/Qipo` (enable interprocedural optimization). The results are the best of five runs, on an Intel Xeon Workstation with an Intel Xeon CPU, X5680 @ 3.33 GHz (two processors, supporting a total of 24 hardware threads).

FIGURE 6-1: The output of the Mandelbrot application

TABLE 6-1: Time Taken to Run the Example Application

FUNCTION	TIME
Calculating	3.433
Printing	2.206
Total	5.638

ACTIVITY 6-1: BUILDING THE EXAMPLE APPLICATION

In this activity you build and run the Mandelbrot program.

1. Copy the source code in Listing 6-1 and place each script in a separate file.

2. Open an Intel Parallel Studio XE command prompt.

3. Build the program with the following command:

```
icl  /O2 /Qipo wtime.c main.cpp mandelbrot.cpp ppm.cpp -o 6-1.exe
```

4. Run the program you have just created and record the time taken.

```
6-1.exe
```

5. Examine the generated `default.ppm` file with a PPM viewer.

Instructions for Linux Users

All the activities in this chapter can be carried out on a Linux platform, but you'll need to use the Linux compiler `icc` instead of `icl`. You will also need to find the equivalent Linux compiler options by following the instructions in the section "A Note for Linux Users."

SOURCING THE COMPILER AND AMPLIFIER XE

To make the Parallel Studio XE tools available from a shell, source the following scripts (or add the commands to your `./bash_profile`):

```
source /opt/intel/composerxe/bin/compilervars.sh intel64
source /opt/intel/vtune_amplifier_xe/amplxe-vars.sh
source /opt/intel/inspector_xe/inspxe-vars.sh
```

This assumes you've installed Parallel Studio XE in the default location.

VIEWING THE PPM FILE

Your Linux systems should have a default PPM viewer installed, such as `gthumb`, `eog`, or `gwenview`.

HOTSPOT ANALYSIS USING THE INTEL COMPILER

A well-kept secret is that the Intel compiler has its own profiler and viewer. These are different products from Amplifier XE and rely on the compiler instrumenting your code.

With the profiler and viewer you can:

➤ Profile functions

➤ Profile loops

➤ View the output in a standalone viewer

➤ Read the results from a text file

Profiling Steps

Figure 6-2 shows the steps for profiling an application:

1. Compile the source code using the `/Qprofile-functions` and `/Qprofile-loops` options. The compiler instruments each loop and each function with extra code that will track each time they are used.

2. Run the program. This produces a text file for each profile (having the `.dump` extension) and an XML file.

3. View the results with the command `loopprofileviewer`, passing it the name of the XML file that has just been generated.

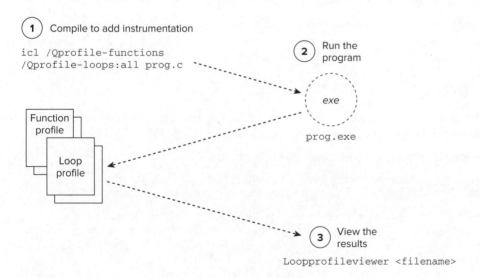

FIGURE 6-2: Using the Intel compiler to find the hotspots

If you do not want to use the profile viewer or the XML, you can read the results from the `.dump` file. You can disable the generating of an XML file by setting the `INTEL_LOOP_PROF_XML_DUMP` environment variable to zero. Table 6-2 lists the options for controlling the profiling.

TABLE 6-2: Profiling Options and Their Arguments

OPTION	ARGUMENTS
/Qprofile-functions	None
/Qprofile-loops:<arg>	Inner, outer, all
/Qprofile-loops-report:<arg>	1 or 2 (times, or times and counts)

INLINING: WHERE ARE MY SYMBOLS?

When doing a Hotspot analysis with interprocedural optimization (IPO) or inlining enabled, some functions end up being inlined and are not visible in the Hotspot analysis. Here are three different strategies you can use to get better visibility:

➤ Don't use IPO. You can disable it with the compiler option /Qipo-.

➤ Disable inlining using the /Ob0 or /Ob1 option.

➤ Use the /Qopt-report-phase ipo_inl option to get a list of inlined functions so that you can manually reconstruct the call tree.

Note that the first two options improve visibility but may have a detrimental effect on performance.

An Example Session

Taking the Mandelbrot program, which by now you should be familiar with, here is a description of the profiling steps and the output generated. You can try this for yourself in Activity 6-2.

1. The program is compiled with optimization level /O2:

```
icl /Zi /O2 /Qipo wtime.c main.cpp  mandelbrot.cpp  ppm.cpp -o m1.exe  \
    /Qprofile-functions  /Qprofile-loops:all /Qprofile-loops-report:2
```

The /Qprofile-functions option tells the compiler to profile the functions. The /Qprofile-loops:all option tells the compiler to profile both inner and outer loops. The /Qprofile-loops-report option selects the level of detail the report should contain; specifying 2 tells the compiler to report loop times and iteration counts.

2. Running the program gives the usual output:

```
C:\>m1.exe
calculating...
printing...
Time to calc :...3.707
Time to print :...7.548
Time (Total) :...11.25
```

When the program has finished running, the directory will contain the following files:

```
C:\dv\CH6>dir /b
default.ppm
```

```
loop_prof_1317923290.xml
loop_prof_funcs_1317923290.dump
loop_prof_loops_1317923290.dump
m1.exe
m1.ilk
m1.pdb
main.cpp
main.obj
mandelbrot.cpp
mandelbrot.h
mandelbrot.obj
ppm.cpp
ppm.obj
vc90.pdb
```

The names of the XML and dump files are augmented with a time stamp.

3. To call the viewer, the name of the XML file is passed in:

```
loopprofileviewer  loop_prof_1317923290.xml
```

```
(Linux users: loopprofileviewer.sh or loopprofileviewer.csh)
```

Figure 6-3 shows the results displayed in the viewer. The top set of results is the function profile, and the bottom set is the loop profile. You can sort the results by clicking at the tops of the columns. There is also a facility for filtering what is displayed by threshold. For example, you can choose to display only the top 10 percent of hotspots.

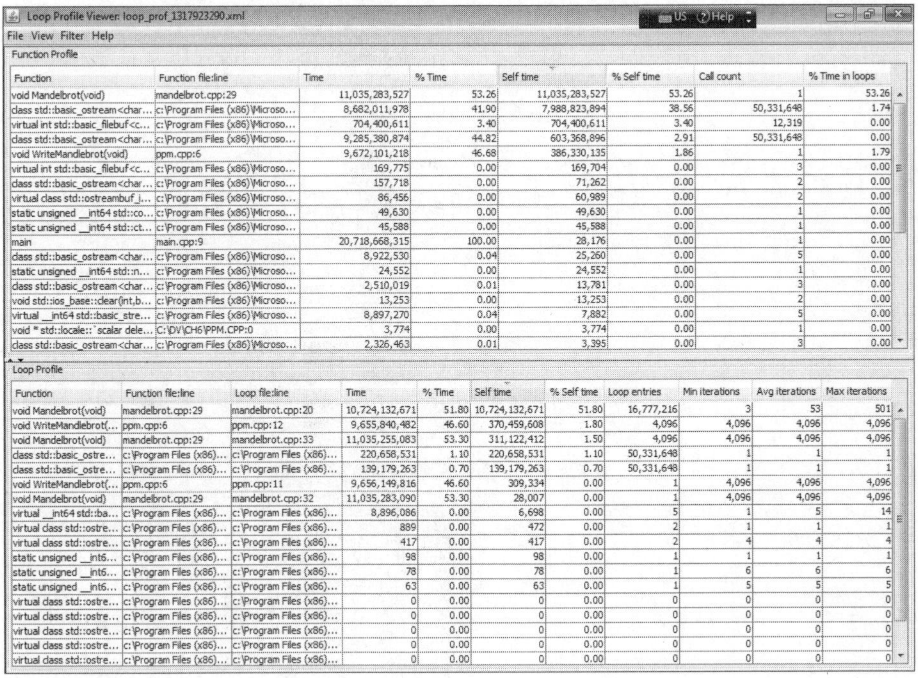

Function	Function file:line	Time	% Time	Self time	% Self time	Call count	% Time in loops
void Mandelbrot(void)	mandelbrot.cpp:29	11,035,283,527	53.26	11,035,283,527	53.26	1	53.26
class std::basic_ostream<char…	c:\Program Files (x86)\Microso…	8,682,011,978	41.90	7,988,823,894	38.56	50,331,648	1.74
virtual int std::basic_filebuf<c…	c:\Program Files (x86)\Microso…	704,400,611	3.40	704,400,611	3.40	12,319	0.00
class std::basic_ostream<char…	c:\Program Files (x86)\Microso…	9,285,380,874	44.82	603,368,896	2.91	50,331,648	0.00
void WriteMandlebrot(void)	ppm.cpp:6	9,672,101,218	46.68	386,330,135	1.86	1	1.79
virtual int std::basic_filebuf<c…	c:\Program Files (x86)\Microso…	169,775	0.00	169,704	0.00	3	0.00
class std::basic_ostream<char…	c:\Program Files (x86)\Microso…	157,718	0.00	71,262	0.00	2	0.00
virtual class std::ostreambuf_i…	c:\Program Files (x86)\Microso…	86,456	0.00	60,989	0.00	2	0.00
static unsigned __int64 std::co…	c:\Program Files (x86)\Microso…	49,630	0.00	49,630	0.00	1	0.00
static unsigned __int64 std::ct…	c:\Program Files (x86)\Microso…	45,588	0.00	45,588	0.00	1	0.00
main	main.cpp:9	20,718,668,315	100.00	28,176	0.00	1	0.00
class std::basic_ostream<char…	c:\Program Files (x86)\Microso…	8,922,530	0.04	25,260	0.00	5	0.00
static unsigned __int64 std::n…	c:\Program Files (x86)\Microso…	24,552	0.00	24,552	0.00	1	0.00
class std::basic_ostream<char…	c:\Program Files (x86)\Microso…	2,510,019	0.01	13,781	0.00	3	0.00
void std::ios_base::clear(int,b…	c:\Program Files (x86)\Microso…	13,253	0.00	13,253	0.00	2	0.00
virtual __int64 std::basic_stre…	c:\Program Files (x86)\Microso…	8,897,270	0.04	7,882	0.00	5	0.00
void * std::locale::`scalar dele…	C:\DV\CH6\PPM.CPP:0	3,774	0.00	3,774	0.00	1	0.00
class std::basic_ostream<char…	c:\Program Files (x86)\Microso…	2,326,463	0.01	3,395	0.00	3	0.00

Function	Function file:line	Loop file:line	Time	% Time	Self time	% Self time	Loop entries	Min iterations	Avg iterations	Max iterations
void Mandelbrot(void)	mandelbrot.cpp:29	mandelbrot.cpp:20	10,724,132,671	51.80	10,724,132,671	51.80	16,777,216	3	53	501
void WriteMandlebrot(…	ppm.cpp:6	ppm.cpp:12	9,655,840,482	46.60	370,459,608	1.80	4,096	4,096	4,096	4,096
void Mandelbrot(void)	mandelbrot.cpp:29	mandelbrot.cpp:33	11,035,255,083	53.30	311,122,412	1.50	4,096	4,096	4,096	4,096
class std::basic_ostre…	c:\Program Files (x86)…	c:\Program Files (x86)…	220,658,531	1.10	220,658,531	1.10	50,331,648	1	1	1
class std::basic_ostre…	c:\Program Files (x86)…	c:\Program Files (x86)…	139,179,263	0.70	139,179,263	0.70	50,331,648	1	1	1
void WriteMandlebrot(…	ppm.cpp:6	ppm.cpp:11	9,656,149,816	46.60	309,334	0.00	1	4,096	4,096	4,096
void Mandelbrot(void)	mandelbrot.cpp:29	mandelbrot.cpp:32	11,035,283,090	53.30	28,007	0.00	1	4,096	4,096	4,096
virtual __int64 std::ba…	c:\Program Files (x86)…	c:\Program Files (x86)…	8,896,086	0.00	6,698	0.00	5	1	5	14
virtual class std::ostre…	c:\Program Files (x86)…	c:\Program Files (x86)…	889	0.00	472	0.00	2	1	1	1
virtual class std::ostre…	c:\Program Files (x86)…	c:\Program Files (x86)…	417	0.00	417	0.00	2	4	4	4
static unsigned __int6…	c:\Program Files (x86)…	c:\Program Files (x86)…	98	0.00	98	0.00	1	1	1	1
static unsigned __int6…	c:\Program Files (x86)…	c:\Program Files (x86)…	78	0.00	78	0.00	1	6	6	6
static unsigned __int6…	c:\Program Files (x86)…	c:\Program Files (x86)…	63	0.00	63	0.00	1	5	5	5
virtual class std::ostre…	c:\Program Files (x86)…	c:\Program Files (x86)…	0	0.00	0	0.00	0	0	0	0
virtual class std::ostre…	c:\Program Files (x86)…	c:\Program Files (x86)…	0	0.00	0	0.00	0	0	0	0
virtual class std::ostre…	c:\Program Files (x86)…	c:\Program Files (x86)…	0	0.00	0	0.00	0	0	0	0
virtual class std::ostre…	c:\Program Files (x86)…	c:\Program Files (x86)…	0	0.00	0	0.00	0	0	0	0
virtual class std::ostre…	c:\Program Files (x86)…	c:\Program Files (x86)…	0	0.00	0	0.00	0	0	0	0

FIGURE 6-3: The standalone loop-profiling viewer

TABLE 6-3: Results of the Loop Profiling with Inlining Enabled

FUNCTION	LOOP	PERCENTAGE OF TIME	PERCENTAGE OF SELF TIME	NUMBER OF LOOP ENTRIES	MINIMUM ITERATIONS	AVERAGE ITERATIONS	MAXIMUM ITERATIONS
main	mandelbrot.cpp:19	54.80	54.80	16,777,216	3	53	501
WriteMandelbrot	ppmt.cpp:12	43.80	2.60	4,096	4,096	4,096	4,096
std::operator<<	ostream:810	53.30	1.40	50,331,648	1	1	1
main	mandelbrot.cpp:32	1.10	1.00	4,096	4,096	4,096	4,096

TABLE 6-4: Results of the Loop Profiling with Inlining Disabled

FUNCTION	LOOP	PERCENTAGE OF TIME	PERCENTAGE OF SELF TIME	NUMBER OF LOOP ENTRIES	MINIMUM ITERATIONS	AVERAGE ITERATIONS	MAXIMUM ITERATIONS
CalcMandelbrot	mandelbrot.cpp:19	28.30	28.80	16,777,216	3	53	501
WriteMandelbrot	ppmt.cpp:12	69.10	1.20	4,096	4,096	4,096	4,096
Mandelbrot	mandelbrot.cpp:32	30.70	0.90	4,096	4,096	4,096	4,096
std::operator<<	ostream:810	0.60	0.70	50,331,648	1	1	1

Table 6-3 shows the results of profiling the Mandelbrot program `M1.exe` with inlining enabled. The biggest hotspots are the three loops at the top of the table. *Time* refers to the time the loop takes including any function calls. *Self time* refers to the time the loop takes without including any called functions.

The first loop at `mandelbrot.cpp:19` is reported as being in the `main` function, but this is not true. The cause of the apparent error is that the function in which the loop resides has been inlined. Using the options `/Qopt-report-phase ipo_inl` and `/Qopt-report-routine:main` shows that the nested function calls to `CalcMandelbrot()`, `SetZ()`, and `Mandelbrot()` have all been inlined:

```
-> INLINE: ?Mandelbrot@@YAXXZ(2905) (isz = 71) (sz = 74 (31+43))
  -> INLINE: ?SetZ@@YAXHHMM@Z(2906) (isz = 51) (sz = 62 (19+43))
    -> INLINE: ?CalcMandelbrot@@YAMMM@Z(2907) (isz = 26) (sz = 36 (17+19))
```

4. Rebuilding the application with inlining disabled (using the `/Ob0` option) improves visibility but has a huge impact on the `WriteMandelBrot()` function. Instead of taking fewer than 4 seconds to complete, it now takes more than 40 seconds. Table 6-4 shows the loop analysis with inlining disabled.

5. The next thing to decide is which loop should be made parallel. Two criteria are important:

➤ There should be a decent number of iterations of the loop.

➤ The individual loops should do a reasonable amount of work.

As shown in Table 6-4, two loops have a large number of iterations, `ppmt.cpp:12` and `mandelbrot.cpp:32`. Both have a self time of around 1 percent, which translates to about a third of a second — this is plenty of work to consider making parallel. You can view the exact value in the `loopprofileviewer`.

There are other considerations, such as loop dependencies, to take into account when it comes to implementing the parallelism. At this stage, however, the only task is to identify the hotspots.

Overhead Introduced by Profiling

Using the profiling option of the compiler adds an overhead to the run time. Table 6-5 records the time taken for each type of profiling. On the Mandelbrot program, with all the profiling options enabled, the program runs twice as slow as when no profiling is carried out.

TABLE 6-5: Time Taken to Run the Example Application

TYPE OF PROFILING	TIME	SPEEDUP
No profiling	5.638	1
Functions	7.953	0.71
Functions and outer loops (time)	10.68	0.53
Functions and outer loops (time and count)	10.86	0.52
Functions and all loops (time)	10.98	0.51
Functions and all loops (time and count)	11.25	0.50

PROS AND CONS OF PROFILING WITH THE INTEL COMPILER

➤ Pros

    ➤ Easy to use

    ➤ Everything you need is available with the compiler, including a standalone viewer

    ➤ Profiles loops as well as functions

➤ Cons

    ➤ Very basic functionality

    ➤ Requires code to be instrumented, introducing a compile-time and a runtime overhead, which can be significant

    ➤ No call tree, so you have to construct the call stack manually

    ➤ No comparison facility

ACTIVITY 6-2: USING THE COMPILER'S LOOP PROFILER

In this activity you use the Intel compiler to instrument the Mandelbrot program and then find the busiest hotspots using the `loopprofileviewer`.

1. Make sure you have carried out Activity 6-1.

2. Rebuild the application, adding the `/Zi` option to generate debug information, and the `/Qprofile` options so that the compiler instruments the code:

```
icl /Zi /O2 /Qipo wtime.c main.cpp  mandelbrot.cpp  ppm.cpp -o 6-2.exe \
    /Qprofile-functions  /Qprofile-loops:all /Qprofile-loops-report:2
```

3. Run the program you have just created and record the time taken:

```
6-2.exe
```

4. Start the `loopprofileviewer` from the command line, and browse to the XML file that has just been generated.

Dealing with the Lack of Symbol Visibility

One of the difficulties of profiling an optimized application is that the compiler will inline some function calls.

5. Repeat steps 2 to 4, adding the option `/Ob0` to the end of the build options.

6. Repeat steps 2 to 4 again, but this time use the following options:

```
icl /Zi /O2 /Qipo wtime.c main.cpp  mandelbrot.cpp  ppm.cpp -o 6-2.exe \
    /Qprofile-functions  /Qprofile-loops:all \
/Qprofile-loops-report:2 ./Qopt-report-phase ipo_inl \
/Qopt-report-routine:main
```

7. Look at the report the compiler prints to the screen. This should help you to identify which functions have been inlined.

Instructions for Linux Users

Refer to the "Instructions for Linux Users" section in Activity 6-1 before carrying out this activity.

HOTSPOT ANALYSIS USING THE AUTO-PARALLELIZER

The Intel compiler has an auto-parallelizer that can automatically add parallelism to loops. By default, the auto-parallelizer is disabled, but you can enable it with the /Qparallel option. Some developers use this feature to give hints on where best to parallelize their code.

The auto-parallelizer does four things:

➤ Finds loops that could be candidates for making parallel

➤ Decides if there is a sufficient amount of work done to justify parallelization

➤ Checks that no loop dependencies exist

➤ Appropriately partitions any data between the parallelized code

Profiling Steps

Figure 6-4 shows the steps for profiling with the help of the auto-parallelizer:

1. Compile the sources with the /Qparallel option. To get superior results, it's always best to enable interprocedural optimization (/Qipo). The option /Qpar-report2 instructs the compiler to generate a parallelization report, listing which loops were made parallel.

2. Look at the results from the compiler and make a note of any lines that were successfully parallelized.

3. Add your own parallel constructs to the identified loops.

4. Rebuild the application without the /Qparallel option.

You might ask, "Why not just accept the results of the parallelizer?" The following are two of the common reasons:

➤ The auto-parallelizer (at the time of writing) uses OpenMP. Many developers prefer to use a more composable parallelism, such as that provided with Cilk Plus or Threading Building Blocks. In this context, "composability" refers to how well a parallel model can be mixed with other models.

➤ Some developers don't like relying on automatic features. They prefer to have more control over where and when threading is implemented.

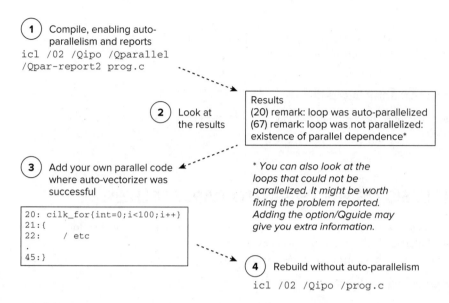

1 Compile, enabling auto-parallelism and reports

```
icl /02 /Qipo /Qparallel
/Qpar-report2 prog.c
```

2 Look at the results

Results
(20) remark: loop was auto-parallelized
(67) remark: loop was not parallelized: existence of parallel dependence*

3 Add your own parallel code where auto-vectorizer was successful

```
20: cilk_for{int=0;i<100;i++}
21:{
22:    / etc
.
45:}
```

* You can also look at the loops that could not be parallelized. It might be worth fixing the problem reported. Adding the option/Qguide may give you extra information.

4 Rebuild without auto-parallelism

```
icl /02 /Qipo /prog.c
```

FIGURE 6-4: Using the auto-parallelizer to find hotspots

An Example Session

Here's an example session of finding hotspots with the auto-parallelizer. You can try this out for yourself in Activity 6-3.

1. The serial version of the code is run so that you have some results to compare against:

```
C:\ >serial.exe
calculating...
printing...
Time to calc :...3.667
Time to print :...2.311
Time (Total) :...5.978
```

2. The Mandelbrot application is then built with auto-parallelism enabled (/Qparallel). The optimization level must be at least /O1 to engage the auto-parallelizer:

```
icl /Zi /O2 wtime.c main.cpp mandelbrot.cpp ppm.cpp -o m1.exe \
/Qparallel /Qipo /Qpar-report2
```

The compiler will report on every loop it finds, including the header files, so the screen will get filled with messages. Here are the ones related to the source code:

```
main.cpp(14):(col.3) remark: LOOP WAS AUTO-PARALLELIZED
main.cpp(14):(col.3) remark: loop was not parallelized: insufficient inner loop
main.cpp(14):(col.3) remark: loop was not parallelized: existence of parallel dependence
.
.
ppm.cpp(11):(col.3) remark: loop was not parallelized: existence of parallel dependence
ppm.cpp(12):(col.5) remark: loop was not parallelized: existence of parallel dependence
```

As an experiment, running the parallelized code shows that the time taken to do the calculations is much better than the 3.667 seconds that was previously achieved without parallelism:

```
C:\>parallel.exe
calculating...
printing...
Time to calc :...0.596
Time to print :...2.272
Time (Total) :...2.868
```

3. The parallelized loop reported at line 14 of `main.cpp` is examined. The first thing you will discover is that there is no loop, but rather a call to `Mandelbrot()`!

```
main.cpp 12: std::cout << "calculating..." << std::endl;
main.cpp 13:    double start = wtime();
main.cpp 14:    Mandelbrot();
main.cpp 15:    double mid = wtime();
```

The loop in question is in the `Mandelbrot()` function in `Mandelbrot.cpp`, but it has been inlined by the use of the option `/Qipo`:

```
mandelbrot.cpp 27:  void Mandelbrot ()
mandelbrot.cpp 28:  {
mandelbrot.cpp 29:    float xinc = (float)deltaX/(maxI-1);
mandelbrot.cpp 30:    float yinc = (float)deltaY/(maxJ-1);
mandelbrot.cpp 31:    for (int i=0; i<maxI; i++) {
mandelbrot.cpp 32:      for (int j=0; j<maxJ; j++) {
mandelbrot.cpp 33:      SetZ(i, j, xinc, yinc);
mandelbrot.cpp 34:      }
mandelbrot.cpp 35:    }
mandelbrot.cpp 36:  }
```

To make the code parallel using the Cilk Plus method, replace the outer `for(..)` with `cilk_for()` and add the Cilk `include` file to the top of the `Mandelbrot.cpp` file:

```
mandelbrot.cpp  0:  #include "mandelbrot.h"
mandelbrot.cpp  1:  #include <cilk/cilk.h>
mandelbrot.cpp 30:    float yinc = (float)deltaY/(maxJ-1);
mandelbrot.cpp 31:    cilk_for (int i=0; i<maxI; i++) {
mandelbrot.cpp 32:      for (int j=0; j<maxJ; j++) {
```

4. Building and running the program gives a better performance improvement than with the auto-parallelism:

```
icl /Zi /O2 wtime.c main.cpp mandelbrot.cpp ppm.cpp -o myparallel.exe /Qipo


C:\>myparallel.exe
calculating...
printing...
Time to calc :...0.2475
Time to print :...2.178
Time (Total) :...2.426
```

Programming Guidelines for Auto-Parallelism

Although this chapter is about using the auto-parallelizer to find hotspots, this is a good time to mention how you can help the auto-parallelizer to do its job better. For auto-parallelism to succeed, you must follow certain guidelines:

➤ The loop must be countable at compile time. Try to use constants where possible.

➤ There must be no data dependencies between loop iterations.

➤ Avoid placing structures in loop bodies (for example, function calls, pointers with ambiguous indirection to globals, and so on).

➤ Don't use the option /Od (or /Zi) on its own. Auto-parallelism will work only at optimization levels /O1 or greater.

➤ Use IPO (/Qipo). IPO gets applied before auto-parallelism and can improve the chance of the code being made parallel.

➤ Try to help the compiler by using the #pragma parallel option. (See the section "Using #pragma parallel.")

Additional Options

Table 6-6 lists other options that you can use. Refer to the compiler help for more information.

TABLE 6-6: Some Auto-Parallelizer Options

OPTION	DESCRIPTION
Qpar-affinity	Specifies thread affinity
Qpar-num-threads	Specifies the number of threads to use in a parallel region
Qpar-report	Controls the diagnostic information reported by the auto-parallelizer
Qpar-runtime-control	Generates code to perform runtime checks for loops that have symbolic loop bounds
Qpar-schedule	Specifies a scheduling algorithm or a tuning method for loop iterations
Qpar-threshold	Sets a threshold for the auto-parallelization of loops
Qparallel	Tells the auto-parallelizer to generate multithreaded code for loops that can be safely executed in parallel
Qparallel-source-info	Enables or disables source location emission when OpenMP or auto-parallelization code is generated
Qpar-adjust-stack	Tells the compiler to generate code to adjust the stack size for a fiber-based main thread

Helping the Compiler to Auto-Parallelize

To ensure correct code generation, the compiler treats any assumed dependencies as if they were proven dependencies, which prevents any auto-parallelization. The compiler will always assume a dependency where it cannot prove that it is not a dependency. However, if the programmer is certain that a loop can be safely auto-parallelized and any dependencies can be ignored, the compiler can be informed of this in several ways.

Using #pragma parallel

Used immediately before a loop, the `#pragma parallel` option instructs the compiler to ignore any assumed loop dependencies that would prevent correct auto-parallelization. It complements, but does not replace, the fully automatic approach; the loop will still not be parallelized if the compiler can prove that any dependencies exist.

Any loop being parallelized must conform to the `for-loop` style of an OpenMP work-sharing construct. The pragma can be used by itself or in conjunction with a selection of clauses, such as `private`, which acts in a similar way to the clauses used in the OpenMP method.

Currently, the clauses include the following:

➤ `always[assert]`, which overrides the compiler heuristics that determine whether parallelizing a loop would increase performance. Using this clause forces the compiler to parallelize if it can, even if it considers that doing so might not improve performance. Adding `assert` causes the compiler to generate an error if it considers that the loop cannot be vectorized.

➤ `private( var1[ :expr1][, var2[ :expr2] ] … )`, where `var` is a scalar or array variable. When parallelizing a loop, private copies of each variable are created for each thread. `expr` is an optional expression used for array or pointer variables, which evaluates to an integer number giving the number of array elements. If `expr` is absent, the rules are the same as those used in the OpenMP method, and all the array elements are privatized. If `expr` is present, only that number of elements of the array are privatized. Multiple `private` clauses are merged as a union.

➤ `lastprivate( var1[ :expr1][, var2[ :expr2] ] … )`, where `var` and `expr` are the same as for `private`. Private copies of each variable are used within each thread created by the parallelization, as in the `private` clause; however, the values of the copies within the final iteration of the loop are copied back into the variables when the parallel region is left.

Following is an example of using #pragma parallel:

```
(41)    #pragma parallel private(b)
(42)    for( i=0; i<MAXIMUS; i++ )
(43)    {
(44)        if( a[i] > 0 )
(45)        {
(46)            b = a[i];
(47)            a[i] = 1.0/a[i];
(48)        }
(49)        if( a[i] > 1 )a[i] += b;
(50)    }
```

This results in the loop being both vectorized and parallelized, with the following messages:

```
C:\Test.cpp(42): (col. 4) remark: LOOP WAS AUTO-PARALLELIZED.
C:\Test.cpp(42): (col. 4) remark: LOOP WAS VECTORIZED.
```

Using #pragma noparallel

You can use the `#pragma noparallel` option immediately before a loop to stop it from being auto-parallelized.

Note that both `#pragma parallel` and `#pragma noparallel` are ignored unless the `/Qparallel` option is set.

PROS AND CONS OF PROFILING WITH THE AUTO-PARALLELIZER

➤ Pros

➤ Easy to carry out

➤ Quickly helps you spot the right places to parallelize

➤ Auto-parallelized loop can be compared with your own manually implemented parallelism

➤ Cons

➤ Can easily be confounded by nontrivial code

➤ Difficult to identify loops when IPO is enabled

ACTIVITY 6-3: USING THE AUTO-PARALLELIZER TO HELP FIND HOTSPOTS

In this activity you enable the Intel compiler's auto-parallelizer and use the location of the successfully parallelized loops to add your own parallel code.

1. Make sure you have carried out Activity 6-1. You will need the results of running the application to compare with the results in this activity.

2. Rebuild the application, adding the `/Qparallel` option to enable auto-parallelism, and the `/Qpar-report2` option to tell the compiler to generate a report:

```
icl /Zi /O2 /Qipo wtime.c main.cpp mandelbrot.cpp ppm.cpp -o 6-3.exe \
    /Qparallel /Qpar-report2
```

3. Examine the messages from the compiler. You should find that one of the loops has been auto-parallelized.

4. Run `6-3.exe`. Calculate the speedup compared to `6-1.exe`, which you created in Activity 6-1. The application should be faster.

You can calculate the speedup using the following formula. *New time* is the time taken by 6-3.exe, and *original time* is the time taken by 6-1.exe.

speedup = new time / original time

5. Add a cilk_for and an include to the loop that the auto-parallelizer has identified:

```
#include <cilk/cilk.h>
.
.
.
 cilk_for (...etc ) {
.
.
.
```

6. Rebuild the application using the following options. Note that auto-parallelism is no longer enabled.

```
icl /Zi /O2 /Qipo wtime.c main.cpp  mandelbrot.cpp  ppm.cpp -o 6-3b.exe
```

7. Run the program and calculate the speedup.

Instructions for Linux Users

Refer to the "Instructions for Linux Users" section in Activity 6-1 before carrying out this activity.

HOTSPOT ANALYSIS WITH AMPLIFIER XE

The Hotspot analysis used in Amplifier XE helps you to identify the most time-consuming source code. Hotspot analysis also collects stack and call tree information. The analysis can be used to launch an application/process or attach to a running program/process.

Conducting a Default Analysis

The steps for conducting a Hotspot analysis with Amplifier XE were described in Chapter 3.

To get the best view of the application in Amplifier XE, it is best to disable inlining by using the /Ob0 or /Ob1 compiler options. The /Ob0 option disables all inlining, whereas the /Ob1 inlines only code that has been marked with the keywords inline, __inline__ , __forceinline, _inline, or with a member function defined within a class declaration. (See online help for more information on these keywords.) Figure 6-5 shows the summary page of two Hotspot analysis sessions: one with inlining enabled (a) and one without (b). You can see that when inlining is disabled, the symbol names of the different functions become available.

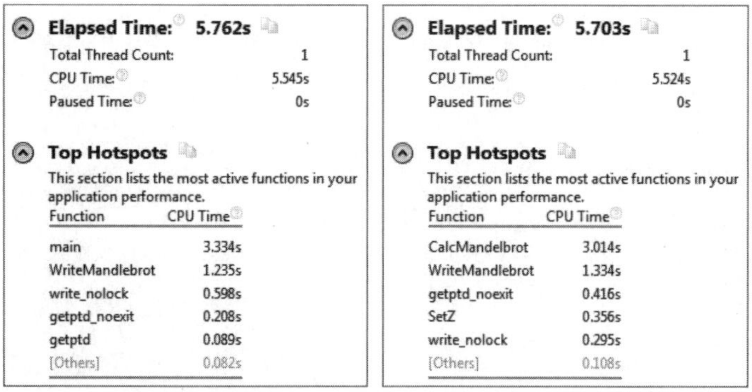

(a) With inlining (b) Without inlining

FIGURE 6-5: Analysis summary with and without inlining

Finding the Right Loop to Parallelize

At the time of writing, Amplifier XE does not have a loop profiler, so you have to manually traverse up the call stack of a hotspot to find the best place to add parallelism. Figures 6-6 through 6-9 show screenshots of doing such a traversal. Clicking on the hotspot in Figure 6-6 displays the source view of the hotspot (Figure 6-7).

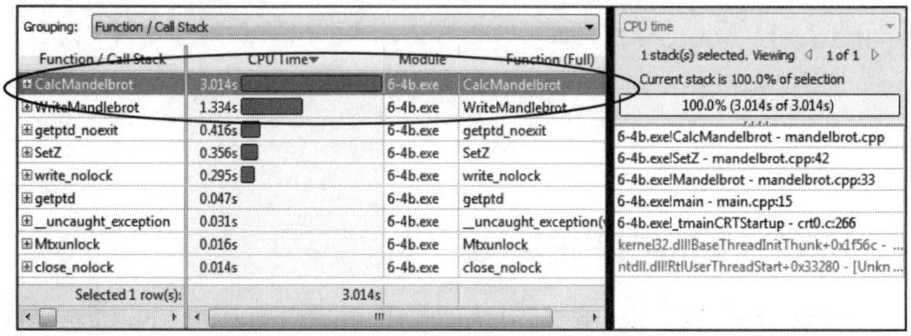

FIGURE 6-6: Bottom-up view of the hotspots

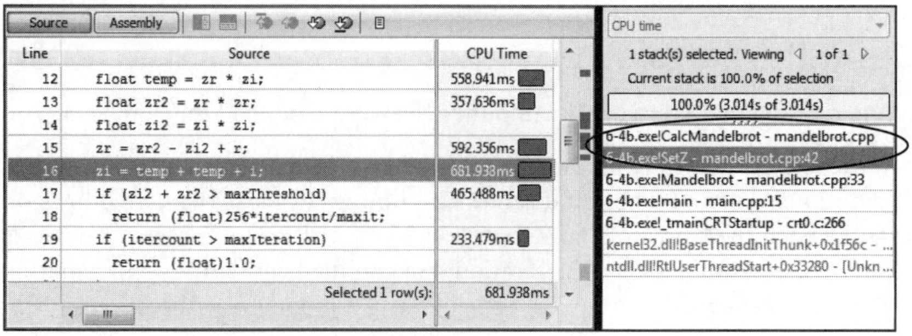

FIGURE 6-7: Source code view of the hotspots

By double-clicking the stack pane on the right (see Figures 6-7 and 6-8), it is possible to traverse up the call stack until an appropriate place to add the parallelism is found, as in Figure 6-9.

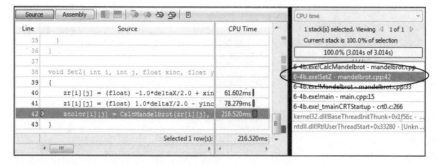

FIGURE 6-8: Source code view, one stack up

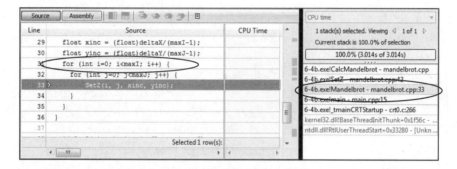

FIGURE 6-9: Source code view, two stacks up

ACTIVITY 6-4: CONDUCTING A HOTSPOT ANALYSIS WITH AMPLIFIER XE

In this activity you carry out a Hotspot analysis on the Mandelbrot program with Amplifier XE.

1. Make sure you have carried out Activity 6-1.

2. Rebuild the application, adding the /Zi flag to generate debug information:

```
icl  /O2 /Qipo /Zi wtime.c main.cpp mandelbrot.cpp ppm.cpp -o 6-4.exe
```

3. Start an Amplifier XE GUI from the command line:

```
amplxe-gui
```

continues

continued

4. Create a new project named Chapter 6.

    a. Select File ⇨ New ⇨ Project.

    b. In the Project Properties dialog, make sure the Application Field points to your Mandelbrot application.

5. Carry out a Hotspot analysis by selecting File ⇨ New ⇨ Hotspot Analysis.

Dealing with the Lack of Symbol Visibility

You've already seen in the previous activities that functions disappear because of compiler inlining. Adding the /Ob1 option to the build improves visibility.

6. Repeat steps 2 to 5, using the following compiler options. You should notice an improvement in what you see.

```
icl  /O2 /Qipo /Zi /Ob1 wtime.c main.cpp mandelbrot.cpp ppm.cpp \
    -o 6-4.exe
```

Traversing Up the Call Stack

7. From the bottom-up view, double-click the largest hotspot. The source view should be displayed.

8. In the stack pane (on the right of the source view), manually trace back up the call stack (by double-clicking the call stack entries) until you find code that has a loop in it.

    You should be able to find the best place to add parallelism by doing this manual stack traversal.

Instructions for Linux Users

Refer to the section "Instructions for Linux Users" in Activity 6-1.

Large or Long-Running Applications

In very large or long-running projects, the amount of data collected may grow to an unmanageable size. The postprocessing of the collected data (finalization) and opening and viewing very large data sets can become very sluggish and almost impractical to use.

Reducing the Size of Data Collected

Some strategies for reducing the amount of data collected include:

➤ Adjust the duration time estimate. Amplifier XE reduces the amount of samples it collects on very long runs. You can change the duration time estimate from "under 1 minute" to "over 3 hours," with some intermediate values, as well.

➤ Automatically stop collection after a short period of time (for example, 30 seconds).

➤ Modify the data-collection limit. The default is 100MB.

➤ Use the Pause and Resume APIs to limit when data is collected.

The first three items in the list are all configurable from the Project Properties dialog (see Figure 6-10), which you can access from the Amplifier XE menu File ➪ Properties.

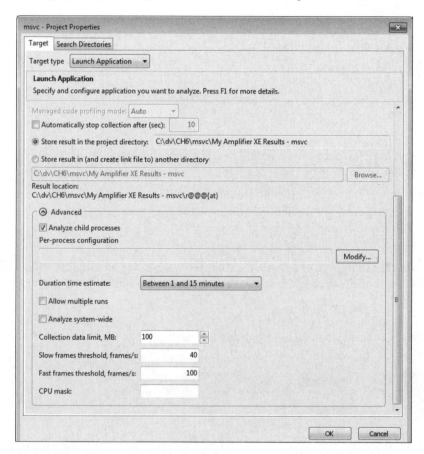

FIGURE 6-10: The Project Properties page

Using the Pause and Resume APIs

You can insert calls to the Pause and Resume APIs in your application to pause and resume data collection, respectively. By doing this you can reduce the amount of data that is collected. These APIs have to be used with caution, especially when analyzing threaded code, because important events may be missed, leading to a meaningless analysis.

The following code snippet shows how to use __itt_pause() and __itt_resume() functions in the Mandelbrot program:

```
#include "ittnotify.h"
```

```
int main()
{
    .
    .
    .
    std::cout << "calculating..." << std::endl;
    double start = wtime();
    __itt_resume();
     Mandelbrot();
    double mid = wtime();

    std::cout << "printing..." << std::endl;
    WriteMandlebrot();
    __itt_pause();
    double end = wtime();
    .
    .
    .
}
```

Once this code is inserted, any Hotspot analysis should be started by clicking the Start Paused button rather than the Start button.

To use the APIs, include the `ittnotify.h` header file. If you get an unresolved symbol at link time, you may have to add the `libittnotify.lib` library, which you can find in the `Amplifier XE\lib32` or `Amplifier XE\lib64` folders. Use the lib64 version if you are building a 64-bit application; otherwise, use the lib32 version.

Table 6-7 shows the difference in the size of data that is collected when doing a normal Hotspot analysis versus doing one with pauses and waits. As you can see, there is a significant saving in the amount of data collected.

TABLE 6-7: Amount of Data Collected when Profiling with and without the Pause and Resume APIs

METHOD	DATA SIZE
Without pause/resume	253.9k
With pause/resume	172.0k

PROS AND CONS OF PROFILING WITH AMPLIFIER XE

➤ Pros

   ➤ Very small profiling overhead

   ➤ Easy to traverse the call stack

   ➤ No special build needed, other than providing debug symbols

   ➤ Multiple options for collection and viewing

   ➤ Results can be compared

> ➤ Cons
>
>> ➤ No loop profiler
>>
>> ➤ No call graph (but see the comments on manual call stack tra-
>> versing in the section "Finding the Right Loop to Parallelize")

SOURCE CODE

The source code in Listing 6-1 consists of several files and is used in the hands-on activities.

LISTING 6-1: main.cpp

Available for
download on
Wrox.com

main.cpp

```cpp
#include <fstream>
#include <iostream>
#include <iomanip>
#include "mandelbrot.h"

float zr[maxI][maxJ],zi[maxI][maxJ];
float zcolor[maxI][maxJ];
extern "C" double wtime();

int main()
{
  std::cout << "calculating..." << std::endl;
  double start = wtime();
  Mandelbrot();
  double mid = wtime();

  std::cout << "printing..." << std::endl;
  WriteMandlebrot();
  double end = wtime();

  std::cout << "Time to calc :..."<< std::setprecision(4) \
     << mid-start <<std::endl;
  std::cout << "Time to print :..." << end-mid <<std::endl;
  std::cout << "Time (Total) :..." << end-start <<std::endl;
}
```

code snippet Chapter6\main.cpp

mandelbrot.cpp

```cpp
#include "mandelbrot.h"

float CalcMandelbrot(float r,float  i)
{
  float zi = 0.0;
  float zr = 0.0;
```

continues

LISTING 6-1 *(continued)*

```cpp
    int itercount = 0;

    float maxit = (float)maxIteration;
    while(1) {
    itercount++;
    float temp = zr * zi;
    float zr2 = zr * zr;
    float zi2 = zi * zi;
    zr = zr2 - zi2 + r;
    zi = temp + temp + i;
    if (zi2 + zr2 > maxThreshold)
      return (float)256*itercount/maxit;
    if (itercount > maxIteration)
      return (float)1.0;
    }
    return 1;
}

void SetZ( int i, int j, float xinc, float yinc )
{
  zr[i][j] = (float) -1.0*deltaX/2.0 + xinc * i;
  zi[i][j] = (float) 1.0*deltaY/2.0 - yinc * j;
  zcolor[i][j] = CalcMandelbrot(zr[i][j], zi[i][j] ) /1.0001;
}

void Mandelbrot ()
{
  float xinc = (float)deltaX/(maxI-1);
  float yinc = (float)deltaY/(maxJ-1);
  for (int i=0; i<maxI; i++) {
    for (int j=0; j<maxJ; j++) {
      SetZ(i, j, xinc, yinc);
    }
  }
}
```

code snippet Chapter6\mandelbrot.cpp

mandelbrot.h

```cpp
#ifndef __MANDLE_H__
#define __MANDLE_H__
const int factor = 8;
const int  maxThreshold = 96;
const int  maxIteration = 500;
const int maxI = 1024 * factor;
const int  maxJ = 1024 * factor;
const float deltaX = 4.0;
const float deltaY = 4.0;
```

```
extern float zr[maxI][maxJ],zi[maxI][maxJ];
extern float zcolor[maxI][maxJ];

void Mandelbrot ();
void WriteMandlebrot();
#endif
```

code snippet Chapter6\mandelbrot.h

ppm.cpp

```
#include <fstream>
#include "mandelbrot.h"

// write to a PPM file.
void WriteMandlebrot()
{
  std::ofstream ppm_file("default.ppm");
  ppm_file << "P6 " << maxI << " " << maxJ << " 255" << std::endl;

  unsigned char red, green, blue; // BLUE - did minimal work
  for (int i=0; i<maxI; i++) {
    for (int j=0; j<maxJ; j++) {
      float color = (float)zcolor[i][j] ;
      float temp = color;
      if (color >= .99999)
      {
        red = 255 ; green = 255; blue = 255;
      }
      else
      {
        red = 0 ; green = 0; blue = 0;
      }
      // write to PPM file
      ppm_file << red  << green << blue;
    }
  }
}
```

code snippet Chapter6\ppm.cpp

wtime.c

```
#ifdef _WIN32
#include <windows.h>
double wtime()
{
  LARGE_INTEGER ticks;
  LARGE_INTEGER frequency;
  QueryPerformanceCounter(&ticks);
  QueryPerformanceFrequency(&frequency);
  return (double)(ticks.QuadPart/(double)frequency.QuadPart);
}
```

continues

LISTING 6-1 *(continued)*

```
#else
#include <sys/time.h>
#include <sys/resource.h>
double wtime()
{
  struct timeval time;
  struct timezone zone;
  gettimeofday(&time, &zone);
  return time.tv_sec + time.tv_usec*1e-6;
}
#endif
```

code snippet Chapter6\wtime.c

SUMMARY

This chapter described several methods of finding hotspots within an application. In practice you would probably want to use a combination of the methods to get best results. The identification of the hotspots is essential if you want to avoid wasted effort in attempting parallelism of any existing code.

It is very easy to apply parallelism at every opportunity you see within the code — for example, at every loop. However, many of these loops may not be invoked often enough nor do enough work, to make the effort of their parallelism worthwhile. Some loops that are tempting to parallelize may not really contribute much to the overall run time.

Finding the parallelization opportunities within your code is the goal of Hotspot analysis. It is an essential first step in adding parallelism to your code. Without this knowledge of your program, you are in danger of making code parallel without seeing any improvement in performance.

Having found the hotspots, the next steps are to implement the parallelism, check for errors, and, finally, tune the threaded application. The next chapter shows how to use different programming models to implement parallelism.

7

Implementing Parallelism

WHAT'S IN THIS CHAPTER?

➤ Parallelizing loops

➤ Parallelizing sections and functions

➤ Parallelizing recursive functions

➤ Parallelizing pipelined applications

➤ Parallelizing linked lists

There are a number of different ways to add parallelism to a program. Figure 7-1 shows how you can use Intel Parallel Studio XE to make your code parallel by using:

➤ **Libraries,** such as the Math Kernel Library (MKL) and the Integrated Performance Primitives (IPP) library.

➤ **Automatic parallelism,** asking the compiler to automatically parallelize your code using the /Qparallel option; you can also use the guided auto-parallelization of the compiler (enabled with the /Qguide option) to help tune the auto-parallelism. You can find more about auto-parallelism in Chapter 6, "Where to Parallelize."

➤ **Programmatic parallelism,** adding parallel constructs to your code using Cilk Plus, OpenMP, Threading Building Blocks (TBB), or native threads (POSIX or WIN32).

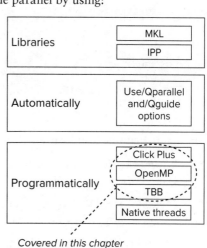

Covered in this chapter

FIGURE 7-1: Adding parallelism using Intel Parallel Studio XE

This chapter shows how to add parallelism to five of the more common serial code patterns: loops, sequential code, recursive functions, pipelined applications, and linked lists. For each pattern, examples are shown using Cilk Plus, OpenMP, and TBB. The MKL, IPP, and native threading examples are not discussed.

Note that the chapter is not a full treatise for each of these parallel languages. The focus here is on is how you can quickly and easily introduce parallelism into your code.

 You already know from reading Chapter 1, "Parallelism Today," that adding parallelism to legacy or preexisting code is one of the biggest challenges that the software industry faces. In line with this challenge, the examples in this chapter assume you have already written some code and want to make it parallel. What isn't covered is how to design a new parallel program from scratch.

C OR C++, THAT IS THE QUESTION

One implementation detail can have a big impact on which parallel construct you decide to use—C or C++.

Cilk Plus and TBB are very C++ friendly, whereas OpenMP is not. Table 7-1 gives some suggestions on which parallel models to use depending on how C++-like your code is.

TABLE 7-1: Parallel Model Suggestions

SOURCE CHARACTERISTIC	CILK PLUS	TBB	OPENMP
.c	Y	N	Y
.cpp, but code is really C	Y	Y	Y
.cpp files, using C++ features	Y	Y	N

Other factors that might influence which mode you choose include:

➤ When using Cilk Plus in .c files, Cilk reducers are awkward to use, requiring use of many C macros.

➤ Multiple OpenMP programs running on the same system do not always share the threading resources very well, and can lead to oversubscription.

➤ TBB is heavily C++ oriented. Use TBB only if you are comfortable with concepts such as classes and templates and operator overloading. Having said that, you will easily understand most of the TBB examples in this chapter even if you are uncomfortable with C++.

TAKING A SIMPLE APPROACH

All three of the programming models used in this chapter — Cilk Plus, OpenMP, and TBB — support different levels of complexity and abstraction. The intention of this chapter is to keep to a higher level of abstraction as possible by:

➤ Thinking in terms of **tasks, not threads.** All the programming examples concentrate on what work needs to be done without being concerned about threads. Emphasis is on work-sharing and relying on automatic scheduling. The question "How many threads do I have?" is not asked.

➤ Using **lambda functions rather than body objects** (TBB specific). When TBB was first released, the snippets of parallel code had to be embedded within new C++ classes, which in turn were used to create body objects. Since the introduction of the C++11 standard, you can now use lambda functions instead for many of the TBB templates. This reduces the amount of boilerplate code you have to write, leading to much simpler code.

➤ **Keeping it simple.** There is no attempt made to describe solutions that are complex. All the examples use high-level abstractions, avoiding anything that is intricate. If your parallel programming requires that you have a fine level of control, or if you need to use a different kind of scheduling, the higher-level parallel abstractions used in the examples may not suit your requirements.

➤ The code examples are **ANSI C-like rather than fully blown C++.** If you are passionate about writing good C++ programs, this will no doubt annoy you. The reason for doing this is so that the code can be accessible to non-C++ programmers. The code examples here are fairly easy to classify (as in writing C++).

This chapter is not intended to teach you everything about Cilk Plus, OpenMP, or TBB. You can read more on how to deal with data races in Chapter 8, "Checking for Errors," and more on scheduling and tuning in Chapter 9, "Tuning Parallel Applications."

THE BEAUTY OF LAMBDA FUNCTIONS

Lambda functions are included in the C++11 standard (formerly known as C++0x) and provide a means of declaring the body of a function in-place. They are sometimes referred to as *anonymous functions* or *functors*.

Figure 7-2 shows the syntax of a lambda function. Within the body of the function you can refer to external variables; the capture_mode options define how these variables get their values.

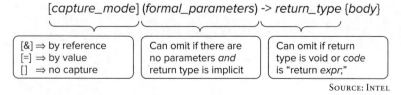

SOURCE: INTEL

FIGURE 7-2: The syntax of the lambda functions

Listing 7-1 shows an example of using a lambda function with the Standard Template Library (STL) `for_each` method. The program examines each character of the `Message` string and counts how many spaces there are.

LISTING 7-1: Using a lambda function

```
1: #include <iostream>
2: #include <algorithm>
3: using namespace std;
4: int main()
5: {
6:    int Spaces = 0;
7:    char Message[]="The Beauty of Lambda!";
8:
9:    for_each(                              // use STL for_each
10:      Message,                            // beginning of string
11:      Message + sizeof(Message),          // end of string
12:
13:      // The lambda function
14:      [&Spaces] (char c) { if (c == ' ') Spaces++;}
15:    );                                    // end of for_each
16:
17:    cout "'"<< Message << "'"<< " has " << Spaces <<" spaces <<endl;
18: }
```

code snippet Chapter7\7-1.cpp

Line 14 contains the lambda function, which takes the `c` parameter and checks to see if it is a space. If so, the function increments the `Spaces` variable, which has been explicitly captured in the lambda function by reference. You don't have to capture variables explicitly; you can rely on the compiler to capture them for you automatically. For example, you could use the following code in place of line 14:

```
[&] (char c) { if (c == ' ') Spaces++;}
```

The beauty of lambda function in the context of parallelism is that you can wrap existing code in a lambda function and then use the wrapped function in your parallelism strategy. This leads to fewer code changes when parallelizing your code and can simplify the use of some parallel constructs.

Be sure to enable the lambda support in the compiler! In the Intel compiler, use the `/Qstd=c++0x` *option.*

PARALLELIZING LOOPS

Loops provide one of the most natural places to add parallelism. The following two requirements need to be satisfied before a loop can be usefully parallelized:

➤ There must be a sufficient amount of work being done in each loop. Any loop being parallelized should be a hotspot. See Chapter 6, "Where to Parallelize," to find out more about hotspots in your code.

➤ Each loop iteration must be independent of any other. For example, iteration n must not depend on iteration n-1 to be able to perform correctly.

The order in which the loops are executed is not important.

This chapter considers two loop constructs, the for loop and the while loop, along with two variants, the nested for loop and the reduction for loop.

The for Loop

You can use the Cilk Plus cilk_for, the OpenMP #pragma omp for, and the TBB parallel_for to parallelize a C/C++ for loop.

The Cilk Plus cilk_for Loop

Cilk Plus has its own equivalent of the serial for loop. By replacing a standard for loop with the cilk_for loop, the iterations within the loop are shared between the available workers. The following code shows a simple cilk_for loop:

```
#include <cilk/cilk.h>

cilk_for (int i=0; i < 100;i++)
{
  work(i);
}
```

Here's an example of a cilk_for loop that uses STL vectors and iterators:

```
cilk_for (T::iterator i(vec.begin()); i != vec.end(); ++i)
{
    Work(i);
}
```

A cilk_for loop must follow these guidelines:

➤ The loop variable can be declared in advance in C, but not in C++.

➤ There must be only one loop control variable.

➤ The loop control must not be modified in the body of the loop.

➤ Termination conditions should not be changed once the loop has started.

➤ No break or return statement is allowed in the loop body.

➤ You can use a `goto` as long as the target is within the loop body.

➤ Loops cannot wrap around.

➤ Infinite loops are not allowed.

Load balancing is carried out automatically by the Cilk Plus run time. The `cilk_for` loop uses a divide-and-conquer strategy. The loops are repeatedly divided into chunks, until a minimum size, known as the *grain size*, is reached. Each chunk is then shared among the available workers.

You can influence the performance of the loop by changing the grain size and the number of workers.

Grain Size

The grain size is used to control the maximum number of loops each chunk can contain. Normally, you do not need to be concerned about setting a value for the grain size; the Cilk Plus run time sets the value automatically. You can specify the grain size using the `cilk_grainsize` pragma:

```
#pragma cilk_grainsize = 1
```

Increasing the grain size reduces the overhead of parallelization, but can lead to poorer parallelism.

The default grain size will have a value between 8 and 512, and is calculated using the following formula:

Grain size = min (512, number-of-loops /(8 * number-of-workers))

Number of Workers

You can set the number of workers using the environment variable `CILK_NWORKERS` or by using the Cilk Plus API command `__cilkrts()`. This command sets the number of workers to 20:

```
__cilkrts("nworkers", "20");
```

Loop Control Variable

You can use different types, including your own custom types, for the loop control variable. Whatever type you use, it must have:

➤ A means of determining the loop range size

➤ An operator to work out the difference between two such variables

➤ An operator to increment or decrement the variable

For more information on this topic, refer to the Intel Composer XE online help.

The OpenMP for Loop

The `#pragma omp for` statement is a work-sharing construct that causes the loops to be executed in parallel by a pool of threads. In the following code example, a pool of threads is created by the `#pragma omp parallel` statement. The loops of the `for` statement are then executed in parallel by the different threads.

```
#pragma omp parallel
{
  #pragma omp for
  for (int i=0; i < 100;i++)
  {
    work(i);
  }
} // end of parallel region
```

The two pragmas in this code can be concatenated into a single pragma, `#pragma omp parallel for`.

At the end of the loop, there is an implicit barrier where all the threads wait until the last thread has completed. If you add a `nowait` clause to the `#pragma omp for` statement, there will be no barrier and the threads will be free to continue on to the next section of code.

Influencing the Scheduling

You can modify the runtime behavior of the `for` loop with the `schedule` clause. The following are the three most common clauses used:

➤ `#pragma omp for schedule(`**static,** `chunk_size)` —The number of threads is divided into `chunk_size` and scheduled in a round-robin fashion among the pool of threads. When no `chunk_size` is specified, the number of chunks is the same as the number of threads.

➤ `#pragma omp for schedule (`**dynamic,** `chunk_size)` —The chunks are requested by the threads. When a thread becomes free, it requests a new chunk. When no `chunk_size` is specified, the `chunk_size` is 1.

➤ `#pragma omp for schedule (`**guided,** `chunk_size)` —Each thread is assigned a chunk of work that is greater than the `chunk_size`. As each thread requests new chunks, the size of the chunk is decreased until it becomes `chunk_size`. When no `chunk_size` is specified, the `chunk_size` is 1.

Number of Threads

You can set the number of threads by using the environment variable `OMP_NUM_THREADS` or the API call `omp_set_num_threads(num)`. If you build an application that includes the following code, and then set the environment variable to be two (`set OMP_NUM_THREADS=2`), the first loop will be shared between two threads, and the second loop will be shared between five threads.

```
void do_work()
{
  #pragma omp parallel for
  for (int i=0; i < 100;i++)
  {
    work(i);
  }
```

```
    omp_set_num_threads(5)
    #pragma omp parallel for
    for (int j=0; j < 100;j++)
    {
      work(j);
    }
  } // end of parallel region
```

Loop Control Variable

The loop control variable can be a signed/unsigned integer, a C++ iterator, or a pointer type. For example, the following code uses a pointer as the control variable:

```
    #include <stdio.h>
    int main()
    {
      char mem[10] = {'a','b','c','d','e','f','g','h','i','j'};
      #pragma omp parallel for
      for (char *p = &mem[0]; p < &mem[10]; p++)
      {
        printf("0x%p:%c\n",p,*p);
      }
      return 0;
    }
```

The TBB for Loop

The following example uses a compact version of the `parallel_for` construct that can iterate over a range of integers. The code being executed is wrapped in a lambda function.

```
    #include <tbb.h>
    .
    .
    parallel_for (size_t(0), 100,[=](size_t i) {
        work(i);
      } // end of lambda code
    ); // end of parallel _for
```

Nested for Loops

When you parallelize a nested loop, it is usually to parallelize just the outer loop. However, on some occasions you should consider parallelizing the inner loop as well as, or instead of, the outer loop. Consider, for example, the following code:

```
    for(int i = 0;  i<5;i++)
      for(int j = 0; j < 100; j++)
    {
      Work(i*100 + j);
    }
```

You can see that

> ➤ The outer loop has a low trip count, much lower than the inner loop.

> ➤ The outer loop trip count could well be less than the number of hardware threads that can be supported.

If you were to run the code on a 24-core PC, the maximum speedup you could obtain by parallelizing the outer loop would only be 5, even though the hardware can support a speedup of up to 24.

A variation on this example might be if the inner and outer loops both have a low trip count:

```
for(int i = 0; i<5;i++)
  for(int j = 0; j < 5; j++)
  {
    Work((i*5) + j);
  }
```

To achieve a better parallelization of these kinds of nested loops, you should do one of the following:

➤ Parallelize the inner loop instead of the outer loop.

➤ Parallelize both inner and outer loops.

➤ Rewrite the loops so the inner and outer loops are swapped, and then parallelize the new outer loop.

In OpenMP, you can collapse loops together using the COLLAPSE clause. In the following code example, the outer two `for` statements are collapsed together:

```
#pragma omp parallel for collapse(2)
for (int i=0; i < 2;i++)
  for (int j=0; j < 10;j++)
    for (int k=0; k < 100;k++)
    {
      Work(k);
    }
```

Using nested parallelism in Cilk Plus and TBB should not cause a problem as long as the inner loop does a sufficient amount of work. The act of work-stealing performed by their respective schedulers will automatically load-balance the work.

In OpenMP, the situation is slightly more complicated. If nested parallelism is enabled, a fresh pool of threads is created for each parallel region. Nested parallelism can lead to oversubscription, where the number of threads running exceeds the number the hardware can support.

By default, nested parallelism is disabled. If you want, you can enable nested parallelism by using the `omp_set_nested(expression)` API command or the environment variable OMP_NESTED. Likewise, you can check if nested parallelism is enabled using the `omp_get_nested()` API command.

For more information on this and other OpenMP features, look at the OpenMP standard, which you can download from www.openmp.org.

The for Loop with Reduction

On some occasions you will want to combine the results of several parallel computations—a technique known as *reduction*. In loop reduction, each parallel strand manipulates its own reduction variable(s), which are combined at the end of the parallel region.

Take, for example, the loop in Figure 7-3. Here the loops are split into three chunks and executed in parallel. When each parallel strand has completed, the value of each r is combined together using the addition operator. You can perform reduction using different operators as well as the addition operator. Cilk Plus, OpenMP, and TBB all support reduction.

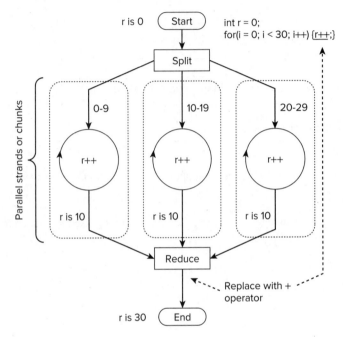

FIGURE 7-3: A for loop with reduction

Cilk Plus Reduction

Cilk Plus provides special objects known as *reducers* to support reduction. You can find a list of reducers in Chapter 2 (Table 2-3), along with a code example in Listing 2-2, "An example of using a Cilk Plus reducer."

OpenMP Reduction

The following code gives an example of reduction:

```
int r = 0;
#pragma omp parallel for reduction(+:r)
for (i=0; i < 29; i++)
{
    r++;
}
```

The reduction clause causes each thread to have its own private copy of the r variable. The values of each private copy are combined back together using the + operator at the end of the for loop. You can use the following operators with the reduction clause: +, *, -, &, |, ^, &&, ||, max, and min.

TBB Reduction

TBB provides the `parallel_reduce` template to support reduction. Listing 7-2 shows how to use it with lambda functions. You must provide two lambda functions: one for the code you want to execute in the loop, and a second one that provides the reduction operator.

LISTING 7-2: Parallel reduction using TBB

```cpp
#include "tbb/parallel_reduce.h"
#include "tbb/blocked_range.h"
using namespace tbb;
float ParallelSum( float array[], size_t n )
{
  return parallel_reduce(
    // range
    blocked_range<float*>( array, array+n ),
    // identity
    0.f,
    // lambda function
    [](const blocked_range<float*>& r, float init)->float
    {
      for( float* a=r.begin(); a!=r.end(); ++a )
      init += *a;
      return init;
    },
    //lambda function providing the reduction operator
    []( float x, float y )->float
    {
      return x+y;
    }
  );
}
```

code snippet Chapter7\7-2.cpp

The while Loop

You can use the Cilk Plus `cilk_spawn`, the OpenMP `#pragma omp task`, and the TBB `parallel_do` to parallelize a C/C++ `while` loop.

Cilk Plus

The simplest way to make a `while` loop parallel is to use the `cilk_spawn` keyword in each iteration. However, if the amount of work done in a loop is low, you may find that the program runs slower than the original serial version. In the following code, the `Prime` function is `cilk_spawned` 100 times:

```cpp
int j = 0;
while (j < 100)
{
  cilk_spawn Prime(Pri);
  j++;
}
```

If your `while` loop has a precomputable trip count, as in the preceding example, you could consider converting it to a `cilk_for` loop, which employs a divide-and-conquer work-stealing algorithm.

In some circumstances part of the `while` loop will need to stay sequential because of some loop dependency, with only part of the `while` loop being able to run in parallel. In the following example, the traversal through the linked list has to be sequential, but as each link is traversed, the call to `Work()` can be parallelized by using `cilk_spawn`:

```
#include <cilk/cilk.h>
// linked list iteration
void RunThoughLinkedList()
{
  node *pHead = Head;
  while(pHead != NULL)
  {
    cilk_spawn Work(pHead);
    pHead = pHead->next;
  }
}
```

OpenMP

Prior to OpenMP 3.0, `while` loops were difficult to make parallel, requiring the programmer either to convert the loops to a standard `for` loop or to write some handcrafted code. The following code uses OpenMP tasks that were introduced in OpenMP 3.0. The bold lines show where extra code has been added to make the `while` loop parallel.

➤ The `#pragma omp parallel` forms a team of threads and starts parallel execution.

➤ Within the parallel region, the code marked with `#pragma omp single` runs only on one thread.

➤ On each iteration of the `while` loop (that is running on one thread), the `#pragma omp task` statement causes an OpenMP task to be created. The moment a task is created it is free to start executing. Each task has its own initialized copy of the `counter` variable.

➤ When the single thread has completed creating all the tasks, the thread becomes available for use by the OpenMP run time. This only happens because of the `nowait` clause.

➤ There is an implicit barrier at the end of the parallel region. Once all the threads have completed, code execution can continue beyond the end of the parallel region.

```
#pragma omp parallel
{
  #pragma omp single nowait
  {
    int counter = 0;
    while(counter < 10)
    {
      counter++;
      #pragma omp task firstprivate(counter)
```

```
        {
          work(counter);
        }
      }
    }
  } // implicit barrier
```

A `do-while` loop can also be made parallel using the same technique.

TBB

You can use the `parallel_do` template to perform, as the TBB manual describes it, a "cook until done" algorithm. You can use this when you don't know how much data has to be processed. A `parallel_do` creates TBB tasks from a list, finishing when the list is empty and all tasks have completed their execution.

Listing 7-3 shows `parallel_do` iterating through the items in vector s and calling the `Work()` function. The first two parameters of `parallel_do` are STL iterators describing the beginning and end of the vector. The third parameter is the code that is executed within the loop—in this case, a lambda function.

LISTING 7-3: TBB parallel_do

```
#include <tbb.h>
#include <vector>

void Work(int Val){ // do some work here}

Func()
{
  std::vector<int> s;
  s.push_back(0);
  s.push_back(1);
  s.push_back(2);
  s.push_back(3);

  tbb::parallel_do(s.begin(), s.end(),
    [&](int Val) { Work(Val);});
}
```

code snippet Chapter7\7-3.cpp

PARALLELIZING SECTIONS AND FUNCTIONS

You can parallelize sections of code or a series of function calls using Cilk Plus, OpenMP, or TBB. A sequence of code can be made parallel as long as each block:

➤   Is independent of any other block

➤   Performs enough work

This kind of parallelism is not scalable—that is, the program's performance will not keep increasing once you have matched the number of cores with the number of parallel strands. It is still worth considering, especially if you have two or more blocks of code that consume a significant amount of time. In this section, a short series of function calls are parallelized in two different ways, as shown in Figure 7-4.

Figure 7-4 (a) shows the layout of the serial program, alongside two parallel patterns. In Figure 7-4 (b) all three functions are run in parallel. Figure 7-4 (c) assumes Work1() and Work2() have a dependency, and so their order of execution must be maintained by running them in the same parallel strand.

The potential speedup for each solution is limited by the number of parallel strands in the program. Figure 7-4 (c), for example, has only two parallel strands, with its maximum potential speedup being achieved on a 2-core CPU. If you ran same the code on a 3-core CPU, it wouldn't run any faster. Similarly, Figure 7-4 (b)'s maximum speedup will be achieved on a 3-core CPU.

At the end of the parallelized sections, there is a barrier that can be crossed only after all the threads have completed executing the individual strands.

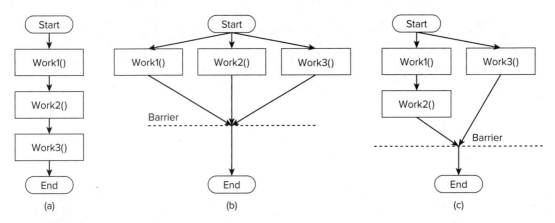

FIGURE 7-4: Functional parallelism

The Serial Version

Listing 7-4 holds the serial version of the code and has three functions: Work1(), Work2(), and Work3(). Each function prints a message at its entry and exit. The Delay() function slows down the execution time by iterating through a large loop.

If you decide to build any of the examples in this section, build them unoptimized using the /Od (Windows) or -O0 (Linux) compiler flag; otherwise, the compiler will "optimize-away" most of the code.

LISTING 7-4: Serial version of code

```c
#include <stdio.h>
void Delay(){for (int i=0; i < 1000000000; i++);}
void Work1(){printf("Start 1\n");Delay();printf("End 1\n");}
void Work2(){printf("Start 2\n");Delay();printf("End 2\n");}
void Work3(){printf("Start 3\n");Delay();printf("End 3\n");}

int main()
{
  Work1();
  Work2();
  Work3();
}
```

code snippet Chapter7\7-4.cpp

Cilk Plus

You can use the `cilk_spawn` keyword to parallelize sections of code. Listings 7-5 and 7-6 show the two versions (b) and (c), respectively. At the end of both examples, the `cilk_sync` keyword is used to place a barrier, as shown in Figure 7-4. In this particular example, `cilk_sync` is not really needed, because the compiler automatically inserts an implicit `cilk_sync` at the end of every function that contains a `cilk_spawn`.

In the first example, all three functions execute in parallel, subject to there being sufficient workers available.

In the second example, you can see how useful lambda functions are in wrapping together `Work1()` and `Work2()` so they execute serially within the same strand, which, in turn, executes in parallel with `Work3()`.

LISTING 7-5: Cilk Plus functional parallelism version (b)

```c
#include <cilk/cilk.h>
.
.
.
int main()
{
  cilk_spawn Work1();
  cilk_spawn Work2();
  Work3();
  cilk_sync;// not really needed, because there is an implicit sync here
}
```

code snippet Chapter7\7-5.cpp

LISTING 7-6: Cilk Plus functional parallelism version (c)

```cpp
#include <cilk/cilk.h>
.
.
int main()
{
  cilk_spawn []{
    Work1();
    Work2();
  }
  Work3();
  cilk_sync;// not really needed, because there is an implicit sync here
}
```

code snippet Chapter7\7-6.cpp

OpenMP

In OpenMP, you can use the `sections` construct to divide and execute blocks of code, as shown in Listings 7-7 and 7-8. The `sections` construct has to reside in a parallel region. In the following examples, the `parallel` and `section` constructs are concatenated together into a single statement.

In the first example, `Work1()`, `Work2()`, and `Work3()` execute in parallel. In the second example, the first block of code containing `Work1()` and `Work2()` runs in parallel with `Work3()`.

LISTING 7-7: OpenMP functional parallelism version (b)

```cpp
int main()
{
  #pragma omp parallel sections
  {
    #pragma omp section
    Work1();
    #pragma omp section
    Work2();
    #pragma omp section
    Work3();
  }
}
```

code snippet Chapter7\7-7.cpp

LISTING 7-8: OpenMP functional parallelism version (c)

```cpp
int main()
{
  #pragma omp parallel sections
  {
    #pragma omp section
```

```
    Work1();
    Work2();
    #pragma omp section
    Work3();
    }
}
```

code snippet Chapter7\7-8.cpp

TBB

Listings 7-9 and 7-10 show how to use the TBB `parallel_invoke` template to run the three functions in parallel. At the time of writing, the maximum number of parameters you can pass to `parallel_invoke` is ten.

LISTING 7-9: TBB functional parallelism version (b)

```
#include <tbb/tbb.h>
 .
 .
 .
int main()
{
  tbb::parallel_invoke(
    []{Work1();},
    []{Work2();},
    []{Work3();}
  );
}
```

code snippet Chapter7\7-9.cpp

LISTING 7-10: TBB functional parallelism version (c)

```
#include <tbb/tbb.h>
 .
 .
int main()
{
  tbb::parallel_invoke(
    []{
        Work1();
        Work2();
    },
    []{Work3();}
  );
}
```

code snippet Chapter7\7-10.cpp

Again, you can see how useful the lambda functions are in simplifying the calls to `parallel_invoke`.

PARALLELIZING RECURSIVE FUNCTIONS

Recursion is a very common pattern found in many programs and is relatively easy to parallelize. Figure 7-5 shows a recursive function, Work().

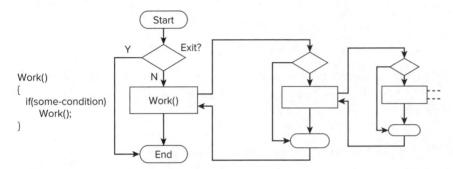

FIGURE 7-5: The recursive construct

A recursive function has three features:

➤ The function calls itself.

➤ There is an exit condition that is eventually reached.

➤ As in any C function, each called function has its own stack, holding its own variables and parameters.

Like any body of code that is to be threaded, the body of your recursive function should perform a decent amount of work; otherwise, you may end up just slowing down the code. If the body of your recursive function does not do much work, you might find it better to convert your recursive code to be loop-oriented, and then use one of the parallel loop structures that have already been discussed.

The Serial Version

Listing 7-11 shows a recursive function, Work(). When the function is first called, it is passed the i parameter, which has been initialized to zero. Each time Work() makes a call to itself, it passes in the value i + 1.

On entry to the function, the exit condition if(i>4) is queried. If the test is satisfied, the function returns; otherwise, it proceeds with the recursive call. Work() prints a message before and after the recursive call.

In this example the recursion will nest four levels deep before returning, unrolling its stack as it returns through the recursive calls.

LISTING 7-11: A serial recursive function

```
#include <stdio.h>
void Delay(){for (int i=0; i < 1000000000; i++);}
void Work(int i)
{
  if(i > 4)
    return;
  printf("S%d\n",i);
  Work(i + 1);
  Delay();
  printf("E %d\n",i);
}

int main()
{
  int i = 0;
  Work(i);
}
```

code snippet Chapter7\7-11.cpp

Cilk Plus

You can use the `cilk_spawn` keyword to parallelize a recursive function. In Listing 7-12, the only modification to the serial version is the addition of `cilk_spawn` in front of the recursive call to `Work()`.

LISTING 7-12: A Cilk Plus recursive function

```
#include <cilk/cilk.h>
void Delay(){for (int i=0; i < 1000000000; i++);}

void Work(int i)
{
  if(i > 4)
    return;
  printf("S%d\n",i);
  cilk_spawn Work(i + 1);
  Delay();
  printf("E %d\n",i);
}

int main()
{
  int i = 0;
  Work(i);
}
```

code snippet Chapter7\7-12.cpp

OpenMP

The recursive OpenMP example in Listing 7-13 uses tasks. In the `main()` function, a parallel region is declared containing a single threaded brace. Within the brace is a call to the `Work()` function.

The recursive call within `Work()` is encapsulated in an OpenMP task. The moment the task is created, it is free to start execution. Each recursive call results in a new task being created, which is then free to be run in parallel with any existing tasks.

LISTING 7-13: An OpenMP recursive function

```
void Work(int i)
{
  if(i > 4)
    return;
  #pragma omp task firstprivate(i)
  {
    printf("S%d\n",i);
    Work(i + 1);
    Delay();
    printf("E %d\n",i);
  }
}

int main()
{
  int i = 0;
#pragma omp parallel
#pragma omp single
  {
    Work(i);
  }
}
```

code snippet Chapter7\7-13.cpp

TBB

The recursive program in Listing 7-14 uses TBB tasks. The code is parallelized in three steps:

➤ By declaring of the `task_group` variable g.

➤ By wrapping the body of the `Work()` function in a lambda function, which is then spawned as a new task using the `g.run()` method.

➤ By adding a `g,wait()` barrier in `main()`, after the call to `Work()`.

LISTING 7-14: A TBB recursive function

```
#include <stdio.h>
#include <tbb/tbb.h>
void Delay(){for (int i=0; i < 1000000000; i++);}
tbb::task_group g;
```

```
void Work(int i)
{
  if(i > 4)
    return;
  g.run(
    [=]{      // spawn a task
      printf("S%d\n",i);
      Work(i + 1);
      Delay();
      printf("E %d\n",i);
    }
  );
}

int main()
{
  int i = 0;
  Work(i);
  g.wait();      // wait for tasks to complete
}
```

code snippet Chapter7\7-14.cpp

PARALLELIZING PIPELINED APPLICATIONS

The software pipeline pattern mimics a common assembly line in a factory. During the manufacturing process, the object being made is passed from one station to the next, with each station being responsible for carrying out a specific task.

Figure 7-6 (a) shows a pipelined application. The complete pipeline reads a set of numbers from the file Test.data, calculates the square root of the numbers, and then stores the results in a second file, Root.data.

The pipeline consists of three phases, or steps, as shown in Figure 7-6 (b). In the first phase, GetLine reads a line of numbers from the input file. In the second step, SqRoot calculates the square root for all the numbers in the line. Finally, PutLine writes the results into an output file.

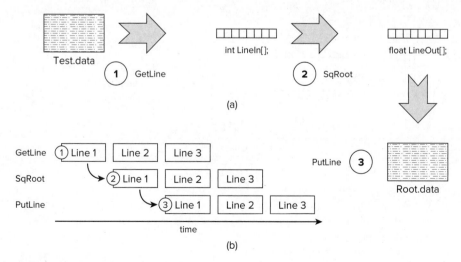

FIGURE 7-6: The recursive construct

The relation between each pipeline stage is that of producer/consumer. The first stage, GetLine, produces data that is consumed by the second stage, SqRoot. This second stage then becomes the producer for data that will be consumed by the last stage, PutLine.

Parallel Pipelined Patterns

To make a pipeline parallel, you allocate each pipeline station to a separate thread. You should only consider parallelizing course-grained pipeline applications, where each pipeline stage is doing a reasonable amount of work.

Within a particular pipeline stage you may also be able to introduce parallelism. In the example used in this chapter, stages 1 and 3 use file I/O and are therefore kept serial. The middle stage, however, performs calculations that are independent of each other, so parallelism can be added here. Figures 7-7 and 7-8 show two different approaches you can take to parallelizing the middle stage:

➤ In Figure 7-7, a single consumer/producer is threaded, so the contents of the current line are manipulated in parallel.

➤ In Figure 7-8, multiple consumer/producers are spawned, and so can manipulate multiple lines at the same time.

The thread IDs in the two diagrams are not significant; they merely indicate that the different pipeline stages are running on different threads or parallel strands.

When parallelizing a pipelined application, you have to take care how you pass the data between the different stages. In the serial version (see Listing 7-15), a single array is used to hold the current line. Once the pipeline is made parallel, several lines may need to be queued or stored, so they can be manipulated in parallel without causing data races.

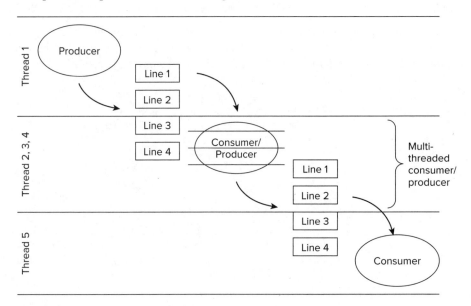

FIGURE 7-7: Using a single consumer/producer

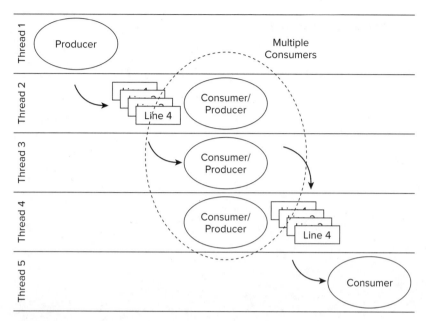

FIGURE 7-8: Using multiple consumer/producers

The parallel examples in this chapter simply make the `LineIn` and `LineOut` arrays two-dimensional so that each line has its own storage area. Another approach to storing the data that is passed along the pipeline is to dynamically allocate separate variables for each line as they are read in. Once the data has been consumed, the variable can then either be freed or passed back to the first pipeline for reuse.

The two parallel examples are based on OpenMP and TBB. There is no Cilk Plus example, but you can find an example of a pipelined application at `http://software.intel.com/en-us/articles/a-parallel-bzip2/`.

The Serial Version

Listing 7-15 shows the serial version of the pipelined application. The outer `for` loop in `main()` applies the three pipeline stages, one line at a time.

➤ In the first stage, a line of the file `Test.data` is read, and the data is placed in the array `LineIn`.

➤ The second stage of the pipeline calculates the square root of all the integers stored in `LineIn`. Rather than using a library call to calculate the square root, a slower, hand-rolled `sqroot()` function is used. Using this slower function helps to give the pipeline sufficient work to do, which is helpful for demonstration purposes. The results of the square root operation are stored as floats in `LineOut`.

➤ The last stage of the pipeline writes the results held in `LineOut` to the file `Root.data`.

LISTING 7-15: A serial pipelined application

```c
#include <stdio.h>
#include <stdlib.h>

#define LINE_LENGTH 8000
#define NUM_LINES 100
#define NUM_ENTRIES LINE_LENGTH * NUM_LINES

int LineIn[LINE_LENGTH];
float LineOut[LINE_LENGTH];

float sqroot(int n)
{
  float i = 0;
  float x1, x2;
  while( i*i<= n )
    i+=0.1;
  x1 = i;
  for(int j=0; j<10; j++)
  {
    x2 = n;
    x2 = x2/x1;
    x2 = x2+x1;
    x2 = x2/2;
    x1 = x2;
  }
  return x2;
}

int main()
{
  FILE *pFile = fopen(".\\Test.Data","r");
  if(!pFile){ printf("Couldn't open Test.Data");exit(999);}

  FILE *pOutputFile = fopen("Squared.Data","w");
  if(!pOutputFile){ printf("Couldn't open Squared.Data");exit(999);}

  // for every line in file ...
  for (int i = 0; i < NUM_LINES; i++)
  {
    // Pipeline STAGE 1
    for (int j = 0; j < LINE_LENGTH; j++)
      fscanf( pFile,"%d ",&LineIn[j]);

    // Pipeline STAGE 2
    for (int j = 0; j < LINE_LENGTH; j++)
      LineOut[j]=sqroot((float)LineIn[j]);

    // Pipeline STAGE 3
    for (int j = 0; j < LINE_LENGTH; j++)
      fprintf(pOutputFile,"%f ",LineOut[j]);
    fprintf(pOutputFile,"\n");
  }
```

```
        fclose(pFile);
        fclose(pOutputFile);
        return 0;
    }
```

code snippet Chapter7\7-15.cpp

OpenMP

Listing 7-16 implements a pipeline using OpenMP. You will see that

➤ The first and third stages of the pipeline need to run on single threads because of the file I/O operations that are serial in nature.

➤ The second stage of the pipeline uses a single consumer/producer. The processing of the individual numbers in the LineIn array is performed in parallel using the #pragma omp for construct.

➤ The nowait clauses in the first and third stages are added to improve performance.

➤ The arrays LineIn and LineOut that are used to pass data from the different pipeline stages are converted to a two-dimensional array so that each line can be manipulated without causing a data race.

➤ The first line from the file is read before the start of the parallel region and the subsequent reads fetch the line number i + 1.

LISTING 7-16: An OpenMP pipelined application

Available for
download on
Wrox.com

```
int main()
{
    FILE *pFile = fopen(".\\Test.Data","r");
    if(!pFile){ printf("Couldn't open Test.Data");exit(999);}

    FILE *pOutputFile = fopen("OpenMP_Squared.Data","w");
    if(!pOutputFile){ printf("Couldn't open OpenMP_Squared.Data");exit(999);}

    // preload line 0
    for (int j = 0; j < LINE_LENGTH; j++)
        fscanf( pFile,"%d ",&LineIn[0][j]);

    #pragma omp parallel
    {
        for (int i = 0; i < NUM_LINES; i++)
        {
            // Pipeline STAGE 1
            #pragma omp single nowait
            {
                // start reading the next line
                // Don't read beyond end
```

continues

LISTING 7-16 *(continued)*

```
        if(i <  NUM_LINES-1);
        {
          for (int j = 0; j < LINE_LENGTH; j++)
          fscanf( pFile,"%d ",&LineIn[i+1][j]);
        }
      }

      // Pipeline STAGE 2
#pragma omp for schedule(dynamic)
        for (int j = 0; j < LINE_LENGTH; j++)
          LineOut[i][j]=sqroot((float)LineIn[i][j]);

      // Pipeline STAGE 3
#pragma omp single nowait
      {
        for (int j = 0; j < LINE_LENGTH; j++)
          fprintf(pOutputFile,"%f ",LineOut[i][j]);
        fprintf(pOutputFile,"\n");
      }
    }
  }
  fclose(pFile);
  fclose(pOutputFile);
  return 0;
}
```

code snippet Chapter7\7-16.cpp

The OpenMP version of the pipeline is based on an idea from T. G. Mattson and B. Chapman's tutorial from the ACM/IEEE Conference on Supercomputing (2005), titled "OpenMP in Action." You can get a copy of the slides from `http://openmp.org/wp/presos/omp-in-action-SC05.pdf`.

TBB

You can use the TBB `parallel_pipeline` template to parallelize the pipeline code, as shown in Listing 7-17. The different pipeline stages are handled by filters, which can operate either in serial or in parallel.

To construct a pipeline using TBB, you should

1. Instantiate the pipeline class. This is done in the example using the `parallel_pipeline` template.

2. Add filters. Listing 7-17 uses lambda functions to provide the filter code.

3. Run the pipeline. This is done automatically when using the `parallel_pipeline` template.

Notice that the outer loop from the original serial code no longer exists. Iteration through the Test .data file is controlled by incrementing variable i in the first stage of the pipeline.

You can pass tokens between the filters. In the example here, the value of the variable i is passed in and out of the different filters.

The ntoken parameter controls the level of parallelism. In Listing 7-17, all the filters are of type filter::serial_in_order, so the value of ntoken has no effect.

Listing 7-18 shows an alternate middle filter, which is of type filter::parallel. By doing this you will be changing the design so that the middle pipeline stage is using multiple consumer/producers, as shown in Figure 7-8. When this filter is used, multiple tokens can be processed by the filter. In this situation the parameter ntokens limits the number of tokens that can be in flight at any one time.

The flow_control fc object is used to control the pipeline and indicates to the scheduler when the pipeline should stop.

As in the OpenMP version, the LineIn and LineOut arrays are promoted to be two-dimensional arrays.

LISTING 7-17: A pipelined application using TBB

```cpp
using namespace tbb;

int main()
{
    int i = 0;
    int ntokens = 24;
    FILE *pFile = fopen(".\\Test.Data","r");
    if(!pFile){ printf("Couldn't open Test.Data");exit(999);}

    FILE *pOutputFile = fopen("TBB_Squared.Data","w");
    if(!pOutputFile){ printf("Couldn't open OpenMP_Squared.Data");exit(999);}

    parallel_pipeline(
        ntokens,
        tbb::make_filter<void,int>(
            filter::serial_in_order, [&i,&pFile](flow_control& fc)->int {
                if (i < NUM_LINES)
                {
                    for (int j = 0; j < LINE_LENGTH; j++)
                        fscanf( pFile,"%d ",&LineIn[i][j]);
                    return i++;
                }
                else
                    fc.stop();

                return -1;
        }) &

        tbb::make_filter<int,int>(
            filter::serial_in_order, [](int i)->int {
                parallel_for (size_t(0), (size_t)LINE_LENGTH,[&](size_t j){
```

continues

LISTING 7-17 *(continued)*

```
            LineOut[i][j]=sqroot((float)LineIn[i][j]);
            });
            return i;
        }) &

    tbb::make_filter<int,void>(
        filter::serial_in_order, [&pOutputFile](int i) {
        for (int j = 0; j < LINE_LENGTH; j++)
            fprintf(pOutputFile,"%f ",LineOut[i][j]);
        fprintf(pOutputFile,"\n");
        })
    );
}
```

code snippet Chapter7\7-17.cpp

LISTING 7-18: Using an alternate TBB filter

```
    tbb::make_filter<int,int>(
        filter::parallel, [](int i)->int {
        {
            for (int j = 0; j < LINE_LENGTH; j++)
            LineOut[i][j]=sqroot((float)LineIn[i][j]);
            return i;
        }
    }) &
```

code snippet Chapter7\7-18.cpp

PARALLELIZING LINKED LISTS

A *linked list* consists of a number of data nodes that are daisy-chained together via a pointer, as shown in Figure 7-9. The end of the iteration space is not known in advance, and has to be detected by looking for a NULL value in the Next pointer. Linked lists can have nodes inserted or deleted dynamically.

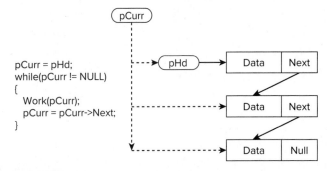

```
pCurr = pHd;
while(pCurr != NULL)
{
   Work(pCurr);
   pCurr = pCurr->Next;
}
```

FIGURE 7-9: The linked list construct

Listing 7-19, which is taken from Listings 7-23, 7-24, and 7-25 at the end of the chapter, traverses through the linked list until the pointer `pHead` has the value `NULL`.

The parallel versions use techniques that have been described earlier in this chapter.

Serial Iteration of the Linked List

Listing 7-19 shows the serial code to iterate through the linked list. You can find the complete version in the source code at the end of this chapter.

LISTING 7-19: Serial iteration of linked list

```cpp
// linked list iteration
void RunThoughLinkedList()
{
  node *pHead = Head;
  while(pHead != NULL)
  {
    Work(pHead);
    pHead = pHead->next;
  }
}
```

code snippet Chapter7\7-19.cpp

Parallel Iteration of the Linked List

Listings 7-20, 7-21, and 7-22 show how to parallelize the linked list iteration using Cilk Plus, OpenMP, and TBB, respectively. All three listings follow the same strategy:

➤ The iteration of the linked list is done in serial.

➤ As each node is visited, a task that runs the function `Work()` is launched.

➤ The tasks can run in parallel.

LISTING 7-20: Linked list iteration using Cilk Plus

```cpp
#include <cilk/cilk.h>
// linked list iteration
void RunThoughLinkedList()
{
  node *pHead = Head;
  while(pHead != NULL)
  {
    cilk_spawn Work(pHead);
    pHead = pHead->next;
  }
}
```

code snippet Chapter7\7-20.cpp

LISTING 7-21: Linked list iteration using OpenMP

```cpp
// linked list iteration
void RunThoughLinkedList()
{
  #pragma omp parallel
  {
    #pragma omp single
    {
      node *pHead = Head;
      while(pHead != NULL)
      {
        #pragma omp task firstprivate(pHead)
        {
          Work(pHead);
        }
        pHead = pHead->next;
      }
    }
  }
}
```

code snippet Chapter7\7-21.cpp

Listing 7-22: Linked list iteration using TBB

```cpp
void RunThoughLinkedList()
{
  tbb::task_group g;
  node *pHead = Head;
  printf("Starting Linked List\n");
  while(pHead != NULL)
  {
    g.run([=]{Work(pHead);});
    pHead = pHead->next;
  }
  g.wait();
}
```

code snippet Chapter7\7-22.cpp

ACTIVITY 7-1: PARALLELIZING THE SAMPLE APPLICATION

In this activity you parallelize the source code in Listings 7-23, 7-24, and 7-25 using some of the techniques described in this chapter.

Building the Program

If you haven't already done so:

1. Copy the three files from the end of the chapter into a directory.

2. Check that the program builds:

```
icl  /O2 main.cpp prime.cpp wtime.c
(LINUX: icc -O2 main.cpp prime.cpp wtime.c)
```

3. Run the program and record the time taken between each phase of the program:

```
[sblairch@localhost ssa]$ ./main
Start of application
*** glibc detected *** ./main: double free or corruption
    (top): 0x0000000007078010 ***
```

Implementing Parallelism

4. Choose one programming model, either Cilk Plus, OpenMP, or TBB.

5. Identify the loops in the program and implement a parallel solution for each one.

Hint: You may want to run Amplifier XE to do a Hotspot analysis to find the busiest parts of the program.

Moving on to the Next Model

6. Work your way through the other programming models, repeating the parallelization steps.

SOURCE CODE

Using the techniques highlighted in this chapter, you should be able to speed up the source code in Listings 7-23, 7-24, and 7-25. The source code is split into three files: main.cpp, wtime.cpp, and prime.c.

The code is somewhat artificial, in that it doesn't do anything particularly useful. Its sole purpose is to provide a "playgound" for you to experiment with parallelization.

With the source code you will find loops and linked lists that you can make parallel using Cilk Plus, OpenMP, and TBB. Activity 7-1 gives some suggestions for you to try out.

LISTING 7-23: Serial version of the example application

```cpp
#include <stdio.h>
#include <memory.h>
extern int Prime(int end);
extern int PrimeRecursive(int end);
extern "C" double wtime();

#define PRIME_NUMS 1000000
#define PRIME_NUMS_RECURSE 20000
#define NUM_NODES 5

enum Op { OpPrime,OpPrimeRecursive};
```

continues

LISTING 7-23 *(continued)*

```cpp
struct node
{
  int ValueIn;
  Op Operation;
  int NumPrimes;
  double Start;    // time
  double End;      // time
  node *next;      // the reference to the next node
  void Init(int v,Op o,node* n){ValueIn = v;Operation=o;next=n;}
  node(){Start=0;End=0;next=NULL;};
};

node List[NUM_NODES];
node * Head;

void Init()
{
  memset(List,'\0',sizeof(List));
  // set up the link
  List[0].Init(PRIME_NUMS,OpPrime,&List[4]);
  List[1].Init(PRIME_NUMS_RECURSE,OpPrimeRecursive,&List[2]);
  List[2].Init(PRIME_NUMS,OpPrime,NULL);
  List[3].Init(PRIME_NUMS_RECURSE,OpPrimeRecursive,&List[1]);
  List[4].Init(PRIME_NUMS,OpPrime,&List[3]);
  Head = &List[0];
}


void Work( node * pHead )
{
  pHead->Start = wtime();
  switch(pHead->Operation)
  {
  case OpPrime:
    pHead->NumPrimes=Prime(pHead->ValueIn);
    break;
  case OpPrimeRecursive:
    pHead->NumPrimes=PrimeRecursive(pHead->ValueIn);
    break;
  };
  pHead->End = wtime();
  printf("Work Time  %7.2f\n",pHead->End-pHead->Start);
}

// linked list iteration
void RunThoughLinkedList()
{
  node *pHead = Head;
  while(pHead != NULL)
  {
    Work(pHead);
    pHead = pHead->next;
  }
}
```

```cpp
// manual iterations
void RunExplicit()
{
  Work(&List[0]);
  Work(&List[1]);
  Work(&List[2]);
  Work(&List[3]);
  Work(&List[4]);
}

int main()
{
  Init();
  double start = wtime();
  double start_linked_list = wtime();
  RunThoughLinkedList();
  double end_linked_list = wtime();
  double start_explicit = wtime();
  RunExplicit();
  double end_explicit = wtime();
  double end = wtime();

  printf("Time through Linked List %7.2f\n"
    "Time through explicit %7.2f\n"
    "Total Time taken %7.2f\n",
    end_linked_list-start_linked_list,
    end_explicit-start_explicit,
    end-start
    );
}
```

Chapter7\\main.cpp

LISTING 7-24: A utility to measure time taken

```c
#ifdef _WIN32
#include <windows.h>
double wtime()
{
  LARGE_INTEGER ticks;
  LARGE_INTEGER frequency;
  QueryPerformanceCounter(&ticks);
  QueryPerformanceFrequency(&frequency);
  return (double)(ticks.QuadPart/(double)frequency.QuadPart);
}
#else
#include <sys/time.h>
#include <sys/resource.h>
double wtime()
{
  struct timeval time;
  struct timezone zone;
  gettimeofday(&time, &zone);
  return time.tv_sec + time.tv_usec*1e-6;
}
#endif
```

Chapter7\ wtime.c

LISTING 7-25: Code to check if a number is prime

```cpp
#include <math.h>
long  gPrimes[1000000];



bool isPrimeRecurse(int p, int i=2)
{
  if (i==p) return 1;//or better  if (i*i>p) return 1;
  if (p%i == 0 || p == 1) return 0;
  return isPrimeRecurse (p, i+1);
}



bool isPrime(int val)
{
    int limit, factor = 3;
    limit = (long)(sqrtf((float)val)+0.5f);
    while( (factor <= limit) && (val % factor))
        factor ++;
    return (factor > limit);
}

int Prime(int Num)
{
  int NumPrimes = 0;
  for( int i = 3; i <= Num; i += 2 )
  {
      if( isPrime(i) )
          gPrimes[NumPrimes++] = i;
  }
  return NumPrimes;
}

int PrimeRecursive(int Num)
{
  int NumPrimes = 0;
  for( int i = 3; i <= Num; i += 2 )
  {
    if( isPrimeRecurse(i) )
      gPrimes[NumPrimes++] = i;
  }
  return NumPrimes;
}
```

Chapter7\prime.cpp

SUMMARY

This chapter demonstrated that making code parallel is not as difficult as it initially may seem. Cilk Plus, OpenMP, and TBB all offer ways of parallelizing loops, recursive calls, blocks of code, and pipelined applications.

Note that this chapter has not addressed the thorny problem of data races and how to deal with shared variables.

In earlier chapters you saw how reducers in Cilk Plus and private and shared variables in OpenMP can be used to prevent data races. The next chapter shows how to detect memory and threading errors using Intel Parallel Inspector XE, and how you can fix such errors in Cilk Plus, OpenMP, and TBB.

8

Checking for Errors

WHAT'S IN THIS CHAPTER?

➤   Detecting threading errors

➤   Fixing data races

➤   Detecting memory errors

➤   Controlling the right level of detail

➤   Creating a custom analysis

Using multiple threads with common memory can easily lead to parallel-type errors, such as data races and deadlocks. Resolving these errors can often be frustrating and time-consuming, so it is vital that you detect them at an early stage of development.

You can use several different tools from Parallel Studio XE to help debug your parallel programs:

➤   **Parallel Advisor** — Advisor guides developers to add parallelism within their existing C/C++ programs. However, you need to add Advisor notations to identify the possible parallel regions. For more details, see Chapter 10, "Parallel Advisor–Driven Design."

➤   **Parallel Debugger Extension** — This extension pairs the parallel tools provided for developing multithreaded applications with the debug extensions, to allow for parallel features within the debugger. See Chapter 11, "Debugging Parallel Applications," for more details.

➤   **Static Security analysis** — Static Security analysis is carried out by the compiler and identifies both coding errors and security vulnerabilities through deep analysis of the source code. However, no final execution file is produced. For more details, see Chapter 5, "Writing Secure Code."

This chapter describes the operation of Intel Parallel Inspector XE, which you can use to find threading and memory errors after you have attempted parallelization. Creating parallel programs introduces the prospect of new types of errors involved with concurrent threading. These errors can have serious consequences on the efficiency and correctness of your parallel programs. Without tools such as Inspector XE, these threading errors can be notoriously difficult to find. You can also use Inspector XE to find many types of memory errors.

You have already used Inspector XE in Chapter 3, "Parallel Studio XE for the Impatient." If you haven't read that chapter or tried its hands-on activities, now would be a good time to do so.

PARALLEL INSPECTOR XE ANALYSIS TYPES

Chapter 3 describes the four steps you can use to make your code parallel: analyze, implement, debug, and tune. In the debug step you must check to see if you have introduced any parallel-type errors into your program. This is where you can use Inspector XE.

Inspector XE has predefined analysis types to help you (see Figure 8-1). These are split into three categories:

➤ **Memory Error analysis** — Detects and locates memory leaks, and finds other memory problems

➤ **Threading Error analysis** — Detects and locates data races and deadlocks

➤ **Custom analysis types** — Stores your own analysis types

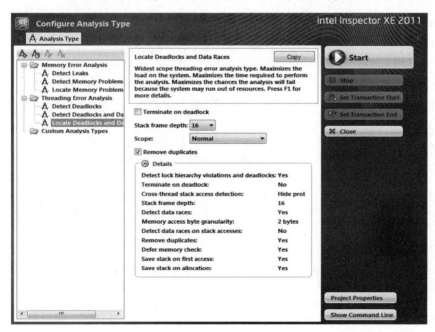

FIGURE 8-1: Inspector XE's Configure Analysis Type window

Each analysis type performs analysis to a different scope; the wider the scope, the more impact the analysis has on the time taken to run the program under test. Table 8-1 describes the likely impact of each scope. The descriptions are taken directly from the Configure Analysis Type window.

TABLE 8-1: The Scope of Each Analysis Type

SCOPE	ANALYSIS TYPES	IMPACT ON PROGRAM UNDER TEST
Narrowest	Detect Leaks Detect Deadlocks	Minimizes the load on the system. Minimizes the time required to perform the analysis. Increases the chances the analysis will complete successfully, particularly on large applications/large data sets.
Medium	Detect Memory Problems Detect Deadlocks and Data Races	Increases the load on the system. Increases the time required to perform the analysis. Increases the chances the analysis will fail because the system may run out of resources.
Widest	Locate Memory Problems Locate Deadlocks and Data Races	Maximizes the load on the system. Maximizes the time required to perform the analysis. Maximizes the chances the analysis will fail because the system may run out of resources.

You can find more details on exactly what options each analysis type uses in the section "Creating a Custom Analysis" later in this chapter.

If you are working on very large applications, it is best that you perform your first analysis using the narrowest scope level, and then when you have fixed all the problems at one scope level, move on to the next.

DETECTING THREADING ERRORS

You already know how to run a threading analysis session; you did this back in Chapter 3. Using Listing 8-4 (at the end of the chapter), this section reminds you how to look for threading errors. You can try this analysis out for yourself in Activity 8-1 and Activity 8-2.

Types of Threading Problems

Inspector XE can report the following types of problems:

➤ Thread information

➤ Potential privacy infringement

➤ Data races

➤ Deadlocks

Thread Information

Inspector XE provides information about the location and number of threads created during the execution of the program; it does not mean that there is a problem. Typically in a parallel program, a pool of threads is created, with the number of threads based on the number of cores in the machine or a user-specified number. If Inspector XE reports only a single thread being created, you may be running a serial program or be executing on a single-core machine. For some parallel models, for example, OpenMP, you also need to specifically enable the right compiler options to enable the parallelism.

Potential Privacy Infringement

Privacy infringement can occur when one thread accesses the stack memory of another thread. Inspector XE reports a potential problem when it detects variables of one thread being accessed by another thread. This is actually a remark only, giving an advisory message that there may potentially be some problem; in many cases it may not matter. Accessing cross-stack data can cause unexpected behavior, including a crash, if no protocols are in place to ensure safe accesses.

Variables involved in data races can be the cause of privacy infringements. Where possible, it is better not to allow threads to share variables on the stack.

Data Races

A data race occurs when multiple threads are trying to access the same memory location without proper synchronization — for example, when one or more threads is reading a variable while another thread is concurrently writing to it. Threads that read the variable before the writing thread updates the variable will obtain a different value from any threads reading the variable after the update.

Deadlocks

A deadlock is a situation where one thread is waiting for another thread to finish with a mutually exclusive resource, while at the same time that thread is waiting for the first thread to finish with its mutually exclusive resource. Neither thread can finish; therefore, a deadlock ensues.

Deadlocks are a common problem in multiprocessing, and are particularly troublesome because there is no general solution to avoid them.

An Example Application Involving Deadlocks

The code in Listing 8-4 uses approximate integration to calculate the values of pi. Figure 8-2 shows the principle used. By adding up the area of each bar under the curve, an approximation of pi is calculated.

The code is parallelized using the OpenMP sections directive, but it has errors. The code is not intended to be an example of how to write good threaded code; rather, it is written to help demonstrate the different threading errors that you can detect in Inspector XE. The following lines in Listing 8-4 provide the parallelism:

➤ **Line 32** — The for loop is responsible for iterating over every bar. On each iteration of the loop, the area of four bars is calculated.

➤ **Lines 35–63** — The OpenMP sections directive contains two section directives. Each section runs in parallel and calculates the area of two bars. The results of the calculations from each section are stored by calling the SafeAdd() function.

➤ **Lines 10–18** — The SafeAdd() function adds the values held in the parameters sum1 and sum2 into the global variables gsum1 and gsum2, respectively. Two OpenMP locks, lock1 and lock2, are used to protect access to the two global variables.

We know that:

$$\int_0^1 \frac{4.0}{(1+x^2)} \, dx = \pi$$

We can approximate the integral as a sum of rectangles:

$$\sum_{i=0}^{N} F(x_i)\Delta x \approx \pi$$

Where each rectangle has width Δx and height $F(x_i)$ at the middle of interval i.

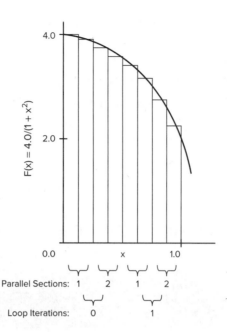

FIGURE 8-2: Calculating pi

Because of the programming errors in the code, the program will not run correctly. Figure 8-3 shows the output from the program once you have corrected all the errors.

FIGURE 8-3: The output window of the application

DETECTING DEADLOCKS

Detecting deadlocks using Inspector XE is straightforward. Even if a deadlock does not actually happen, you should be able to detect it — that is, as long as you have executed the code path on which the deadlock resides.

When you run the pi program from Listing 8-4, you will see that the log reports a deadlock, as shown in Figure 8-4.

The Summary window shows the results of running a Detect Deadlocks analysis on the code from Listing 8-4 in more detail (see Figure 8-5). The two reported problems, P1 and P2, are related. P2 is a deadlock and is caused by the lock hierarchy violation, as reported in problem P1. The snippets of code in the Code Locations pane show the source of the P2 deadlock problem. In total, six observations associated with the deadlock are detected, and are labeled X7 to X12.

Sometimes you will find it useful to look at the Timeline view (see Figure 8-6). You can access the Timeline view by clicking the Timeline tab at the top right of the Code Locations pane.

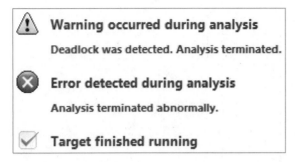

FIGURE 8-4: The log report from Inspector XE

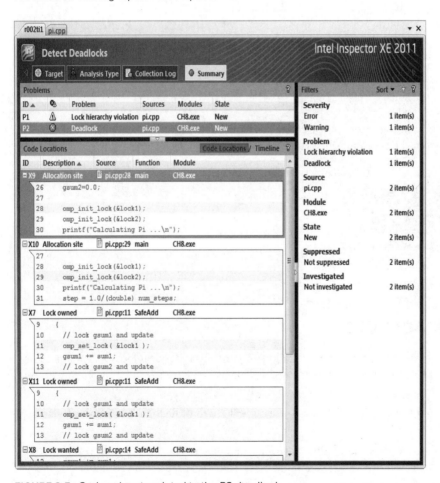

FIGURE 8-5: Code snippets related to the P2 deadlock

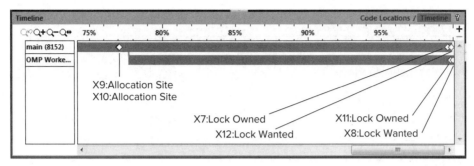

FIGURE 8-6: The Timeline view

The two horizontal bars are the two threads that were running. The four diamond markers show the time where the six events (X7 to X12) happened. Events X9 and X10 are located at the first diamond. If you hover the mouse over the diamond markers, the names of the events are displayed. If you then examine the locks associated with these six events, by looking at the code displayed in the Code Locations pane (as in Figure 8-5), the sequence of events looks like this:

First event, X9, Thread 0: Allocation Site - lock1

Second event, X10, Thread 0: Allocation Site - lock2

Third event, X7, Thread 0: Lock Owned - lock1

Fourth event, X11, Thread 1: Lock Owned - lock1

Fifth event, X12, Thread 0: Lock Wanted - lock2

Sixth event, X8, Thread 1: Lock Wanted - lock2

You immediately should be suspicious of what you see:

➤ Apparently both threads own lock1 (at events X7 and X11). This is impossible; two threads cannot own the same lock at the same time.

➤ No thread owns lock2, yet the lock is wanted at X12 and X8.

Something must be really wrong with the program. With a bit more investigation you will realize that the cause of the problem is the order in which the locks are being used when calling the SafeAdd() function. The order of the locks has been accidently swapped in Lines 48 and 61 of Listing 8-4:

```
48:         SafeAdd(sum1,sum2,lock1,lock2);
61:         SafeAdd(sum1,sum2,lock2,lock1);
```

You can resolve the deadlock problem relatively easily. If both threads use the same locks in the same order, no deadlock will result. By changing the order of the parameters lock1 and lock2 so that both calls to SafeAdd() use them in the same sequence, you can fix the deadlock:

```
48:         SafeAdd(sum1,sum2,lock1,lock2);
61:         SafeAdd(sum1,sum2,lock1,lock2);
```

This was a relatively simple case. However, deadlocks can be very difficult to detect without the right tools, which is where the use of Inspector XE comes into its own.

ACTIVITY 8-1: DETECTING AND FIXING A DEADLOCK

In this activity you use Inspector XE to detect and fix a deadlock. You can run this activity on Linux or Windows.

Building and Running the Program

1. Copy the source code in Listing 8-4 into a file named `pi.cpp`.

2. Open an Intel Parallel Studio XE command prompt.

3. Build the program with the following command:

WINDOWS

```
icl  /Od /Qopenmp /Zi pi.cpp -o 8-1.exe
```

LINUX

```
icc  -O0 -openmp -g pi.cpp -o 8-1.exe
```

4. Run the program:

```
8-1.exe
```

You should see that the program will hang.

Detecting and Fixing the Deadlock

5. Start the Inspector XE GUI from the command line:

```
inspxe-gui
```

6. Create a new project named `Chapter 8`:

  ➤ Select File ⇨ New ⇨ Project.

  ➤ In the Project Properties dialog, fill in the application details.

7. Carry out a Detect Deadlocks analysis:

  ➤ Select File ⇨ New ⇨ Analysis.

  ➤ Highlight the Detect Deadlocks analysis.

  ➤ Make sure the Terminate on Deadlock box is selected.

  ➤ Click the Start button.

8. After the analysis is displayed, look at the problem(s) reported to ensure you understand the issue.

9. Fix the deadlock issue by editing lines 48 and 61 of `pi.cpp` to look like this:

```
48:        SafeAdd(sum1,sum2,lock1,lock2);
61:        SafeAdd(sum1,sum2,lock1,lock2);
```

10. Rebuild the application (see step 3 and step 4) and then run the program. The program should run to completion without hanging.

11. Rerun the deadlock analysis (see step 7). No errors should be reported.

In this activity you used Detect Deadlocks analysis to find the deadlock. The program also has a data race, but it was not detected. In Activity 8-2, you use Inspector XE to detect and fix the data race.

DETECTING DATA RACES

Once the deadlock from Listing 8-4 has been fixed, it's time to look for any data races by running the Detect Deadlocks and Data Races analysis. The steps are identical to what you did when you ran a Detect Deadlocks analysis, except you choose a different prebuilt analysis type.

Running the Threaded Program

Before running the analysis you should run the program several times to see if the results are deterministic. Table 8-2 shows the value of pi for ten runs of the program. In the first five runs, the program ran in parallel; in the last five runs, only one thread was made available by setting the OMP_NUM_THREAD=1 environment variable. You can see that when the program runs with more than one thread, the value of pi varies.

TABLE 8-2: The Value of pi

ATTEMPT #	VALUE	OMP_NUM_THREADS
1	3.145416887792414700000	Not Set
2	3.141616771104690700000	Not Set
3	3.141592656670666500000	Not Set
4	3.142346075956167900000	Not Set
5	3.142247551357102900000	Not Set
6	3.141592653641859900000	1
7	3.141592653641859900000	1
8	3.141592653641859900000	1
9	3.141592653641859900000	1
10	3.141592653641859900000	1

First Results of the Analysis

When you run a Detect Deadlocks and Data Races analysis, you should get results similar to Figure 8-7. Three data races, P1, P2, and P3, are detected. With the P1 error highlighted, you can see that the problem is related to simultaneously reading from and writing to the variable x1. Similarly, P2 and P3 relate to variables x2, sum1, and sum2.

You can fix these data races by modifying line 35 so that each thread has its own private copy of x1, x2, sum1, and sum2:

```
35:     #pragma omp parallel sections private(x1,x2,sum1,sum2)
```

With the problem fixed, when you rerun the program you will see that:

➤ The value of pi stays the same value when you run the program several times.

➤ Running a fresh Inspector XE analysis gives the result "No Problems Found."

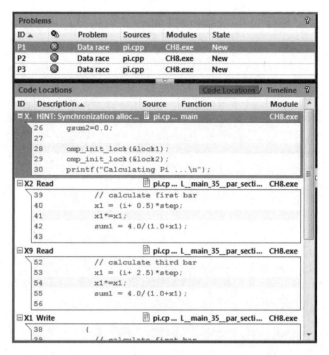

FIGURE 8-7: Three data race problems are revealed after the resolving deadlock

You can try out these steps for yourself in Activity 8-2.

ACTIVITY 8-2: DETECTING AND FIXING DATA RACES

In this activity you use Inspector XE to help detect and fix a data race. You can run this activity on Linux or Windows.

Building and Running the Program

1. Continue to work with the modified version of Listing 8-4. This step assumes you have fixed the deadlock identified in Activity 8-1.

2. Build the program 8-2.exe with the following command:

WINDOWS

```
icl  /Od /Qopenmp /Zi pi.cpp -o 8-2.exe
```

LINUX

```
icc  -O0 -openmp -g pi.cpp -o 8-2.exe
```

3. Run the program several times to make sure it works:

```
8-2.exe
```

4. Set the number of threads to be 1 using the OMP_NUM_THREADS environment variable, and then run the program several times and note its behavior:

Controlling the Right Level of Detail

The pi program is very small and has only a few data races. You may have many more errors in your programs. You need to avoid two extremes when analyzing your code:

➤ Failing to test all the code paths

➤ Collecting and/or displaying too much information

Testing All the Code Paths

When you perform an analysis, it's important that you choose the right test data so that all your code paths are executed. You might find it quite hard to test some of your code, especially if it is in a path that is not normally executed (for example, error handling code). To help overcome this, you can:

➤ **Build your program in debug mode with optimization disabled** — This ensures that none of your code paths are optimized away, and all the functions and symbols will be available in your results. For example, no inlining of functions will occur.

➤ **Write test cases that exercise the less obvious paths through your code** — That is, manipulate the data to force the program to run down the obscure pathways through your code. Don't assume a pathway will never occur in general operation; they always will.

➤ **Do a Static Security analysis** — As described in Chapter 5, "Writing Secure Code," this kind of analysis tests all the paths in the code, although it cannot detect every kind of threading problem. Some problems can be detected only when you actually run your program.

Avoiding Being Overwhelmed by the Amount of Data

The more information you collect, the slower your analysis session will take to run. The analysis might even fail to complete if you generate too much data. Strategies you can use for reducing the amount of data include:

➤ Use a minimum test set. For example, where a loop is involved, reduce the loop count to a minimum.

➤ Don't use a higher depth of analysis than you need. Deeper depth investigations take longer and generate more data. In the predefined analysis pane, the first items in the list are the ones that have the lowest overhead. See the "Creating a Custom Analysis" section for more information on what each analysis type contains.

➤ Use the one-click filters to display a subset of the results. You can filter the results based on severity, problem type, source file, module, state, and suppression mode. You can read more about the one-click filters in the "Investigating the Results of the Analysis" section in Chapter 5.

➤ Use suppression files where large numbers of problems exist to help reduce the information to manageable chunks.

Using Suppression Files

The threading example used in this chapter is fairly simple and creates only a few errors that can be easily managed. In other, more complex and extensive situations, the sheer quantity of problems and observations may well overwhelm and confuse you. You may also know that some errors are false positives and can be ignored.

Creating Suppression Files

You can suppress problems and observations in Inspector XE using suppression rules. In effect, these rules declutter the overview of problems and their observational events, making it easier for you to focus on a subset of the problems reported. You can experiment with suppression rules by using the output from Activity 8-1 (refer to Figure 8-7).

Assume that you want to suppress the results of the first data race, P1. To do this, perform the following steps:

1. Click the data race P1 within the Problems pane.

2. Right-click the first observation event (X15) within the Code Locations pane, and select Suppress from the drop-down menu.

   In the Create Private Suppression window (Figure 8-8), three related observations are checked. The rule will take effect only when all the selected observations are present. You can selectively choose whether to have all entries or just one entry checked.

3. Note the default file being used, default.sup. You can change this to one of your own, if required.

4. Click the Create button.

Upon creating this new suppression rule, the summary display will be changed, as shown in Figure 8-9. Notice that P1 and its associated observations have been crossed through.

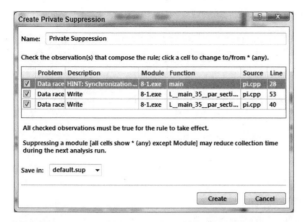

FIGURE 8-8: The pop-up window for creating private suppressions

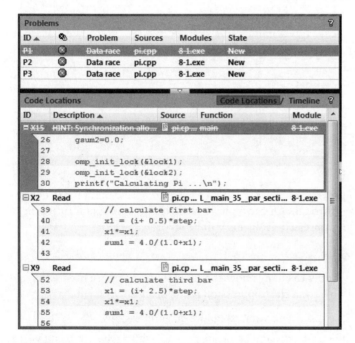

FIGURE 8-9: Simple suppression of the first data race

Deleting Suppression Files

To remove the private suppression rule you just made:

1. Right-click, as before, on an observation.

2. In the drop-down menu, select Do Not Suppress.

3. In the pop-up window, check the box next to the filename and click the Remove button.

After you have removed this suppression rule, notice that problem P1 and its associated observations are no longer crossed through.

Suppressing by Type Rather Than by Instance

You can also choose to suppress not just a single occurrence of a type of problem, but all occurrences of the type:

1. Click the first data race (P1) within the Problems pane.

2. Right-click the first observation event (X15) within the Code Locations pane, and select Suppress from the drop-down menu.

3. In the Create Private Suppression window, click the line numbers and select * (any) (see Figure 8-10).

4. Click the Create button.

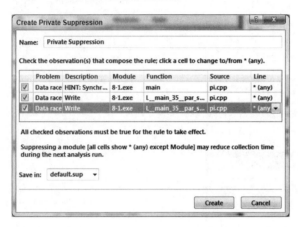

FIGURE 8-10: Suppressing all data races

A new suppression rule is created suppressing all data races. You should notice that all three data race problems have now been crossed through. Once you have created the suppression rules, the next time you run an analysis all the suppressed problems will be ignored.

Changing the Suppression Mode

You can use the Project Properties window to change how the suppression rules are used (see Figure 8-11). Three options are available from the Suppression mode drop-down menu:

➤ **Do not use suppressions** — Use this if you want to ignore all suppressions.

➤ **Mark problems** — Displays the problems and associated events with each item being written through.

➤ **Delete problems** — This is the default behavior. Any events that match the suppression rules will not be displayed. There will be no hint that they have been supressed!

 When a suppression file is being used, and you use Delete problems suppression mode, it is almost impossible to tell from the results of any analysis that some errors have been deleted. It is strongly recommended that as a sanity check, you should always run a final analysis with the suppression mode being either Do not use suppressions or Mark problems.

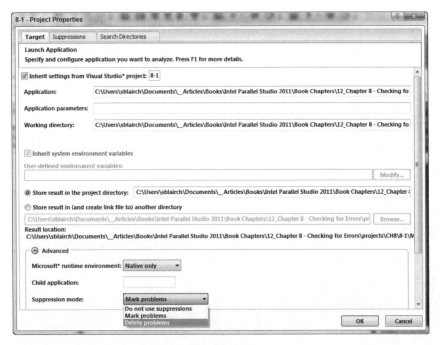

FIGURE 8-11: Changing how suppression filters are used

Suppressing known problems can aid with development. If you are already aware of certain problems, you can suppress them, which enables you to focus on and fix those problems of which you were not aware. At the end of this chapter is a discussion on different ways of fixing data races in Cilk Plus, OpenMP, and TBB.

The next section of this chapter shows how to detect memory errors. Before you read that, however, you can use Activity 8-3 to experiment with suppression files.

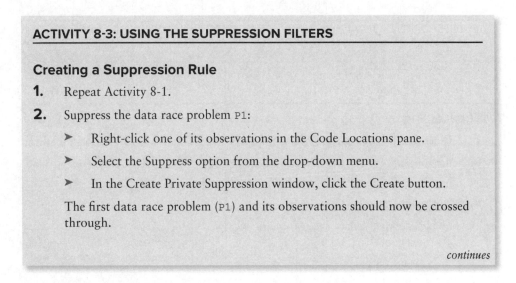

ACTIVITY 8-3: USING THE SUPPRESSION FILTERS

Creating a Suppression Rule

1. Repeat Activity 8-1.

2. Suppress the data race problem P1:

➤ Right-click one of its observations in the Code Locations pane.

➤ Select the Suppress option from the drop-down menu.

➤ In the Create Private Suppression window, click the Create button.

The first data race problem (P1) and its observations should now be crossed through.

continues

continued

3. Run a new analysis:

➤ Select File ⇨ New ⇨ Analysis.

➤ Highlight the Detect Deadlocks and Data Races analysis.

➤ Click the Start button.

You should notice that all the previous errors are no longer displayed.

Deleting a Suppression Rule

4. Start a new analysis, but before clicking the Start button, modify the suppression mode in the Project Properties window:

➤ Select File ⇨ New ⇨ Analysis.

➤ Highlight the Detect Deadlocks and Data Races analysis.

➤ Click the Project Properties button.

➤ In the Advanced section of the Project Properties dialog, set the suppression mode to Mark problems, and then click OK.

➤ Click the Start button.

5. In the new analysis:

➤ Right-click one of its observations within the Code Locations pane.

➤ Select the Do Not Suppress option from the drop-down menu.

➤ In the Delete Private Suppressions window, check the box for the name of the file (in the top half of the window).

➤ Click the Remove button.

The first data race problem (P1) and its observations are no longer crossed through.

6. Run a new analysis.

You should see that the P1 problem is now displayed.

Suppressing by Type

7. Delete all the suppression rules (as in steps 4 to 6).

8. Run a new analysis, but before you click Start, make sure that Delete problems is selected in the Project Properties window.

9. Suppress all data races:

➤ Select the P1 data race problem.

➤ Right-click one of its observations within the Code Locations pane.

> ➤ Select the Suppress option from the drop-down menu.
>
> ➤ In the Create Private Suppression window, click in the line number column of the first entry. This enables you to access a drop-down menu, where you should select *(any).
>
> ➤ Repeat this for the remaining lines.
>
> ➤ Click the Create button.
>
> All data race problems are now shown as crossed through. Notice that the Read observation of P1 problem that is not crossed through. This is because when you created the suppression rule, the lines all had the Write description.
>
> **10.** If you like, you can re-create the suppression rule and change the Write entries to *(any), as in step 9. Now all observations will be suppressed.

FIXING DATA RACES

After detecting deadlocks or data races in your program, you need to fix them. Cilk Plus, OpenMP, and TBB each have their own constructs that will help. Don't forget that you can borrow constructs from one parallel model and use them in another (see the section "Choosing the Right Parallel Constructs" in Chapter 1).

You can use the following strategies to deal with data races:

➤ Use local variables rather than shared variables.

➤ Restructure your code or change your algorithm.

➤ Use objects that are designed to be safely shared across threads.

➤ Use atomic operations.

➤ Use locks or other synchronization constructs to enforce mutual exclusion.

Before deciding to use a construct, you should see if you can fix your data race problem by using local variables or restructuring your code.

Using Cilk Plus

You can use three different kinds of Cilk Plus objects to handle shared data:

➤ Reducers

➤ Holders

➤ Home-grown reducers

Home-grown reducers are not covered in the book. You can find more information about them in the online help that is distributed with the Intel compiler.

Cilk Plus does not have any locks available, but you can use synchronization objects from TBB or system locks provided by the OS.

Cilk Plus Reducers

Cilk Plus reducers are objects that address the need to use shared variables in parallel code. Conceptually, a reducer can be considered to be a shared variable. However, during run time each thread has access to its own private copy, or *view*, of the variable, and works on this copy only. As the parallel strands finish, the results of their views of the variable are combined asynchronously into the single shared variable. This eliminates the possibility of data races without requiring time-consuming locks.

Listing 3-3 in Chapter 3 uses a `cilk::reducer_opadd` to overcome the data races caused by the sum and `total` shared variables. Each type of reducer has its own default initialization value, but you can initialize them yourself when they are declared. In Listing 3-3 the values are explicitly set to zero (which also happens to be the default value for the `reducer_opadd`):

```
// define check sum and total as reduction variables
cilk::reducer_opadd<long int> sum(0);
cilk::reducer_opadd<double> total(0.0);
```

Each type of Cilk Plus reducer has its own header file that should be included. For the `reducer_opadd` this is:

```
#include <cilk/reducer_opadd.h>
```

To obtain the final merged values of the reduction variables, use the `get_value()` method:

```
printf("Time Elapsed %10d mSecs  Total=%lf   Check Sum = %ld\n",
       (int)elapsedtime, total.get_value(), sum.get_value() );
```

If none of the reducers available in the Cilk Plus reducer library fit your need, you can write your own. You can find an example of writing your own reducer in the online help that is distributed with the Intel compiler.

Cilk Plus Holders

Holders are similar to Cilk Plus reducers in that you can use them to provide variables that can be used in parallel code. However, Cilk Plus holders do not preserve all the views beyond the parallel strands. One view will be maintained, based on the holder policy, which can be one of `holder_keep_indeterminate, include holder_keep_last, holder_keep_last_copy, holder_keep_last_swap`, and `holder_keep_last_move`. For more information on these policies, refer to the Intel compiler online help. The default policy in the template definition is `holder_keep_indeterminate`:

```
template <typename Type,
          holder_policy Policy = holder_keep_indeterminate,
          typename Allocator = std::allocator<Type> >
class holder
{
  //etc.
};
```

You can use holders to provide the equivalent of thread-local storage. You can even wrap holders with your own class to reduce the amount of code edits you have to make. Chapter 16, "Parallelizing Legacy Code," contains an example of defining your own wrappers.

Listing 8-1 gives an example of using Cilk Plus holders and how you can create your own wrapper.

LISTING 8-1: Using Cilk Plus holders

```
1:  #include <cilk/holder.h>
2:
3:  cilk::holder<int> g;
4:
5:  // code that uses Cilk Plus holder
6:  void test1()
7:  {
8:    int i;
9:    g() = 8;
10:   cilk_spawn[]
11:   {
12:     g()=100;
13:     i = g();
14:   }();
15:   g()= 37;
16:   cilk_sync;
17: }
18:
19: // template for wrapper
20: template <typename T>
21: class myholder
22: {
23:   private:
24:     cilk::holder<T> m_holder;
25:   public:
26:     myholder<T> & operator=(const T &rhs)
27:     {
28:       m_holder() = rhs;return *this;
29:     }
30:     operator T &(){return m_holder();}
31: };
32:
33: // code that uses the wrapper
34: myholder<int> h;
35: void test2()
36: {
37:   int i;
38:   h = 8;
39:   cilk_spawn[]
40:   {
41:     h=100;
42:     i = h;
43:   }();
44:   h = 37;
45:   cilk_sync;
46: }
```

code snippet Chapter8\8-1.cpp

Line 3 declares a `cilk::holder`, which is used in the `cilk_spawn`/`cilk_sync` parallel code (lines 10–16). Notice that to access the values of the g variable, the function operator has to be used:

```
12:     g()=100;
13:     i = g();
```

At line 34, the h variable uses a wrapper template, the wrapper being defined in lines 20–31. You will immediately notice that the access to the h variable does *not* need to use a function operator:

```
41:     h=100;
42:     i = h;
```

Both the `cilk::holder` and the `myholder` templates provide variables that are safe to use in parallel code. Each parallel strand treats the variables as its own private variable without any data races occurring.

Using OpenMP

OpenMP provides a number of constructs that you can use to implement mutual exclusion, including locks, critical sections, atomic operations, and reduction clauses.

Using Locks

You've already seen how you can use OpenMP locks to enforce mutual exclusion earlier in the chapter. Be careful when you use locks; it is very easy to forget to release a lock. Many programmers prefer not to use any locks in their code. If you can, avoid locks.

Using Critical Sections

The following code shows how you can protect a shared variable with a `#pragma omp critical` construct. You could use this code in place of the existing code in lines 10–17 of Listing 8-3. In this example, the critical constructs have been given a name (you can use any name).

```
#pragma omp critical(gsum1)
gsum1 += sum1;

#pragma omp critical(gsum2)
gsum2 += sum2;
```

Any `#pragma omp critical` statements that do not have a name are all given the same anonymous name.

Using Atomic Operations

The following code shows how you can use an atomic operation to enforce mutual exclusion. You can use atomic operations to protect a memory update. For example, placing the `#pragma omp atomic` directive before the variable gsum1 ensures that there is no data race:

```
#pragma omp atomic
gsum1 += sum1;

#pragma omp critical
gsum2 += sum2;
```

Atomic operations are much more efficient than using locks or critical sections.

Using a reduction Clause

For an example of using an OpenMP `reduction` clause, see the section "Parallelizing Loops" in Chapter 7, "Implementing Parallelism."

Using TBB

By using the algorithms in TBB, you should be able to avoid concurrent access. TBB also provides a number of concurrent containers that you can use to avoid data races. The containers are very similar to the STL containers.

Listing 8-2 is an example of using the `tbb::concurrent_queue`. The queue is first filled with values from 0 to 99 using `queue.push()`. Two `while` loops, each embedded in its own lambda function, are then executed in parallel using `parallel_invoke`. Each parallel strand pops values off the queue until the queue is empty. The `try_pop()` function returns `true` if an item has been returned from the queue; otherwise, it returns `false`.

LISTING 8-2: Using a TBB container

```
1:  #include <tbb/tbb.h>
2:  #include <stdio.h>
3:  int main()
4:  {
5:    int a,b;
6:    tbb::concurrent_queue<int> queue;
7:    for(int i =0; i< 100; i++)
8:      queue.push(i);
9:
10:   tbb::parallel_invoke(
11:   [&]{
12:        while(queue.try_pop(a)){
13:          printf("a%d ",a);
14:        }
15:     },
16:   [&]{
17:        while(queue.try_pop(b)){
18:          printf("b%d ",b);
19:        }
20:      }
21:   );
22: }
```

code snippet Chapter8\Memory8-2.cpp

On rare occasions, you may want to introduce mutual exclusion into your code to prevent some race condition or enforce some deterministic behavior into your code. You can use TBB mutexes and atomic operations to enforce mutual exclusion.

Variants of the mutex include `spin_mutex`, `queueing_mutex`, `spin_rw_mutex`, and `queueing_rw_mutex`. Like all C++ variables, mutexes work within the scope they are declared. Once a mutex goes out of scope, its destructor is called, which releases the lock.

The `atomic<T>` template class provides a single atomic operation on a single variable. Methods include `read`, `write`, `fetch-and-add`, `fetch-and-store`, and `compare-and-swap`.

Listing 8-3 shows the use of a `tbb::mutex` and a `tbb::atomic`. Within the `cilk_for` loop, three variables (a, b, and c) are incremented. Variable a is protected by the TBB mutex `m.lock()` and `m.unlock()` methods; variable b is declared to be a `tbb::atomic` operation; and variable c has no protection against data races. When the code is built and run, the values of the incremented variables are printed to the screen. All the values are incremented 1,000 times, but the value of c will almost certainly be wrong due to a data race.

LISTING 8-3: Using TBB locks

```
1: #include <cilk/cilk.h>
2: #include <tbb/mutex.h>
3: #include <stdio.h>
4: int main()
5: {
6:    int a = 0;
7:    tbb::atomic<int> b;
8:    b = 0;
9:    int c = 0;
10:   tbb::mutex m;
11:
12:   cilk_for(int i =0; i< 10000; i++)
13:   {
14:     m.lock();
15:     a++;
16:     m.unlock();
17:     b++;
18:     c++;
19:   }
20:   printf("a:%d, b:%d, c:%d\n",a,b,c);
21:}
```

code snippet Chapter8\8-3.cpp

DETECTING MEMORY ERRORS

Inspector XE has three predefined analysis types dedicated to finding memory errors (refer to Figure 8-1):

➤ **Detect Leaks** — Use this to detect where memory or resources are allocated but never released. This is the narrowest scope of analysis and will have the least impact on your code. For large applications, it is best to start an analysis with this type.

➤ **Detect Memory Problems** — Use this to detect memory leaks (as in the previous bullet) and invalid or uninitialized access to memory.

➤ **Locate Memory Problems** — Use this to perform the most detailed analysis. In addition to detecting memory problems, the analysis has enhanced checks for dangling pointers (a pointer that has been used after it has been freed) and enables guard zones. Inspector XE adds guard zones to the end of allocated memory to test for any memory access that strays beyond the end of a memory block. Of the three analysis types, this analysis will have the most impact on your application. On large applications, the analysis may fail due to insufficient resources.

Types of Memory Errors

You can use Inspector XE to detect memory errors in both parallel and nonparallel code. Parallel programs can be much more sensitive to memory errors than serial programs. A memory error often can introduce unpredictable behavior; when you run a program with a memory error, it's not always obvious that there is a problem. It is important that you don't forget to run a memory analysis on your code.

You can detect several types of memory errors, including the following:

➤ **GDI resource leak** — This occurs when a Graphics Device Interface (GDI) object is created but never deleted.

➤ **Incorrect memcpy call** — This occurs if you use the `memcpy` function with two pointers that overlap. This error is checked only on Linux systems; on Windows, the overlapping of `memcpy` pointers is considered safe.

➤ **Invalid deallocation** — This happens when you try to call a deallocation function with an address pointing to memory that has not been allocated dynamically.

➤ **Invalid memory access** — This occurs when a read or write instruction references invalid memory. This can happen, for example, when you use stale or dangling pointers. A dangling pointer is one that has been freed but has not been set to the value NULL.

➤ **Invalid partial memory access** — This occurs when a block of memory is accessed that is partially invalid. Often the cause of such errors is the miscalculation of the size of an object before dynamically allocating it.

➤ **Kernel resource leak** — This happens when a kernel object handle is created but never closed.

➤ **Memory growth** — This happens when memory is allocated but not deallocated during application execution. For example, the continual allocation of memory in a loop without the memory being deallocated will lead to memory growth.

➤ **Memory leak** — This occurs when a block of memory is allocated but never released.

➤ **Mismatched allocation/deallocation** — This happens, for example, when you attempt to deallocate memory with the `delete` function that was allocated with the `malloc` function.

➤ **Missing allocation** — This occurs when you attempt to free a previously freed block of memory, or free a memory block that was never allocated.

➤ **Uninitialized memory access** — This occurs when you read memory that has not been initialized (for example, when you dynamically create a block of memory and start reading from it without first initializing its values).

➤ **Uninitialized partial memory access** — This occurs when you read memory that has been only partially initialized (for example, if you dynamically create a `struct` but initialize only some of the members, and start reading from one of the uninitialized members).

An Example Application for Memory Analysis

Listing 8-5 (at the end of the chapter) shows an example program that reveals several types of memory errors. Each potential memory error has been explicitly commented on within the example program. The program has an outer loop within which the following actions take place:

➤ **Line 23** — A drawing object is created, but never deleted. This creates a GDI resource leak, where each iteration of the outer loop uses up more resources allocated for graphical purposes. Eventually, the limits of these resources will be used up and the program will stop. These types of memory errors are notoriously difficult to detect because they do not affect the correct operation of the program; only after the program has been running for some time will graphical allocation limits be reached and the program stop running. This code is included only if you are building under Windows.

➤ **Line 26** — A region of memory in heap space is reserved by the dynamic allocation call to `calloc` and used as a temporary array to hold data for some calculations that follow. However, the space is never freed. Each iteration of the outer loop will reserve a new region of heap without freeing the previous ones. This is a memory leak. Unless corrected, eventually all the heap space will be used up. Again, this sort of error does not affect the immediate running of the program; only later, when all the heap space has been consumed, will the program fail to carry on running.

➤ **Line 35** — A second region of heap space is reserved and used as another temporary array. However, the program accesses the array with an index beyond its limits (lines 40–43). This is an invalid memory access error. Pointer operations of this type would not be picked up by the compiler.

➤ **Lines 42 and 45** — This second reserved space is then released; however, the released pointer is then used to access memory. This is another invalid memory access error.

➤ **Line 47** — An attempt is then made to free the second reserved space again, which creates a missing allocation error. Although this will not affect the outcome of the program or stop its operation, it does use up valuable executing time.

➤ **Line 48** — An uninitialized pointer is then used to allocate memory. This is another invalid memory access error.

Because these activities lie within a loop, any activities not tightly controlled will be found by the inspection — for example, allocation of heap space without associated release of this space.

As before, with the threading errors example, it is advisable to use a small representative data set when inspecting. To this end, the example program has been altered to run only once through its outer loop.

Run a new inspection of the example program using Inspector XE's Locate Memory Problems analysis, the fullest and most comprehensive analysis possible for memory errors (see Activity 8-4).

After a successful analysis, the output shown in Figure 8-12 will result. All six possible memory errors are accounted for, marked as problems P1 to P6 in the Problems pane of the Inspector XE's output. Clicking each problem results in the corresponding associated observations event data for that problem being shown in the Code Locations pane (the lower-left pane).

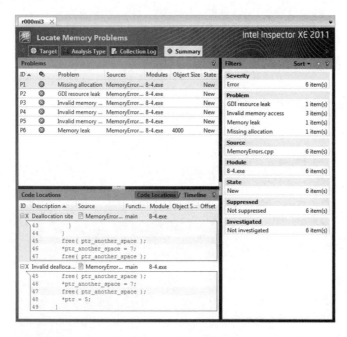

FIGURE 8-12: Inspector XE output from the memory errors example

The Filters pane shows a summary of problems, including how many of each. To filter the problems by type, you can just select (by clicking) one of the problem types. For example, clicking on Invalid memory access results in Figure 8-13, which shows only invalid memory access errors. Filtering like this concentrates the mind onto a particular error type, before moving onto the rest. Clicking the All button brings all the memory problems back.

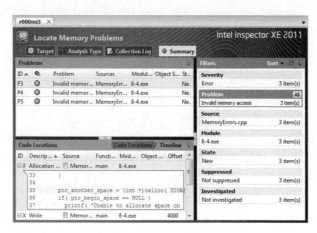

FIGURE 8-13: Filtered memory errors observations

Clicking one of the squares to the left of any event in the Code Locations pane brings up a snippet of code that is responsible for that observation. This is demonstrated for problem P4 in Figure 8-14, where events X4, X6, and X7 have been selected. The summary information to the right has been closed to give a better view of the code.

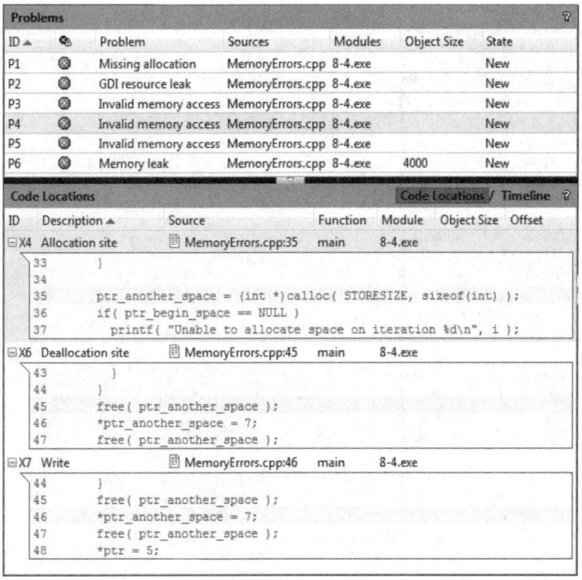

FIGURE 8-14: Code snippets associated with events of problem P5

Alternatively, you can reveal these same code snippets by double-clicking the problems themselves within the Problems pane, as shown in Figure 8-15, where problem P1 has been selected. In this example, the problem X2 occurs when a deallocation was attempted.Also shown is the associated event X1 where the original deallocation was carried out. Obviously, you cannot deallocate a memory address that has already been deallocated. You can solve the P1 problem simply by removing the second deallocation.

The P2 problem is a GDI resource leak, caused by hDefpen (see line 23 of Listing 8-5) being repeatedly created but never deleted. As new pens are continually created for each loop iteration, the graphical resources may eventually be used up, causing the program to fail. Problems of this sort are notoriously hard to predict.

In this example, although there is only a single outer loop for testing purposes, and therefore the leak cannot cause a program failure because the closing of the application will automatically release any resources it uses, Inspector XE will still flag it as a potential problem.

Figure 8-16 shows the code snippet associated with the P2 problem, clearly indicating that there is a problem with pen creation. You can solve this by deleting the pen at the end of each loop iteration.

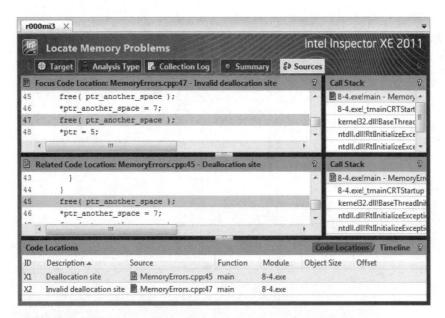

FIGURE 8-15: Revealing the offending code responsible for the P1 problem

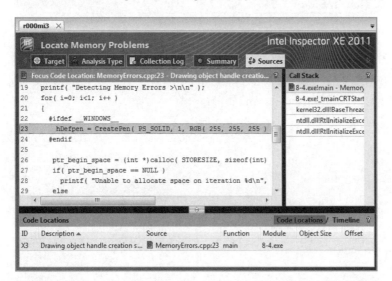

FIGURE 8-16: Revealing the offending code responsible for the P2 problem

The memory leak problems are similarly caused by continuously reserving space within the heap space without freeing up any of it. Again, eventually all the heap space will be used up and the application will fail. This is clearly shown for problem P6 by the code snippet shown in Figure 8-17.

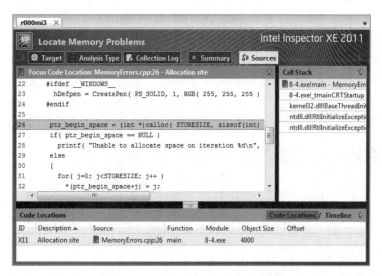

FIGURE 8-17: Revealing the offending code responsible for the P12 problem

ACTIVITY 8-4: DETECTING MEMORY ERRORS

In this activity you use Inspector XE to detect and analyze some memory errors.

Building and Running the Program

1. Copy the source code in Listing 8-5 into a file named `MemoryErrors.cpp`.

2. Open an Intel Parallel Studio XE command prompt.

3. Build the program with the following command:

WINDOWS

```
icl /Od /Zi MemoryErrors.cpp -D__WINDOWS__ gdi32.lib -o 8-4.exe
```

LINUX

```
icc  -O0 -g MemoryErrors.cpp -o 8-4.exe
```

4. Run the program to make sure it works:

```
8-4.exe
```

Detecting Memory Problems

5. Start the Inspector XE GUI from the command line:

```
inspxe-gui
```

6. Create a new project named `Chapter 8-memory`:

➤ Select File ➪ New ➪ Project.

➤ In the Project Properties dialog, fill in the application details.

7. Carry out a Detect Memory Problems analysis:

➤ Select File ➪ New ➪ Analysis.

➤ Highlight the Detect Memory Problems analysis.

➤ Click the Start button.

The results are shown in Figure 8-12.

8. After the analysis is displayed, look at the problem(s) reported. Make sure you understand the issues.

9. Work through each problem and fix them in the code. As you fix a problem, change its state on the Summary page:

➤ Highlight the problem you have fixed.

➤ Right-click and select Change State from the context menu.

➤ Change the state to Fixed.

10. After fixing all the problems, rebuild the application (see step 3), and run a fresh analysis (see step 7).

CREATING A CUSTOM ANALYSIS

When you select a new analysis for Inspector XE, the Configure Analysis Type window appears. This window enables you to select the analysis type and to configure it to your own requirements. Six analysis types are offered; however, you can also create a customized analysis of your own.

To create a custom analysis type, right-click on the Custom Analysis Type in the Configure Analysis Type window (see Figure 8-18).

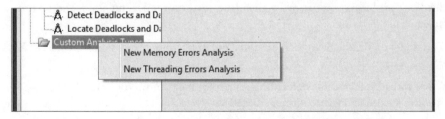

FIGURE 8-18: Creating a custom analysis type

You can select a new Memory Errors analysis or a new Threading Errors analysis, or you can copy the analysis you have currently selected. When creating a new analysis, you can configure a number of options. The following descriptions are taken directly from the tooltips in Inspector XE's Custom Analysis dialog box:

➤ **Memory Errors analysis options**

> ➤ **Detect memory leaks** — Detect problems where a block of memory is allocated but never released. Extremely low cost, especially if used only with "Remove duplicates" selected.

> ➤ **Detect resource leaks** — Detect problems where a kernel object handle is created but never closed, or where a GDI object is created but never deleted. Useful when analyzing Windows GUI applications. Low cost.

> ➤ **Detect invalid/uninitialized accesses** — Detect problems where a read or a write instruction references memory that is logically or physically invalid, or a read instruction accesses an uninitialized memory location. Medium cost.

> ➤ **Analyze stack access** — Analyze invalid and uninitialized accesses to thread stacks. High cost.

> ➤ **Enable enhanced dangling pointer check** — Detect if an application is trying to access memory after it was logically freed. Medium to high cost.

> ➤ **Byte limit before reallocation** — Set the amount of memory Inspector XE defers returning to the pool of available memory.

> ➤ **Enable guard zones** — Show offset information if Inspector XE detects memory use beyond the end of an allocated block. Useful when an application exhibits unexpected behavior or when you need more context about heap allocations to interpret invalid memory access problems. Low cost.

> ➤ **Stack frame depth** — A high setting is useful when analyzing highly object-oriented applications. A higher number does not significantly cost.

> ➤ **Remove duplicates** — When deselected, reports all instances of detected errors on the timeline. Low cost.

➤ **Threading Errors analysis options**

> ➤ **Detect lock hierarchy violations and deadlocks** — Useful when an application has complicated synchronization and it is hard to verify correctness, or when you suspect deadlock problems that are not yet evident. Low cost unless an application has a significant number of locks.

> ➤ **Terminate on deadlock** — Stop analysis and application execution if Inspector XE detects a deadlock. Low cost.

> ➤ **Cross-thread stack access detection** — Set alert mechanism for when a thread accesses stack memory of another thread. Low cost.

> ➤ **Stack frame depth** — A high setting is useful when analyzing highly object-oriented applications. The higher the number, the higher the cost.

> ➤ **Detect data races** — Detect problems where multiple threads access the same memory location without proper synchronization and at least one access is a write. High cost.

> ➤ **Memory access byte granularity** — Set the byte size of the smallest memory block on which Inspector XE should detect data races.

➤ **Detect data races on stack accesses** — Detect data races for variables on the stack.

➤ **Remove duplicates** — When deselected, reports all instances of detected errors on the timeline. Low cost.

➤ **Defer memory check** — Do not allocate shadow memory for given block until second thread access.

➤ **Save stack on first access** — Report as much information as possible on all threads involved in a data race. High cost.

➤ **Save stack on allocation** — Identify the allocation site of dynamically allocated memory objects involved in a data race. Medium cost.

THE SOURCE CODE

Listing 8-4 contains a program with threading errors and is used in Activities 8-1, 8-2, and 8-3. Listing 8-5 contains a program with memory errors and is used in Activity 8-4.

LISTING 8-4: A program with threading errors

```
1: #include <stdio.h>
2: #include <omp.h>
3: static long num_steps = 10000 * 4;
4: double step;
5: double gsum1;
6: double gsum2;
7:
8: void SafeAdd(double sum1, double sum2, omp_lock_t &lock1, omp_lock_t &lock2 )
9: {
10:   // lock gsum1 and update
11:   omp_set_lock( &lock1 );
12:   gsum1 += sum1;
13:   // lock gsum2 and update
14:   omp_set_lock( &lock2 );
15:   gsum2 += sum2;
16:   omp_unset_lock( &lock2 );
17:   omp_unset_lock( &lock1 );
18:}
19:
20:int main()
21:{
22:   int i;
23:   double x1,x2;
24:   omp_lock_t  lock1, lock2;
25:   gsum1=0.0;
26:   gsum2=0.0;
27:
28:   omp_init_lock(&lock1);
29:   omp_init_lock(&lock2);
30:   printf("Calculating Pi ...\n");
31:   step = 1.0/(double) num_steps;
32:   for (i=0;i< num_steps; i+=4)
```

continues

LISTING 8-4 *(continued)*

```
33:  {
34:    double sum1,sum2;
35:    #pragma omp parallel sections
36:    {
37:      #pragma omp section
38:      {
39:        // calculate first bar
40:        x1 = (i+ 0.5)*step;
41:        x1*=x1;
42:        sum1 = 4.0/(1.0+x1);
43:
44:        // calculate second bar
45:        x2 = (i+ 1.5)*step;
46:        x2*=x2;
47:        sum2 = 4.0/(1.0+x2);
48:        SafeAdd(sum1,sum2,lock1,lock2);
49:      }
50:      #pragma omp section
51:      {
52:        // calculate third bar
53:        x1 = (i+ 2.5)*step;
54:        x1*=x1;
55:        sum1 = 4.0/(1.0+x1);
56:
57:        // calculate fourth bar
58:        x2 = (i+ 3.5)*step;
59:        x2*=x2;
60:        sum2 = 4.0/(1.0+x2);
61:        SafeAdd(sum1,sum2,lock2,lock1);
62:      }
63:    }
64:  }
65:
66:  // calc value of pi
67:  double pi = step * (gsum1+gsum2);
68:  printf("pi: %2.21f\n",pi);
69:  omp_destroy_lock( &lock1 );
70:  omp_destroy_lock( &lock2 );
71:}
```

code snippet Chapter8\pi.cpp

LISTING 8-5: A program with memory errors

```
1: #include <stdio.h>
2: #include <stdlib.h>
3: #ifdef __WINDOWS__
4: #include <windows.h>
5: #endif
6: #include <omp.h>
7:
8: #define STORESIZE 1000
```

```
 9: int main( void )
10:{
11:  int i, j;
12:  int * ptr_begin_space;
13:      int * ptr_another_space;
14:      int * ptr = NULL;
15:    #ifdef __WINDOWS__
16:      HGDIOBJ hDefpen;
17:   #endif
18:
19:      printf( "Detecting Memory Errors >\n\n" );
20:      for( i=0; i<1; i++ )
21:      {
22:          #ifdef __WINDOWS__
23:           hDefpen = CreatePen( PS_SOLID, 1, RGB( 255, 255, 255 ) );
24:          #endif
25:
26:          ptr_begin_space = (int *)calloc( STORESIZE, sizeof(int) );
27:          if( ptr_begin_space == NULL )
28:              printf( "Unable to allocate space on iteration %d\n", i );
29:          else
30:          {
31:              for( j=0; j<STORESIZE; j++ )
32:                  *(ptr_begin_space+j) = j;
33:          }
34:
35:          ptr_another_space = (int *)calloc( STORESIZE, sizeof(int) );
36:          if( ptr_begin_space == NULL )
37:              printf( "Unable to allocate space on iteration %d\n", i );
38:          else
39:          {
40:              for( j=0; j<STORESIZE+1; j++ )
41:              {
42:                  ptr_another_space[j] = j;
43:              }
44:          }
45:          free( ptr_another_space );
46:          *ptr_another_space = 7;
47:          free( ptr_another_space );
48:          *ptr = 5;
49:      }
50:      return 0;
51:  }
```

code snippet Chapter8\MemoryErrors.cpp

SUMMARY

Eliminating parallel-type errors such as deadlocks and data races from programs has always been a major problem. As programs become increasingly complex, the ability to find and eliminate such problems becomes more difficult. In addition, you have to overcome all the extra problems that can be created when running parallel concurrent code. The greatest obstacle to solving these problems is finding them in the first place. Many problems can be subtle in their operation, showing up only under ideal circumstances. Software tools that can find all these types of errors become invaluable.

Intel Parallel Inspector XE is a sophisticated and versatile tool capable of finding a wide range of potential problems within both parallel and serial programs. Its flexibility and the presentation of its results make it a powerful tool for developers. This chapter has demonstrated just some of Inspector XE's capabilities. The case studies in Part III will amplify these capabilities even further.

The next chapter shows how to use Amplifier XE to tune the parallelism in your programs.

Tuning Parallel Applications

WHAT'S IN THIS CHAPTER?

➤ Using Amplifier XE to profile a parallel program

➤ The five tuning steps

➤ Using the Intel Software Autotuning Tool

Chapters 6–8 described the first three steps to make your code parallel — analyze, implement, and debug. This chapter discusses the final challenge — tuning your parallel application so that it is load-balanced and runs efficiently.

The chapter begins by describing how to use Amplifier XE to check the concurrency of your parallel program, and then shows how to detect and tune any synchronization problems. The chapter concludes by describing the experimental Intel Software Autotuning Tool (ISAT).

Note that all the screenshots and instructions in this chapter are based on Windows XE; however, you can run the hands-on activities on Linux, as well.

INTRODUCTION

Amplifier XE provides two predefined analysis types to help tune your parallel application:

➤ **Concurrency analysis** — Use this to find out which logical CPUs are being used, to discover where parallelism is incurring synchronization overhead, and to identify potential candidates for further parallelization.

➤ **Locks and Waits analysis** — Use this to identify where your application is waiting on synchronization objects or I/O operations, and to discover how these waits affect your program performance.

In this chapter, you use the Concurrency analysis as the main vehicle for parallel tuning. If your program has a lot of synchronization events, you may find the Locks and Waits analysis useful. Because both of these analysis types run in user mode, you can use them on both Intel and non-Intel processors.

Figure 9-1 shows the different tuning steps carried out in this chapter. You should have already fixed any data races and deadlocks (refer to Chapter 8, "Checking for Errors") before starting to tune your parallel application.

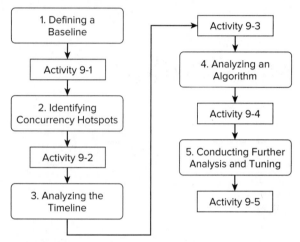

FIGURE 9-1: The five steps for tuning parallel applications

DEFINING A BASELINE

The first step to undertake for any performance tuning is to create a baseline to compare against. Ideally, the baseline test should give the same results each time you run it; otherwise, it would be very difficult to be certain that an improvement in performance is not just due to some random behavior of your program or system.

Ensuring Consistency

If the program you are testing gives wildly different results, try the following:

➤ Turn off Turbo Boost, speed-step, and hyper-threading in the BIOS of your computer (but do *not* turn off multi-core support). These options can cause huge variations from one run to the next of your program. For more discussion on this point, see Chapter 4, "Producing Optimized Code." Once you have finished performance tuning, you should remember to turn these features back on.

➤ If possible, disable any antivirus software. If this is not possible, run your program twice after each rebuild. Often the antivirus software will kick in only on the first run of a program.

➤ Run the program more than once, and take an average result of any timing values.

Measuring the Performance Improvements

When tuning parallel programs you need to keep an eye on two things:

➤   The total time the program runs (assuming time taken is the key performance measure).

➤   Performance improvements of the parallel part of the program within your code.

In the prime numbers example used in this chapter (`ParallelPrime.cpp`, from Listing 9-4 at the end of the chapter), three different timing values are available:

➤   The time it takes to calculate the prime numbers, as printed out in the program.

➤   The elapsed time, as recorded by Amplifier XE.

➤   The time taken to execute the parallel region, as recorded by Amplifier XE.

Most of the time you should concentrate on performance improvements of the parallel region, but remember to keep an eye on the other figures as well.

Measuring the Baseline Using the Amplifier XE Command Line

You can use the command-line version of Amplifier XE to profile your code and produce a report. If you like, you can then look at the results generated from the command line with the GUI version of Amplifier XE.

In Activity 9-1 you build and test a program that calculates prime numbers. The program has been parallelized using the OpenMP method. Once the test program has been built, the following command produces a concurrency report, which in this case is the result of running the application on a 12-core machine. Your report may be different.

```
amplxe-cl -collect concurrency ./9-1.exe
100%
Found    13851 primes in  7.7281 secs
Using result path 'C:\CH9\r000cc'
Executing actions 75 % Generating a report
Summary
-------

Average Concurrency:   0.975
Elapsed Time:          8.028
CPU Time:              55.051
Wait Time:             85.423
Executing actions 100 % done
```

You can see that:

➤   The `Average Concurrency` — the measure of how many threads were running in parallel — is very poor. In fact, the program has effectively been serialized.

➤   The `Elapsed Time` — the total time for the program to run — was just over eight seconds. This includes a slight overhead introduced by the act of profiling.

➤ The program has more Wait Time than CPU Time. Wait Time is the amount of time the threads are waiting for a resource. CPU Time is the sum of the time each core has spent executing code.

You can use the Amplifier XE command-line interface to generate a hotspot report. The example shown in Figure 9-2 generates a hotspot report, with the results grouped by openmp-task. This is a convenient way of seeing how much time the parallel for loop (in lines 51–60 of ParallelPrime .cpp) took.

```
amplxe-cl -report hotspots -group-by openmp-task
Using result path `C:\CH9\r000cc'
Executing actions 75 % Generating a report
OpenMP Regions CPU Time Idle:CPU Time Poor:CPU Time Ok:CPU Time Ideal:CPU Time Over:CPU Time
-------------- -------- ------------- ------------- ---------- -------------- -------------
GetPrimes:51-60  54.901   15.739        39.162        0          0              0
[Outside]         0.150    0             0.150         0          0              0
Executing actions 100 % done
```

FIGURE 9-2: A command line hotspot report

Notice that no results folder is passed to Amplifier XE, which causes Amplifier XE to use the most recently generated results.

From the results, you can see the following:

➤ The parallel region consumes most of the execution time of the program. This is good; it means that any improvement you make in the parallel section of the code will positively impact the performance of the whole program.

➤ The concurrency rate of the parallel region is Poor. A well-tuned parallel program should have a concurrency of at least OK.

➤ For 20 percent of the time, the parallel region is Idle. A well-tuned parallel program ideally should have no Idle time.

ACTIVITY 9-1: DEFINING A BASELINE

In this activity you build the code from Listings 9-4 and 9-5 and use Amplifier XE to look at how parallel the resulting program is. You can run this activity on Linux or Windows.

Building and Running the Program

1. Copy the source code in Listing 9-4 into a file named ParallelPrime.cpp, and the source code in Listing 9-5 into a file named wtime.c.

2. Build the program with the following command:

WINDOWS

```
icl /O2 /Zi /Qopenmp /Ob1 ParallelPrime.cpp wtime.c -o 9-1.exe
```

LINUX

```
icc -O2 -g -openmp -inline-level=1 ParallelPrime.cpp wtime.c -o 9-1.exe
The option /Zi (-inline-level=1)
```

3. Run the program and record the time taken:

```
9-1.exe
```

4. If the program does not run for about two to three seconds, edit the value in the #define LAST statement in ParallelPrime.cpp and rebuild and run the program until it runs for about two seconds.

```
#define LAST 300000
```

Using the Command-Line Version of Amplifier XE to Get a Timestamp

5. Start the command-line version of Amplifier XE, and record the elapsed time and average concurrency:

```
amplxe-cl -collect concurrency ./9-1.exe
```

Make a note of the results directory (for example, r000cc). You will need this for Activity 9-2.

6. Generate a report and record the amount of time that is spent in the OpenMP parallel region:

```
amplxe-cl -report hotspots -group-by openmp-task
```

IDENTIFYING CONCURRENCY HOTSPOTS

Having created a baseline of your parallel application, you can start looking at the performance in more detail by examining how well the program is using the CPU cores. You can try this out for yourself in Activity 9-2.

Thread Concurrency and CPU Usage

Thread concurrency and CPU usage will help you get a good feel for how parallel your program is.

➤ **Thread concurrency** is a measure of how many threads are running in parallel. Ideally, the number of threads running in parallel should be the same as the number of logical cores your processor can support.

➤ **CPU usage** measures how many logical cores are running simultaneously.

Figure 9-3 shows the thread concurrency of the application when it is run on a 12-core Windows-based workstation. As you can see, it runs with a low concurrency, with most of the time no threads running concurrently. The concurrency information is split into four regions — Poor, OK, Ideal, and Over — and are colored red, orange, green, and blue, respectively (albeit not shown in the figure).

You can change the crossover point between each region by highlighting and dragging the triangular shaped cursors that are positioned just below the horizontal bar.

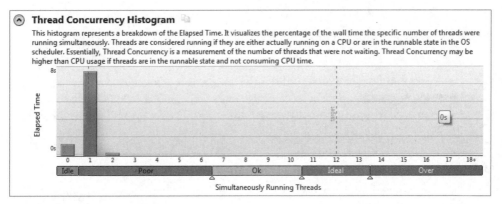

FIGURE 9-3: Concurrency of the Windows application

Figure 9-4 shows the CPU usage of the baseline program on Windows. It shows the length of time when various numbers of CPUs were running concurrently. For example, for almost a second no CPUs were running, and for approximately 1.3 seconds two CPUs were running concurrently. Ideally, there would be a single entry showing 12 CPUs running all the time. In this case you can see that not all the CPUs were in use all the time. The dotted vertical line indicates that the average concurrent CPU usage is almost 7.

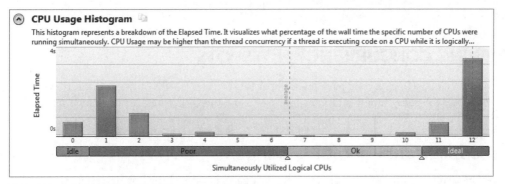

FIGURE 9-4: CPU usage of the Windows application

Identifying Hotspots in the Code

The Bottom-up view of the analysis shows the main hotspots in the system (see Figure 9-5).

The largest hotspot is the `PrintProgress` function, with most of the bar colored red. When you tune any parallel code, your goal is to get the colored bar to be green, indicating that the concurrency is ideal.

Double-clicking the hotspot brings up the Source view of the hotspot (see Figure 9-6).

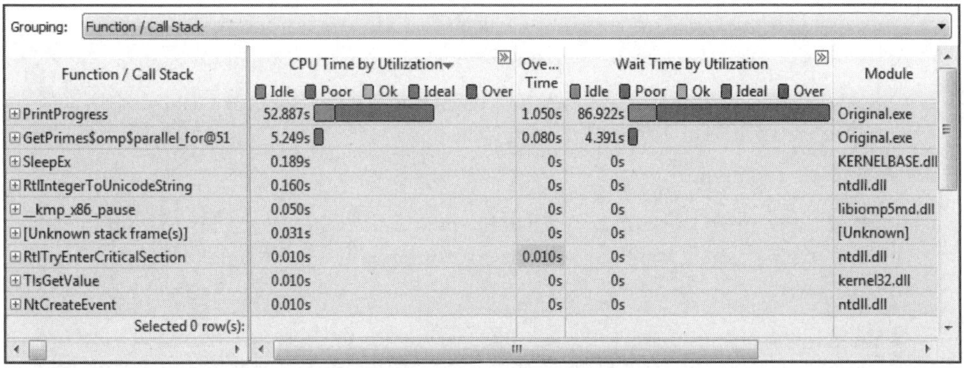

FIGURE 9-5: Source code view of CPU usage

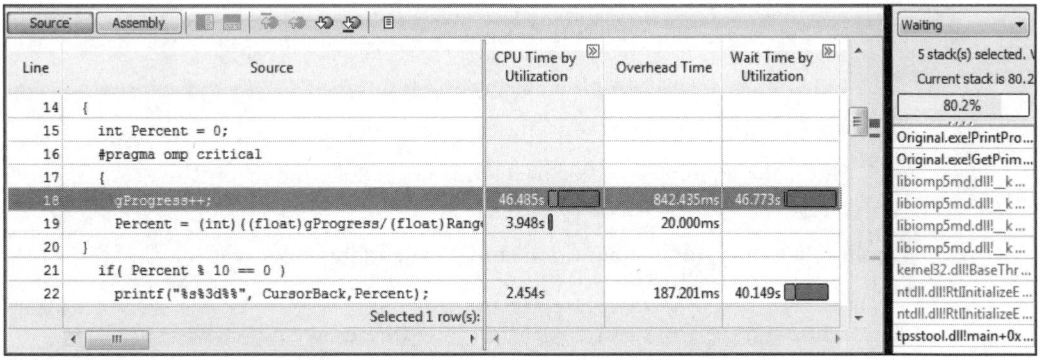

FIGURE 9-6: The biggest hotspot in the code

Notice the following:

➤ The `PrintProgress` function has three hotspots, at lines 18, 19, and 22. Line 18 is the biggest hotspot, with a CPU Time of just over 46 seconds.

➤ Lines 18 and 22 have significant amounts of Wait Time by Utilization. This is discussed more in the section "Analyzing the Timeline."

➤ The stack pane (on the right) reports five stacks, and that the current stack contributes to 80.2% of the hotspot. If you toggle through the five stacks, by clicking the arrow (next to "1 of 5"), the other stacks are reported as contributing 10.1%, 7.6%, 2.0%, and 0.1%. In this program, the call stack information is not needed for tuning purposes, but you may find it useful when you analyze other programs.

ACTIVITY 9-2: IDENTIFYING THE CONCURRENCY HOTSPOTS

In this activity you use the GUI version of Amplifier XE to examine the results from Activity 9-1. You can run this activity on Linux or Windows.

1. Open the GUI version of Amplifier XE, using the results directory that you noted in step 5 of Activity 9-1:

```
amplxe-gui r000cc
```

2. Look at the Thread Concurrency Histogram and the CPU Usage Histogram in the Summary page. (This page will have automatically been displayed in step 1 of this activity.)

3. Display the Bottom-up page by clicking the Bottom-up button, and make note of the biggest hotspot. You will see that most of the time, the hotspot is identified as being Poor. (The horizontal bar will be red.)

4. Look at the timeline view. Notice that there are many transition lines.

➤ Highlight a small part of the timeline.

➤ Right-click and select Zoom in on Selection.

➤ Repeat these steps until you can see about a dozen or so transitions.

➤ Hover the mouse over some of the transition lines and identify which type of transition is occurring.

5. Double-click the main hotspot (in the top pane), and find out which line of code is responsible for the hotspot.

6. Toggle through the different stacks by clicking the arrow and see what percentage the other stacks contribute to the hotspot.

ANALYZING THE TIMELINE

You can use the timeline of an analysis to better understand how your program is behaving. Figure 9-7 shows the timeline of the baseline application. You can glean further information about the program from four distinct areas of the display:

➤ In the *list of threads* (the left-hand side) are twelve OpenMP worker threads plus one master thread. Not all the worker threads are displayed, but you can see them by either scrolling down or resizing the timeline pane.

➤ Each horizontal bar gives more information about the *runtime behavior of each thread*. You can see when a thread is running or waiting. A running thread is colored dark green, and a waiting thread is colored light green. You can also see the transitions between threads. There are so many transitions that the whole of the timeline appears as a solid block of yellow. You can always turn the transitions off by unchecking its box on the right.

➤ The *CPU Usage* chart shows that most of the CPUs are used all the time, but nine rather interesting dips where the CPU usage drops dramatically.

➤ The *Thread Concurrency bar* is empty (that is, no concurrency). It seems that for most of the time, the program is running serially — a fact you already know from the summary analysis.

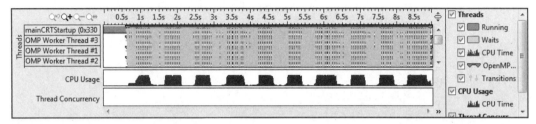

FIGURE 9-7: The application timeline

Questions to Answer

From the information in the timeline, you need to answer three questions:

➤ Why are there so many transition lines?

➤ Why is the concurrency so poor?

➤ What is the cause of the dips in the CPU usage?

The last question is answered in the section, "Analyzing an Algorithm."

When you analyze your own programs, you may see other patterns that need more exploration. The important thing is that you make sure you understand all the patterns you see.

The poor concurrency and the reason for the many transition lines can be deduced from a zoomed-in view of the timeline (see Figure 9-8). There is only ever one thread running at any time; the other threads are waiting. Between each thread is a transition line. If you hover your mouse over a transition line, details about that transition are displayed (as in the figure), which show that a critical section is involved.

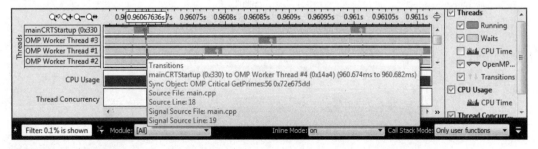

FIGURE 9-8: Zooming in on the transitions

Fixing the Critical Section Hotspot

If you double-click the transition line, the source code of the object is displayed (the same source code that you have already seen in Figure 9-6).

The `#pragma omp critical` construct is used to protect the reading and writing of the `gProgress` shared variable that is being incremented. Without the critical section, there would be a data race. A variable can be incremented much more efficiently by using an atomic operation.

The following code shows how you can use the `#pragma omp atomic` construct to protect the incrementing of `gProgress`. The reading of `gProgress` at line 19 does not need protecting, because a data race occurs only when there are unsynchronized reads *and* writes. Reading shared variables will not cause data races.

```
// old code
16:  #pragma omp critical
17:  {
18:     gProgress++;
19:     Percent = (int)((float)gProgress/(float)Range *200.0f + 0.5f);
20:  }

// new code
16:  #pragma omp atomic
17:  gProgress++;
18:
19:  Percent = (int)((float)gProgress/(float)Range *200.0f + 0.5f);
20:
```

With the fix in place, running a new analysis shows an improvement, as shown in Table 9-1. The program now has a much shorter elapsed time, and the CPU time used in the parallel part of the code has reduced by a factor of almost eight. You can try out Activity 9-3 to see these results for yourself. Often solving simple problems involving just a few of the many lines of program's code can result in large improvements in its operation.

TABLE 9-1: The Results of Replacing the Critical Section with an Atomic Operation

METRIC	ORIGINAL	WITH ATOMIC
Average Concurrency	0.975	0.715
Elapsed Time	8.028	2.777
CPU Time	55.051	7.441
Wait Time	85.423	28.418
Parallel Region CPU Time	54.901	7.090
Parallel Region Idle Time	15.739	3.432

ACTIVITY 9-3: ANALYZING THE TIMELINE

In this activity you use the GUI version of Amplifier XE to examine the timeline from Activity 9-1, and fix a synchronization problem identified. You can run this activity on Linux or Windows.

1. If the GUI version of Amplifier XE is not already open, open it using the results directory that you noted in step 5 of Activity 9-1:

```
amplxe-gui r000cc
```

2. Display the Bottom-up page by clicking the Bottom-up button.

3. In the timeline pane, keep expanding the view until you can clearly see the individual transition lines. You should see that only one thread is ever running at any one time.

4. Hover your mouse over a transition line and read the information displayed.

5. Double-click the transition line, which should take you to the source lines.

6. In `ParallelPrime.cpp`, edit lines 16 to 20 so that they look the same as the following:

```
16:  #pragma omp atomic
17:  gProgress++;
18:
19:  Percent = (int)((float)gProgress/(float)Range *200.0f + 0.5f);
20:
```

7. Rebuild and run the modified program (see steps 2–6 of Activity 9-1). Record the name of the results directory; you will need it in Activity 9-4.

8. Compare the results from Activity 9-1 with your new results. Your results should be similar to Table 9-1.

In the next step, you explore the dips in the CPU usage, which look like they might be caused by a flaw in the algorithm of the program.

ANALYZING AN ALGORITHM

In Figure 9-7 you saw nine distinct dips in the CPU usage. Once you have fixed the data race by adding the `#pragma omp atomic`, the dips are less pronounced but are still clearly visible (see Figure 9-9).

To see what is causing the dips, zoom in and filter on the timeline (see Figure 9-10). Notice that the call stack mode on the bottom right has been set to user + 1 so that the function calling the hotspot is also displayed. You can see that the hotspot is the `printf` function, which has a high Wait Time by Utilization. Notice that all the threads are mostly light green, indicating that they are in a waiting state, with just `OMP Worker Thread #4` showing some activity in the middle of the timeline.

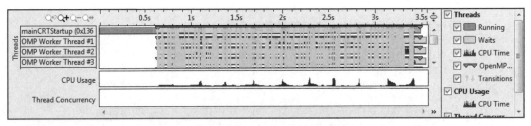

FIGURE 9-9: The timeline after the atomic operation has been introduced

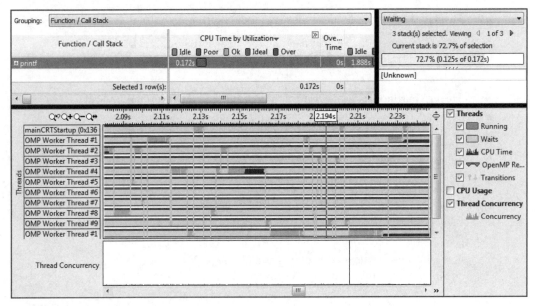

FIGURE 9-10: Examining the CPU usage dips

Looking at the code that calls `printf` in the function `PrintProgress`, you can see that whenever the percent value is a multiple of 10, `printf` is called:

```
21:    if( Percent % 10 == 0 )
22:       printf("%s%3d%%", CursorBack,Percent);
```

The intention is to display the progress on the screen after each 10 percent increment of work.

Looking at the length of the timeline, you can see that it has a length of approximately 0.13 seconds — an awfully long time to do one `printf`! You should suspect that something is wrong with this code and is causing the nine dips in CPU usage.

When you find a section of code that may be causing a problem, one quick test you can try is to comment out the code and see what difference it makes. Figure 9-11 shows the timeline of the application with lines 21 and 22 commented out. You can see that the dips in CPU usage have disappeared, confirming that lines 21 and 22 were the cause.

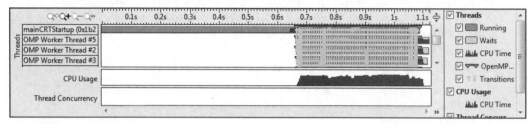

FIGURE 9-11: The application timeline with the printf removed

Amplifier XE will not tell you how to fix problems with your program algorithms, but it will let you observe any odd behavior.

In lines 21 and 22, the problem is caused because the `printf` is not only called when you first reach a percent value that is divisible by ten, but that it is then repeatedly called until `Percent % 10 == 0` evaluates to false.

By modifying the code to look like Listing 9-1 (as you'll do in Activity 9-4), `printf` should be called only once on each 10 percent increment; the changes to the code are highlighted:

LISTING 9-1: The modified PrintProgress function

```
12:  // Display progress
13:  void PrintProgress(int Range )
14:  {
15:    int Percent = 0;
16:    static int lastPercentile = 0;
17:    #pragma omp atomic
18:    gProgress++;
19:    Percent = (int)((float)gProgress/(float)Range *200.0f + 0.5f);
20:    if( Percent % 10 == 0 )
21:    {
22:      // we should only call this if the value is new!
23:      if(lastPercentile < Percent / 10)
24:      {
25:        printf("%s%3d%%", CursorBack,Percent);
26:        lastPercentile++;
27:      }
28:    }
29:  }
```

code snippet Chapter9\9-1.cpp

ACTIVITY 9-4: ANALYZING AN ALGORITHM

In this activity you use the GUI version of Amplifier XE to examine the timeline from Activity 9-1, and fix a synchronization problem identified. You can run this activity on Linux or Windows.

Examining the CPU Utilization Dip

1. Open the GUI version of Amplifier XE, using the results directory that you noted in step 8 of Activity 9-3. (You should replace r000cc with your results directory name.)

```
amplxe-gui r000cc
```

2. Display the Bottom-up page by clicking the Bottom-up button.

3. In the Timeline pane:

➤ Select one of the dips in the CPU utilization.

➤ Right-click and select Zoom in and Filter by Selection.

➤ Change the call stack mode (see bottom right of screen) to user "functions + 1."

You should find that the function involved in the selected timeline is printf, with most threads in a waiting state.

4. (Optional) If you like, prove that the printf function is the problem by commenting out lines 21 and 22 of ParallelPrime.cpp, and then rebuild and rerun the analysis.

Correcting the Problem

5. In ParallelPrime.cpp edit the PrintProgress function so that it looks the same as Listing 9-1.

6. Rebuild and run the modified program (see steps 2–6 of Activity 9-1).

7. Open the GUI version of Amplifier XE, using the results directory that you noted in step 6. (You should replace r000cc with your results directory name.)

```
amplxe-gui r000cc
```

8. Display the Bottom-up page by clicking the Bottom-up button. Look at the timeline. The dips in the CPU usage should have disappeared.

CONDUCTING FURTHER ANALYSIS AND TUNING

You've already carried out some analysis of the code and fixed two programming problems. With the two problems in PrintProgress fixed, a new Concurrency analysis will reveal a different part of the code GetPrimesompparallel_for@57 as the biggest concurrency hotspot (see Figure 9-12).

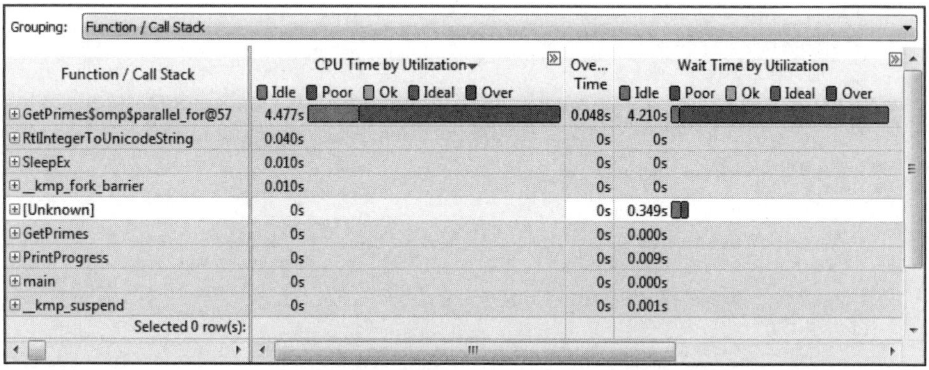

FIGURE 9-12: The new concurrency hotspot

Double-clicking the hotspot `GetPrimes$omp$parallel_for@57` in the Bottom-up page reveals that the hotspot is in a critical section in the function `GetPrimes`, as shown in Figure 9-13. Notice that the line numbers in the figure no longer match those of Listing 9-4 due to the changes made in previous sections. The `GetPrimes` function increments through every even number between a `Start` value and an `End` value, and tests to see if each number is a prime number by calling the `IsPrime` function.

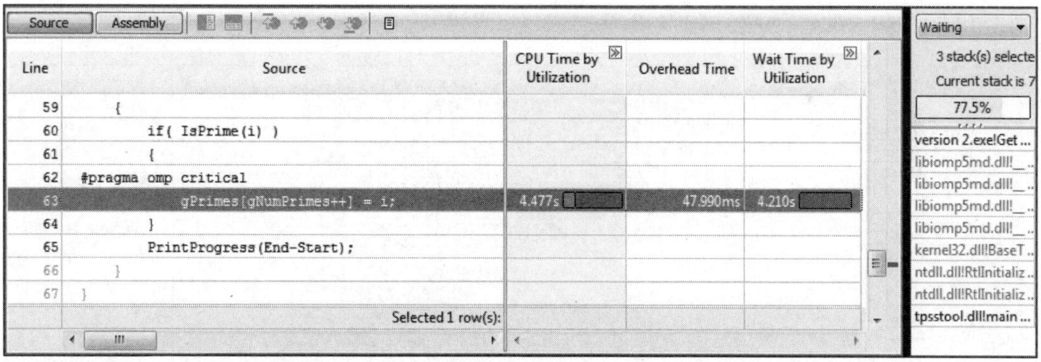

FIGURE 9-13: Source code of the new concurrency hotspot

The critical section is applied to line 57, where the global variable `gNumPrimes` is incremented, and then used as an index so that the current prime (held in the variable `i`) can be stored into the global array `gPrimes`.

By now you should know what you can do to fix this — use an atomic instruction instead of the `#pragma omp critical`. By splitting the line into two lines, you can apply a `#pragma omp critical` to the incrementing of `gNumPrimes`:

```
// old code
56:        #pragma omp critical
57:        gPrimes[gNumPrimes++] = i;

// new code
56:        #pragma omp atomic
```

```
57:          gNumPrimes++;
58:          gPrimes[gNumPrimes] = i;
```

After you implement this code, a new analysis shows a further improvement in performance. Table 9-2 shows the performance improvement of the parallel region over the last three code changes that have been made.

TABLE 9-2: Performance Improvements

VERSION	TIME IN PARALLEL REGION (SECONDS)	COMMENTS
Original	8.308	
#1	2.847	Replaced `critical` with `atomic` in `PrintProgress`
#2	0.403	Rewrote `PrintProgress`
#3	0.015	Replaced `critical` with `atomic` in `GetPrimes`

Figure 9-14 shows the timeline of the parallel region. The darker part of the horizontal bars represents the time that the threads are running. Each of the start and end points of the thread are staggered; when you see such a pattern, it probably means there is scope for further tuning.

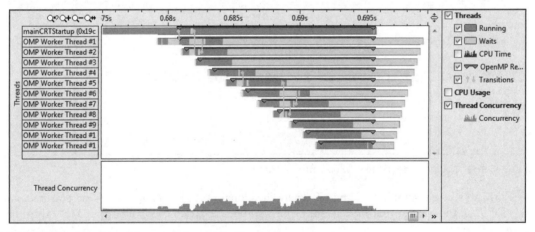

FIGURE 9-14: Timeline of the parallel region before tuning

You can use a `schedule` clause with the `#pragma parallel for` to try to improve the load balancing. (The `schedule` clause was discussed in Chapter 7, "Implementing Parallelism.")

Most developers experiment with the different `schedule` clauses, keeping the one that produces the best results. Listing 9-2 shows a new listing of the `GetPrimes` function with the previous changes and the `schedule` clause added. The ISAT tool was used to find the best combination of schedule type and chunk size. You'll read more about ISAT later in this chapter.

LISTING 9-2: The GetPrimes function with the schedule clause

```cpp
void GetPrimes(int Start, int End)
{
    // Make Start to always be an even number
    Start += Start %2;

    // If Start is 2 or less, then just record it
    if(Start<=2) gPrimes[gNumPrimes++]=2;

    #pragma omp parallel for schedule(guided,512) num_threads(12)
    for( int i = Start; i <= End; i += 2 )
    {
        if( IsPrime(i) )
        {
            #pragma omp atomic
            gNumPrimes++;
            gPrimes[gNumPrimes] = i;
        }
        PrintProgress(End-Start);
    }
}
```

code snippet Chapter9\9-2.cpp

Figure 9-15 shows the results of the schedule clause. Note the following:

➤ All the threads stop running at about the same time.

➤ The length of the parallel region is now shorter (0.010 seconds compared with 0.015 seconds).

➤ The start of the threads is still staggered. Between each thread starting there is about a 1ms delay (0.001 seconds). This is probably a feature of the OpenMP run time that cannot be changed.

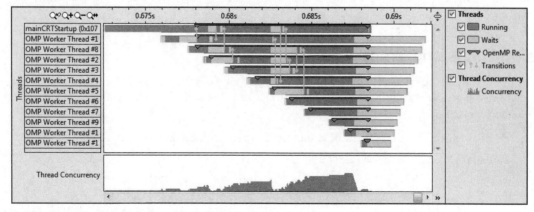

FIGURE 9-15: Timeline of the parallel region after tuning

Using Other Viewpoints

The only analysis type you have used so far is the Concurrency analysis. Within this analysis you can change the viewpoint to see the information captured with differing emphasis.

Figure 9-16 shows the viewpoints available:

➤ Hotspots

➤ Hotspots by CPU Usage

➤ Hotspots by Threading Concurrency

➤ Locks and Waits

You can access this menu by clicking on the spanner icon. In your version of Amplifier XE, additional viewpoints may be available.

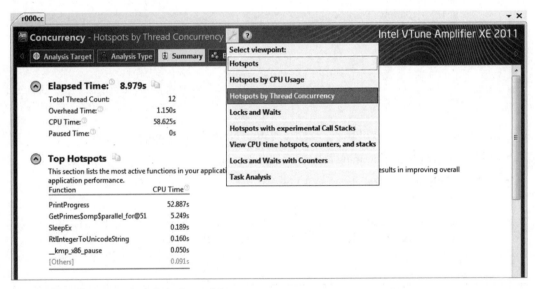

FIGURE 9-16: The menu to switch viewpoints

Using Locks and Waits Analysis

In addition to changing viewpoints, you can use other analysis types. Using the Locks and Waits analysis will give you slightly more information than a locks and waits viewpoint available from the Concurrency analysis.

Here's an example of running the Locks and Waits analysis from the command line:

```
amplxe-cl -collect locksandwaits ./9-1.exe
100%
```

```
Found      13851 primes in  7.6617 secs
Using result path `C:\dv\CH9\Release\r001lw'
Executing actions  0 % Finalizing results
Executing actions 75 % Generating a report
Summary
-------

Average Concurrency:  0.912
Elapsed Time:         7.940
CPU Time:             53.586
Wait Time:            85.153
Executing actions 100 % done
```

Once you have run the Locks and Waits analysis, you can view the results using the GUI version of Amplifier XE:

```
amplxe-gui r001lw
```

Figure 9-17 shows the analysis of the application in Listing 9-4 (without all the corrections you made earlier) using the Locks and Waits analysis. One of the differences between this analysis and a Concurrency analysis is that the hotspots are presented using synchronization objects. The first two synchronization objects listed are both critical sections. Notice that the Spin Times of the first four objects are shaded. A *spinning thread* is one that is executing code in a tight loop, waiting for some resource to become available. While the thread is spinning it is consuming CPU time, but it is not doing any useful work. Amplifier XE shades the values to warn you that the values are unacceptably high.

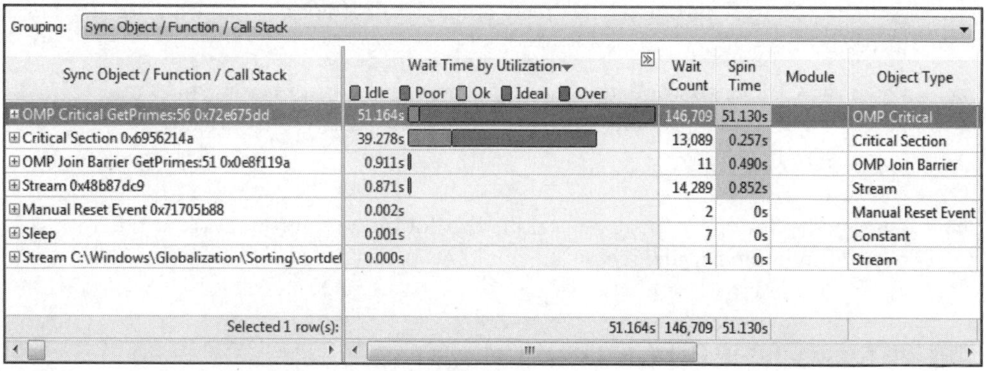

Grouping:	Sync Object / Function / Call Stack							▼
Sync Object / Function / Call Stack	Wait Time by Utilization▾ ▣ Idle ▣ Poor ▣ Ok ▣ Ideal ▣ Over		Wait Count	Spin Time	Module	Object Type
⊞ OMP Critical GetPrimes:56 0x72e675dd	51.164s		146,709	51.130s		OMP Critical
⊞ Critical Section 0x6956214a	39.278s		13,089	0.257s		Critical Section
⊞ OMP Join Barrier GetPrimes:51 0x0e8f119a	0.911s		11	0.490s		OMP Join Barrier
⊞ Stream 0x48b87dc9	0.871s		14,289	0.852s		Stream
⊞ Manual Reset Event 0x71705b88	0.002s		2	0s		Manual Reset Event
⊞ Sleep	0.001s		7	0s		Constant
⊞ Stream C:\Windows\Globalization\Sorting\sortde		0.000s		1	0s		Stream
Selected 1 row(s):			51.164s	146,709	51.130s		

FIGURE 9-17: The hotspots of a Locks and Waits analysis

Other Analysis Types

You can also use other analysis types to help tune your application. Apart from the user analysis types mentioned in this chapter, you can also use Hotspot analysis (described in Chapter 6, "Where to Parallelize") and event-based sampling (described in Chapter 12, "Event-Based Analysis with VTune Amplifier XE").

ACTIVITY 9-5: FURTHER ANALYSIS AND TUNING

In this activity you fix a synchronization overhead in the code, and then tune the OpenMP parallel loop.

Analyzing the New Hotspot

1. Using the Amplifier XE Concurrency analysis that you already have open (from Activity 9-4), click the Bottom-up button and examine the hotspots.

2. Double-click the biggest hotspot and confirm that it is in the GetPrimes function.

3. In ParallelPrime.cpp, edit the GetPrimes function so that it looks like this. (Your line numbers may be different.)

```
// old code
56:        #pragma omp critical
57:        gPrimes[gNumPrimes++] = i;

// new code
56:        #pragma omp atomic
57:        gNumPrimes++;
58:        gPrimes[gNumPrimes] = i;
```

4. Rebuild and run the modified program (see steps 2–6 of Activity 9-1). Amplifier XE will automatically create a new results folder — make a note of its name.

5. Open the GUI version of Amplifier XE, using the results directory that you noted in step 4. (You should replace r000cc with your results directory name.)

```
amplxe-gui r001cc
```

6. Display the Bottom-up page by clicking the Bottom-up button. Look at the time taken in the parallel region. It should be about 20 times shorter than the results from Activity 9-4.

Tuning the OpenMP Parallel Loop

7. Expand the timeline so just the parallel region is displayed. Notice that the start and end positions of the threads are staggered.

8. In ParallelPrime.cpp, edit the GetPrimes function to add the schedule clause to the #pragma omp parallel for loop (so that it looks the same as Listing 9-2).

9. Rebuild and run the modified program. (See steps 2–6 of Activity 9-1.)

10. Open the GUI version of Amplifier XE, using the results directory that you noted in step 9. (You should replace r000cc with your results directory name.)

```
amplxe-gui r002cc
```

11. Display the Bottom-up page by clicking the Bottom-up button. Expand the timeline so just the parallel region is displayed. You should notice the following:

➤ The running threads finish at about the same time.

➤ The execution time of the parallel section is shorter than you saw in step 7.

USING THE INTEL SOFTWARE AUTOTUNING TOOL

The Intel Software Autotuning Tool (ISAT) is an experimental tool that you can use to automatically tune Cilk, OpenMP, and TBB parallel code. You can download the tool from `http://software.intel.com/en-us/articles/intel-software-autotuning-tool`. At the time of this writing, ISAT is available only for use in a Linux environment, although it may eventually be available for Windows as well.

ISAT works by automatically searching for the optimal values of program parameters that have a significant impact on parallel performance. Parameters include scheduling policy and granularity within the OpenMP method, task granularity within the TBB method, and cache blocking factors in matrix-intensive applications.

You control which code should be tuned by inserting directives in the form of pragmas within your existing code.

ISAT produces two outputs:

➤ Source code with the best scheduling parameters automatically added

➤ A graph of all the results (see Figure 9-18)

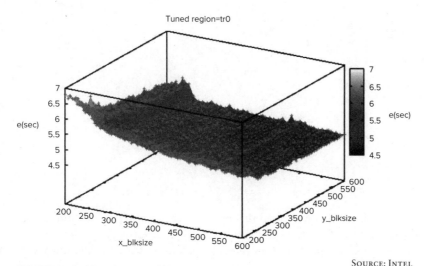

FIGURE 9-18: Visualization of ISAT results

Listing 9-3 shows the ISAT profiling pragmas added to the `ParallelPrime.cpp` code. The first pragma, `#pragma isat tuning scope...`, tells ISAT the names of the start and end of the code to be tuned (`M_begin` and `M_end`, respectively). The three variables in the pragma set the range of values to use for the schedule type, chunk size, and number of threads. For more information, refer to the help that is distributed with ISAT.

LISTING 9-3: The code with **ISAT** macros added

```
// NOTE: this pragma is written on ONE line
#pragma isat tuning scope(M_begin, M_end) measure(M_begin, M_end)
variable(@omp_schedule_type, [static,dynamic,guided])
variable(@omp_schedule_chunk, range(5, 10, 1, pow2))
variable(@omp_num_threads, range(1, $NUM_CPU_THREADS, 1)) search(dependent)

// go through all numbers in range and see which are primes
void GetPrimes(int Start, int End)
{
  // Make Start to always be an even number
  Start += Start %2;

  int Range = End - Start;
  // if start is 2 or less, then just record it
  if(Start<=2) gPrimes[gNumPrimes++]=2;

  #pragma isat marker M_begin
  #pragma omp parallel for
  for( int i = Start; i <= End; i += 2 )
  {
    if( IsPrime(i) )
    {
      #pragma omp atomic
      gNumPrimes++;

      gPrimes[gNumPrimes] = i;
    }
    PrintProgress(Range);
  }
  #pragma isat marker M_end
}
```

code snippet Chapter9\9-3.cpp

SOURCE CODE

Listing 9-4 is a badly tuned implementation of a parallel program that calculates the number of primes between two values, FIRST and LAST. As the values are calculated, the program prints a status message. The message is updated in 10 percent intervals. Listing 9-5 is a timing utility used to measure how long the program takes.

LISTING 9-4: A parallel program to calculate prime numbers

```c
1:  #include <stdio.h>
2:  #include <math.h>
3:  extern "C" double wtime();
4:  #define FIRST 1
5:  #define LAST 300000
6:  #define CursorBack "\b\b\b\b"
7:  // globals
8:  int gProgress  = 0;
9:  int gNumPrimes = 0;
10: int gPrimes[10000000];
11:
12:  // Display progress
13: void PrintProgress(int Range )
14: {
15:   int Percent = 0;
16:   #pragma omp critical
17:   {
18:     gProgress++;
19:     Percent = (int)((float)gProgress/(float)Range *200.0f + 0.5f);
20:   }
21:   if( Percent % 10 == 0 )
22:     printf("%s%3d%%", CursorBack,Percent);
23: }
24:
25: // Test to see if a number is a prime
26: bool IsPrime(int CurrentValue)
27: {
28:   int Limit, Factor = 3;
29:
30:   if( CurrentValue == 1 )
31:     return false;
32:   else if( CurrentValue == 2 )
33:     return true;
34:
35:   Limit = (long)(sqrtf((float)CurrentValue)+0.5f);
36:   while( (Factor <= Limit) && (CurrentValue % Factor))
37:     Factor ++;
38:
39:   return (Factor > Limit);
40: }
41:
42: // Go through all numbers in range and see which are primes
43: void GetPrimes(int Start, int End)
44: {
45:   // Make Start to always be an even number
46:   Start += Start %2;
47:
48:   // If start is 2 or less, then just record it
49:   if(Start<=2) gPrimes[gNumPrimes++]=2;
50:
```

continues

LISTING 9-4 *(continued)*

```
51:    #pragma omp parallel for
52:    for( int i = Start; i <= End; i += 2 )
53:    {
54:      if( IsPrime(i) )
55:      {
56:        #pragma omp critical
57:        gPrimes[gNumPrimes++] = i;
58:      }
59:      PrintProgress(End-Start);
60:    }
61: }
62:
63: int main()
64: {
65:    double StartTime = wtime();
66:    GetPrimes(FIRST, LAST);
67:    double EndTime = wtime();
68:
69:    printf("\nFound  %8d primes in %7.4lf secs\n",
70:        gNumPrimes,EndTime - StartTime);
71: }
```

code snippet Chapter9\ParallelPrime.cpp

LISTING 9-5: A function to find the current time

```
#ifdef _WIN32
#include <windows.h>
double wtime()
{
  LARGE_INTEGER ticks;
  LARGE_INTEGER frequency;
  QueryPerformanceCounter(&ticks);
  QueryPerformanceFrequency(&frequency);
  return (double)(ticks.QuadPart/(double)frequency.QuadPart);
}
#else
#include <sys/time.h>
#include <sys/resource.h>
double wtime()
{
  struct timeval time;
  struct timezone zone;
  gettimeofday(&time, &zone);
  return time.tv_sec + time.tv_usec*1e-6;
}
#endif
```

code snippet Chapter9\wtime.c

SUMMARY

This chapter showed how you can use Amplifier XE to help tune a parallel program. Using Amplifier XE's predefined analysis types, you can quickly find out how much concurrency your program exhibits and observe how well any synchronization objects are performing.

The examples in the chapter used OpenMP, but you can use Amplifier XE to profile Cilk Plus, TBB, and native threading code as well.

The next chapter shows how to model parallelism in your code using Intel Parallel Advisor.

10

Parallel Advisor–Driven Design

WHAT'S IN THIS CHAPTER?

➤ Using Parallel Advisor

➤ Surveying the application

➤ Adding annotations

➤ Assessing suitability

➤ Checking for correctness

➤ Moving from annotations to parallel implementations

This chapter introduces a parallel development cycle that uses Intel Parallel Advisor. Advisor helps programmers become more productive, because it reveals the potential costs and benefits of parallelism by modeling (simulating) this behavior before programmers actually implement the parallelism in their code.

USING PARALLEL ADVISOR

The problem that Advisor helps you solve is to parallelize existing C/C++ programs to obtain parallel speedup. Advisor's value is increased productivity; it enables you to quickly and easily experiment with where to add parallelism so that the resulting program is both correct and demonstrates effective performance improvement. The experiments are performed by modeling the effect of the parallelism, without adding actual parallel constructs.

Advisor is a time-tested methodology for successfully parallelizing code, along with a set of tools to provide information about the program. Advisor has several related personas:

➤ A design tool that assists you in making good decisions to transform a serial algorithm to use multi-core hardware

➤ A parallel modeling tool that uses Advisor annotations in the serial code to calculate what might happen if that code were to execute in parallel as specified by the annotations inserted by the user

➤ A methodology and workflow to educate users on an effective method of using parallel programming

The objective of parallelization is to find the parallel program lurking within your serial program. The parallelism may be hiding due to the serial program being over-constrained — for example, having read-write global variables that cause no problems for serial code but inhibit parallelism.

Advisor is not an automatic parallelization tool. It is aimed at code that is larger and messier than simple loop nests. Instead, it guides you through the set of decisions you must make, and provides data about your program at each step. In summary, Advisor provides a lightweight methodology that allows you to easily experiment with parallelism in different places.

Your parallel experiments with Advisor may all fail, which can be a blessing in disguise — you can avoid wasting time trying to parallelize an inherently serial algorithm. You may need to investigate alternative algorithms that can be parallelized, or just leave your program serial and investigate serial optimizations.

Who can use Advisor?

➤ **Architects** — To design where introducing parallelism will provide the best return on investment (ROI): improved performance for a reasonable development cost.

➤ **Developers** — To discover opportunities for parallelization and modify the program to make it parallel-ready. A program is parallel-ready when there is a predicted parallel speedup and no predicted data-sharing (correctness) issues exist.

The key technology in Advisor is the use of *parallel modeling of the serial program*. You don't actually add parallelism to your code — you just indicate where you want to add it and the Advisor tools model how that parallel code would behave. This is a huge advantage over having to immediately add parallel constructs. Your still-serial program doesn't crash or produce incorrect results because of incorrect and likely nondeterministic parallel execution (such as unprotected data sharing among tasks). Test suites generate identical results, because your serial program will not show the nondeterminism caused by parts of the program running in different orders due to parallelism. This also enables you to refactor your program to remove data-sharing errors and make it parallel-ready, while it is still serial.

Advisor does have some disadvantages, compared with plunging ahead and immediately adding parallel constructs:

➤ You have to add annotations to describe where you want to experiment with parallelism. Later, you convert them to parallel constructs.

➤ Analyzing (modeling) the correctness of the pretend tasks' use of shared memory can be significantly slower than the program's normal execution time. Not only do you use a Debug build, but the Correctness tool also must instrument and track every load and store as the program runs to detect these kinds of errors. But it has the advantage of relatively quickly finding problems that are otherwise difficult to uncover using traditional debugging techniques.

➤ The tools analyze your running program, so they tell you only about parts of the program that are actually executed. However, you would encounter this same limitation by attempting to introduce parallelism immediately.

Understanding the Advisor Workflow

Intel Parallel Advisor guides you through a series of steps (see Figure 10-1). In practice, programmers usually move back and forth between some of the steps until they achieve good results.

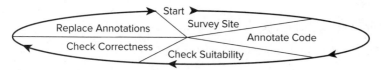

FIGURE 10-1: The five-step Advisor workflow

The Advisor Workflow tab guides you through these steps, highlighting the current step in blue (see Figure 10-2). The Start buttons are used to launch each analysis, and the Update buttons are used to re-run an analysis tool. You can view the results by pressing the blue right arrow button.

The following five basic steps help you find hidden parallel programs:

1. Use the Survey tool to determine where your program spends most of its time.

2. Insert *Advisor annotations* into your source code, which indicate to the Advisor tools where you might like to use parallelism.

3. Use the Suitability tool to determine whether these locations will provide suitable parallel speedups.

4. Use the Correctness tool to discover which data dependencies and shared data problems will occur with this parallelism, and then fix them. Can you correctly tease a parallel program out of the serial one? If you modify the annotations or source code, you need to run the Suitability and Correctness tools again.

5. Convert your serial program to a parallel program by replacing annotations with parallel constructs.

Now that you have a parallel program, you can apply the rest of Parallel Studio.

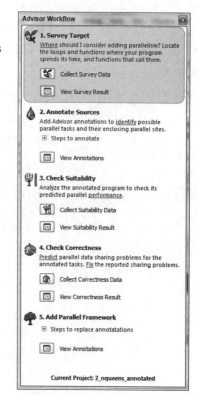

FIGURE 10-2: The Advisor Workflow tab

You can follow several strategies for investigating multiple parallel region (site) opportunities:

➤ **Depth-first** — Take a region through all steps before picking another region; you can focus on the behavior of one region of code.

➤ **Breadth-first** — Take all regions through the steps together; you can focus on the purpose and information provided by each tool.

➤ **Modified depth-first** — Take each region through the final correctness checking step, and then convert all regions to parallel constructs together; your program remains serial for as long as possible, preserving the benefit of identical test suite results.

Finding Documentation

Advisor provides copious documentation, which you can access in one of the following ways:

➤ Help ⇨ Intel Parallel Studio 2011 ⇨ Parallel Studio Help ⇨ Advisor Help

➤ Help ⇨ Intel Parallel Studio 2011 ⇨ Getting Started ⇨ Advisor Tutorial

➤ The Workflow tab and its hot links into Advisor help

➤ Visual Studio context-sensitive F1 help

➤ Right click in any Advisor report, and choose "What should I do next?"

Getting Started with the NQueens Example Program

This chapter uses the NQueens example program that ships with Advisor to demonstrate how Advisor works. Listing 10-1 shows the two functions, setQueen() and solve(), that are the focus of the analysis.

LISTING 10-1: The setQueen() and solve() functions

```
void setQueen(int queens[], int row, int col)
{
    int i = 0;
    for (i=0; i<row; i++) {
        // vertical attacks
        if (queens[i]==col)
        return;
        // diagonal attacks
        if (abs(queens[i]-col) == (row-i) )
        return;
    }

    // column is ok, set the queen
    queens[row]=col;

    if (row==g_nsize-1)
    {
```

```
            nrOfSolutions ++;
        }
        else {
            // try to fill next row
            for (i=0; i<g_nsize; i++)
                setQueen(queens, row+1, i);
        }
    }
}

void solve(int size)
{
    g_nsize = size;

    for(int i=0; i<g_nsize; i++)
    {
        // create separate array for each recursion
        int* pNQ = new int[g_nsize];

        // try all positions in first row
        setQueen(pNQ, 0, i);

        delete pNQ;
    }

}
```

The NQueens program computes the number of ways you can place *n* queens on an nxn chessboard with none being attacked. It prints the result and the elapsed time. The program's default value for *n* is 13. The NQueens algorithm proceeds in the following way. The loop in the solve() function places a queen in each of the size columns of the first row, and then calls the setQueen() function to place queens in the remaining rows. The setQueen() function tries a queen in each column of the next row. If it doesn't "fit," setQueen() goes to the next column. If more rows exist, it calls itself recursively on the next row; otherwise, a solution has been found and the nrOfSolutions global variable is incremented — and in these cases setQueen() also goes on to the next column.

You can find the nqueens_Advisor.zip file that ships with Advisor in the Samples\<locale> folder in the Parallel Studio 2011 install folder, usually C:\Program Files\Intel\Parallel Studio 2011. Unzip the file into a writable folder. Start Visual Studio 2005, 2008, or 2010, and open the solution file nqueens_Advisor\nqueens_Advisor.sln in that folder; for VS 2008 or 2010, the .sln file will be converted — follow the wizard's directions.

Figure 10-3 shows the Advisor toolbar, which appears in the Visual Studio toolbar area. It provides one of the several ways of invoking Advisor and the Advisor tools.

You should start by opening the Workflow tab. In addition to using the toolbar, you can start the three analysis tools from the Workflow tab either by clicking the corresponding button or by selecting VS Tools ⇨ Intel Parallel Advisor 2011.

FIGURE 10-3: The Advisor toolbar

SURVEYING THE SITE

Recall the discussion of Amdahl's Law in Chapter 1, "Parallelism Today," which says that parallel speedup is limited by the execution time of the portion of the program that remains serial. The obvious conclusion is that you need to discover where your serial program spends the most time and focus there in order to find the most effective parallel speedup.

This is what the Survey tool helps you do: it runs and profiles the program to show where the program spends its time.

Your goal in this step is to find candidate parallel regions. You make the decisions — the Survey tool provides timing information and helps you navigate your program. You may already have candidate regions in mind, but run a Survey analysis anyway so that you have quantitative data about how much time is spent in each portion of the program.

If you were doing serial optimization, you would find hotspots that have the highest Self Time and reduce the time there (that is, by reducing the number of executed instructions). Looking elsewhere will not help serial execution time!

In contrast, with parallel optimization you don't need to focus just on a hotspot — you can also look along the chain of loops and function calls from the application's entry point to the hotspot for candidate parallel regions that have high Total Time — time spent there and in called functions (including the hotspot). This is because the objective of parallel optimization is to *distribute* the execution time (the executed instructions) over as many tasks/cores as possible. The parallel program typically executes more instructions than the serial program (due to task overhead), but it consumes less *elapsed* time because the work is spread among multiple tasks at the same time on multiple cores.

Running a Survey Analysis

To run a Survey analysis, begin by building a release configuration of your program. For best results, turn on debug information so that the Survey tool can access symbols, and turn off inlining so that all functions in the source-level call chain appear in the Survey Report. Survey analysis has low overhead — it allows the program to execute at nearly full speed — so employ a data set that exercises the program the way it is normally used. Start the Survey analysis using the Advisor toolbar, Workflow tab, or the Tools ⇨ Intel Parallel Advisor 2011 menu.

The Survey Report

The Survey Report for NQueens has several columns (see Figure 10-4):

➤ **Function Call Sites and Loops** — Call/loop chains starting from the main entry point (upper left). All distinct chains appear, sorted by highest Total Time toward the top. You can use the [+] or [–] to open/close a call chain, respectively.

➤ **Total Time % (and Total Time)** — The percentage of and actual elapsed time, respectively, spent in a function or loop and all functions called from this location (used to estimate the time that could be covered by a parallel region).

➤ **Self Time** — Elapsed time spent in only the function or loop (used to find hotspots).

➤ **Source Location** — The file name and line number of the function or loop.

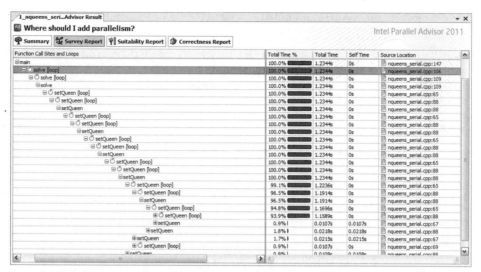

FIGURE 10-4: The Survey Report for NQueens

Finding Candidate Parallel Regions

The basic strategy is to look along hot call/loop chains in the Function Call Sites and Loops column from the upper left toward the lower right for candidate parallel regions:

➤ **Data parallelism** — Loops can be promising parallel regions because if each instance of the loop body can be a task, then you naturally create numerous tasks (one per iteration) over which to distribute the execution. This is why the Survey Report displays loops as well as calls.

➤ **Task parallelism** — Alternatively (or in addition on the same call/loop chain as a candidate loop), look for a high Total Time function F that makes direct calls to several functions G and H that also have high Total Times — for example, F: 60%, G: 40%, H: 20%. The calls to G and H could be put in two different tasks that can execute in parallel, assuming G and H are "independent." This can provide scaling that seems to be limited to 2 cores (but see the following "nested parallelism" bullet).

➤ **Nested parallelism** — Several candidate regions along the same call chain; inner parallel regions are "nested" within outer parallel regions. For example:

➤ Several directly nested loops. If you select the m outer iterations and the n inner iterations as tasks, there will be $m*n$ parallel tasks executing the body of the inner loop.

➤ Task parallelism in a recursive function. For example:

```
Qsort(array) {
    Partition array into [less_eq_array, "center" element, greater_array];
    Qsort(less_eq_array);
    Qsort(greater_array);
    }
```

With task parallelism the two recursive `Qsort` calls occur in different tasks. At each level of the recursion you get 2, 4, 8, 16, ... parallel tasks. So, with this *recursive decomposition* you are not limited to a fixed number of tasks, even though you see only two tasks in the source code.

➤ **Easy and hard cases** — If you can find a candidate parallel region that covers 90 percent of the total time you may be in good shape. In contrast, if you have ten candidates each covering 10 percent of the time, you may have to work harder to get the full parallel speedup.

The Survey Source Window

Double-clicking a loop or function call in the Survey Report takes you to the Survey Source window, which shows the source code to help you determine if this is a good parallel site (see Figure 10-5). The information displayed includes:

➤ **Total Time** — Shows the total time spent in a function. Values appear only on some statements.

➤ **Loop Time** — Represents the total time over all of the statements in a loop. The value appears on some statement in the loop, often the loop header.

➤ **Call Stack with Loops** — Shows the chain of calls used. You can navigate to the source for different locations in the stack by clicking the corresponding stack entry.

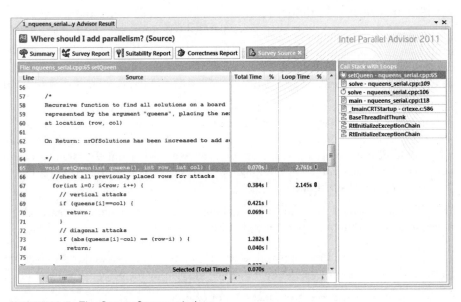

FIGURE 10-5: The Survey Source window

Double-click in the Survey Source window to enter the Visual Studio editor on the corresponding file. Return to the Survey Report from the editor by selecting the My Advisor Results tab for the current Visual Studio project, or click the arrow icon in the "1. Survey Target" section of the Workflow tab. To return from Survey Source to the Survey Report, click the Survey Report button or the arrow icon.

How Survey Analysis Works

When you start a Survey analysis, it runs the current program. Occasionally it takes a sample of where the program is executing, computing the call chain and also noting locations along the chain that are in a loop. When the program completes, the analysis scales the samples to determine the Self Time and the Total Time, sorts the call/loop chains by highest Total Time, and displays the Survey Report. Because the Survey Report employs coarse sampling, there is usually minimal slow-down of the program. The coarse sampling is sufficient because the Survey Report is trying to identify high-frequency events: hotspots and hot call chains.

ACTIVITY 10-1: SURVEYING THE NQUEENS APPLICATION

In this activity you will run a Survey analysis on the serial version of the NQueens application, and examine the resulting report.

1. Unzip and open a copy of the NQueens example shipped with Parallel Studio 2011. You should find the project in

    ```
    C:\Program Files (x86)\Intel\Parallel Studio 2011\Samples\en_US
    \nqueens_Advisor.zip
    ```

    or

    ```
    C:\Program Files\Intel\Parallel Studio 2011\Samples\en_US
    \nqueens_Advisor.zip
    ```

    Notice that the solution has three projects, `1_nqueens_serial`, `2_nqueens_annotated`, and `3_nqueens_cilk`.

2. Set the `1_nqueens_serial` project to be the startup project, and build its release configuration.

3. Run the project without debugging; the window shows the results for 13 queens and tells the elapsed execution time.

4. Run a Survey analysis on the program.

5. Explore the Survey Report.

    a. Open and close call/loop chains.

    b. Go to the Survey Source window and back.

    c. Go to the Survey Source window and to the editor, and back.

6. Pick some candidate parallel regions in the `nqueens_serial.cpp` file and roughly estimate the parallel speedup on 4 cores. For example, if you pick a loop with 40% total time, it will take 10% on 4 cores, assuming perfect scaling, plus 60% for the remaining serial portion, or (100%)/(10%+60%) = 1.4x).

7. Extra credit: Look for a case of potential (recursive) nested parallelism.

ANNOTATING YOUR CODE

You communicate to Advisor where you want to try candidate parallel regions by adding *annotations* to your program. This section describes the parallel model that annotations simulate, the common annotations and parallel constructs they can represent, and how to add them to your program. Recall that Advisor is an inexpensive way to try parallelism in different places. Annotations are cheap — feel free to experiment!

Advisor's Suitability and Correctness tools run your serial program and *model* how it would behave if it were parallel as specified by the annotations — that is, they pretend it is running in parallel.

Site Annotations

Advisor tools model fork-join parallelism as expressed by the following Advisor annotations:

➤ `ANNOTATE_SITE_BEGIN(<site name>);` — After you execute this annotation, subsequently created tasks belong to this site and pretend to run in parallel with other tasks of this site. This is sort of a pretend "fork" point, except tasks are not created until you execute `ANNOTATE_TASK_BEGIN`.

➤ `ANNOTATE_SITE_END(<same site name>);` — Execution of `SITE_END` is a "join" point for all tasks created in this site; execution pretends to wait here until all owned tasks have completed — that is, the tasks do *not* run in parallel with code at the same syntactic level following the `SITE_END`. Note that if the site is (dynamically) nested within another site, tasks of the nested site may run in parallel with other tasks belonging to the parent site.

➤ `ANNOTATE_TASK_BEGIN(<task name>);` — Execution of `TASK_BEGIN` pretends that the code from here to the execution of the matching `ANNOTATE_TASK_END(<same task name>);` executes in parallel with other "tasks" belonging to the owning site.

➤ `ANNOTATE_TASK_END(<same task name>);` — Execution of `TASK_END` simulates the completion of the execution of the corresponding named task.

Fork-join parallelism is sufficient to model Intel Cilk Plus, OpenMP, and most of the parallel algorithms in Intel Threading Building Blocks (TBB). Following are some examples of Advisor annotations for parallel regions:

➤ **Loop parallelism** — To model that the bodies of all iterations of the loop may execute in parallel (also referred to as *data parallelism*):

```
ANNOTATE_SITE_BEGIN(big_loop);
    for (i = 0; i < n; i++) {
        ANNOTATE_TASK_BEGIN(loop);
            Statement1;
            …
            Statementk;
        ANNOTATE_TASK_END(loop);
    }
ANNOTATE_SITE_END(big_loop);
```

➤ **Task parallelism** — To model that the two Qsort calls may execute in parallel. Notice that this example also uses recursion:

```
// Qsort sorts the array a in place, and uses modeled recursive parallelism
void Qsort(array a){
// If a is small enough, sort it directly and return.
// Otherwise, pick an element e from array a.
// Rearrange the elements within a so that it is partitioned in 3 parts
// a == [elements <= e; e; elements > e]
// Let array less_eq_qsort be a reference to the first partition of a
// Let array greater_qsort be a reference to the last partition of a
// Recursively apply Qsort to each of these array references, in parallel.
ANNOTATE_SITE_BEGIN(qsort);
      ANNOTATE_TASK_BEGIN(qsort_low);
            Qsort(less_eq_array);
      ANNOTATE_TASK_END(qsort_low);

      ANNOTATE_TASK_BEGIN(qsort_high);
            Qsort(greater_array);
      ANNOTATE_TASK_END(qsort_high);
ANNOTATE_SITE_END(qsort);
}
```

➤ **Nested parallelism** — This example is an extract from the Tachyon ray tracing example that ships with Advisor:

```
// Inner loop nest (simplified) from Ray Tracing sample program tachyon_Advisor.
// Two nested loops on y and x, each inner iteration renders
// one pixel in a rectangular grid.
// Processing one pixel is independent of every other pixel, so they
// can all be done in parallel. This is modeled using nested parallelism.
ANNOTATE_SITE_BEGIN(allRows);
   for (int y = starty; y < stopy; y++){
      ANNOTATE_TASK_BEGIN(eachRow);

            ANNOTATE_SITE_BEGIN(allColumns);
                for (int x = startx; x < stopx; x++) {
                    ANNOTATE_TASK_BEGIN(eachColumn);
                        color_t c = render_one_pixel (x, y, …);
                        put_pixel(c);
                    ANNOTATE_TASK_END(eachColumn);
                    }
                ANNOTATE_SITE_END(allColumns);

      ANNOTATE_TASK_END(eachRow);
      }
ANNOTATE_SITE_END(allRows);
```

Lock Annotations

Lock annotations can be used to pretend to protect access to shared data by multiple tasks. Note that you usually add lock annotations only after you have run the Correctness tool and have found cases of unprotected data sharing that need to be fixed.

➤ `ANNOTATE_LOCK_ACQUIRE(<address>);` — After a task executes this annotation, modeling pretends that no other task may enter a region protected by `LOCK_ACQUIRE` of the same address — that is, only one task at a time can execute any protected region.

➤ `ANNOTATE_LOCK_RELEASE(<address>);` — Execution of this annotation ends the locked region corresponding to `<address>` — that is, modeling can pretend that another "waiting" task can enter the protected region.

The following example shows how to protect the incrementing of a shared variable inside a task using lock annotations:

```
ANNOTATE_LOCK_ACQUIRE(0);  // zero is a convenient address
      shared_variable ++;
ANNOTATE_LOCK_RELEASE(0);
```

Although the preceding examples show paired site and task annotations that match statically in the source code, the paired annotations actually must match at execution time, because they have their parallel modeling effect at run time. So, if multiple execution paths are exiting such a region, it is necessary to have multiple "closing" annotations (two lock-releases in this case):

```
static int my_lock;
ANNOTATE_LOCK_ACQUIRE(&my_lock);
if (shared_variable == 0) {
            ANNOTATE_LOCK_RELEASE(&my_lock);
            return; }
shared_variable ++;
ANNOTATE_LOCK_RELEASE(&my_lock);
```

Some other special-purpose annotations are explained in the Advisor documentation.

Adding Annotations

Advisor has some features to simplify adding annotations to your code in the editor. Note that you make the decisions about parallel regions; Advisor helps you generate the correct syntax. To add annotations, follow these steps:

1. Navigate to the location in the source file where you want to insert annotations: for example, double-click a line in the call/loop chain in the Survey Report to see the Survey Source window, and double-click again to reach the editor.

2. Use the mouse (left-click and drag) to select a code region to be surrounded by an annotation pair.

3. Right-click and select Intel Parallel Advisor 2011.

4. You can select one of the annotation types displayed in Figure 10-6. This will cause the

FIGURE 10-6: The Annotation menu in the editor

annotation pair to be entered into the source around the selected code, with a unique name chosen as the argument.

Alternatively, select Annotation Wizard, which guides you through several steps for selecting annotation kinds and argument names. It also explains the semantics of the selected annotation kind. Figure 10-7 shows the Annotation Wizard, where Annotate Task has been selected as the annotation type from the pull-down menu. The two panes show what the code will look like near the ANNOTATE_TASK_BEGIN and ANNOTATE_TASK_END annotations.

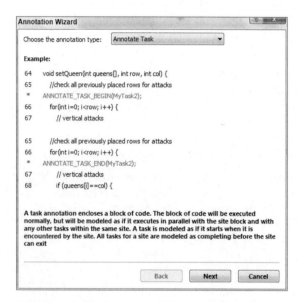

FIGURE 10-7: The Annotation Wizard window

Recall that if the flow of control can leave a region by different paths (for example, a return), it may be necessary to have multiple ending annotations. The Annotation Wizard does not handle this case, so you will need to recognize this situation and insert the additional *END annotation by hand.

Annotations are actually C/C++ macros that expand into calls to null functions with special names; the Advisor tools recognize the names and model the corresponding behavior. And because annotations are just macros, you can employ any C/C++ compiler to build your annotated program.

Every source file using annotations needs to include the file advisor-annotate.h, which defines the annotation macros:

```
#include "advisor-annotate.h"
```

The Annotation Wizard in the editor can help with this step. This include file is located in the directory $(ADVISOR_2011_DIR)/include, so you also need to add this include path to the Additional Include Directories in Build Configurations under Properties ➪ C/C++ ➪ General for all projects and configurations using annotations.

ACTIVITY 10-2: ADDING ANNOTATIONS TO NQUEENS

In this activity you add annotations to the NQueens application.

1. In the 1_nqueens_serial project, enter the VS editor on a source file and use the Annotation Wizard to add several annotation kinds. Use the editor's Undo command to remove them.

2. In the same project, add site and task annotations for all the candidate parallel regions you selected in Activity 10-1. Add the include file to the source file(s). Also add the include path to the build configurations. Build the program and correct any compilation errors.

3. One way of parallelizing NQueens is to select the loop in the solve() function as a parallel site. It covers 100 percent of the Total Time, so it has the potential for being a good site. The source file nqueens_serial.cpp in project 1_nqueens_serial contains commented-out annotations at this loop, as well as a commented out #include of advisor-annotate.h. Uncomment this code, add the include path to the build configurations, and then rebuild the project.

4. Alternatively, move to the 2_nqueens_annotated project, which already has annotations added at this site (see the nqueens_annotated.cpp file). Set this as the startup project and build it. This project is used in the next two sections.

CHECKING SUITABILITY

Suitability analysis provides coarse-grained speedup estimates for the annotated code. The purpose of the performance information is to guide your decisions about these sites:

➤ If the estimate is good, keep going with this site.

➤ If the estimate is bad, either adjust the site or abandon the experiment.

In either case, you have made progress with a small expenditure of effort because you are using modeling.

You can answer other questions. Does the performance match your expectations from the Survey Report? Are there parallelization-related performance issues (for example, overhead items)?

If you have fixed correctness issues by adding locks or restructuring the code (on the previous iteration through the Advisor workflow), the projected parallel performance may have changed since the last time you ran the Suitability analysis. So, you need to run it again after modifying your annotations or your code.

Running a Suitability Analysis

To run a Suitability analysis, begin by building a release configuration of your program (similar to a Survey analysis, but the program now has annotations) and use the same data set. Start the Suitability analysis from the Advisor toolbar, Workflow tab, or from the Tools menu. The Suitability tool runs the program, analyzing what its performance characteristics might be. There is typically less than a 10 percent slowdown compared to normal program execution. However, if many task instances have a small number of executed instructions, the modeling overhead could be higher and the accuracy of the estimates may suffer. For example, if the average time for tasks is less than 0.0001 seconds (displayed in the Selected Site pane), the instrumentation overhead in the Suitability tool may cause the predicted speedups to be too small.

The Suitability Report

The Suitability Report for NQueens appears in Figure 10-8. It displays the following panes of information. All performance data consists of *modeled estimates* about how the program might behave if it were parallel.

➤ **All Sites** — Summarizes performance information about parallel sites and the whole program and contains:

➤ *Maximum Program Gain For All Sites* — The speedup of the whole program due to all sites, for the current Target CPU Number.

➤ A list of each site with their individual Maximum Site Gain (speedup), contribution to Maximum Total Gain of the program, Average Instance Time, and Total Time.

➤ *Model parameters* — Drop-down lists for changing the Target CPU Number and Threading Model. You can select different values to see how the results behave.

➤ **Selected Site** — Shows details about the currently selected site in the All Sites pane. The information includes:

➤ *Scalability of Maximum Site Gain graph* — A log-log graph of the site's maximum gain versus the number of CPUs. Each vertical bar shows the range of values for that number of cores, and the ball on the bar shows the estimate with the current set of *model parameters* and *parallel choices*.

➤ Green area — Good speedup (linear, or close to linear scaling)!

➤ Yellow area — Some speedup but there may be opportunities for improvement.

➤ Red area — No (or negative) speedup; may need significant effort to improve, or perhaps this site should be abandoned.

➤ A list of tasks and locks associated with the current site along with performance information such as maximum, average, and minimum times.

➤ *Changes I will make to this site to improve performance* — Lists five parallel choices you make about sites, tasks, and locks. This area of the pane indicates if any of these items impact performance, and if so, Advisor may recommend how to reduce the impact and what speedup might be achieved. You can change a choice by clicking in the corresponding box. (Click the underlined name for additional documentation.)

➤ *Reduce Site Overhead* — The time to create and complete a parallel site.

➤ *Reduce Task Overhead* — The time to start and stop a task.

➤ *Reduce Lock Overhead* — The time to acquire and release a lock.

➤ *Reduce Lock Contention* — The time spent in one task waiting for another task to release a lock.

➤ *Enable Task Chunking* — Combining multiple tasks into a single task to reduce the task overhead (for example, in a parallelized loop, performing numerous consecutive iterations in one task). Several parallel frameworks, such as Intel Cilk Plus, Intel TBB, and OpenMP, perform task chunking by default.

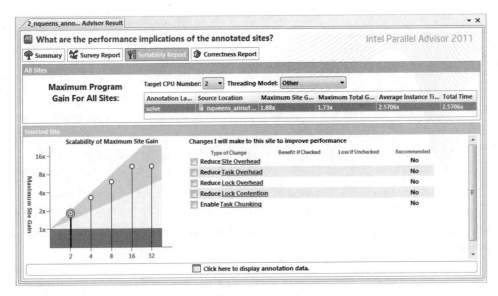

FIGURE 10-8: The Suitability Report for NQueens

Double-clicking a site or task name displays the corresponding source code in the Suitability Source window. Return to the Suitability Report by clicking the Suitability Report.

A summary of all your annotations is provided in the Summary Report. This is described in the later section "Replacing Annotations." An example appears in Figure 10-13.

Parallel Choices

This section describes the meaning and effect of the parallel choice boxes in the Selected Site pane of the Suitability Report.

Figure 10-9 shows the Selected Site pane for a program with lock annotations. In the scalability graph, the balls indicating current estimated gain are in the red, meaning no speedup. However, the bars reach into the green and indicate that there is a range of performance depending on the parallel choices listed to the right. In particular, Advisor shows that a 5.35x speedup can be achieved if you select Reduce Lock Contention, and also recommends that you do so.

Figure 10-10 shows the result of clicking the Reduce Lock Contention box. The balls in the graph are now in the green, representing very good speedup. By clicking the box, you have agreed to take some action(s) to reduce lock contention when you convert to actual parallel constructs. Note that

Advisor only predicts the effect of reducing lock contention — *you* have the responsibility of implementing that decision later when you add parallel code!

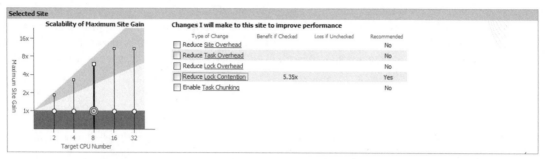

FIGURE 10-9: The Selected Site pane *before* making a parallel choice

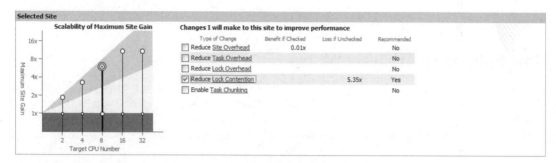

FIGURE 10-10: The Selected Site pane after making a parallel choice

Using the Suitability Report

You have multiple ways to use the Suitability Report to determine what parallel performance your program might have, and what you might change to achieve improvements. First look at the Maximum Program Gain, and then for each site examine the scalability graph and the parallel choices. Is the program gain what you expected? Change the number of CPUs to check the scalability or to match the number of CPUs on your target platform. Answer the same questions about the gain for each site, and study the scalability graph for each site.

If a site's speedup is low, click it and examine its Selected Site pane:

➤ In which region of the scalability graph (green, yellow, red) is the result?

➤ Are there recommended changes to the parallel implementation choices? If so, try clicking the corresponding box.

➤ How many task instances are there for each site instance? Too few may limit scalability.

➤ If there are numerous tasks with very small average time, you probably already have recommendations to Reduce Task Overhead and/or to Enable Task Chunking. Task times less than 0.0001 second can cause the instrumentation overhead of the Suitability tool to degrade the accuracy of the speedup estimates.

➤ Compare Total Time for the tasks with that of the site. Recall that if the tasks cover only 50 percent of the site's time, then Amdahl's Law says the speedup limit is 2x.

➤ If you have a small number of tasks and a large time deviation, there may be a problem with load balancing (see Chapter 9, "Tuning Parallel Applications"). The large tasks continue running while some tasks finish early and there are no other tasks to run, so some CPUs will be idle. Try to make the amount of work in each task similar, or at least cause the large tasks to start executing first.

➤ Is the number of locking instances large? This will probably also show up in Reduce Lock Overhead.

➤ Is the Total Time in locks similar to that for tasks? This may also show up as a Reduce Lock Contention recommendation.

You can also experiment with the sensitivity of the performance by varying the model parameters and the parallel choices, looking for significant changes in the results. This Sensitivity analysis is fast because all the results have been precomputed — Suitability analysis is not run again.

How Suitability Analysis Works

When you start a Suitability analysis, it runs the current program, keeping track of site, task, and lock annotations, and the time spent in each. It then models what the performance of the program would be if it were run in parallel as specified by the annotations, and for all combinations of modeling parameters and parallel choices. It then displays the coarse-grained estimates in the Suitability Report.

Here is a more detailed description of the Suitability analysis:

➤ **Data collection** — While the program runs, the Suitability tool collects timestamps for the beginning and end of each site, task, and lock region, and computes the elapsed times. (Recall that annotation macros expand into calls to specially named null functions; the tool identifies the kind of annotation by the name of the function.) Data collection generates a program trace as a stream of ordered times and information about the regions. It also compresses the data. For example, if 100 consecutive instances of task(foo) are similar, each with about the same elapsed time of 3 seconds, then this could be represented as "100 * task(foo) total 300 seconds."

➤ **Construct task execution tree** — The next step is to build an ordered tree representing the sites and their contained tasks (and nested sites and their tasks) from the ordered stream coming from data collection. Under each tree node for a task are also the instances of locked regions that were executed in the task. The ordering in the tree represents the serial execution order of the regions. To keep the amount of memory consumed by the tree reasonable, the tree is limited to a fixed number of nodes. This is accomplished by employing another kind of compression: if the size limit is reached and more data is still arriving, the tree-building process aggregates the effects of the leaves of a node into the node, and then deletes the leaves. For example, the times for the tasks belonging to a site can be summed and stored in the site's tree node before the tasks' nodes are removed.

➤ **Modeling** — The purpose of creating the tree is to provide a structure for modeling the performance characteristics of parallel executions of the program as represented by the annotations. The modeling is performed by *simulating* the execution of the program in parallel on a fixed number of *simulated cores*, where the only operations simulated are the beginnings and ends of sites and tasks, and the acquiring and releasing of locks. Time is estimated by using *simulated clocks* for each core. When a task "runs" on a core, the core's clock is incremented by the time the task took during the data collection run (as stored in the tree).

A key component of parallel modeling is the *task scheduler*. It has a queue of tasks that are ready to "execute." The scheduler assigns tasks to cores as the cores complete other tasks. The simulator keeps track of the simulated elapsed time for the sites, tasks, and locks. Note that the simulation does not take into account cache or memory effects from tasks running on different cores. The only inter-task performance impacts are from locks.

The simulation is run for every combination of number of CPUs, threading model, and the five parallel choices, and then the results are saved. When you change one of the values in the Suitability Report, the new result is displayed immediately because it has been precomputed. The reason for building the execution tree is that it is used multiple times for the simulations.

The *Target CPU Number* affects how many cores are available for the scheduler to allocate to tasks. The *Threading Model* affects the overheads of individual site, task, and lock operations. The *parallel choices* have different impacts. For example, the option "fix task overhead" is modeled by having the simulator use zero for task overhead. For the option "fix lock contention," the simulator never makes a task wait for a lock. (Normally, the simulator causes a task to wait for the lock to be free and records the additional *simulated* elapsed time for that task.)

ACTIVITY 10-3: RUNNING THE SUITABILITY ANALYSIS ON NQUEENS

In this activity you run a Suitability analysis on the annotated NQueens application and explore the effect choosing different modeling parameters.

1. Run the Suitability analysis on the program with your annotations from Activity 10-2, or use the 2_nqueens_annotated project.

2. Examine the different sections of the Suitability Report.

3. Change the number of CPUs and the threading model parameters. Are there any parallel choice recommendations to select?

CHECKING FOR CORRECTNESS

You have run the Suitability analysis and are feeling good because you have found some sites that are projected to provide parallel speedups. Now it's time for a reality check; if you parallelize your program in these locations, will there be data-sharing problems or deadlocks that will cause the parallel program to be incorrect? The purpose of checking correctness is to predict if these issues will occur.

Not only does correctness modeling tell you if errors exist, but it also helps you navigate to all of the source locations participating in a data-sharing error or a deadlock. You need this in order to fix the problem.

Or, you may decide that the correctness errors are too difficult to fix or will take too much development time relative to the projected speedup for a parallel site. So, if the return on investment (ROI) is too small, abandon this site and remove its annotations. You have been able to quickly experiment with this site, and now you can go on to other sites.

Running a Correctness Analysis

To run a Correctness analysis, begin by building a debug configuration on your program, making sure that the build configuration uses the dynamic runtime library (Configuration Properties ➪ C/ C++ ➪ Code Generation ➪ Runtime Library is /MD or /MDd). Correctness needs optimization off so that all memory references are retained in the generated code, and retained in their original program order, because the modeling tracks all the loads and stores. Correctness modeling causes a significant slowdown of the program, such as 100 times slower. Thus, you should use a reduced input data set to minimize the run time. However, the reduced data set should cause the program to traverse all the paths within the sites. For example, if the Survey or Suitability input data set causes a "parallel" loop to execute one million iterations, it is probably sufficient for correctness modeling if the reduced data set causes the loop to execute only a few iterations. Start the Correctness analysis using the Advisor toolbar, Workflow tab, or Tools ➪ Intel Parallel Advisor 2011 menu.

As mentioned, performing a Correctness analysis can cause a significant expansion of execution time. So when the Correctness tool is running your program, it displays each "observation" as the program runs. If enough error observations have occurred, you can stop the program by clicking the red Stop button on the Advisor toolbar, or by closing your program's window. A Correctness Report will be created for these observations, even though the program has not run to completion.

The Correctness Report

The Correctness Report for NQueens displays several panes of information (see Figure 10-11):

➤ **Problems and Messages** — Correctness combines multiple "observations" into a single "problem"; for example, if an error occurs on the currently indexed element of an array on every iteration of a one-million-iteration loop, you will see one problem instead of having to sift through a million observations on the individual elements of the array.

➤ **Memory reuse: Observations** — For the currently selected problem (for example, P1 in Figure 10-11), this section displays a highlighted source line and a surrounding source code "snippet" for the distinct observations (for example, X4, X5) associated with the problem. Clicking the [–] for an observation eliminates the source code lines and shrinks it to a single line describing the observation; clicking the [+] redisplays the source snippet.

➤ **Filter** — Lists a number of problems and messages by different categories. Click a line to display only problems and messages in the upper-left pane satisfying that filter category. For example, you can display only problems in a particular file, or only errors (omitting warnings and remarks).

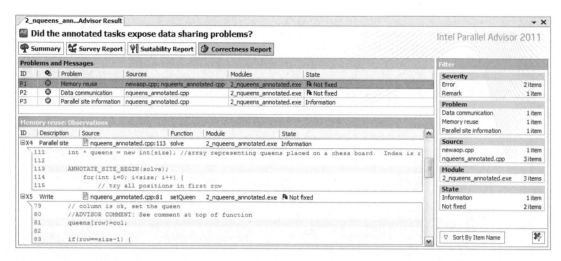

FIGURE 10-11: The Correctness Report for NQueens

The Correctness Source Window

You can navigate to the Correctness Source window by double-clicking the corresponding line in the Correctness Report. Figure 10-12 shows the Correctness Source window for the P1 memory reuse. The following panes of information appear:

➤ **Source code snippets for two observations for the problem (upper-left panes)** — Shows more lines of code than in the Correctness Report window. Double-clicking a line navigates to the VS editor.

➤ **Call Stacks for the two source snippets (upper-right panes)** — Shows the call stack to get to the displayed source observation. Clicking a function in the stack displays the corresponding source code for that level in the stack.

➤ **Memory reuse: Observations (lower-left pane)** — Shows one line for each of the observations for the problem. Double-clicking an observation opens the corresponding source view in the upper pane.

➤ **Relationship Diagram (lower-right pane)** — Shows dependencies among the critical observations of the problem. This identifies the important observations and how they relate to each other, which can help you understand the problem.

Double-click a snippet in the Correctness Source window to enter the Visual Studio editor on the corresponding file. Return to the Correctness Report from the editor by selecting the My Advisor Results tab for the current VS project, or click the arrow in the "4. Check Correctness" section of the Workflow tab. To return from the Correctness Source window to the Correctness Report, click either the Correctness Report button or the arrow.

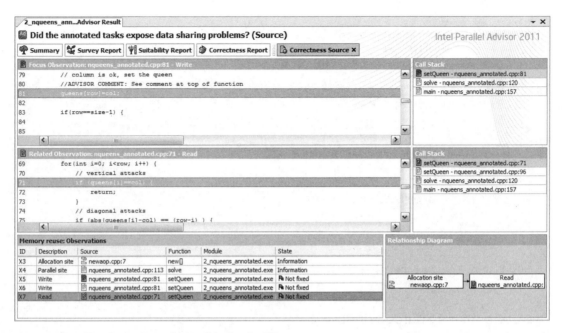

FIGURE 10-12: The Correctness Source window for NQueens

Understanding Common Problems

Correctness analysis discovers the following four problem categories that you need to understand and fix (or abandon the site). The components of the Correctness Report attempt to assist you in deciphering the cause of the problem.

> ➤ **Memory reuse** — A shared object is referenced by multiple tasks, and in the serial program some tasks that write to the object do so before reading from it. Because multiple tasks are reading and writing the object, this would cause data-sharing problems if the program were actually parallel. However, no values flow from one task to another — they are just "reusing" the same memory. This is called *incidental sharing*. The tasks are sharing an object but do not need the sharing; instead, each task could use its own copy of the object. *Privatizing* — providing a private object for each task — is exactly the way to fix this problem.
>
> Refer to problem P1 in Figure 10-11, which is an instance of memory reuse. The following program fragment shows another instance, where the `temp` variable declared outside of the parallel site is used to temporarily hold the value of an array element:

```
static int temp;
…
ANNOTATE_SITE_BEGIN(big_loop);
    for (i = 0; i < n; i++) {
        ANNOTATE_TASK_BEGIN(loop);
            temp = a[i];
            b[i] = … temp …;
        ANNOTATE_TASK_END(loop);
    }
ANNOTATE_SITE_END(big_loop);
```

When the loop body becomes a task, all the task instances will (potentially) be using the single `temp` at the same time. Changing the program, as follows, to declare a `temp` automatic variable inside the loop causes each task to have its own copy of `temp` — problem solved!

```
ANNOTATE_SITE_BEGIN(big_loop);
    for (i = 0; i < n; i++) {
        ANNOTATE_TASK_BEGIN(loop);
            int temp;
            temp = a[i];
            b[i] = … temp …;
        ANNOTATE_TASK_END(loop);
    }
ANNOTATE_SITE_END(big_loop);
```

➤ **Data communication** — A shared object is referenced by multiple tasks, at least one of which performs a write. In the serial program, values flow from a write in one task to a read in another. This is another instance of a data-sharing problem, but it may be more difficult to resolve than memory reuse. In solving this kind of problem you have to work out whether the data values are independent of each other:

> ➤ *Independent updates* — This is a case where the tasks are updating an object and the final result does not depend on the order in which the tasks update the object. For example, each task is adding a value to a counter; it does not matter in what order the updates are done, as long as multiple tasks do not access the object at the same time. You can solve this problem by using a lock, which will enforce that only one task at a time is allowed to update the object.

> Problem P2 in Figure 10-10 is a data communication error, which is actually a case of independent updates of the `nrOfSolutions` variable. (You will investigate and fix this error in Activity 10-4.) Another instance is shown in the following program fragment, which shows a `counter` that every task (iteration) increments:

```
static int counter = 0;
…
ANNOTATE_SITE_BEGIN(big_loop);
    for (i = 0; i < n; i++) {
        ANNOTATE_TASK_BEGIN(loop);
            …
            counter++ ;
            …
        ANNOTATE_TASK_END(loop);
    }
ANNOTATE_SITE_END(big_loop);
```

> It does not matter in what order the increments occur — they just must occur one at a time. The following fragment shows the corrected example with lock annotations added:

```
static int counter = 0;
static int my_lock;
…
ANNOTATE_SITE_BEGIN(big_loop);
    for (i = 0; i < n; i++) {
        ANNOTATE_TASK_BEGIN(loop);
```

```
            …
            ANNOTATE_LOCK_ACQUIRE(&my_lock);
                counter++ ;
            ANNOTATE_LOCK_RELEASE(&my_lock);
            …
        ANNOTATE_TASK_END(loop);
    }
ANNOTATE_SITE_END(big_loop);
```

> ➤ *True dependence* — If the serial order of access to the object must be retained so that the correct answer is achieved, then the problem is more difficult to fix. It may be necessary to move task boundaries or to combine multiple tasks into a single task (for example, so that multiple references are in a single task), or it may be necessary to abandon this site altogether.

➤ **Inconsistent lock use** — A shared object is protected by one lock at one location in the code and by a different lock (or is unprotected) when referenced at another location in the code. Your goal is to protect the object from a data communication error since a lock is used in at least one place. However, because the same lock is not used *every* time, there might still be a sharing problem. The usual fix is to consistently employ the same lock at all points of reference. The following example demonstrates inconsistent lock use:

```
ANNOTATE_LOCK_ACQUIRE(&lock1);
    counter++;
ANNOTATE_LOCK_RELEASE(&lock1);
…
ANNOTATE_LOCK_ACQUIRE(&lock2);
    // protected by different lock
    counter++;
ANNOTATE_LOCK_RELEASE(&lock2);
…
// not protected by any lock
counter++;
```

In the preceding code, the counter variable is *inconsistently* protected by lock1 in the first use, by lock2 in the second use, and is unprotected in the third use.

➤ **Lock hierarchy violations** — This is a case where two tasks have nested locked regions, and the locks are acquired in different orders in the two regions. This can cause a deadlock, as described in Chapter 8, "Checking for Errors." The following example demonstrates a lock hierarchy violation:

```
//Region 1
ANNOTATE_LOCK_ACQUIRE(&lock1);
    ANNOTATE_LOCK_ACQUIRE(&lock2);
    …
    ANNOTATE_LOCK_RELEASE(&lock2);
ANNOTATE_LOCK_RELEASE(&lock1);
…
//Region 2
ANNOTATE_LOCK_ACQUIRE(&lock2);
    ANNOTATE_LOCK_ACQUIRE(&lock1);
```

```
...
        ANNOTATE_LOCK_RELEASE(&lock1);
ANNOTATE_LOCK_RELEASE(&lock2);
```

Imagine that two tasks execute the code snippet above. Suppose that task 1 is about to execute Region 1, and task 2 is about to execute Region 2 at the same time. Task 1 acquires lock1 and task 2 acquires lock2. In order for task 1 to acquire lock2, it has to wait for task 2 to complete Region 2 and release lock2. But in order for task 2 to acquire lock1, it has to wait for task 1 to complete Region 1 and release lock1. Both tasks will wait forever — this is a deadlock.

The fix is to have all tasks that acquire multiple locks acquire them in the identical order. In other words, they must use the same hierarchy of locks.

Using the Correctness Report

There are several approaches to using the Correctness Report and Correctness Source window to find, understand, and fix sharing problems that would occur if your program were parallel.

Diagnose in detail what is causing each problem by exploring the corresponding source locations and call stacks. The problem statement and observation code snippets in the Correctness Report may be sufficient for discovering the error. For example, if you are incrementing a global counter, you need a lock.

In other cases, the Correctness Source window provides more details about what leads to the occurrence of the problem. One complication is that you have to comprehend the distinct code that two tasks might be executing at the same time, which can cause the interference. Another is that the object being shared might be a parameter, so it may have different names in the two tasks. This is where the call stack is handy; it enables you to examine the source code at different levels of the stack so that you can track how an object is passed through multiple function calls.

Decide if there are too many hard problems to fix for this site, in which case you can either change the location of the site and tasks or abandon the site altogether. Otherwise, fix the problems by employing your understanding of each problem, picking a strategy to fix it, and using the source locations to enter the editor at the appropriate places to make the required source changes.

Rebuild the modified program and run a fresh Correctness analysis to verify that your changes do in fact fix the identified problems and do not introduce new problems. (And after converting your program to parallel constructs, use Intel Parallel Inspector XE to determine if any other classes of memory-sharing problems exist.) Now return to the Suitability analysis step to see what impact these changes may have on performance.

Correctness Analysis Limitation

There is a case of a potential data-sharing problem that Correctness analysis cannot distinguish from the safe usage of a local variable. The potential error is not reported because it would also report errors on the safe case, thus causing false positives. This is one reason you should always run Intel Parallel Inspector XE after adding parallel constructs — Inspector can distinguish these two cases.

The following code fragment demonstrates both a data-sharing issue and a safe usage:

```
void foo(…) {
    int relatively_global = 0;
    …
    ANNOTATE_SITE_BEGIN(big_loop);
        for (i = 0; i < n; i++) {
            ANNOTATE_TASK_BEGIN(loop);
                int relatively_local = 0;
                …
                relatively_local++ ;   //safe
                relatively_global++ ; //unprotected sharing!
                …
            ANNOTATE_TASK_END(loop);
        }
    ANNOTATE_SITE_END(big_loop);
```

The `relatively_global` variable is local to the `foo` function but global relative to the tasks in the loop. All the tasks share the object, so when it is incremented in the tasks in the parallel program, there is a data-communication error. In contrast, the `relatively_local` variable is declared within the tasks, and when the program is parallel, each task will have its own copy. So, incrementing `relatively_local` will not cause a sharing problem.

The issue is that in the *serial* program, the compiler creates both variables as local stack variables of the `foo` function. Therefore, the Correctness tool cannot distinguish the two different cases. The design choice was to report either both as errors or neither as errors. The decision was made to avoid annoying false positives and rely on Inspector to catch any true sharing errors. Note that this situation arises only when the task is in a function and the variable declaration (for example, `relatively_global`) occurs in the same function or the calling function.

How Correctness Analysis Works

When you start a Correctness analysis, it runs the current program, tracking all memory references and annotations that occur. It models which references to the same object could occur in different tasks at the same time if the program were run in parallel, taking into consideration the constraints of which tasks can run at the same time, and lock regions. It then combines related observations into problems and displays them in the Correctness Report.

Here is a more detailed description of Correctness analysis:

➤ **Data collection** — While the program runs, Correctness data collection captures the loads and stores them for every object, and also tracks the start and end of each site, task, and lock region.

➤ **Construct task execution tree** — The Correctness tool builds an ordered tree representing the sites and their contained tasks (and nested sites and their tasks). The tree is used to answer the question: if two tasks reference the same object, can they be executing at the same time in a parallel program? This is one condition necessary for a data-sharing issue to occur. For efficiency, the tree is constructed and destroyed on-the-fly. For example, if a parallel site is not nested in any other sites, when it finishes executing, it and its tasks can be removed from the tree because they will never be able to execute in parallel with subsequent tasks. So, the answer to the question will be no if one of the tasks is not in the tree.

➤ **Locksets** — The set of locks (*lockset*) that is held by a task at an instant of execution is all the locks that have been acquired without yet being released. If two tasks reference the same object, the tasks can execute in parallel (answer from the tree), and one of the references is a write, then there *may* be a data-sharing error. If at the time of the two references the tasks hold a lock in common (`lockset(task1) & lockset(task2) != NULL`), then that lock will prevent them from executing the references at the same instant — thus, no error. However, if the intersection of the locksets is `NULL` (that is, the locksets are disjoint), a data-sharing problem could occur in a parallel execution.

➤ **Modeling** — As the serial program runs, for each load or store, the Correctness tool stores the following information into the model's database associated with the object's address:

   ➤ The object's address and size

   ➤ Whether it is a read or write

   ➤ The current task identity

   ➤ The task's lockset

The Correctness modeler then examines other references to this same object in the database, looking for other tasks that:

   ➤ Can execute at the same time as the current task.

   ➤ Has a disjoint lockset.

   ➤ Has at least one reference that is a write.

If these conditions hold, then this data-sharing *error observation* is passed to the Correctness Report. Actually, only a small number of entries need to be kept in the database for each object; data-sharing errors will still be found. In spite of this optimization, the sheer number of loads and stores to be processed can cause Correctness modeling to take up to 100 times longer than the original program.

➤ **Correctness Report** — Correctness Report processing combines similar observations into single *problems* that are displayed. For example, there may be multiple observations with different object addresses and task instances, but the referencing instructions have the same line number. This is probably a case of a "parallel" loop iterating through a data structure — you want this reported as only a single problem to be fixed.

➤ **References** — The first paper describes the Intel Thread Checker, a tool similar to Advisor's Correctness analysis that models parallelism while executing a serial program. It uses the compiler to insert instrumentation code, whereas Correctness instruments the program as it runs. The second paper describes the use of locksets for finding race conditions.

   ➤ P. Petersen and S. Shah. OpenMP Support in the Intel Thread Checker. *Proceedings of WOMPAT 2003*, LNCS Springer Lecture Notes in Computer Science, 2716:1–12, 2003.

   ➤ S. Savage, M. Burrows, G. Nelson, P. Sobalvarro, and T. Anderson. Eraser: A Dynamic Race Detector for Multithreaded Programs. *ACM Transactions on Computer Systems (TOCS)*, 15(4): 391–411, November 1997.

ACTIVITY 10-4: RUNNING A CORRECTNESS ANALYSIS ON NQUEENS

In this activity you run a Correctness analysis on the annotated NQueens application, and then fix the errors that are detected.

1. Build a debug configuration of the `2_nqueens_annotated` project, and run a Correctness analysis. The debug configuration solves a smaller problem to reduce the execution time: *n* is 8, not 13 (as is used for the release configuration).

2. In the Correctness Report, click each problem and scroll through the corresponding observations.

3. Explore the Filter pane. Click different items to see what problems are displayed, and return to all problems by clicking All.

4. From the Correctness Report, navigate to the Correctness Source window by clicking on a problem or an observation. Click different levels of the call stack to see the corresponding source code, and then return to the Correctness Report.

5. From the Correctness Report, navigate to the VS editor on the source corresponding to a problem or an observation, and then return to the Correctness Report.

6. Fix each problem, and then rebuild and rerun the Correctness analysis. Are all the problems gone?

7. Make a release build and run a Suitability analysis. Is the projected performance still good?

In the `nqueens_annotated.cpp` source file in the `2_nqueens_annotated` project, comments and commented-out code in the `solve()` and `setQueen()` functions describe how to fix the memory reuse and data communication errors, respectively. Uncomment the code and rebuild. Run the Correctness tool again to make sure the problems were fixed.

REPLACING ANNOTATIONS

When you have a site or sites with good predicted performance and the correctness issues have been resolved, you can convert your parallel-ready program to a true parallel program. First, choose a parallel programming model, such as one of the Intel Parallel Building Blocks, or some other approach. (See Chapter 7, "Implementing Parallelism," for descriptions of parallel models and how to use them.) Then replace each Advisor annotation with the corresponding parallel construct. This section shows some of these mappings; Advisor documentation contains a more complete set of mappings for Intel Threading Building Blocks and Intel Cilk Plus.

The Summary Report

Figure 10-13 shows the Summary Report, which you can display either by clicking the Summary button at the top of the Advisor window or by clicking the arrow icon for the "5. Add Parallel Framework" step in the Workflow tab.

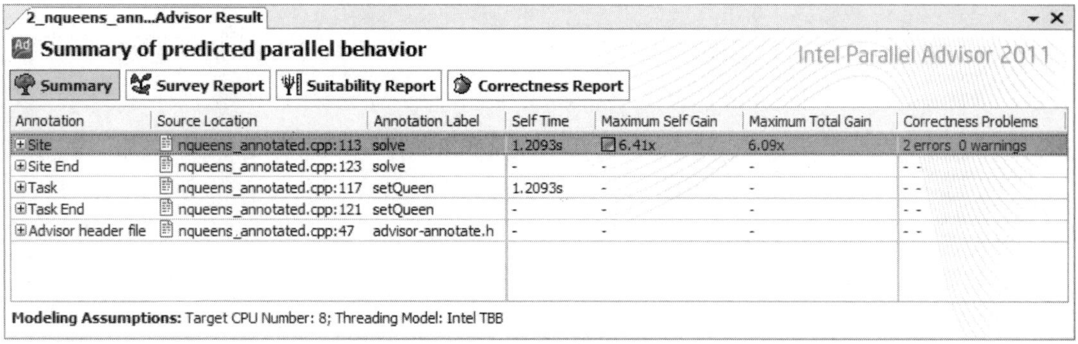

FIGURE 10-13: The Summary Report for NQueens

The Summary Report provides a high-level overview of the progress on sites, suitability, and correctness in the program. It shows the kind and location of every annotation in the program. For each site, the report displays the estimated speedup of the site and the entire program (if Suitability analysis has been run) and the number of correctness problems (if Correctness analysis has been run). Figure 10-13 shows the Summary Report for NQueens before the data-sharing problems have been fixed (there are still two errors). The bottom of the report shows the modeling assumptions used (for example, eight CPUs), which you compare against the speedups.

An ROI comparison can be performed from the Summary Report. For a program with numerous parallel sites, you can use the Summary Report to balance the amount of speedup against the amount of development work needed to fix the correctness problems for a site, and then compare the sites to each other to prioritize sites where you can expect the best ROI.

The Summary Report is also the natural place to start when you are moving to parallel constructs, because all the annotations in the program are listed here. Navigate to each annotation so that it can be replaced by a parallel construct, double-click a line for an annotation in the Summary Report to take you into the Visual Studio editor on the file at the line containing that annotation, and then insert the corresponding parallel construct.

Common Mappings

This section shows simple mappings from annotations representing loop parallelism and task parallelism to Intel Threading Building Blocks (Intel TBB) and Intel Cilk Plus. It also demonstrates how to replace lock annotations with the Intel TBB `spin_mutex` for both Intel TBB and Intel Cilk Plus.

➤ Loop parallelism

```
ANNOTATE_SITE_BEGIN(big_loop);
    for (i = 0; i < n; i++) {
        ANNOTATE_TASK_BEGIN(loop);
            Statement;
        ANNOTATE_TASK_END(loop);
    }
ANNOTATE_SITE_END(big_loop);
```

  ➤ Intel TBB (using lambda expression)

```
#include <tbb/tbb.h>
...
```

```
tbb::parallel_for(0, n,
    [&](int i) {statement;}
);
```

> ➤ Intel Cilk Plus

```
#include <cilk/cilk.h>
…
cilk_for (i = 0; i < n; i++) {
    Statement;
}
```

➤ Task parallelism

```
ANNOTATE_SITE_BEGIN(qsort);
    ANNOTATE_TASK_BEGIN(qsort_low);
        Qsort(less_eq_array);
    ANNOTATE_TASK_END(qsort_low);

    ANNOTATE_TASK_BEGIN(qsort_high);
        Qsort(greater_array);
    ANNOTATE_TASK_END(qsort_high);
ANNOTATE_SITE_END(qsort);
```

> ➤ Intel TBB (using lambda expressions)

```
#include <tbb/tbb.h>
…
tbb::parallel_invoke(
    [&] { Qsort(less_eq_array);},
    [&] { Qsort(greater_array);}
);
```

> ➤ Intel Cilk Plus

```
#include <cilk/cilk.h>
…
// version 1 for function calls
cilk_spawn Qsort(less_eq_array);
Qsort(greater_array);
cilk_sync;

// version 2 for general statements wrapped in lambda expressions
cilk_spawn [&] {statement-1}();
statement-2
cilk_sync;
```

The first version is simple because the two statements are function calls. Note that `cilk_spawn` is not needed on the last task before the `cilk_sync`. The second version assumes arbitrary statements, so lambda expressions are used to create functions for all but the last statement.

➤ Locks for Intel TBB and Intel Cilk Plus

```
static int my_lock;
…
```

```
ANNOTATE_LOCK_ACQUIRE(&my_lock);
shared_variable ++;
ANNOTATE_LOCK_RELEASE(&my_lock);
```

The following Intel TBB `spin_mutex` has low overhead for a low-contention lock, and can be used for both Intel TBB and Intel Cilk Plus. Intel TBB's other mutex types would be used in the same manner.

```
#include "tbb/spin_mutex.h"
…
static tbb::spin_mutex my_mutex;
…
{ // Declare my_lock in its own scope; on scope exit
  // the destructor will unlock it.
  tbb::spin_mutex::scoped_lock my_lock(my_mutex);

shared_variable ++;
}
```

You could avoid using locks altogether by declaring `shared_variable` to be a Cilk Plus reducer. If you look at the `3_nqueens_cilk` project, you will see how to do this.

ACTIVITY 10-5: IMPLEMENTING PARALLELISM IN NQUEENS

In this activity you convert the annotated NQueens application to a parallel program, first using TBB and then Cilk Plus.

1. Explore the Summary Report for the `2_nqueens_annotated` project. Navigate to the editor for each annotation.

2. Convert the annotations in `nqueens_annotated.cpp` to Intel TBB. Set the current project to `3_nqueens_tbb` and examine the `nqueens_tbb.cpp` file, comparing it to the changes you made in `nqueens_annotated.cpp`. Change the configuration to `Release_TBB`, which has directory paths for the include files, the library files, and the shared library files. Build and run the Intel TBB version on a multi-core machine. Is it faster than the original serial version?

3. Convert the annotations in `nqueens_annotated.cpp` to Intel Cilk Plus. Set the current project to `3_nqueens_cilk` and examine the `nqueens_cilk.cpp` file, comparing it to the changes you made in `nqueens_annotated.cpp`. (Note that this project uses the Intel Parallel Composer compiler, which supports the Intel Cilk Plus extensions. You could use Intel Composer XE, which also supports Intel Cilk Plus.) Change the configuration to `Release_Cilk`, which has directory paths for the include files, the library files, and the shared library files. Build and run this version on a multi-core machine. Is it faster than the original serial version?

SUMMARY

Intel Parallel Advisor is a unique tool that helps you add parallelism to your programs. This chapter has demonstrated how to use Advisor effectively:

➤ The modeling provides information about your parallel experiments.

➤ Advisor's methodology takes you through the necessary steps, but you remain in control; Advisor does not automatically change your program.

➤ You progressively refactor your serial program into a parallel solution.

You should now understand the value of parallel modeling:

➤ The modeling maintains your original application's semantics and behavior.

➤ You can quickly experiment with parallelism in different regions and transform the predicted most promising regions to be parallel-ready.

11

Debugging Parallel Applications

WHAT'S IN THIS CHAPTER

➤ Introducing the Intel Debugger and its workflow

➤ Detecting data races

➤ Observing the runtime behavior of a threaded program

This chapter shows how to use the parallel debugging features of the Intel Debugger on your parallel or threaded application. One of the biggest challenges in parallel programming is tracking down data races. In this chapter you use the debugger to detect data races as you debug.

Unlike the error-finding techniques presented in other chapters, with a debugger you can single-step into your code and examine your parallel applications to confirm that the program is running as you expect. You can, as it were, sit inside your program and observe what is happening around you.

INTRODUCTION TO THE INTEL DEBUGGER

You are probably reading this chapter because you are developing or debugging a parallel program. Compared to pure serial software, parallel programs introduce additional issues that can produce problems that are difficult to track down and debug. The most common error is a *data race*, where one thread tries to read data that is being written by another thread. Programmers solve data races by inserting synchronization primitives in the code so that only one thread at a time can access shared data. Adding these primitives may solve the data race issue, but could inadvertently introduce a deadlock, with both threads waiting for each other to release the shared resource.

In addition to the risk of introducing data races and deadlocks, making a program parallel could break its integrity, with the program no longer working as intended. The newly parallelized program needs to be correct, free from programming and algorithmic errors.

Debuggers help developers to solve such software issues in real time by following, examining, and modifying a program's runtime execution. Intel Parallel Studio XE has a debugger dedicated to debugging the parallel features of your program. The debugger has two variants:

➤ **Intel Parallel Debugger Extension (PDE)** — A Windows plug-in to Visual Studio

➤ **Intel Debugger (IDB)** — A Linux Eclipse-based standalone debugger

 This chapter uses the term Intel Debugger *(or simply* debugger*) to refer to both the Windows version and the Linux version. Where comments refer to a particular version, the chapter uses the terms* PDE-Windows *and* IDB-Linux.

The debugger enables you to:

➤ Identify data races in Cilk, OpenMP, and native (WIN32 and POSIX) threaded programs.

➤ Investigate a program's parallel behavior, by checking that the parallelized version runs the same way as the serial version.

➤ Filter out data race events that are of no interest.

➤ Detect events from a defined "focus" region.

➤ Serialize a threaded region to compare serial and parallel execution.

➤ Display OpenMP tasks, locks and barriers, call stack, and task hierarchy.

➤ Display Cilk Plus call stacks (PDE-Windows only).

In addition, the IDB-Linux version, which is a fully featured symbolic debugger, helps programmers to:

➤ Debug programs.

➤ Disassemble and examine machine code and examine machine register values.

➤ Debug programs with shared libraries.

➤ Debug multithreaded applications.

This chapter concentrates on the parallel debugging features that are common to both PDE-Windows and IDB-Linux.

 To use the Intel parallel debugging features, your code must be built with the Intel compiler.

The Parallel Debugger Workflow

You can use the debugger in two ways:

➤ **Curative** — To fix errors and problems

➤ **Preventative** — To ensure a program runs as you expect

Figure 11-1 shows a suggested workflow for both approaches. You should fix parallel issues during run time, using a short, repetitive debug cycle, where very little time is spent between identifying and fixing problems.

The starting point assumes you have seen some strange behavior in the parallel program you are developing, so you run the Intel Debugger to try to find the problem.

Usually, it is best to identify and fix one problem at a time before moving on to the next problem. (This is the approach taken in this chapter.) However, some developers prefer to identify a whole series of problems before fixing them.

The first step is to serialize the code by turning off the threading. Serialization is available only for Cilk and OpenMP code. If rerunning the program shows the problem still exists, you should debug the program in serial mode and fix it.

If serialization makes the problem disappear, the problem is caused by the parallelism in the code. You should turn off serialization, thus reenabling the parallelism, before continuing.

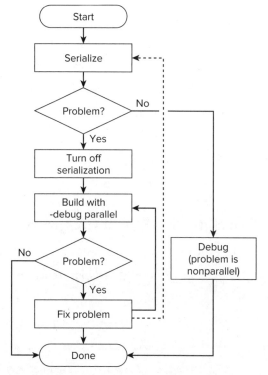

FIGURE 11-1: Parallel Debugger workflow

 To use the data race detection feature in the Intel Debugger, you need to rebuild the application with the Intel compiler with the added -debug parallel *option.*

For each problem, use the debugger to pinpoint the source of the error, looking for data races or unexpected behavior. Each time you fix a problem, you should rebuild and test. If you prefer, after each error has been fixed, you can go back to the serialization stage (refer to the dotted line in Figure 11-1).

USING THE INTEL DEBUGGER TO DETECT DATA RACES

Most of the activities in this chapter use the Tachyon ray-tracing application that ships with Composer XE. The Tachyon example is quite large — much bigger than a simple "hello world" program and more like a real-world example.

In ray tracing, the paths of light in an image are simulated, displaying the shadows and reflections that will occur. The example program draws a set of colored balls along with shadows. In the parallel version of the program, the picture has some blemishes caused by data races.

The program consists of a ray tracer in which a very busy loop calculates the value of each pixel. For the sake of simplicity, the main focus is on the parallelization of this loop, without discussing the rest of the program. The purpose is to improve execution performance.

You perform the following steps to detect the data races in the program:

1. Build and run the serial program.

2. Add parallelism.

3. Observe the results by looking at the picture.

4. Use the debugger to discover any faults, especially data races.

5. Fix the data races.

Building the Serial Program

The Tachyon example consists of several projects:

➤ `Build_serial` — Nonparallel version of program

➤ `Build_with_cilk` — Uses Cilk Plus

➤ `Build_with_openmp` — OpenMP version

➤ `Build_with_tbb` — Uses Threading Building Blocks

➤ `Tachyon.common` — Shared between all other projects

You can build the serial version of the Tachyon program by completing Activity 11-1.

ACTIVITY 11-1: BUILDING AND RUNNING THE SERIAL VERSION

In this activity you build and run the serial version of the Tachyon ray-tracing program. Use steps 1–5 if you are using Windows, and steps 6–10 if you are using Linux.

PDE-Windows

1. Unzip the Tachyon example to a directory for which you have read/write access (usually located at `<Parallel Studio XE Installation directory>\Samples\en_US\C++\tachyon_compiler.zip`).

2. Open the `tachyon_compiler.sln` project, which you can find in the `vc8` folder. (Visual Studio conversion will take place.)

3. Make sure `build_serial` is set as the start-up project by selecting it in the Solution Explorer and then selecting Project ➪ Set as StartUp Project.

4. Build the program by selecting Build ➪ Build build_serial.

5. Press Ctrl+F5 to run the program.

IDB-Linux

6. Untar the Tachyon example to a directory for which you have read\write access:

```
tar xvfz /opt/intel/composerxe/Samples/en_US/C++/tachyon.tar.gz ./
```

7. Build the `build_serial` (Debug) solution:

```
make build_serial_debug
```

8. Run the program:

```
./tachyon.serial dat/balls.dat &
```

Adding Parallelism

The sample code uses OpenMP to add parallelism. The solution is purposefully naïve; the intention is to show how to use the debugger, not how to write perfect parallel code.

Listing 11-1 is a modified version of the `draw_task` function from `build_with_openmp.cpp`. (You'll be using this listing in Activity 11-1.) The function draws the ray-traced picture on the screen. The `#pragma omp parallel for` statement causes the loop iterations to be shared among the available threads.

Available for download on Wrox.com

LISTING 11-1: The imperfectly parallelized code

```
static void draw_task (void)
{
    unsigned int serial = 1;
    int ison=1;
    unsigned int mboxsize = sizeof(unsigned int)*(max_objectid() + 20);
    unsigned int * local_mbox = (unsigned int *) alloca(mboxsize);
    memset(local_mbox,0,mboxsize);

    // Add parallelism - NOTE THIS WILL INTRODUCE DATA RACES!
    #pragma omp parallel for

    // each iteration will draw a raster
    for(int y = starty; y < stopy; y++) {
      if (ison) {
        drawing_area drawing(startx, totaly-y, stopx-startx, 1);

        // draw the individual line
        for (int x = startx; x < stopx; x++) {
        // work out the right color
        color_t c = render_one_pixel (x, y, local_mbox, serial,
                                      startx, stopx, starty, stopy);
        // draw the pixel
        drawing.put_pixel(c);
      }
```

continues

LISTING 11-1 *(continued)*

```
        ison = video->next_frame();
    }
  }
}
```

code snippet Chapter11\11-1.cpp

As the parallel program runs, each thread writes a series of rasters to the screen. The left-hand picture in Figure 11-2 shows the program running on a machine that has two 6-core CPUs with Simultaneous Multi Threading, giving support for 24 hardware threads. The snapshot was taken part way through the picture being drawn.

FIGURE 11-2: Noisy image generated by the parallel program

The middle picture in Figure 11-2 is complete. Although it looks almost right, a closer look shows that there is some "noise" in the resulting image. The right-hand picture enlarges the top corner of the middle picture. You can clearly see that the background is not very clean.

ACTIVITY 11-2: BUILDING THE OPENMP VERSION

In this activity you make the ray-tracing program parallel using OpenMP. When you run the parallelized program, the displayed image will be imperfect. Use steps 1–9 if you are using Windows, and steps 10–14 if you are using Linux.

PDE-Windows

1. If not already open, open the `tachyon_compiler.sln` project.

2. Make sure the `build_with_openmp` is the start-up project:

    a. Highlight the `build_with_openmp` project.

    b. Right-click and select Set as StartUp Project from the drop-down menu.

3. Open the `build_with_openmp.cpp` file.

4. Replace the `draw_task` function with the code in Listing 11-1.

5. Make sure the debug version is selected from the solution configuration.

6. Make sure that OpenMP has been enabled in the project properties by selecting Project ➪ Properties ➪ C/C++ ➪ Language ➪ OpenMP support.

7. Build the debug version from the menu Build ➪ Build build_with_openmp.

8. Press Ctrl+F5 to run the program.

9. Compare the picture with the one in Activity 11-1. You should notice a degradation in quality.

IDB-Linux

10. Open the `src/build_with_openmp/build_with_openmp.cpp` file.

11. Replace the `draw_task` function with the code in Listing 11-1.

12. Build the debug version:

```
make build_openmp_debug
```

13. Run the program:

```
./tachyon.serial dat/balls.dat &
```

14. Compare the picture with the one in Activity 11-1. You should notice a degradation in quality.

Using the preceding hypothetical case as a real-life debugger issue, you should next investigate the issue using the debugger. It is intuitive that many errors are introduced with the very rough parallelization code. Looking more closely at the picture, you can see that the differences with the neighbor pixels are really high. It's time to start a data-race analysis.

Observing the Results

Imagine that you have just received from your quality assurance team a defect report pointing out the noisy image and you are not sure what is causing the problem. It could be an incorrect implementation of the algorithm or a mistake in the parallelization of the algorithm. If the underlying algorithm is wrong, the defect should be observable, whether the code is running parallel or not. The first step is to run the code with parallelism turned off — that is, to serialize the application.

Serializing the Parallel Code

With the debugger you can serialize a parallel application at the click of the Serialize button. When working on Cilk code, the debugger stops the Cilk scheduler from stealing work; for OpenMP code, the debugger sets the number of threads available in a parallel region to one.

You can serialize a parallel application three different ways:

➤ By clicking the Serialize button on the debugger toolbar

➤ By selecting Debug ➪ Intel Parallel Debugger Extension ➪ Serialize Execution

➤ By using the commands (IDB-Linux only) `idb set openmp-serialization on` and `idb set cilk-serialization on` in the control window

Figure 11-3 shows the PDE-Windows toolbar with the sixth button from the left (the serialization button) pressed. The dark line around the icon indicates the serialization is active. The IDB-Linux also has a similar looking toolbar.

FIGURE 11-3: Parallel Debug Extension toolbar with the serialization button pressed

In the case of the Tachyon program, when you click the serialization button and the program is executed, the image is completely clean. This means two things: the program algorithm is okay, and problems exist with the parallel part of the code. Try out the serialization for yourself in Activity 11-3.

ACTIVITY 11-3: TURNING ON SERIALIZATION

In this activity you use the PDE serialization button to serialize the parallel program to confirm that it runs okay when just one thread is used. Use steps 1–4 if you are using Windows, and steps 5–7 if you are using Linux.

PDE-Windows

1. Modify the `tachyon_compiler` solution to use the Intel compiler solution. Be sure to convert the whole solution, which contains five projects:

    a. Highlight the `tachyon_compiler` solution in the Solution Explorer.

    b. Right-click and select Intel C++ Composer XE 2011 ➪ Use Intel C++ from the drop-down menu.

2. Build the debug version of the `build_with_openmp` project by selecting Build ➪ Build build_with_openmp.

3. Click the serialization button on the toolbar. This sets the number of OpenMP threads to one.

4. Press F5 to start debugging the program. (Notice that you do not press Ctrl.) Compare the picture with the one from Activity 11-1. The picture quality should be the same.

IDB-Linux

5. Start the debugger:

```
idb -args tachyon.with_openmp dat/balls.dat
```

6. Select Parallel ➪ Serialize Execution to enable serialization.

7. Press F5 to start debugging. Compare the picture with the one from Activity 11-1. The picture quality should be the same.

Detecting Data Races

Once you suspect that your code contains data races, whether by seeing inconsistent results or any other reason, it is time to start a data sharing analysis.

Before conducting a data sharing analysis, you need to enable two features:

➤ **Enable Parallel Debug Checks (in the compiler)** — This option adds extra helper or instrumentation code to the application so that the debugger can handle the parallel code appropriately. It is important to apply this option to all code you are interested in. In the Tachyon example, the option should be applied to all the code; otherwise, there is a danger of missing some data races. Figure 11-4 shows enabling parallel debug checks in the compiler tab of the project properties page. This is equivalent to using the compiler option `/debug::parallel` (in Linux, use `-debug parallel`).

➤ **Parallel Debug Environment (required only in PDE-Windows)** — Figure 11-5 shows enabling the parallel debug environment in the project properties page.

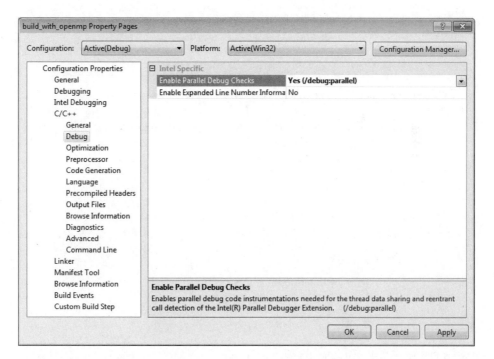

FIGURE 11-4: Enabling parallel debug checks in the compiler

To start a data sharing analysis, follow these steps:

1. Click the data sharing analysis button — the second from the left in the toolbar (see Figure 11-6). In IDB-Linux you can also use the `idb sharing on` command in the console window.

You can also enable data sharing analysis through the menu Debug ➪ PDE ➪ Thread Data Sharing Detection ➪ Enable Detection.

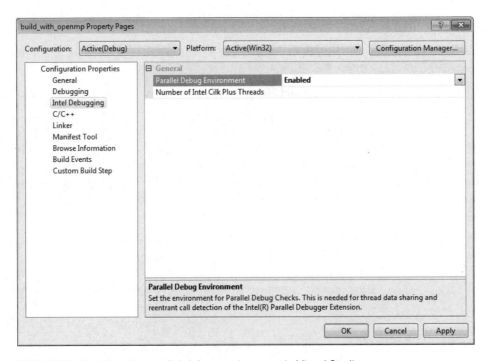

FIGURE 11-5: Enabling the parallel debug environment in Visual Studio

2. Start debugging your code by either single-stepping though it or by running the program with the debugger. You can use these function keys:

➤ PDE-Windows

➤ Single step: <F10>

➤ Run with debugging: <F5>

➤ IDB-Linux

➤ Single step: <F11>

➤ Run with debugging: <F5>

FIGURE 11-6: The toolbar's data sharing analysis button
in the state of performing an analysis

When you execute code that involved a data race, the debugger presents a list of events, showing the operation (read/write), the code location or data involved, and the thread performing that operation (see Figure 11-7).

After detecting an event, you need to examine the code to determine whether the problem is genuine or just a false positive. You may see that there is a data race but decide it is harmless. If you want to ignore an event, you can apply a filter to stop the event from appearing in the events list.

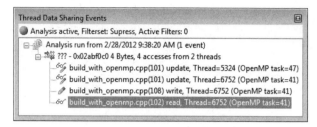

FIGURE 11-7: A list of data sharing events

Using Filters

Filtering events is a very important step of the data sharing analysis. Filters enable you to find the source of the current issue and reduce the performance penalty caused by the analysis itself.

Filtering operates in two different modes:

➤ Suppression

➤ Suppression filters discard events.

➤ Suppression filters work by exclusion.

➤ Focus

➤ Focus filters home in on code or data ranges that you specify.

➤ Focus filters work by inclusion.

It's quite normal to use both kinds of filters in the same analysis session, swapping between filter sets as you narrow down a problem. The following examples use two different approaches to using the filters. In the first example, when an error is detected, you apply a suppression filter and then search for the next data race. The second example assumes that you have a good idea which part of the code is causing a problem. You then set up focus filters to home in on this area.

Using Suppression Filters to Discard Unwanted Events

The `build_with_openmp` program has several data races that have already been identified. Clicking the data sharing analysis button and starting a debug session results in the debugger stopping at the first data race event. The debugger displays the region of the code where the data race is located.

 There is no guarantee in which order the data races occur, so the events presented here may appear in a different location for every run.

The debugger stops at the source location where a data sharing issue occurs (see Figure 11-8). The `serial` variable seems to be the source of the problem.

Three events are captured, as shown in Figure 11-9. Three threads are accessing the same `serial` variable. Two of them are trying to read from and write into the `serial` variable, and one is reading from it. Two threads are incrementing the `serial` variable at line 101, and one thread is reading `serial` at line 102 (`primary.serial = serial`).

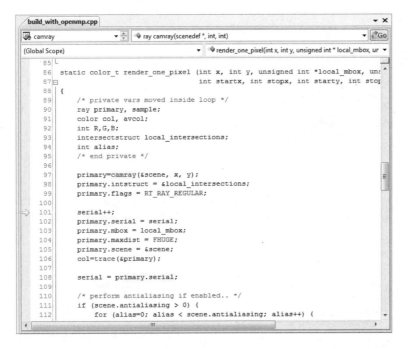

FIGURE 11-8: The source location where a data-sharing issue was detected

After detecting an issue, you should investigate the origin of the variable and which other functions are using it. Looking at the call stack will help. The `serial` variable is instantiated in the `draw_task` function and is passed by reference to the `render_one_pixel` function.

The `render_one_pixel` routine is not a thread-safe routine because it alters the parameters passed to it. The `serial` variable is shared between all the threads and needs to be made thread safe (which you will do in Activity 11-5).

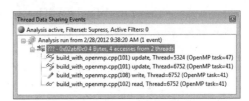

FIGURE 11-9: The Thread Data Sharing Events window, displaying and logging the events that have been detected

Creating the Filters

At this point you can use the debugger to:

➤ Try to solve the problem, recompile the program, and run the analysis again.

➤ Single-step a little further in the code to help your investigations. Here you are "stepping through" code causing the date race condition.

➤   Suppress this detection and look for the next error.

You might find it more interesting to take the second approach — that is, continue the investigation to get a more comprehensive overview of the damage caused by sharing variables.

To filter out issues coming from the `serial` variable, right-click one of the events in the Thread Data Sharing Events window and select Add Filter. The option Add Filter ⇨ To This Data Object suppresses all the events coming from the `serial` variable (see Figure 11-10). Once a filter has been created, it is listed in the Thread Data Sharing Filters window (see Figure 11-11).

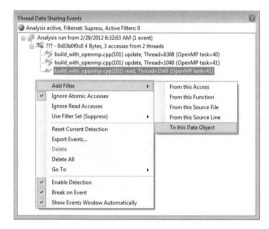

FIGURE 11-10: Inserting a filter from the Thread Data Sharing Events window

FIGURE 11-11: The suppression filters

Once you have inserted the filter for `serial`, you can continue the debugging. You will see that most data races involve data passed by parameter from `draw_task` to each thread.

You will find that one of the data races deserves special mention. The `mbox` variable is an array (see Figure 11-12). After creating a filter for an array, you can adjust the range of the filter so that it spans the address space of the array. This means that any data race on any element of the `mbox` variable will be filtered.

FIGURE 11-12: A data race derived from the mbox variable

ACTIVITY 11-4: DETECTING AND FILTERING DATA RACES

In this activity you build the code with the Intel compiler, adding special options to support parallel debugging. A data race is detected, and you create a filter so that the data race events are ignored. Use steps 1–7 if you are using Windows, and steps 8–14 if you are using Linux.

PDE-Windows

1. Highlight the two projects, build_with_openmp and tachyon.common. Open the project properties page by pressing Alt+F7 and ensure the following options are set:

> Intel Debugging ⇨ Parallel Debug Environment: Auto

> C/C++ ⇨ Debug ⇨ Enable Parallel Debug Checks: Yes

2. Rebuild the debug version using the menu Build ⇨ Build build_with_openmp.

3. Make sure the serialization button is not selected!

4. Click the data sharing analysis button.

5. Press F5 to start debugging the program. The program should stop at a data race (probably in the `render_one_pixel at serial++` function). Press F5 again.

6. In the Thread Data Sharing Events window, highlight the event and from the context menu select Add Filter ⇨ To This Data Object.

7. Press F5. The program will ignore all events associated with the object identified in step 6, and will stop at the next data race.

IDB-Linux

8. Rebuild the debug version (note the extra command):

```
export CXXFLAGS="-debug parallel"
make clean
make build_openmp_debug
```

9. Launch the debugger:

```
idb -args tachyon.with_openmp dat/balls.dat &
```

10. Make sure the serialization button is not selected.

11. Choose Parallel ⇨ Enable Detection to enable data race detection.

12. Press F5 to start debugging the program. The program should stop at a data race (probably in the `render_one_pixel` at `serial++` function). Press F5 again.

13. In the Thread Data Sharing Events window, highlight the event and from the context menu select Add Filter ⇨ To This Data Object.

14. Press F5. The program will ignore all events associated with the object identified in step 6, and will stop at the next data race.

Fixing the Data Races

Having identified the data races, you now need to come up with a solution. Listing 11-2 gives one possibility. If you place the start of the parallel region using the `#pragma omp parallel` construct before the declaration of `ison`, `serial`, `mboxsize`, and `local_mbox`, each variable will become thread-local.

LISTING 11-2: Fixing data races by moving the parallel region

```cpp
static void draw_task (void)
{
  // Start a parallel region
  #pragma omp parallel
  {
    // each thread will have its own copy of these variables
    int ison             = 1;
    unsigned int serial  = 1;
    unsigned int mboxsize = sizeof(unsigned int)*(max_objectid() + 20);
    unsigned int * local_mbox = (unsigned int *) alloca(mboxsize);
    memset(local_mbox, 0, mboxsize);
     // workshare the loops between the threads
    #pragma omp for
    for(int y = starty; y < stopy; y++) {
      if (ison) {
        drawing_area drawing(startx, totaly-y, stopx-startx, 1);
        for (int x = startx; x < stopx; x++) {
          color_t c = render_one_pixel (x, y, local_mbox, serial, startx,
                                        stopx, starty, stopy);
          drawing.put_pixel(c);
        }
        ison = (video->next_frame()? 1 : 0);
      }
    }
  }
  return;
}
```

code snippet Chapter11\11-2.cpp

After you recompile and rerun the application, the image should be completely clean. If you run a data sharing analysis again, you will still detect some issues. Those are mainly related to image display, and in practice are not relevant for the image generation, so they will not be resolved here.

ACTIVITY 11-5: FIXING THE OPENMP DATA RACE

In this activity you fix the data races. On closer examination, however, the picture still has imperfections. Use steps 1–5 if you are using Windows, and steps 6–10 if you are using Linux.

PDE-Windows

1. Open the `build_with_openmp.cpp` file and replace the `draw_task` function with the code in Listing 11-2.

2. Build the debug version from the menu Build ⇨ Build build_with_openmp.

3. Press Ctrl+F5 to run the program.

4. Compare the picture with the one in Activity 11-1. You should notice degradation in quality.

5. Use the PDE to see if any data races still exist. (See steps 2–5 of Activity 11-4.)

IDB-Linux

6. Open the `build_with_openmp.cpp` file and replace the `draw_task` function with the code in Listing 11-2.

7. Build the debug version:

```
export CXXFLAGS="-debug parallel"
make build_openmp_debug
```

8. Run the program:

```
./tachyon.with_openmp dat/balls.dat
```

9. Compare the picture with the one in Activity 11-1. You should notice degradation in quality.

10. Use the Debugger to see if any data races still exist. (See steps 2–5 of Activity 11-4.)

Using the suppress filters presents a straightforward model of detecting and finding data races in the code. However, this mode has as a side effect: there will be a high performance penalty because every file is taking part in the data sharing detection. A more efficient way is to use focus filters.

Using Focus Filters to Examine a Selected Portion of Code

When working with more complex examples, focusing on a specific region may be a more efficient way of working. In the suppression mode, data race detection is applied to every file that has been instrumented with the Intel compiler. This can lead to a large number of events being generated that have to be examined. If you are working on a large project written by several developers, you may want to focus on just the code that you have written. You can do this in the debugger by setting it to focus mode.

To enable focus mode, choose Use Filter Set (Focus) ⇨ Focus in the Thread Data Sharing Events window (see Figure 11-13).

Before adding and creating any filters, you could modify the code example to fix some of the data races you are already aware of. In Listing 11-3, the `serial` and `ison` stack variables are declared to be `firstprivate` in the `#pragma omp` statement. By doing this, each thread gets its own initialized copy of those variables.

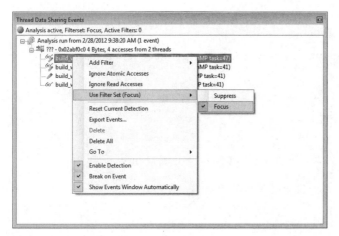

FIGURE 11-13: Setting the filter mode to focus

LISTING 11-3: Image generated by the Tachyon example

```cpp
// This code fixes some of the data races but not all of them!
// WARNING: THERE ARE STILL SOME DATARACES IN HERE
static void draw_task (void)
{
  unsigned int serial = 1;
  int ison=1;
  unsigned int mboxsize = sizeof(unsigned int)*(max_objectid() + 20);
  unsigned int * local_mbox = (unsigned int *) alloca(mboxsize);
  memset(local_mbox,0,mboxsize);

  // Each thread has its own initialized copy of serial and ison
  #pragma omp parallel for firstprivate(serial, ison)
  for(int y = starty; y < stopy; y++) {
    if(ison) {
      drawing_area drawing(startx, totaly-y, stopx-startx, 1);
      for (int x = startx; x < stopx; x++) {
        color_t c = render_one_pixel (x, y, local_mbox, serial,
                                      startx, stopx, starty, stopy);
        drawing.put_pixel(c);
      }
      ison = video->next_frame();
    }
  }
  return;
}
```

code snippet Chapter11\11-3.cpp

Note that running the program now produces a near perfect image. However, if you enlarge the image, you will see that some pixels still have the wrong color, as shown in Figure 11-14.

FIGURE 11-14: A close examination shows some pixels are wrong

Creating the Filters

Before running the data sharing analysis, you have to define the region that you are interested in. For the purpose of this exercise, the local_mbox stack variable was not declared to be firstprivate, so all the threads are still sharing it. Any half-decent programmer would have already fixed this by now, but it was ignored; so, a data sharing error still exists.

Before inserting any kind of filter, you should identify the chain of functions that make use of local_mbox. The variable is first used in the render_one_pixel function, which, in turn, passes a reference to the trace, intersect_object, and grid_intersect functions.

To insert a filter:

1. Right-click the Thread Data Sharing Filters window and select New Code Range Filter.

2. Specify the function {,,build_with_openmp.exe}function_name.

After doing this for each of the trace, intersect_object, grid_intersect, and render_one_pixel functions, the window will look similar to Figure 11-15.

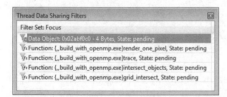

FIGURE 11-15: The Thread Data Sharing Filters window

When the filters are first created, their state will be marked as *pending*. Once you start a debug session, the state of the filters will change to *active*.

After enabling the data-race analysis and debugging, the first problem detected is in the grid_intersect function in grid.cpp. The variable ry->mbox is originally derived from the previously mentioned local_box stack variable:

```
static void grid_intersect(grid * g, ray * ry)
{
  // .
  // code omitted
  // .

  while (1) {
    if (tmax.x < tmax.y && tmax.x < tmax.z) {
      cur = g->cells[voxindex];
        // iterate through a linked list
        while (cur != NULL) {
        if (ry->mbox[cur->obj->id] != ry->serial) {
         // THIS CODE CAUSES A DATA RACE!
         ry->mbox[cur->obj->id] = ry->serial;
          cur->obj->methods->intersect(cur->obj, ry);
        }
        // go to next link in the list
        cur = cur->next;
      }
  // .
  // code omitted
  // .
  }
}
```

ACTIVITY 11-6: USING A FOCUS FILTER

In this activity you fix some of the data races. You create a filter to focus on captur-ing data races in four functions. Use steps 1–6 if you are using Windows, and steps 7–12 if you are using Linux.

PDE-Windows

1. Open the `build_with_openmp.cpp` file and replace the `draw_task` function with the code in Listing 11-3.

2. Build the debug version from the menu Build ➪ Build build_with_openmp.

3. Right-click the Thread Data Sharing Events window and select Use Filter Set (Focus) ➪ Focus.

4. Right-click the Thread Data Sharing Filters window and select New Code Range Filter. In the Entire Function field, add the text **{,,build_with_openmp. exe}render_one_pixel**, and then click OK.

5. Repeat step 4 using the following function names:

   ```
   {,,build_with_openmp.exe}trace
   {,,build_with_openmp.exe}intersect_objects
   {,,build_with_openmp.exe}grid_intersect
   ```

6. Press F5 to debug the program.

IDB-Linux

7. Open the `build_with_openmp.cpp` file and replace the `draw_task` function with the code in Listing 11-3.

8. Build the debug version:

```
export CXXFLAGS="-debug parallel"
make build_openmp_debug
```

9. Right-click the Thread Data Sharing Events window and select Use Filter Set (Suppress) ⇨ Focus.

10. Right-click the Thread Data Sharing Filters window and select New Code Range Filter. In the Entire Function field, add the text {,,**build_with_openmp. exe}render_one_pixel**.

11. Repeat step 4 using the following function names:

```
{,,build_with_openmp.exe}trace
{,,build_with_openmp.exe}intersect_objects
{,,build_with_openmp.exe}grid_intersect
```

12. Press F5 to debug the program.

Correcting the mbox Data Race

At this point you must decide where to perform the fix — either on the parallelized loop or in the function where the problem was detected.

One way to fix the error would be to insert a `#pragma critical` statement immediately before the data race. The shared variable is used twice, so adding a local variable called `localID` will work:

```
#pragma critical
int localID = cur->obj->id;
    if (ry->mbox[localID] != ry->serial) {
            ry->mbox[localID] = ry->serial;
```

The code is now thread safe, but inserting the critical section in the code introduces a performance penalty because only one thread can access this code at any time; all the other threads have to wait. A much better solution is to create an independent buffer for every thread. Listing 11-4 does exactly this.

The code in Listing 11-4 defines a new `ParameterForRendering` class, with member items `_ison`, `_serial`, `_mboxsize`, and `_local_mbox` being used to replace the original stack variables. The initialization code for `_local_mbox` is moved from its original place into the constructor `ParameterForRendering(unsigned int box_size)`.

The `ParameterForRendering (const ParameterForRendering &input)` copy constructor is also implemented because the compiler will implicitly call it in the `firstprivate` clause.

The original stack variables are replaced with an instantiation of the `ParameterForRendering` `pars(mboxsize)` object. In turn, this is declared to be `firstprivate` in the `#pragma omp for` loop, creating an object for every thread.

A `schedule (dynamic)` scheduling clause is added to the OpenMP loop. When you run the code with this scheduling loop, you will see that each raster is drawn in equal time. In the original program some rasters were completed much earlier than others.

LISTING 11-4: Using an object to pass the parameters

```cpp
// A new class used to hold the former stack variables
class ParameterForRendering {
public:
  int           _ison;
  unsigned int  _serial;
  unsigned int  _mboxsize;
  unsigned int *_local_mbox;
public:
  // constructor
  ParameterForRendering(unsigned int box_size) :
    _ison(1),
    _serial(1),
    _mboxsize(box_size),
    _local_mbox(NULL) {
      _local_mbox = (unsigned int *) malloc(_mboxsize);
      memset(_local_mbox, 0, _mboxsize);
    }

  // copy constructor
  ParameterForRendering(const ParameterForRendering &input) :
    _ison(input._ison),
    _serial(input._serial),
    _mboxsize(input._mboxsize),
    _local_mbox(NULL) {
      _local_mbox = (unsigned int *) malloc(_mboxsize);
      memset(_local_mbox, 0, _mboxsize);
    }
  // destructor
  ~ParameterForRendering() {
    free (_local_mbox);
  }
};


static void draw_task (void)
{
  unsigned int mboxsize = sizeof(unsigned int)*(max_objectid() + 20);

  // instantiate class object
  ParameterForRendering pars(mboxsize);

  // share loop iterations between threads
  // each thread gets its own initialized copy of 'pars'
  #pragma omp parallel for firstprivate (pars) schedule (dynamic)
  for(int y = starty; y < stopy; y++) {
```

```
    if (pars._ison) {
      drawing_area drawing(startx, totaly-y, stopx-startx, 1);
       for (int x = startx; x < stopx; x++) {
        color_t c = render_one_pixel (x, y, pars._local_mbox, pars._serial,
                         startx, stopx, starty, stopy);
        drawing.put_pixel(c);
      }
      pars._ison = (video->next_frame()? 1 : 0);
    }
  }
  return;
}
```

code snippet Chapter11\11-4.cpp

After you implement the preceding modifications, the image is generated without any defect. You can try this for yourself in Activity 11-7. An interesting task is to compare the performance of this solution against a version that uses a critical section.

Data race issues still exist in the display routines, but they are not addressed here.

ACTIVITY 11-7: FIXING THE DATA RACE

In this activity you fix the remaining data races. Use steps 1–3 if you are using Windows, and steps 4–6 if you are using Linux.

PDE-Windows

1. Open the `build_with_openmp.cpp` file and replace the `draw_task` function with the code in Listing 11-4. Notice the listing also adds a new `ParameterForRendering` class that will be used to pass parameters.

2. Build the debug version from the menu Build ⇨ Build build_with_openmp.

3. Press F5 to debug the program. There should be no data races detected in the four functions that are being monitored.

IDB-Linux

4. Open the `build_with_openmp.cpp` file and replace the `draw_task` function with the code in Listing 11-4. Notice the listing also adds a new `ParameterForRendering` class that will be used to pass parameters.

5. Build the debug version.

6. Press F5 to debug the program. There should be no data races detected in the four functions being monitored.

MORE ABOUT FILTERS

Filters are an important part of the debugger. They help you to determine where and what to investigate when analyzing data races in your code. As you have already seen, two different kinds of filters exist: *suppress filters* and the *focus filters*. You don't have to apply the filters to all your code; you can instead apply the filters to a specific range within your code. Table 11-1 shows how to apply the filters to different ranges.

TABLE 11-1: Specifying the Filter Range

RANGE	PURPOSE	INPUT
Entire function	Used when you are not interested/ interested in the detections coming from a specific function.	{function,[source],[module] }
Entire source file	Used when you are not interested/ interested in the detections coming from a specific source file.	{,source,[module] }
Address range	Used to filter (out/in) the complete address range of a translation unit. It can be set by line range or address range.	{,source,[module] }@line
Data range/ Filter	Used to filter (out/in) events coming from any specific data.	Symbol name or address. If you reference arrays, you must also state their size.

You can insert filters in two ways: either straight from an event in the Thread Data Sharing Events window or by right-clicking the Thread Data Sharing Filters window. After inserting a filter, you can modify its properties in a dialog box (see Figures 11-16 and 11-17), which you can reach by right-clicking the filter name in the Thread Sharing Filters Window.

FIGURE 11-16: The Modify Data Range Filter dialog

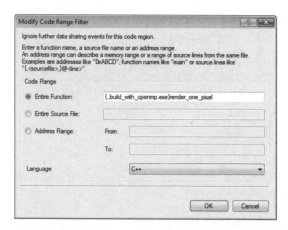

FIGURE 11-17: The Modify Code Range Filter dialog

RUNTIME INVESTIGATION: VIEWING THE STATE OF YOUR APPLICATION

As shown in Table 11-2, the debugger offers several specialized windows to help you investigate the current state of your application and its threads.

TABLE 11-2: Intel Debugger Windows

WINDOW	DESCRIPTION	MODEL
Tasks	Displays the state of a task, the parent task, and the number of spawned tasks.	OpenMP
Spawn Tree	Displays a tree of spawned tasks; tasks that have not spawned anything are shown as leaf nodes.	OpenMP
Locks	Displays the state a lock, the type of lock, the number of threads holding the lock, and references to the lock.	OpenMP
Barriers	Displays the state of a barrier, the number of threads that have reached the barrier, and the location of the barrier.	OpenMP
Teams	Displays the team of threads that supports a parallel region.	OpenMP
Taskwaits	Displays the state of a taskwait, the number of tasks the taskwait is waiting for, and the location of the taskwait.	OpenMP
Cilk Thread Stack	Displays a call stack of worker threads.	Cilk Plus

The OpenMP windows give information about the team hierarchy and the relationship between tasks and source code. This will help you to identify what code the thread is executing.

You can access the OpenMP windows either by clicking the corresponding buttons on the toolbar (see Figure 11-18) or by selecting Debug ➪ Intel Parallel Debugger Extension ➪ Windows ➪ OpenMP ➪ [*window*] (see Figure 11-19).

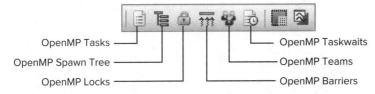

OpenMP Tasks ———
OpenMP Spawn Tree ———
OpenMP Locks ———
——— OpenMP Taskwaits
——— OpenMP Teams
——— OpenMP Barriers

FIGURE 11-18: The OpenMP windows toolbar

FIGURE 11-19: Accessing the OpenMP window from the menu

Using the OpenMP Tasks Window to Investigate Variables Within a Parallel Region

Using the Tachyon solution in Listing 11-3, you can use the OpenMP windows to investigate what happened to the variables created inside of the `#pragma omp parallel` region. However, at first, it doesn't appear obvious how to find out what code (and thread) a particular OpenMP task has used.

You can use the information from the Tasks window and the Spawn Tree window to associate a parallel task to a specific thread. You can then examine the call stack for that thread (and the local variables) all the way back to the point where the thread was first created within the parallel region.

Figure 11-20 shows the windows needed to map the OpenMP task to the correct call stack. You can examine the contents of an OpenMP task's call stack as follows:

1. Get the thread ID of a task in OpenMP's Tasks window. In the example, task 47 has a thread ID of 3400.

2. Double-click thread 3400 in the Threads window.

3. Examine the Locals window to see the stack variables. These are thread-specific in the example.

4. Examine the Call Stack window to see the function hierarchy.

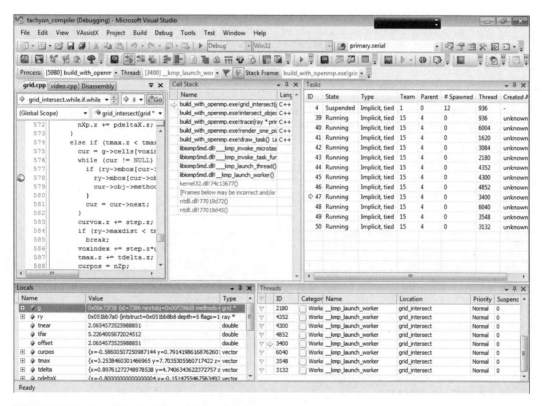

FIGURE 11-20: Examining the OpenMP task states

Using the OpenMP Spawn Tree Window to View the Behavior of Parallel Code

You can use the OpenMP Spawn Tree window to confirm that your OpenMP parallelism is working as intended. For example, consider the Fibonacci number calculator. Fibonacci numbers are integer numbers that follow the sequence 0, 1, 1, 2, 3, 5, 8, 13, and so on. Each Fibonacci number is the sum of the previous two numbers in the sequence. The first two numbers in the sequence are always 0 and 1. Listing 11-5 contains a parallel version. The bolded code makes the program parallel. If you delete that code, you will end up with the original serial version.

LISTING 11-5: Simple implementation of a Fibonacci calculator

```c
// This code has an ERROR in it which will cause a SEGMENTATION fault!
#include <stdio.h>
long long int fibonacci(int n) {
  if (n > 1) {
    long long int r_1, r_2;
    // create a task to calculate the n-1 number
    #pragma omp task  default(none) shared(r_1,n)
    {
      // recursive call
      r_1 = fibonacci(n - 1);
    }
    // create a task to calculate the n-2 number
    #pragma omp task  default(none) shared(r_2,n)
    {
      // recursive call
      r_2 = fibonacci(n - 2);
    }
    return r_1 + r_2;
  } else {
    // exit point for the recursion
    // this seeds the first two numbers in the sequence
    // ie 0 and 1
    if (n==0) return 0;
    return 1;
  }
}

int main()
{
  int i = 50;
  long long int t  =0 ;
  // create a parallel region
  #pragma omp parallel
```

```
{
    // run as a single thread
    #pragma omp single
    // calculate the 50th number in the fibonacci sequence
    t = fibonacci(i);
}
printf("%d\n",t);
return 0;
}
```

code snippet Chapter11\11-5.cpp

Two independent OpenMP tasks are used to add parallelism to the `fibonacci` function. The first task calculates `fibonacci(n-1)`, and the second calculates `fibonacci(n-2)`. This should generate a tree of spawned tasks, branching twice for every execution of the `fibonacci` function.

If you compile and execute the code, a segmentation fault occurs. Figure 11-21 shows the OpenMP spawn tree at the point the fault happens. Although you can see that two tasks are spawned from task 55, a strange pattern is displayed that does not match the expected behavior for the task hierarchy.

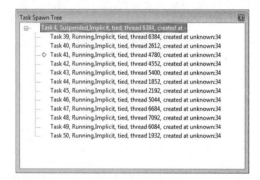

FIGURE 11-21: The spawning tree for the wrong parallelization suggested for the Fibonacci example

The cause of the problem is a missing `taskwait` clause (see the bold code in Listing 11-6). This missing statement causes each task to overlap, corrupting the stack and causing a segmentation fault and chaos on the spawned tree. Inserting a `#pragma omp taskwait` statement before the `return` statement in the `fibonacci` function should eliminate this effect. With this addition, both tasks run to completion.

Listing 11-6 shows the modified code with the `taskwait` clause, and Figure 11-22 shows the spawn tree of the corrected code.

LISTING 11-6: Right parallelization for the Fibonacci example

```c
#include <stdio.h>
long long int fibonacci(int n) {
  if (n > 1) {
    long long int r_1, r_2;

    // create a task to calculate the n-1 number
    #pragma omp task  default(none) shared(r_1,n)
    {
      r_1 = fibonacci(n - 1);
    }

    // create a task to calculate the n-2 number
    #pragma omp task  default(none) shared(r_2,n)
    {
      r_2 = fibonacci(n - 2);
    }
     // wait here until both tasks have finished running.
     #pragma omp taskwait

    return r_1 + r_2;
  } else {
    // exit point for the recursion
    // this seeds the first two numbers in the sequence
    if (n==0) return 0;
    return 1;
  }
}

int main()
{
  int i = 50;
  long long int t  =0 ;
  // create a parallel region
  #pragma omp parallel
  {
    // run as a single thread
    #pragma omp single
   // calculate the 50th number in the fibonacci sequence
    t = fibonacci(i);
  }
  printf("%d\n",t);
  return 0;
}
```

code snippet Chapter11\11-6.c

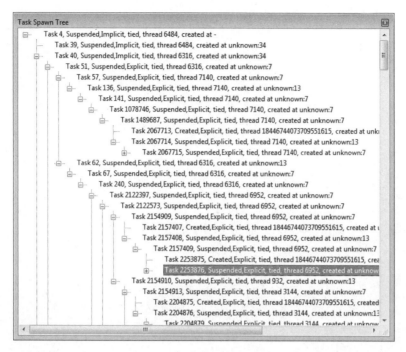

FIGURE 11-22: The spawn tree after the correction of the parallel Fibonacci example

SUMMARY

Viewing a parallel program while it is running is a very different experience from error-detection techniques described in other chapters. Finding data races and observing program behavior becomes a dynamic process rather than a batch-driven process.

Using the Intel Debugger to detect data races brings a new level of visibility and confidence when debugging. In this chapter you used the debugger to fix data races in the Tachyon ray-tracing program, and corrected the execution order in a Fibonacci calculator. You can see another example of using the debugger in Chapter 14, "Nine Tips to Parallel-Programming Heaven," where you use it to detect data races in a Cilk Plus program.

Chapter 12, "Event-Based Analysis with VTune Amplifier XE," shows how to use Amplifier XE to see how well your program is using the CPU architecture.

12

Event-Based Analysis with VTune Amplifier XE

WHAT'S IN THIS CHAPTER?

➤ Using the cycles per instruction retired (CPI) metric to spot potentially unhealthy programs

➤ Using Amplifier XE's General Exploration analysis to identify performance issues in your program

➤ Drilling down into architectural hotspots

➤ Using Amplifier XE's APIs to control data collection

When we are ill, most of us know how to check the obvious. Do we have a fever? Are we aching anywhere? Is our pulse rate normal? Wouldn't it be great if there were an easy way of measuring the health of a program? The good news is that some equivalent indicators can be used to monitor the health of an application, and Amplifier XE can be used to get those measurements.

This chapter shows how to check the health of an application using Amplifier XE's architectural analysis types. Starting with a system-wide view of your system, you learn how to observe how well different programs are performing.

TARGET ARCHITECTURE

The principles described in this chapter can be applied to any CPU architecture. However, Amplifier XE's architectural analysis features are specifically targeted at Intel devices. You will not be able to carry out the activities in this chapter on a non-Intel device.

TESTING THE HEALTH OF AN APPLICATION

When looking at the health of an application, several facts need to be ascertained. Like people, each piece of software has its own unique traits. Even if two programs do the same thing — for example, predicting the weather — they may work quite differently internally. These internal differences often have a direct impact on how quickly a program runs and how well the software makes use of the CPU. A well-written "healthy" program will run efficiently, whereas a poorly written "sick" program may run slowly and waste CPU resources.

The following are basic questions to ask when optimizing software:

➤ How long does the program run?

➤ How much work does the program do?

➤ Does the program have any inefficiencies?

Fortunately, all Intel CPUs have hardwired into them electronics that can measure myriad parameters and statistics. Two fundamental parameters (*clock ticks* and *instructions retired*), and an associated ratio (*cycles per instruction retired*), can be used to quickly spot unhealthy software.

➤ **Clock ticks** show how many CPU cycles a program consumed. They are a measure of time. Depending on the processor you are running on, clock ticks might be measured per logical core or per CPU.

➤ **Instructions retired** measure the number of instructions that have progressed all the way through the CPU pipeline and have not been abandoned along the way. The retired instructions represent the real work being done by the program.

➤ **Cycles per instruction retired (CPI)** gives an average figure of how much time each executed instruction took in cycles. The formula is as follows:

$$CPI = \text{clock ticks} / \text{instructions retired}$$

You can use this ratio to measure a program's efficiency. The lower the CPI value, the more efficient the program is. Low is good, high is bad.

What Causes a High CPI?

In modern CPUs, it is theoretically possible to have four instructions retired on each cycle, giving a CPI of 0.25; however, this low of a figure is rarely achieved. If your application has a CPI of below 1, you are doing pretty well. In the hands-on activities you will see CPI values varying from 26, which is terrible, down to about 0.4, which is excellent.

If you take every cycle of a program, you will find that each cycle can be classed in one of three ways (see Figure 12-1).

> ➤ Cycles where instructions are executed and usefully employed (A)

> ➤ Cycles where the CPU is doing nothing (B)

> ➤ Cycles where instructions are read and possibly executed but are then abandoned or "thrown away" (C)

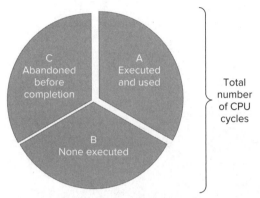

Total cycles consumed = A + B + C

FIGURE 12-1: Every cycle the CPU consumes can be categorized based on how they use instructions

A healthy program will have very few of categories B and C, with most of the cycles being executed and used. An unhealthy program will have a lot of cycles that are not doing anything useful. The more B or C type cycles, the worse the CPI. (Note that the terms A, B, and C have no special significance; they are used merely to help identify the segments in Figure 12-1.)

You will probably find that your application is dominated by one of the segments. You can use Amplifier XE to detect these different cycles by looking for the hotpots in your code.

Is CPI on Its Own a Good Enough Measure of Health?

Although CPI can be used to indicate that some programs have wasted cycles and hence present optimization opprtunities, using just CPI can occasionally be misleading.

In Activities 12-3 and 12-4 later in the chapter, you will see that the speed of the matrix multiplication program improves but the CPI gets worse.

When doing any optimization work, always keep an eye on the most fundamental measurement — that is, how long a program took to run; otherwise, you may spend a lot of unfruitful time improving the CPI but ending up with a slower program.

Conducting a System-Wide Analysis

It's sometimes educational to do a system-wide analysis on a PC with Amplifier XE to see which programs have the best CPI and which have the worst. To perform a system-wide analysis, you first set the project properties to Profile System, as shown in Figure 12-2, and then launch a Lightweight Hotspots analysis. This kind of hotspot uses the performance monitoring capabilities of the CPU, has a very low impact on the running programs, and is capable of sampling everything that running on your PC.

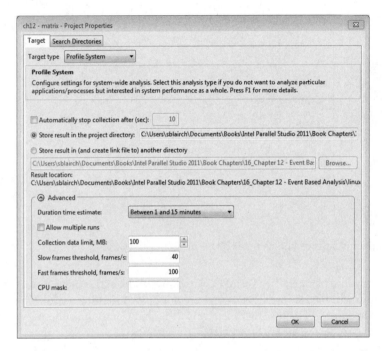

FIGURE 12-2: Editing the project properties to enable system-wide profiling

Once you've run a profiling session, you'll probably be fascinated by the results. Figure 12-3 shows the results of doing an analysis on a dual core laptop (the one that was used to write this chapter). Notice that `autocheck.exe` has a huge CPI of nearly 36. As it happens, this value is expected. `Autocheck.exe` is part of Windows and is designed to be non-CPU-intensive, running in the background doing some maintenance activities. Amplifier XE highlights the CPIs to alert you to values that need further investigation.

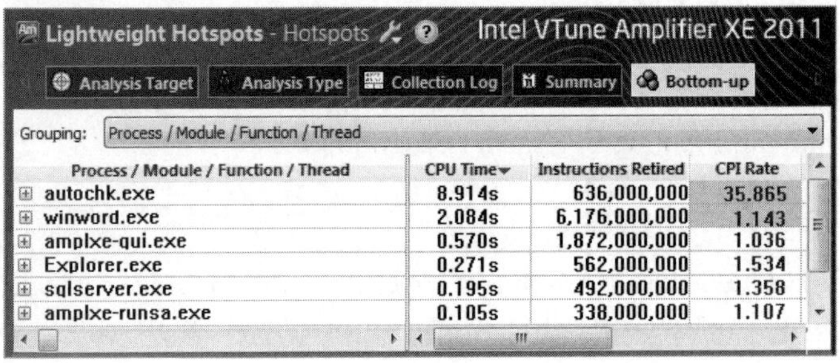

FIGURE 12-3: A system-wide analysis reveals the CPI rate of every program

Looking at CPI of different programs is entertaining, but there is a serious part to exercise as well. Apart from CPI spotting, you can use the same system-wide analysis to see if one particular program is hogging all the CPU time, as the following story illustrates.

In a recent code-optimization training session at a university, a student complained that his "optimized" applications ran unexpectedly slow. By running a system-wide analysis with Amplifier XE, the reason for the slowdown became obvious. Another user was logged on to the same node and running an MP3 player; the player had been running for the last five days! After a little further exploration, the user of the MP3 software was identified as being someone from the university's IT department. Once the MP3 player was killed, the application ran as expected.

> *When installing Amplifier XE on a cluster or other high-performance computing (HPC) environment, make sure your administrator knows Amplifier XE's capabilities.*

ACTIVITY 12-1: CONDUCTING A SYSTEM-WIDE ANALYSIS

In this activity you perform a system-wide analysis to see how well the programs are running on your machine. You can run this activity on Linux or Windows.

1. Start Amplifier XE GUI from the command line:

```
amplxe-gui
```

2. Create a new `Chapter 12` project by selecting File ➪ New ➪ Project. In the Project Properties dialog, select Profile System from the Target tab.

3. Carry out a Hotspot Analysis by selecting File ➪ New ➪ Analysis... ➪ Algorithm Analysis ➪ Lightweight Hotspots.

4. Stop the data collector after about ten seconds or so.

5. Explore the results and find the following:

➤ The application with the largest CPI

➤ Any fields highlighted in pink

CONDUCTING A HOTSPOT ANALYSIS

Once it is established that someone is not well, a more detailed diagnosis is needed, with the doctor prodding, poking, and asking appropriate questions. The doctor will need to work out what the problem is in order to decide on the best treatment. Someone complaining of feeling hot and having stomach pain should be dealt with quite differently from someone with a suspected broken leg. Knowing the location and nature of any discomfort or pain is essential for a correct diagnosis.

In the same way, once you've identified that your program is running poorly by looking at the CPI and the time the program took to run, you should conduct a hotspot analysis to find out where the bottlenecks are in your code. After identifying the hotspots, you then need to find the cause of the hotspots and apply suitable remedies.

Hotspot Analysis Types

Amplifier XE has two hotspot analysis types:

➤ **Lightweight Hotspots analysis** — This uses hardware event-based sampling and samples all the processes running on a system. The overhead of this type of collection is very low. No stack information is collected in this analysis type. The lightweight hotspot analysis can be applied either to a single application or to the whole system, depending on whether you choose *Profile System* or *Launch Application* in the project properties. If you choose Launch Application, only information about the application will be displayed; the rest will be filtered out.

➤ **Hotspots analysis** — This employs user-mode sampling and, unlike lightweight hotspots, will collect stack and call tree information. You cannot use this kind of analysis to do a system-wide analysis; it is used to analyze a single application or process. You can find more information on this kind of analysis in Chapter 6, "Where to Parallelize."

 To reduce confusion about the terms "Lightweight Hotspots analysis" and "Hotspots analysis," the rest of this chapter refers to the latter as User Mode Hotspots analysis.

User Mode Hotspots Versus Lightweight Hotspots

It's worth spending a few minutes looking at the difference between the two types of analysis. The screenshots in this section use the code from `matrix.cpp` in Listing 12-3 (at the end of the chapter). The machine used has a second-generation Intel Core Architecture (aka Intel Sandy Bridge) 3.0 GHz processor, 8GB of memory running Centos 5 (64-bit 2.6.18 Kernel). The CPU has 4 cores and supports hyper threading, giving a total availability of 8 logical CPUs.

The Results Tabs

Amplifier XE displays the data collected from a hotspot analysis in different tabs (see Figure 12-4). Notice that the User Mode Hotspots analysis has five tabs, whereas the Lightweight Hotspots analysis has only four tabs. The extra tab, Top-down Tree, is available only in the User Mode Hotspots analysis because only this analysis collects stack and call graph information.

(a) Lightweight Hotspot

(b) User Mode Hotspot

FIGURE 12-4: The results tabs

The Summary Tab

When you select the Summary tab, the Lightweight Hotspots analysis gives two extra pieces of information: Instructions Retired and CPI Rate (see Figure 12-5). Notice that the Lightweight Hotspots analysis lists what seems to be two OS-related functions: vmlinux and _dl_relocate_object. The *Paused Time* records the amount of time the analysis ran with the collector paused.

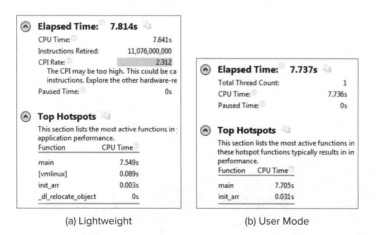

(a) Lightweight

(b) User Mode

FIGURE 12-5: A summary page showing the two types of hotspot analysis

The Bottom-up Tab

You can group and display the results in the Bottom-up tab according to different objects, such as Process, Module, Thread, and so on. Table 12-1 lists the different objects used in the two types of hotspot analysis. Most terms will be familiar to you or will be explained later; however, the following two terms need a quick explanation now:

➤ **Package** refers to the physical CPUs. A dual-CPU system has two packages.

➤ **H/W context** refers to logical CPUs.

TABLE 12-1: Objects Used in the Bottom-up Results Grouping

OBJECT	LIGHTWEIGHT	USER MODE
Process	Y	N
Module	Y	Y
Thread	Y	Y
Source file	Y	Y
Function	Y	Y
Basic nlock	Y	N
Code location	Y	N
Class	Y	Y
H/W context	Y	N
Package	Y	N
Frames	Y	Y
Call stack	N	Y
OpenMP regions	N	Y
Task type	N	Y

Figure 12-6 shows an example of lightweight hotspots grouped by module/function.

Grouping:	Module / Function					
Module / Function	CPU Time▼	Instructions Ret...	CPI Rate	Function (Full)	Module Path
⊟ ijk.gcc.exe	7.552s	11,062,000,000	2.286		/home/sblairch ...
main	7.549s	11,022,000,000	2.293	main	/home/sblairch ...
init_arr	0.003s	40,000,000	0.450	init_arr(double*)	/home/sblairch ...
⊟ vmlinux	0.089s	12,000,000	27.000		vmlinux
[vmlinux]	0.089s	12,000,000	27.000	[vmlinux]	vmlinux
⊟ ld-2.5.so	0s	2,000,000	0.000		/lib64/ld-2.5.so
_dl_relocate_object	0s	2,000,000	0.000	_dl_relocate_obj ...	/lib64/ld-2.5.so
Selected 1 row(s):	7.552s	11,062,000,000			

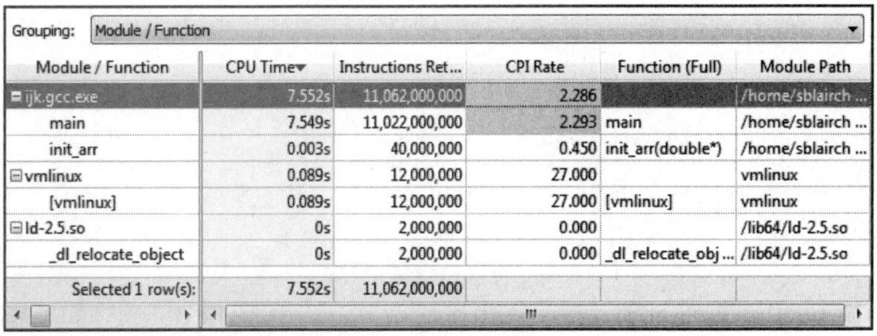

FIGURE 12-6: Lightweight hotspots grouped by module/function

The Top-down Tree Tab

Only the User Mode Hotspots analysis has a top-down view. This view displays the call stack and timeline view as shown in Figure 12-7.

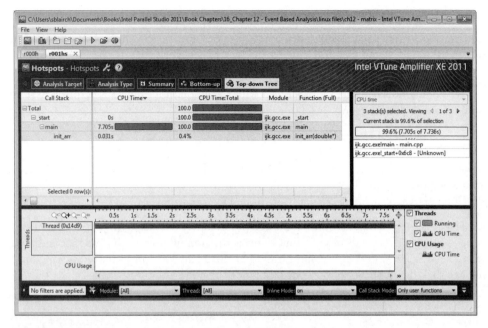

FIGURE 12-7: The Top-down Tree tab of the User Mode Hotspots analysis

Viewpoints

All analysis types have a default view. You can change the view by clicking the spanner next to the analysis title (see Figure 12-8). The Lightweight Hotspots analysis has four views, whereas the User Mode Hotspots analysis has only two views. *Viewpoints* are simply different ways of presenting the collected data. Because the User Mode Hotspots analysis does not collect any hardware events, only two viewpoints are available.

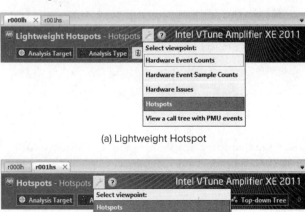

(a) Lightweight Hotspot

(b) User Mode Hotspot

FIGURE 12-8: Different viewpoints for the two types of analysis

To summarize, the major differences between the two types of hotspot analysis are as follows:

➤ Lightweight Hotspots analysis is system wide but does not collect call stack information. It collects CPU events, and therefore can display metrics such as CPI.

➤ User Mode Hotspots analysis is not system wide but does provide call stack information. This type of analysis is primarily concerned with the amount of time each part of a program takes. It cannot display events or CPI.

Finding Hotspots in Code

Back to the task at hand. The purpose of doing a hotspot analysis is to determine the health of your code and to understand the nature of any bottlenecks. For this type of analysis you need to use a Lightweight Hotspots analysis rather than a User Mode Hotspots analysis.

As shown in Figure 12-6, the biggest lightweight hotspot in `ijk.gcc.exe` is the `main()` function, which is using just over 7.5 seconds of CPU time. This is the sum of how much time each individual hardware thread used. The CPI is 2.293, indicating that there may be a problem. By clicking on the hotspot, you can drill down to the source code (see Figure 12-9).

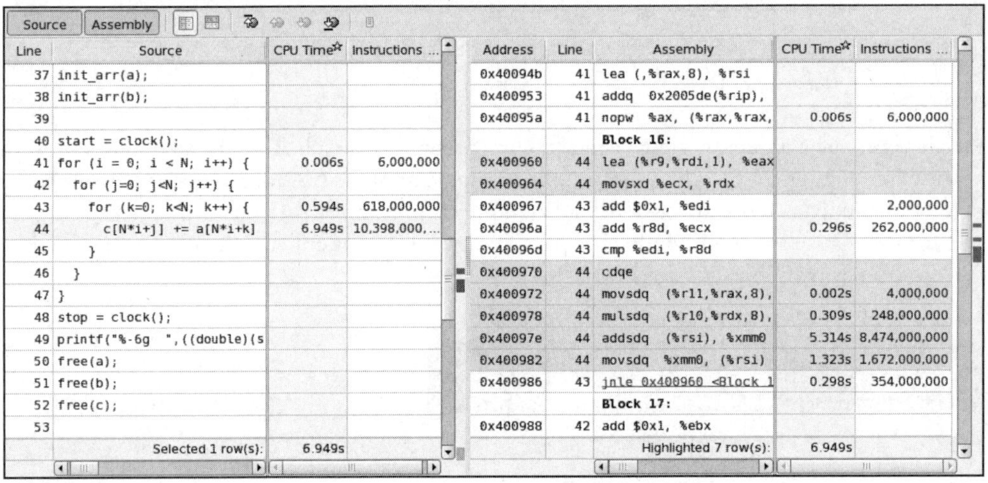

Line	Source	CPU Time	Instructions ...		Address	Line	Assembly	CPU Time	Instructions ...
37	`init_arr(a);`				0x40094b	41	`lea (,%rax,8), %rsi`		
38	`init_arr(b);`				0x400953	41	`addq 0x2005de(%rip),`		
39					0x40095a	41	`nopw %ax, (%rax,%rax,`	0.006s	6,000,000
40	`start = clock();`						**Block 16:**		
41	`for (i = 0; i < N; i++) {`	0.006s	6,000,000		0x400960	44	`lea (%r9,%rdi,1), %eax`		
42	` for (j=0; j<N; j++) {`				0x400964	44	`movsxd %ecx, %rdx`		
43	`  for (k=0; k<N; k++) {`	0.594s	618,000,000		0x400967	43	`add $0x1, %edi`		2,000,000
44	`   c[N*i+j] += a[N*i+k]`	6.949s	10,398,000,...		0x40096a	43	`add %r8d, %ecx`	0.296s	262,000,000
45	` }`				0x40096d	43	`cmp %edi, %r8d`		
46	`}`				0x400970	44	`cdqe`		
47	`}`				0x400972	44	`movsdq (%r11,%rax,8),`	0.002s	4,000,000
48	`stop = clock();`				0x400978	44	`mulsdq (%r10,%rdx,8),`	0.309s	248,000,000
49	`printf("%-6g ",((double)(s`				0x40097e	44	`addsdq (%rsi), %xmm0`	5.314s	8,474,000,000
50	`free(a);`				0x400982	44	`movsdq %xmm0, (%rsi)`	1.323s	1,672,000,000
51	`free(b);`				0x400986	43	`jnle 0x400960 <Block 1`	0.298s	354,000,000
52	`free(c);`						**Block 17:**		
53					0x400988	42	`add $0x1, %ebx`		
	Selected 1 row(s):	6.949s					Highlighted 7 row(s):	6.949s	

FIGURE 12-9: The Source view

Looking at the C code of the hotspot, you can see that three arrays (a, b, and c) are accessed:

```
for (i = 0; i < N; i++) {
    for (j=0; j<N; j++) {
        for (k=0; k<N; k++) {
            c[N*i+j] += a[N*i+k] * b[N*k+j];
```

```
        // printf("%p,%p,%p\n", &c[N*i+j],&a[N*i+k],&b[N*k+j]);
    }
  }
}
```

The right side of the Source view in Figure 12-9 shows the disassembly window (duplicated in Table 12-2). The instructions that take the most time are addsdq and movsdq.

TABLE 12-2: The Assembly Lines

ADDRESS	LINE	ASSEMBLY	CPU TIME
0x400970	44	cdqe	
0x400972	44	movsdq (%r11,%rax,8), %xmm0	0.002s
0x400978	44	mulsdq (%r10,%rdx,8), %xmm0	0.309s
0x40097e	44	addsdq (%rsi), %xmm0	5.314s
0x400982	44	movsdq %xmm0, (%rsi)	1.323s
0x400986	43	jnle 0x400960 <Block 16>	0.298s

Both of the addsdq and movsdq instructions access memory, so the underlying problem might be related to memory. If you are not an expert on assembler instructions, you can use the online context-sensitive help to display the instruction description, as shown in Figure 12-10.

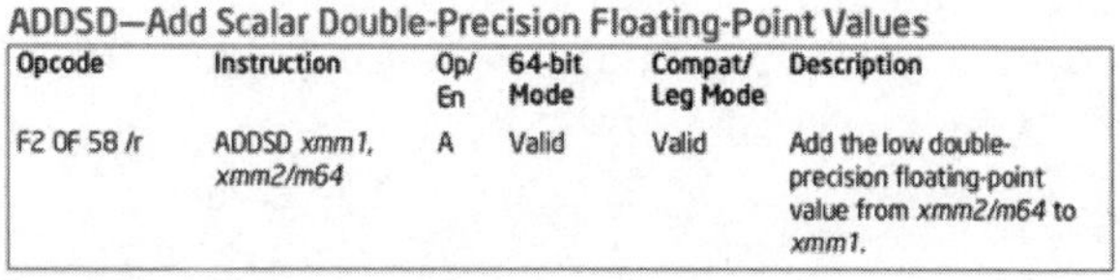

ADDSD—Add Scalar Double-Precision Floating-Point Values

Opcode	Instruction	Op/ En	64-bit Mode	Compat/ Leg Mode	Description
F2 0F 58 /r	ADDSD xmm1, xmm2/m64	A	Valid	Valid	Add the low double-precision floating-point value from xmm2/m64 to xmm1.

FIGURE 12-10: Online instruction help

The code was built as a 64-bit application using GNU GCC version 4.1.2. If you have built a 32-bit application or used a different compiler, you may get different assembler instructions. The events that have been captured do not yet tell exactly what is happening in the CPU, although depending on your profiling experience you might be able to guess as to what the underlying cause is.

Try out a Lightweight Hotspots analysis for yourself using the instructions in Activity 12-2.

ACTIVITY 12-2: CONDUCTING A LIGHTWEIGHT HOTSPOTS ANALYSIS

In this activity you look for the hotspots in the application `memory.exe`. You can run this activity on Linux or Windows.

1. Build the `matrix.cpp` application from Listing 12-3 (at the end of the chapter):

LINUX

```
g++ matrix.cpp -g -O2 -o matrix.exe
```

WINDOWS

```
cl matrix.cpp /Zi /O2 -o matrix.exe
```

2. In the Amplifier Project you already have open (from Activity 12-1), start a new Amplifier analysis and choose Lightweight Hotspots (File ⇨ New ⇨ Analysis... ⇨ Algorithm Analysis ⇨ Lightweight Hotspots).

3. In the Project Properties Target tab, select Launch Application.

4. Start the analysis by pressing the Start button.

5. When the analysis is complete, find the biggest hotspot in from the Bottom-up tab.

6. Double-click the hotspot and find the following in the source code:

> ➤ The C line taking up the most time

> ➤ The assembler instruction taking up the most time

> ➤ The CPI rate of the bottleneck

7. Look in the Summary window and confirm that the hotspot you discovered is the same as the one mentioned on the summary page. (Figure 12-4 shows the summary button that you can use to display the summary page.)

CONDUCTING A GENERAL EXPLORATION ANALYSIS

A good doctor will find the underlying cause of an illness. Sometimes the reason will be obvious, and sometimes finding the exact cause will be difficult. You have the same set of challenges when examining your software.

You already know where the bottleneck is, so now you need to dig a little deeper to find out what is causing the hotspot. Amplifier XE's General Exploration analysis is designed to help you do this. The General Exploration analysis looks for hardware issues that can cause problems. Amplifier XE has multiple versions of this analysis type that are dedicated to different CPUs. This chapter uses the version for Intel Microarchitecture Code Name Sandy Bridge. If you use a different version (because your system is from a different CPU family), the results may be categorized differently.

When an analysis has completed, the Bottom-up window is displayed, as shown in Figure 12-11. Several fields are highlighted to draw your attention to potential problems.

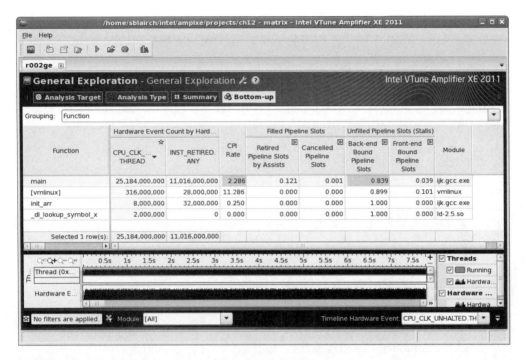

FIGURE 12-11: The Bottom-up window with each issue highlighted

As shown in Figure 12-12, the summary page identifies four hardware issues: *CPI Rate, Back-end Bound Pipeline Slots, LLC Miss,* and *DTLB Overhead.* Figure 12-12 shows only the top part of the summary page; more entries are available further down the list, but none of them are highlighted.

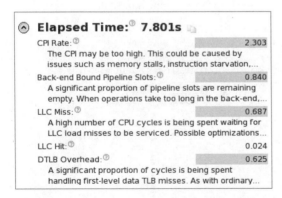

FIGURE 12-12: A summary of the General Exploration analysis

 If you hover the mouse over each highlighted field, a description of the problem and the threshold value formula are displayed. When a ratio exceeds the threshold value, Amplifier highlights the field in pink.

Every ratio, apart from CPI, has a value between 0 and 1. The nearer the value is to 0, the better the performance. Before exploring further what these entries mean, try out Activity 12-3.

ACTIVITY 12-3: CONDUCTING A GENERAL EXPLORATION ANALYSIS

In this activity you run a General Exploration analysis on `matrix.cpp` and discover the underlying hardware issue. You can run this activity on Linux or Windows.

1. If you haven't already done so, build the `matrix.cpp` application from Listing 12-3:

LINUX

```
g++ matrix.cpp -g -O2 -o matrix.exe
```

WINDOWS

```
cl matrix.cpp /Zi /O2 -o matrix.exe
```

2. Start new Amplifier analysis and choose General Exploration.

> File ⇨ New ⇨ Analysis...

3. In the Project Properties Target tab, select Launch Application and make sure the application to launch is `matrix.exe`.

4. In the list of prebuilt analysis types, chose < *CPU architecture* > ⇨ General Exploration, where *CPU architecture* will be one of the following:

> ➤ Advanced Intel Core 2 Processor Family Analysis
>
> ➤ Advanced Intel Microarchitecture Code Name Nehalem Analysis
>
> ➤ Advanced Intel Microarchitecture Code Name Sandy Bridge Analysis
>
> ➤ Advanced Intel Atom Processor Analysis

Amplifier XE will only let you choose the analysis type that fits your CPU. If you choose an invalid option, the message `This analysis type is only defined for processors based on...` will be displayed, and the Start button will be disabled.

5. Start the analysis by selecting the Start button.

6. When the analysis is complete, look at the summary page. You should see some fields highlighted in pink.

7. Browse the Bottom-up view and find the biggest hotspot.

8. Navigate to the source code by double-clicking the hotspot and identify which source line is causing the problem.

A Quick Anatomy Class

One of the most daunting aspects of optimizing code is coming to grips with the internals of the CPU. Fortunately, Amplifier XE helps out by providing predefined analysis types along with helpful on-screen explanatory notes. Here's an example of the explanatory note attached to the CPI ratio:

> "Cycles per instruction retired, or CPI, is a fundamental performance metric indicating approximately how much time each executed instruction took, in units of cycles. Modern superscalar processors issue up to four instructions per cycle, suggesting a theoretical best CPI of .25. But various effects (long latency memory, floating-point, or SIMD operations; nonretired instructions due to branch mispredictions; instruction starvation in the front-end) tend to pull the observed CPI up. A CPI of 1 is generally considered acceptable for HPC applications but different application domains will have very different expected values. Nonetheless, CPI is an excellent metric for judging an overall potential for application performance tuning"

CPU Internals

Just as knowing what to call different parts of your anatomy is helpful when describing your aches and pains to the doctor, it is helpful to know a few terms to help describe bottlenecks.

Figure 12-13 shows a high-level view of a typical processor, split into two halves: the *front-end* and the *back-end*.

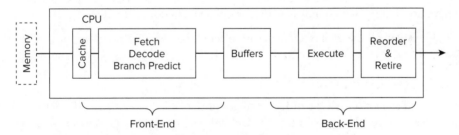

FIGURE 12-13: The basic blocks of a CPU

The *front-end* is responsible for the following:

➤ Fetching instructions from memory.

➤ Decoding instructions into micro-operations, a format the CPU understands.

➤ Predicting the direction branch instructions will take and prefetching those instructions ahead of when they are actually needed.

The *back-end* is responsible for the following:

➤ Executing the micro-operations. Several execution engines can run in parallel, thus providing instruction-level parallelism. Some engines are dedicated to specific types of instructions.

➤ Retiring the instructions.

➤ Preserving the order layout of retired instructions. Some of the micro-operations will be executed out of order. The reorder mechanism makes sure that all retired instructions will be retired in the same order they appeared in the original source code.

The buffers between the front-end and back-end help to mitigate against delays known as *stalls*. As long as micro-operations are stored in the buffer, even if there is a stall in the front-end, the back-end can still be fed micro-operations from the buffer. This reduces the chance of a front-end stall causing a back-end stall. In fact, many buffers throughout the CPU are not shown in Figure 12-13.

Categories of Execution Behavior

As mentioned previously (in the section "What Causes a High CPI?"), a program's cycles can be split between cycles where something useful is done and cycles where nothing useful is done. The different cycle categories are caused by how the code is executing on the CPU. The categories of execution can be split into the following four types, all of which can indicate that there are tuning optimizations to be had:

➤ Retirement-dominated execution

➤ Front-end-bound execution

➤ Back-end-bound execution

➤ Cancellation-dominated execution

In each of the following diagrams (Figures 12-14 to 12-17), the flow of instructions through the CPU is shown by the arrow. The thickness of the arrow represents the volume of throughput. Some of the blocks within the diagrams are shaded, which represents a lot of activity (or bottlenecks), whereas others have no shading, which indicates that the blocks are doing very little.

Your program could display all these characteristics in different parts of the program, or it could be dominated by one particular type of behavior.

Retirement-Dominated Execution

In retirement-dominated execution, all the different stages of the CPU are working efficiently with no significant stalls (see Figure 12-14). Typically, the CPI will be low (less than, say, 0.4), and the percentage of CPU utilization will be approaching 100 percent. The main opportunity for optimization is in reducing the amount of code that needs to be executed.

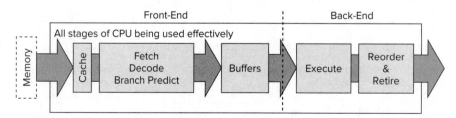

FIGURE 12-14: Retirement-dominated execution

Front-End-Bound Execution

As shown in Figure 12-15, front-end-bound code does not provide enough micro-operations to the back-end. Front-end problems are usually caused by:

➤ Delays in fetching code — for example, due to instruction cache misses

➤ Time taken to decode instructions

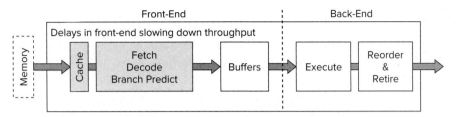

FIGURE 12-15: Front-end-bound execution

Back-End-Bound Execution

Back-end-bound code is not able to accept micro-operations from the front-end. The front-end supplies more micro-operations than the back-end can handle, leading to the back-end's internal queues being full. This usually is caused by the back-end's data structures being taken up by micro-operations that are waiting for data in the caches.

The hollow arrows in Figure 12-16 are intended to show that the front-end is capable of providing many instructions but cannot because of a busy back-end.

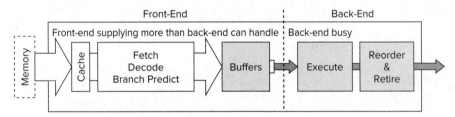

FIGURE 12-16: Back-end-bound execution

Cancellation-Dominated Execution

In cancellation-dominated execution, many micro-operations are cancelled or "thrown away" (see Figure 12-17). The most common reason for this type of behavior is the front-end mispredicting branch instructions. You often see this kind of behavior in database applications or in code that is doing a lot of pointer chasing, such as in linked lists.

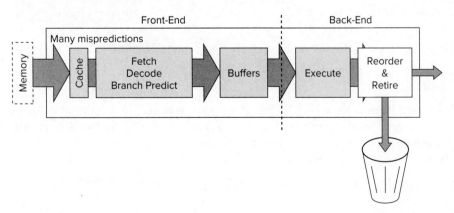

FIGURE 12-17: Cancellation-dominated execution

FIXING HARDWARE ISSUES

An experienced doctor will consider the facts he knows, filter out the unimportant data, and make a diagnosis based on his knowledge and experience. Ideally, after making the right diagnosis, the doctor will procure the correct remedy.

You've seen that Amplifier XE does a great job of collecting the facts and filtering out the unimportant data, eventually coming up with a list of four problems. You probably didn't notice it, but the General Exploration analysis you carried out captured more than 33 different types of events and checked every hotspot against at least 26 different rules.

The next step in the process is to fix the problems identified. It sounds so simple, doesn't it? The question is, which problem should be fixed first? Here are some guidelines that will help you:

➤ Always fix one problem at a time. Even if you know how to fix more than one problem at once, always focus on just one. Quite often fixing one problem will have a radical effect on other problems; therefore, it's best to go one step at a time, doing a fresh analysis between each fix.

➤ You can choose in which order to fix the problems either by fixing the problem with the highest ratio or by using Table 12-3, which lists the most common issues in their rough order of likelihood.

TABLE 12-3: Suggested Order of Fixing Problems

PRIORITY	PROBLEM	CHARACTERISTIC
1	Cache misses	Back-end-bound
2	Contested access	Back-end-bound
3	Other data-access issues	Back-end-bound
4	Allocation stalls	Back-end-bound
5	Micro assists	Retirement-dominated
6	Branch mispredictions and machine clears	Cancellation-dominated
7	Front-end stalls	Front-end-bound

As shown previously in Figure 12-12, the four problems identified by Amplifier XE are as follows:

➤ **CPI Rate** — The high CPI rate is a result of the other hardware issues. Once the issues are fixed, the CPI will drop.

➤ **Back-end-Bound Pipeline Slots** — On the machine these tests were run on (a Sandy Bridge), the front-end could provide up to 4 micro-operations per cycle to the back-end. Back-end-bound means the back-end was not able to accept enough operations to match the rate at which the front-end was supplying them.

➤ **LLC Miss** — An LLC miss is one of the most common causes of poor performance.

> ➤ **DTLB overhead** — The Data Translation Look-aside Buffer is used to support memory access. Partial copies of this table are normally held in cache. If a program accesses a memory address that is not referenced by the DTLB in cache, the new DTLB entries have to be loaded from external memory, causing a high overhead.

Using Table 12-3 as a guide, the LLC miss is tackled first.

Reducing Cache Misses

The code used for the matrix multiplication, `matrix.cpp`, is accessing memory in a cache-inefficient way. Figure 12-18 shows two 4x4 matrices, a and b being multiplied together, with the results in matrix c. In Figure 12-18(a) the nested loop uses the variables i, j, and k, with the outermost loop using i, and the innermost loop using k. The diagram shows each of the matrices sitting in the L1 cache and taking up two cache lines.

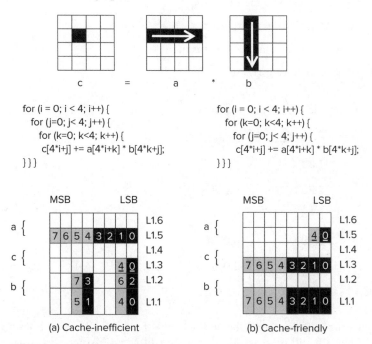

```
for (i = 0; i < 4; i++) {
  for (j=0; j< 4; j++) {
    for (k=0; k<4; k++) {
      c[4*i+j] += a[4*i+k] * b[4*k+j];
}}}
```

```
for (i = 0; i < 4; i++) {
  for (k=0; k<4; k++) {
    for (j=0; j< 4; j++) {
      c[4*i+j] += a[4*i+k] * b[4*k+j];
}}}
```

(a) Cache-inefficient   (b) Cache-friendly

FIGURE 12-18: Cache-inefficient and cache-friendly access

The numbers inside the cells are to show which cell is accessed in each iteration of the nested loop. The underlined numbers represent a sequence of four accesses on the same cell.

In Figure 12-18(a) you can see the following:

> ➤ Matrix a is accessed sequentially on each iteration.

> ➤ The first cell of matrix c is accessed on loops 0 to 3, and the second cell is accessed on loops 4 to 7.

> ➤ The access to the cells of matrix b is not sequential, with the cache line boundary being traversed between alternate loops.

Although this diagram shows only a 4×4 matrix, you can imagine that in very large matrices the code in Figure 12-18(a) would result in huge gaps in the address accessed between each read of matrix b, along with cache misses as far back as the Last Level Cache.

You can solve the cache misses by changing the loop sequence so that i and j are swapped. This results in the access to each cell becoming sequential, as shown in Figure 12-18(b).

Rerunning the code with this modification results in the application running much quicker. Table 12-4 shows the results of a General Exploration analysis on the modified application. You can see the following:

➤ The application runs more than five times faster.

➤ The CPI rate is much improved.

➤ The cache misses (LLC) have reduced by a factor of 10.

➤ The DTLB Overhead likewise is substantially reduced.

➤ The back-end-bound pipeline slot is reduced by a factor of 5.

➤ The front-end-bound pipeline slots have increased.

TABLE 12-4: Comparison of the Original and Loop-swapped Code

ISSUE	ORIGINAL	SWAPPED
Elapsed Time	7.801	1.535
CPI Rate	2.303	0.410
Back-end-Bound Pipeline Slots	0.84	0.159
LLC Miss	0.687	0.073
DTLB Overhead	0.625	0.010
Front-end-Bound Pipeline Slots	0.040	0.163

Having fixed the first problem, it's time to move onto the next issue. Although the back-end-bound pipeline slots are much reduced, they are still present and need to be addressed further.

Using More Efficient Instructions

In the assembler view of the application, you may have already noticed that the multiplication is carried out using the mulsd instruction. This instruction is a *scalar* SSE instruction — that is, it operates only on one value at a time. One way of improving the performance would be to use a *packed* SSE instruction instead. You can tell whether an instruction is scalar or packed by the presence of the letter s and p in the instruction name. The following code snippet shows packed SSE instructions being used in the inner loop:

```
for (j=0; j<N; j++) {
        res = _mm_mul_pd(*pA,pB[j]);
```

```
        res = _mm_hadd_pd ( res , res);
        _mm_store_sd(&c[N*i+j],res);
    }
```

By using the packed instruction, there should be a speedup of about two, because packed SSE instructions can calculate two double-precision floating-point values in one instruction.

Listing 12-4 (at the end of the chapter) has a new version of the main() function in which packed SSE instructions have been inserted into the code. Three major changes are made to the code:

➤ The dynamic allocated memory is aligned to a 16-byte boundary using the _mm_malloc function; it is then freed using the _mm_free function.

➤ Two pointers, pA and pB (of type __m128d), are used to point to the matrices a and b, respectively.

➤ The calculations are carried out using SSE instructions. The _mm_hadd function performs a horizontal add to add together the results of the vectorized multiplication.

Table 12-5 gives the new results, comparing them to the version that already has its loops swapped. The elapsed time has reduced, but note again that the CPI has increased. The two items in bold are highlighted in pink in Amplifier XE, suggesting that they need further investigation.

TABLE 12-5: A Comparison of the Loop-swapped and SSE Code

ISSUE	LOOP-SWAPPED	SSE
Elapsed Time	1.535	0.960
CPI Rate	0.410	0.591
Back-end-Bound-Pipeline Slots	0.159	**0.233**
LLC Miss	0.073	0.178
DTLB Overhead	0.010	0.016
Front-end-Bound Pipeline Slots	0.163	0.144
Machine Clears	0	**0.027**

Obviously, you still have more opportunities to optimize the code, but rather than using SSE intrinsic functions in your code, it's time to try a different strategy by using the Intel compiler to automatically do the optimizations.

Using the Intel Compiler

Up until now in this chapter, the code has been built with GNU GCC. If you use the Intel compiler, you will find that it automatically does both loop swapping and uses SSE instructions. Figure 12-19 shows the results of building Listing 12-3 with the Intel compiler. The first thing to notice is that the speed has improved yet again, even though the CPI got worse.

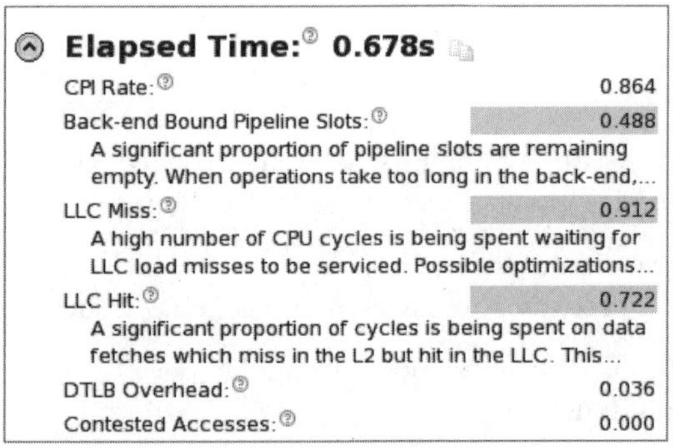

FIGURE 12-19: The results using the Intel compiler

Amplifier XE has identified that there is still more optimization work that could be explored. Because this chapter is mainly about using Amplifier XE, the optimization effort will not be pursued anymore here. If you want to consider some more optimization techniques, refer to Chapter 4, "Producing Optimized Code."

ACTIVITY 12-4: OPTIMIZING THE APPLICATION

In this activity you fix the hardware issue identified in Activity 12-3. In the first two parts, optimization is achieved by modifying the code. In the last part, the optimizations are achieved automatically by using the Intel compiler. You can run this activity on Linux or Windows.

Implementing Loop Swapping

1. Copy the contents of Listing 12-3 into a file named `swapped.cpp`.

2. Swap the three nested loops so that the sequence is as follows:

```
// do the matrix calculation c = a * b
  for (i = 0; i < N; i++) {
    for (k=0; k<N; k++) {
      for (j=0; j<N; j++) {
        c[N*i+j] += a[N*i+k] * b[N*k+j];
      }
    }
  }
```

3. Build `swapped.cpp`:

LINUX

```
g++ swapped.cpp -g -O2 -o swapped.exe
```

WINDOWS

```
cl swapped.cpp /Zi /O2 -o swapped.exe
```

4. Make sure the Project Properties page points to `swapped.exe`.

5. Start a new Amplifier analysis and choose General Exploration (following the same instructions as Step 4 of Activity 12-3).

6. Start the analysis by pressing the Start button.

7. When the analysis is complete, look in the summary window. There should be fields highlighted in pink. (The results may vary, depending on what PC you are running on. You may even find that there are no highlighted fields in your results.)

8. Browse to the Bottom-up view and find the biggest hotspot.

9. Navigate to the source code by double-clicking the hotspot and confirm that the hardware issues from the summary page are associated with that line.

Using SSE Instructions to Speed Up the Code

10. Copy the contents of Listing 12-3 into a file named `sse.cpp`.

11. Replace the `main` function with the code in Listing 12-4.

12. Build `sse.cpp`:

LINUX

```
g++ sse.cpp -msse3 -g -O2 -o sse.exe
```

WINDOWS

```
cl sse.cpp /Zi /O2 -o sse.exe
```

13. Repeat steps 4 to 9, looking at `sse.exe`.

Using the Intel compiler

14. Rebuild the original `matrix.cpp` (which you created in step 1 of this activity) with the Intel compiler:

LINUX

```
icc matrix.cpp -g -O2 -o intel.exe
```

WINDOWS

```
icl matrix.cpp /Zi /O2 -o intel.exe
```

15. Repeat steps 4 to 9, looking at `intel.exe`.

USING AMPLIFIER XE'S OTHER TOOLS

Like all good doctors, you will want to use a choice of instruments to help diagnose an unhealthy application. Amplifier XE's bag of instruments includes:

➤ Predefined analysis types

➤ Viewpoints

➤ APIs

➤ Command-line interface

➤ Context-sensitive help and Internet-based resources

Using Predefined Analysis Types

You've already seen how the clock ticks, the number of instructions retired, and the CPI can be gathered from a Lightweight Hotspots analysis. You've also used the General Exploration analysis to spot issues in your code. To do a yet more detailed examination of your program, you can use one of the other predefined analysis types.

A CPU can generate hundreds of different types of events. Using Amplifier XE's predefined analysis types takes the pain out of choosing the right events. Table 12-6 shows the analysis types available.

TABLE 12-6: Predefined Analysis Types for CPU Architecture-level Analysis

ANALYSIS	DESCRIPTION
General Exploration	As the starting point for advanced analysis, identifies and locates the most significant hardware issues that affect performance
Memory Access	Identifies where memory access issues affect performance
Cycles and uOps	Identifies where micro-operation flow issues affect performance
Bandwidth	Identifies where memory bandwidth issues affect performance
Bandwidth Breakdown	Identifies where memory bandwidth issues affect performance; transactions are broken down into reads and write backs
Front End Investigation	Identifies where front-end issues affect performance
Custom designed	Enables you to create your own analysis type based on any of the predefined types

Using Viewpoints

Amplifier XE has a number of different viewpoints that represent the results of an analysis. The name of the current viewpoint is displayed in the results tabs, just after the name of the analysis type. Figure 12-20 shows the viewpoint menu, which you can access by clicking on the spanner icon.

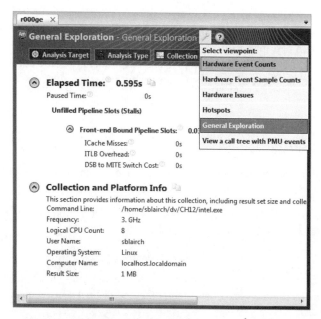

FIGURE 12-20: Changing the viewpoint

Sometimes it is worth switching between the different viewpoints. For example, while in the General Exploration viewpoint, you might want to see the actual event counts by flipping to the Hardware Event Counts viewpoint. Figure 12-21 shows the summary page of such a viewpoint. In the different viewpoints Amplifier XE uses the existing data but presents it in a different layout. No data is lost or has to be resampled as you swap between viewpoints.

FIGURE 12-21: The Hardware Event Counts viewpoint

Using APIs

Amplifier XE has a number of APIs that you can insert into a program to control an analysis. Table 12-7 lists some of the commonly used APIs when doing an event-based analysis. Some additional user-mode APIs are also available, which have already been described in earlier chapters.

TABLE 12-7: Supported APIs

PAUSE/RESUME API	DESCRIPTION
`__itt_pause`	Inserts a pause command so that application continues to run but no profiling information is being collected.
`__itt_resume`	Inserts a resume command so that the application continues to run and profiling information is collected.
FRAME APIS	
`__itt_domain_create`	Creates a domain to hold frame data. You can create multiple domains to help you separate the data into distinct groupings in the GUI.
`__itt_frame_begin_v3`	Marks the start of a frame.
`__itt_frame_end_v3`	Marks the end of a frame.

 At the time of this writing, some API names were going through a name change. If you have unresolved externals when using the API examples, look in the header file <Amplifier XE install dir>/include/ittnotify.h or check the online documentation.

You can use the Pause and Resume API to turn data collection off and on, respectively, from within the application under test. The Frame API is used to measure the time between two markers, or frames. Use the Frame API when you want to get accurate timing information between two positions in your source code.

The Pause and Resume API

Listing 12-1 uses the `__itt_pause()` and `__itt_resume()` functions to pause and resume the data collection, respectively. The code consists of two functions, `LoopOne()` and `LoopTwo()`. The content of these functions is not important; they are added simply to make the example run long enough when profiling. The `ITT_PAUSE` and `ITT_RESUME` user-defined macros are used to include and exclude the API from the code, depending on whether or not the `USE_API` macro is defined.

LISTING 12-1: An example of using the Pause and Resume API

```c
#include <stdio.h>
#define USE_API
#ifdef USE_API
#include "ittnotify.h"
#define ITT_PAUSE  __itt_pause()
#define ITT_RESUME __itt_resume()
#else
#define ITT_PAUSE
#define ITT_RESUME
#endif

int LoopTwo(){int i;for (i = 0 ; i < 100000000; i++);return i;}

int LoopOne(int i)
{
    i++;
    if (i > 50)
        return i;
    for (int j = 0 ; j < 10000000; j++);
    return LoopOne(i);
}

int main(int argc, char * argv[])
{
    int a,b;
    ITT_PAUSE;          // start paused

    a = LoopOne(0);
    printf("LoopOne Returns %d\n",a);

    ITT_RESUME;         // collect data

    b = LoopTwo();
    printf("LoopTwo Returns %d\n",b);
    ITT_PAUSE;          // pause data collection

    return a + b;
}
```

code snippet Chapter12\12-1.cpp

If you try to build this code, you must add `libittnotify.lib`, which you can find in the `Amplifier\lib32` or `Amplifier\lib64` folders. Use the lib64 version if you are building a 64-bit application; otherwise, use the lib32 version.

You can use the Pause and Resume API to reduce the amount of data you collect. Table 12-8 shows the total size of the data collected with and without the pause/resume.

TABLE 12-8: Amount of Data Collected when Profiling Listing 12-1

METHOD	DATA SIZE
No pauses	92.2k
With pauses/resumes	42.0k

The Frame API

Frame rate analysis was added to Amplifier XE to help game programmers analyze how many frames or pictures are being displayed per second. Although developed with game programmers in mind, the Frame API can be applied to any piece of code. Listing 12-2 shows a loop that iterates 100,000 times — this is the *frame* in this example. Within the loop, two delays are inserted to simulate frames with different amounts of time.

LISTING 12-2: An example of using the Frame API

Available for
download on
Wrox.com

```cpp
#include <ittnotify.h>
int main()
{
    __itt_domain* pD = __itt_domain_create( "Time" );
    pD->flags = 1; // enable domain

    for(int i = 0; i < 100000; i++)
    {
        // mark the beginning of the frame
        __itt_frame_begin_v3( pD,NULL);

        // simulate frames with different timings
        if(i%3)
            for(int j = 0; j < 30000; j++);  // a delay
        else
            for(int j = 0;  j < 11200; j++);  // another delay

        // mark the end of the frame
        __itt_frame_end_v3( pD,NULL);
    }
    return 0;
}
```

code snippet Chapter12\12-2.cpp

On Windows the program can be built using the following command:

```
cl /Od /Zi main.cpp -I"%VTUNE_AMPLIFIER_XE_2011_DIR%include"
"%VTUNE_AMPLIFIER_XE_2011_DIR%/lib64/libittnotify.lib"
```

Figure 12-22 shows a zoomed-in view of the analysis. In the timeline view there is an extra bar that displays the frame rate. At the top of the timeline, each frame is marked with a blue line. The Bottom-up pane is organized by Frame Domain/Frame Type/Frame Function. Notice that Amplifier XE splits the frames into fast and slow frames.

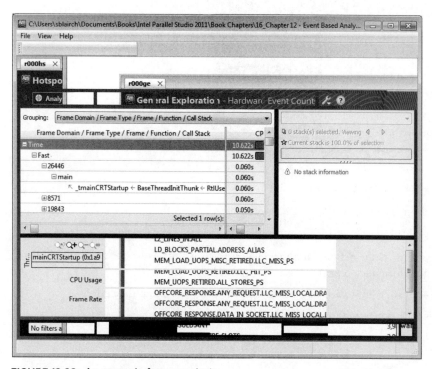

FIGURE 12-22: An example frame analysis

 Chapter 15, "Parallel Track Fitting in the CERN Collider," includes another example of using the Frame API.

Using Amplifier XE from the Command Line

You can use the command-line interface (CLI) to Amplifier to collect, compare, and view profiling data. The tool uses the same data collector as the GUI version, so the data collected has the same level of detail as if the profiling were launched from the GUI. The CLI was designed so that Amplifier could be used in scripted and automated test environments.

You can generate a command line from an existing project by clicking the Get Command Line button in the Analysis Type window (see Figure 12-23).

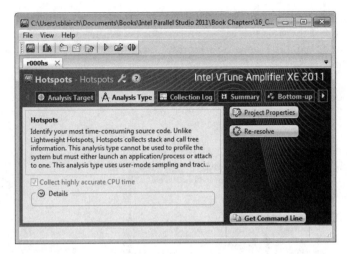

FIGURE 12-23: An Analysis Type window with the Get Command Line button

Here's the command-line syntax:

```
ampl-cl <action-option> [modifier-options] [[--] <target> [target-options]]
```

➤ `<action-option>` is the action Amplifier XE performs — for example, collecting data or generating a performance report.

➤ `[modifier-options]` are various command-line options defining the action.

➤ `<target>` is the application to analyze.

➤ `[target options]` are the options of the analyzed application.

So, for example:

```
$ ampl-cl -collect hotspots -r r001hs -- C:\test\example.exe
```

➤ `-collect` is an action.

➤ `hotspots` is an argument of the action option.

➤ `-r` is a modifier option.

➤ `r001hs` is an argument of modifier option.

➤ `C:\test\example.exe` is the target.

➤ If you have correctly installed Parallel Studio XE, the command `ampl-xe` should be available from the Parallel Studio XE command prompt (Windows) and the command shell (Linux).

Finding More Information

Here are some resources that you might find helpful:

➤ The online help that comes with Amplifier XE

➤ Intel 64 and IA-32 Architectures Software Developers Manuals (`www.intel.com/products/processor/manuals`)

➤ *The Software Optimization Cookbook, Second Edition*: *High-Performance Recipes for IA-32 Platforms*, by Richard Gerber et al. (www.intel.com/intelpress)

➤ *VTune Performance Analyzer Essentials*: *Measurement and Tuning Techniques for Software Developers*, by James Reinders (www.intel.com/intelpress)

➤ User forums, such as at http://software.intel.com/en-us/forums/intel-vtune-performance-analyzer

THE EXAMPLE APPLICATION

Available for download on Wrox.com

LISTING 12-3: matrix.cpp

```cpp
//Naive matrix multiply
//Warning, this implementation is SLOW!
#include <stdio.h>
#include <time.h>
#include <stdlib.h>

#define DEFAULT_SIZE 1000

// pointers for matrices
double *a, *b, *c;
int N;   // stores width of matrix(if N = 2, then matrix will be 2 * 2)

// function prototypes
void init_arr(double a[]);
void print_arr(char* name, double array[]);
void zero_arr(double a[]);
int main(int argc, char* argv[])
{
  clock_t start, stop;
  int i,j,k;

  // if user does not input matrix size, DEFAULT_SIZE is used
  if(argc == 2)
  {
    N = atoi(argv[1]);
  }
  else
  N = DEFAULT_SIZE;

  // allocate memory for the matrices
  a = (double *)malloc(sizeof (double) * N * N);
  if(!a) {printf("malloc a failed!\n");exit(999);}

  b = (double *)malloc(sizeof (double) * N * N);
  if(!b) {printf("malloc b failed!\n");exit(999);}

  c = (double *)malloc(sizeof (double) * N * N);
```

continues

LISTING 12-3 *(continued)*

```c
    if(!c) {printf("malloc c failed!\n");exit(999);}

    init_arr(a);
    init_arr(b);
    zero_arr(c);

    start = clock();

    // do the matrix calculation c = a * b
    for (i = 0; i < N; i++) {
      for (j=0; j<N; j++) {
        for (k=0; k<N; k++) {
          c[N*i+j] += a[N*i+k] * b[N*k+j];
        }
      }
    }
    stop = clock();

    // print how long program took.
    printf("%-6g  ",((double)(stop - start)) / CLOCKS_PER_SEC);

    // free dynamically allocated memory
    free(a);
    free(b);
    free(c);
}

// print out a matrix
void print_arr(char * name, double array[])
{
  int i,j;
  printf("\n%s\n",name);
  for (i=0;i<N;i++){
    for (j=0;j<N;j++) {
      printf("%g\t",array[N*i+j]);
    }
    printf("\n");
  }
}

// initialize array to values between 0 and 9
// this is just to make the printout look better
void init_arr(double a[])
{
  int i,j;
  for (i=0; i< N;i++) {
    for (j=0; j<N;j++) {
      a[i*N+j] = (i+j+1)%10;
    }
  }
}
// initialize array entries to zero
```

```
void zero_arr(double a[])
{
  int i,j;
  for (i=0; i< N;i++) {
    for (j=0; j<N;j++) {
      a[i*N+j] = 0;
    }
  }
}
```

code snippet Chapter12\matrix.cpp

LISTING 12-4: Using SSE instructions to optimize calculations

```
// This code should be used to replace the function main()
// from Listing 12-3.
// NOTE: this is not the BEST solution! The best solution is
// simply to build the original code with the Intel Compiler.

// We need some additional headers
#ifdef _WIN32
  #include <intrin.h>
#else
  #ifndef __INTEL_COMPILER
    #include <pmmintrin.h>
  #else
    #include <xmmintrin.h>
  #endif
#endif

int main(int argc, char* argv[])
{
    clock_t start, stop;
    int i, j,k;

  if(argc == 2)
  {
    N = atoi(argv[1]);
  }
  else
    N = DEFAULT_SIZE;

  // printf("Using Size %d\n", N);
  a = (double *)_mm_malloc(sizeof (double) * N * N,16);
  if(!a) {printf("malloc a failed!\n");exit(999);}

  b = (double *)_mm_malloc(sizeof (double) * N * N,16);
  if(!b) {printf("malloc b failed!\n");exit(999);}

  c = (double *)_mm_malloc(sizeof (double) * N * N,16);
  if(!c) {printf("malloc c failed!\n");exit(999);}

  init_arr(a);
```

continues

LISTING 12-4 *(continued)*

```
    init_arr(b);
    zero_arr(c);

    __m128d *pA;
    __m128d *pB;
    start = clock();

    for (i = 0; i < N; i++) {
      for (k=0; k<N; k+=2) {
        pA=(__m128d *)&a[N*i+k];
        pB =(__m128d *)&b[N*k];
        __m128d res = _mm_setzero_pd();
        for (j=0; j<N; j++) {
          res = _mm_mul_pd(*pA,pB[j]);
          res = _mm_hadd_pd ( res , res);
          _mm_store_sd(&c[N*i+j],res);
        }
      }
    }
    stop = clock();
    printf("%-6g  ",((double)(stop - start)) / CLOCKS_PER_SEC);

    _mm_free(a);
    _mm_free(b);
    _mm_free(c);
}
```

code snippet Chapter12\12-4.cpp

SUMMARY

Detecting the health of a program is not easy. Amplifier XE is a very powerful tool, which you can use to find out how well your program is using the CPU.

By first running a system-wide analysis on your PC, you can see how well your program interacts with its environment. You can use the CPI rate as a first indicator of your program's health. Programs with a poor CPI rate are likely to be good candidates for optimization.

Performing a hotspot analysis will show you where the bottlenecks are. You can then use some of the Amplifier XE's predefined analysis types to get more detailed information about the bottlenecks you have discovered.

Amplifier XE's predefined analysis types helps you spot unhealthy code. By becoming aware of the underlying hardware issues in the various bottlenecks of your code, you can begin to address the problems.

Chapter 13, "The World's First Sudoku 'Thirty Niner,'" is the first of five case studies that show examples of how Intel Parallel Studio XE has been used in different projects.

PART III
Case Studies

13

The World's First Sudoku "Thirty-Niner"

WHAT'S IN THIS CHAPTER?

➤ Lars Peters Endresen and Håvard Graff, two talented engineers from Oslo, share how they created what may be the world's first Sudoku puzzle that has 39 clues

➤ A hands-on exercise that mimics some of the programming techniques they used

This case study solves an intriguing problem: finding a Sudoku puzzle with 39 clues using the latest hardware advances. Multiple execution units, together with multiple cores, enable the modern programmer to tackle engineering problems that in the past would have been doable only on a supercomputer.

This case study uses the Streaming SIMD Extensions (SSE) registers and instructions in an ingenious way. The tricks used here can easily be used in other projects. The code is first optimized to run on one core, and then parallelism is introduced so that the code runs on several cores.

THE SUDOKU OPTIMIZATION CHALLENGE

Sudoku is a number-placement puzzle that uses a 9×9 grid of squares into which the numbers 1 through 9 are placed. The grid is further subdivided into 3×3 boxes, within each of which are 3×3 cells. The puzzle starts with an almost empty grid with some of the cells already filled. The aim of the puzzle is to fill the grid so that every row, every column, and every 3×3 box contains the numbers 1 through 9. This implicitly means that no row, column, or box can have duplicated numbers within it (see Figure 13-1).

								8
					9			
4	9			1	7			
			9			3	2	
	2					6	8	
	1			8				9
9			7	3				1
		8				5		7

1	5	2	3	6	9	4	7	8
8	7	3	4	5	2	9	1	6
4	9	6	8	1	7	3	2	5
6	8	7	5	9	4	1	3	2
5	2	9	7	3	1	6	8	4
3	1	4	6	2	8	7	5	9
9	4	5	2	7	3	8	6	1
2	3	8	1	4	6	5	9	7
7	6	1	9	8	5	2	4	3

FIGURE 13-1: Starting and solved grids for a typical Sudoku puzzle

The challenge Endresen and Graff faced was how to generate a puzzle with 39 clues — one with 38 clues having already been produced by others. Generating Sudoku puzzles using software may seem like an easy exercise, requiring the following steps:

1. Write a solver using some sort of nested loop to traverse the puzzle's grid, writing logic to test that they comply with certain rules.

2. Write a generator that populates the puzzle with clues, using the solver to validate the puzzles being generated.

However, if you were to follow this approach, you would soon discover that the total number of puzzles that have to be processed makes the task almost impossible to achieve because of the length of time it would take to iterate through every possible solution.

The Nature of the Challenge

More than 6×10^{21} different valid Sudoku boards exist. If a developer were to use brute force to try all the combinations of numbers, the programming exercise would be quite easy. However, the algorithm would require the lifetime of the programmer to complete the calculations. It has been estimated that a brute-force approach to producing a valid "thirty-niner" would take approximately 150 years to complete. This time can be reduced to something approaching a month by applying a number of strategies to produce an optimized version of the generator.

Four strategies are used to slim down the execution time:

➤ Use an algorithm that finds shortcuts through the brute-force approach by starting with a partially constructed board.

➤ Modify the code to take advantage of the enhanced execution units available in most of today's CPUs.

➤ Add parallelism to the code.

➤ Enable the generator to be dispatched across a cluster of machines.

The following sections go deeply into the first strategy. Although applied to Sudoku, these same strategies can be applied to a programmer's own complex algorithms in a similar fashion. Techniques learned here will enable programmers to produce fast, optimized code.

A number of other programming and algorithm "tricks" were used under the hood — such as checking for redundant clues — but they are not explained here because they are not important for our actual goals. The development of the code took place over a two-year period, much of it done in the developers' spare time. Figure 13-2 shows one of the first 39-clue puzzles to be discovered and is an example of a difficult Sudoku puzzle.

A puzzle is valid only if it has one unique solution. If more than one solution exists, it cannot be classed as a Sudoku puzzle. A *minimal solution* is one where every clue is integral to the solution — that is, the puzzle has no *redundant clues*. In such a puzzle, removing any one of the clues would result in a puzzle that has more than one solution. Today, the smallest Sudoku puzzle in the world has 17 clues, and the largest puzzle has 39 clues. The race is on to find a puzzle with 40 clues.

			3					
	3	6		7				1
6	4		9	1	3			7
5				3			2	4
7	4			6	2	5		3
	2				5	7	1	
2		5	7	1	6	4		
4		6		2	9	1	7	5
								2

FIGURE 13-2: One of the first 39-clue puzzles

The High-Level Design

The Sudoku program design that was used is made up of two components: the *generator* and the *solver*. To reduce the number of calculations required and increase the chance of success, the generator starts with an existing puzzle. One or two clues are then removed from the puzzle. New clues are then added and a brute-force iterative process is used to call the solver to determine if any valid solutions exist for the new puzzle. This process is repeated for every clue in the original puzzle.

Figure 13-3 shows how to create a new 17-clue puzzle. The generator strips two clues from an 18-clue puzzle, adds a new clue, and then uses the solver to search for any valid solutions.

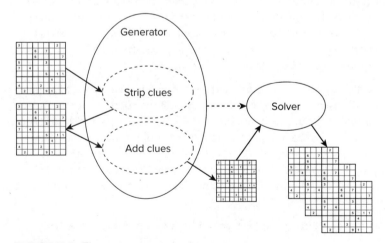

FIGURE 13-3: The generator and solver

As shown in Figure 13-4, clues 3 and 9 in the left-hand puzzle are first removed from the first column. The generator then populates each unsolved cell with a list of valid options (see the middle puzzle). The gray values are values where the cell can hold only one value. The solver then recursively prunes down the options to find a valid puzzle, taking care that no redundant clues exist (see the right-hand puzzle). The gray number 6 is the new clue that has been added.

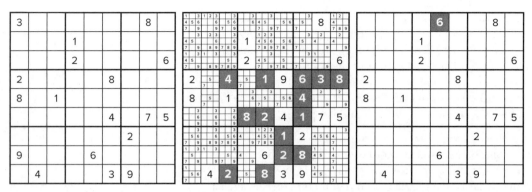

FIGURE 13-4: Creating a 17-clue Sudoku puzzle

This method of creating a new puzzle is known as the *minus-two-plus-one* algorithm. A similar technique is used to find the "thirty-niner." Taking an existing "thirty-eighter," one clue is removed and two new clues are added — in other words, a *minus-one-plus-two* algorithm.

Optimizing the Solver Using SSE Intrinsics

Modern CPUs have instructions that can work on more than one data item at the same time — that is, Single Instruction Multiple Data (SIMD) instructions. Examples of such instructions include MMX and the various Streaming SIMD Extensions (SSE, SSE2, and so forth). Because these instructions work on more than one element of data at a time, the resulting code is referred to as *vectorized code*. Vectorization is covered in detail in Chapter 4, "Producing Optimized Code." Vectorized code runs much faster than code that has not been vectorized.

SSE intrinsics are compiler-generated assembler-coded functions that can be called from C/C++ code and that provide low-level access to SIMD functionality without the need to use an inline assembler. Compared to using an inline assembler, intrinsics can improve code readability, assist instruction scheduling, and help reduce the debugging effort. Intrinsics provide access to instructions that cannot be generated using the standard constructs of the C and C++ languages.

The Intel compiler supports a wide range of architectural extensions, from the early MMX instructions to the latest generation of SSE instructions. By using these SIMD instructions, it is possible to do some quite creative manipulation of the puzzle data. SSE2 (and later) supports 128-bit registers, and the individual bits of these can be used to hold all the data in a Sudoku puzzle. Note that only the first 81 bits need be used to represent all the cells on a Sudoku board. Each bit in the 128-bit array values corresponds to a cell location. The 128-bit value at `BinNum[0]` records any cell containing a 1. `BinNum[1]` records any cell that contains a 2, and so on. Figure 13-5 gives an example of how this happens.

The following code shows how the values in Figure 13-5 would be stored in the `BinNum` array:

```
__m128i BinNum[9];        // Declare array of 128-bit values

BinNum[0] = 0x400100;     // 1's in cells 9 and 23
BinNum[1] = 0x800000000;  // 2's in cell 36
   .
   .
BinNum[8] = 0x80088000;   // 9's in cells 16, 20 and 32
```

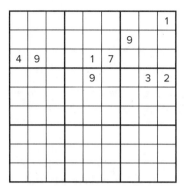

FIGURE 13-5: A typical Sudoku puzzle that stores its numbers into 128-bit variables

To find out if a puzzle holds a particular value, predefined masks are used. The masks are again held in an array of 128-bit SSE variables:

```
__m128i BinBox[9];      // holds binary mask of all boxes
__m128i BinRow[9];      // holds binary mask of all rows
__m128i BinColumn[9];   // holds binary mask of all columns
```

These masks hold binary bitmaps representing a whole row, column, or box, as shown in Figure 13-6. `BinRow[0]` represents the first row; `BinRow[1]` represents the second row; and so on. For example:

```
BinRow[1] = 0x3FE00;    // mask for row 2
BinBox[0] = 0x1C0E07;   // mask for box 1
```

To check if row 2 contains a 3 now only requires the mask of row 2 to be ANDed with the variable for number 3, as follows:

```
Result = BinRow[1]  & BinNum[2];
```

The result will be nonzero if row 1 does contain a 3; otherwise, the result will be zero.

The first version of the Sudoku generator did not use SSE instructions or intrinsics. Reworking the first version of the code to use SSE2 registers took a significant amount of time. Using SSE2 registers and adding SSE intrinsics resulted in a speedup of several hundred times using the same hardware.

Using SSE intrinsics does have drawbacks, because it is possible to end up locking your implementation to a particular generation of architecture. Also, the long names of the SSE functions can make your C++ code almost unreadable, and there is a significant learning curve for the programmer to climb. Only experience can determine when it is advantageous to use intrinsics. However, in the case of the Sudoku generator, the performance improvement far outweighed the extra effort required.

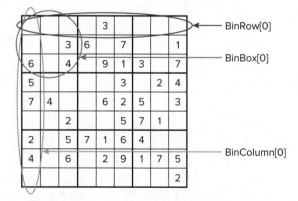

FIGURE 13-6: The rows, columns, and boxes of the Sudoku grid are represented by an array of registers

If you want to examine the code in more detail, download the code that is used in the hands-on section.

Adding Parallelism to the Generator

Intel VTune Performance Analyzer was applied to the Sudoku generator, allowing hotspots to be identified within code. The biggest hotspot, which was found to be in the top hierarchy of the generator, was then parallelized using OpenMP tasks.

OpenMP tasks, introduced in OpenMP 3.0, can be used to add parallelism to loops, linked lists, and recursive calls. OpenMP tasks are good at producing balanced loads, especially when the amount of work between each loop may be uneven; the same is true for linked lists and recursive calls.

OpenMP tasks and load balancing are described in Chapter 7, "Implementing Parallelism," and Chapter 9, "Tuning Parallel Applications."

Listing 13-1 shows how a number of tasks were created in a single-threaded loop. Each task was then scheduled and run by the OpenMP run time. As a thread completes the execution of one task, it is given another task to execute.

Available for download on Wrox.com

LISTING 13-1: Using OpenMP tasks to add parallelism to the generator

```
1: int node;
2: #pragma  omp parallel shared(omp_log, node)
3: {
4:    #pragma omp single nowait
5:    {
6:      for(node = 0; node < Num_SudokuNode ; node++)
7:      {
8:        #pragma omp task firstprivate(omp_log, node)
9:        {
10:          int result = AddClues(SudokuNode[node], omp_log);
11:        }
12:      }
13:    }
14: }
```

code snippet Chapter13\13-1.cpp

The code is part of the minus-one-plus-two algorithm. The SudokuNode[] array holds a number of Sudoku puzzles that have already had one clue removed. For example, when looking for a new "thirty-niner," this array would hold 38 copies of a "thirty-eighter," with one clue having already been removed sequentially from each puzzle. Each puzzle is then filled with an additional two clues by a call to AddClues(), with the number of successfully generated puzzles being returned. The omp_log variable points to a file that is used to store each new "thirty-niner" that is generated.

At line 2, the OpenMP run time creates a pool of threads (as explained in Chapter 7). By default, the number of threads is the same number as the number of hardware threads the environment can support, although the programmer can override this.

The code between lines 4 and 13 will run on just one thread. The enclosed loop is responsible for creating a number of tasks that will be run in parallel, with each thread running one task at a time. At line 8, an OpenMP task is created on each iteration of the loop. The tasks are free to start execution straight away. Variables outside the parallel region, which is defined by the first pair of braces, are visible to all threads by default. To make a thread have a private instance of such a variable, you use the private or firstprivate keyword. In line 2, the shared keyword is redundant, because the default behavior of OpenMP is that all data is shared. The shared keyword is added here as a reminder to the programmer that the variables omp_log and node can be accessed by all the threads.

Adding firstprivate at line 8 causes the OpenMP run time to create private copies of the variables omp_log and node for each created task. A firstprivate variable differs from a private variable in that a firstprivate variable is automatically initialized with the values from the shared variable, whereas a private variable is uninitialized.

There is an implicit barrier at line 13: the end of the omp single thread. To allow the single thread to be made available to execute some of the newly created OpenMP tasks, the nowait keyword has been added at line 4. Without this keyword, once the single thread had completed creating the OpenMP tasks, it would simply sit at line 13 until all the other threads have completed their execution. By adding nowait, the efficiency of the threaded execution is improved by making the single thread available for joining in executing the tasks.

The Results

Once the parallel code was added to the project, it was rewarding to see that on a quad-cored machine running hyper-threading, which can support 12 hardware threads, all 12 hardware threads were kept busy. Figure 13-7 shows that with the parallelism implemented in the code, each hardware thread ran at 100 percent. However, it should be emphasized here that the goal is to reduce overall time, not just to increase CPU utilization.

One of the most difficult aspects of adding OpenMP was grasping how variables were treated. Much of the time taken was used in reworking the code so that there was less need to share data between the different running tasks. Some effort was also spent on reducing the number of dependencies between loops so that they could be easily parallelized. Adding the parallelism took about two weeks of work, which felt like a lot of effort at the time, but in relation to the length of the project, the time was fairly short.

As a result of the work done, three new "thirty-niners" were discovered, as shown in Figure 13-8.

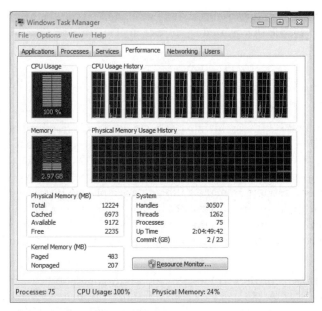

FIGURE 13-7: A fully utilized CPU

Grid 1

		3						
	3	6		7				1
6		4		9	1	3		7
5					3		2	4
7	4			6	2	5		3
		2			5	7	1	
2		5	7	1	6	4		
4		6		2	9	1	7	5
								2

Grid 2

					3			
	3	6		7				1
6		4		9	1	3		7
5					3		2	4
1	4			6	2	5		3
		2			5	1	7	
2		5	1	7	6	4		
4		6		2	9	7	1	5
								2

Grid 3

		1		3	7	6	4	
6		4		9	1	3		7
		2			6			3
1	4			2	3	5		6
3				1	5	4	2	
2		5			9	7		4
4	1			7	2			5
	7			5		2	6	

FIGURE 13-8: The three 39-clue minimal solutions found using the minus-one-plus-two search

HANDS-ON EXAMPLE: OPTIMIZING THE SUDOKU GENERATOR

The code used for this hands-on section shows how to optimize a Sudoku generator by using the same techniques as those used in the project that led to the first "thirty-niner." The sample code does not check for redundant clues or log the results correctly. Some error checking has also been ignored. This was done to make the example simpler and easier to understand and to reduce the required computation time.

The code consists of a solver and a generator. The solver uses a brute-force recursive algorithm to solve a partially populated puzzle. The generator creates a stack of partially populated puzzles that are passed on to the solver. The algorithm used in the generator is the minus-two-plus-one search.

About the Code

The code for the hands-on activities is available for download as a Visual Studio project (`Chapter13\sudoku.zip`). As you work your way through the activities, you will be asked to switch to different configurations, with names such as `STEP_1`, `STEP_2`, and so forth (using the drop-down configuration menu in Visual Studio). As you swap configurations, different preprocessor macros will be automatically added to the build parameters of the project.

A number of header files are associated with the project. Of particular note is `Config.h`, which contains macros to control inclusion of different optimization features. The various source files are as follows:

➤ `File.cpp` contains fairly rudimentary code that reads a single-line text file containing a partially completed Sudoku puzzle.

➤ `Generator.cpp` holds the code for the minus-two-plus-one code.

➤ `Main.cpp` holds the main body of the code for the solver.

➤ `Print.cpp` contains code to print the clues and puzzles to the screen.

Figure 13-9 gives the project structure as seen within Visual Studio.

In this hands-on section there is no need to change any code. All the required changes are added automatically when you choose the correct build configuration. Figure 13-10 shows the seven activities in this hands-on section. Activity 13-1 uses the Microsoft compiler, and then switches to the Intel compiler.

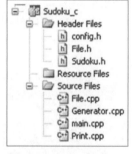

FIGURE 13-9: The code consists of a number of source files and a user-editable Config.h

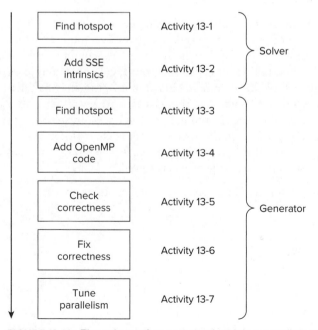

FIGURE 13-10: The solver is first optimized and then parallelism is added to the generator

The reasons for using the Microsoft compiler and then switching to the Intel compiler are as follows:

➤   The original Sudoku project started with the Microsoft compiler.

➤   To show that Intel VTune Amplifier XE can be used with the Microsoft compiler. (This is also true of Inspector and Advisor.)

➤   To show how to swap to the Intel compiler.

➤   To take advantage of the optimized code that the Intel compiler produces.

➤   The Intel compiler supports Open MP tasks, which is not currently the case with the Microsoft compiler.

The running program accepts a single-line file as input, where each cell is represented by a digit. Where there is no clue, a zero is placed instead. The `test.txt` file is used in the hands-on exercise and contains the following:

```
000704005020010070000080002090006250600070008053200010400090000030060090200407000
```

The code used here is not the same code as that used in the "thirty-niner" project. To be able to produce a "thirty-niner," some important features would need to be added to the code, such as the filtering out of nonredundant clues and certain "under-the-hood" algorithmic tricks.

The Solver

Figure 13-11 illustrates the solver's recursive backtracking algorithm.

The solver first is passed a partially completed puzzle (Table A). For simplicity, only the top-left corner of the puzzle is shown. The solver starts at the first empty cell, Idx1 (row 1, column 2), which could be assigned the values 4, 7, or 9 (determined by the clues in the same row, column, and box). The solver is called recursively two more times, taking the cells Idx2 (row 1, column 3) and Idx 20 (row 3, column 3). The table now looks like Table B. Because Idx 20 cannot legitimately be filled with any value, the solver returns, removing the cell content of the cells along the way. The solver returns back to Idx 1 and places the next available clue (7) and in Idx1 and does a fresh recursive call. The solver then fills the next empty cell (Idx 2) with the lowest potential clue (4). This is followed by another recursive call, in which Idx 20 is filled with the value 9. The puzzle now looks like Table C. This recursive procedure is continued until the puzzle is solved.

Listing 13-2 shows the structures used in the solver. The SUDOKU structure contains an array of 81 NODE structs.

LISTING 13-2: Structures used in the solver

```
1:   typedef struct NODE
2:   {
3:       int cell;
```

```
4:      int number;
5:      int TempCellsLeft;
6:  }_NODE;
7:
8:  typedef struct SUDOKU
9:  {
10:     NODE Nodes[NUM_NODES];
11: }_SUDOKU;
```

code snippet Chapter13\13-2.cpp

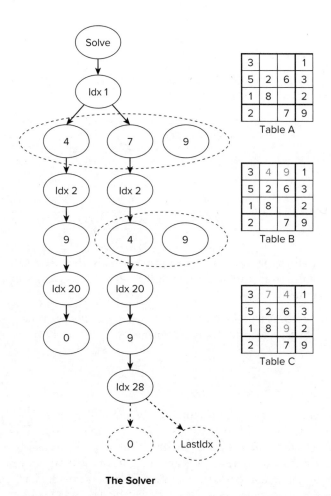

The Solver

FIGURE 13-11: The solver uses a recursive backtracking algorithm to solve the puzzle

Listing 13-3 shows the solver's recursive algorithm. When the solver is first called, it is passed pPuzzle, which is a pointer to the current puzzle, and NodeIdx, which is an index to the current cell that is being considered.

LISTING 13-3: The solver's recursive code

```
 1: bool Solve(SUDOKU *pPuzzle,int PuzzleIdx,int NodeIdx,int &NumRecursions)
 2: {
 3:     NumRecursions ++;
 4:     if (NodeIdx >= NUM_NODES)
 5:         return true;
 6:
 7:     if(!FillPossibilities(pPuzzle,NodeIdx))
 8:         return false;
 9:
10:     NODE BackupNode;
11:     for(int i=1; i<=MAX_NUM; i++)
12:     {
13:         if(Allowed(pPuzzle,NodeIdx,i))
14:         {
15:             StoreNumber(pPuzzle,NodeIdx,BackupNode,NumRecursions,i);
16:             int NewIdx = GetNextIdx(pPuzzle, NodeIdx);
17:
18:             if (!Solve(pPuzzle,PuzzleIdx,NewIdx,NumRecursions))
19:                 ClearNumber(pPuzzle,NodeIdx,BackupNode,i);
20:         }
21:     }
22:     return false;
23: }
```

code snippet Chapter13\13-3.cpp

In line 7, the solver first populates the partially populated puzzle's empty cells with a list of all valid possibilities. The loop at line 11, which iterates from 1 to 9, along with the call to `Allowed`, is used to drive the next recursive call to `Solve` at line 18.

If `Solve` fails, it returns false; otherwise, it returns true — once it has visited all the nodes in the puzzle (line 8). Each time `Solve` is called, the `NewIdx` (line 16) is incremented to point to the next empty cell in the puzzle.

Finding Hotspots in the Solver

The details of using Intel Parallel Amplifier are presented in Chapter 6, "Where to Parallelize," and need not be repeated here. However, Activity 13-1 lists the steps for using Amplifier to find the hotspots within the code. As mentioned in Chapter 6, it is good practice to optimize the serial code first, before making any code parallel. Code that consumes significant amounts of the total run time of the program is the ideal candidate for optimization. After running Amplifier, you can see that the biggest consumer of CPU time is the `NumInRow` function, closely followed by `NumInColumn` (see Figure 13-12).

Examining the code of the first hotspot within Parallel Amplifier shows that the majority of the time consumed is due to two things: the iteration of the array of nodes and the divide calculation (see Figure 13-13).

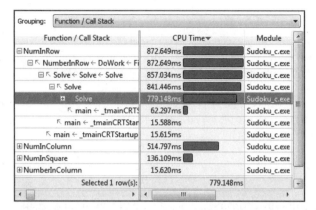

FIGURE 13-12: Intel Parallel Amplifier shows the hotspots in the solver code

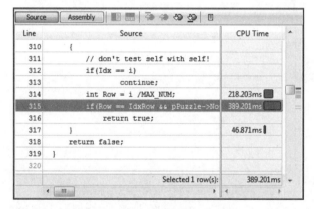

FIGURE 13-13: The code of the solver hotspot

ACTIVITY 13-1: FINDING HOTSPOTS

In this activity you build the serial version of the solver with the Microsoft compiler and then the Intel compiler. You analyze the code for hotspots using Amplifier XE.

1. Open the `suduko_c.sln` project.

2. Build the STEP_1 configuration.

3. Run the program by pressing Ctrl+F5, and record the time taken.

4. Switch to the Intel compiler.

5. Repeat steps 2 and 3.

6. Check for hotspots using Parallel Amplifier.

Optimizing the Code Using SSE Intrinsics

The code in the STEP_2 version of the project has been changed to use SSE intrinsics, as described in the first part of this case study. The following SSEHasNumber function is used for checking the existence of a number in a row column or box:

```
1: bool SSEHasNumber(SUDOKU *pPuzzle,__m128i BinArray[], int i, int j)
2: {
3:     __m128i Tmp1 = ( _mm_and_si128(pPuzzle->BinNum[j-1], BinArray[i]));
4:     __m128i Tmp2 = _mm_setzero_si128();
5:
6:     Tmp2 = _mm_cmpeq_epi32(Tmp2, Tmp1);
7:
```

Once the new code is included in the build (by choosing the STEP_2 build configuration in Visual Studio), the total execution reduces significantly, giving a speed up of 12 when using the same hardware as the serial version (see Table 13-1).

TABLE 13-1: Speedup with and without SSE Intrinsics

	TIME (SECONDS)	SPEEDUP
Without SSE	1.78	1
With SSE	0.14	12

ACTIVITY 13-2: ADDING SSE INTRINSICS

In this activity you build the version of the code that has SSE intrinsics.

1. Build the STEP_2 configuration.

2. Run the program by pressing Ctrl+F5, and record the time taken.

The Generator

The generator uses a minus-two-plus-one search algorithm to remove two clues from an existing puzzle, and then traverses the puzzle, filling in each empty square with a new clue before passing the partially completed puzzle on to the solver.

The code consists of four nested loops:

➤ The outermost loop removes the first clue and creates a copy of the puzzle.

➤ The second nested loop is responsible for removing the second clue.

➤ The third nested loop traverses through each empty cell, using the innermost loop (the fourth loop) to try out all the new potential clues in the current cell.

To summarize, the outermost loop and the second nested loop are responsible for the *minus-two* part of the search, and the other two loops are responsible for the *plus-one* part.

Finding the Hotspots in the Generator

When parallelizing a hotspot, the usual rule of thumb is that it is not the hotspot itself that is parallelized, but rather the parallelism is added higher up in the calling sequence. Activity 13-3 shows the steps involved with running Intel Parallel Amplifier on the generator code to reveal hotspots.

Activity 13-3 reveals that the main hotspot is SSEHasNumber, which is called by Solve, which, in turn, is called by GenDoWork. The GenDoWork function is called from the outermost loop in the generator code. Figure 13-14 shows these relationships.

Grouping:	Function / Call Stack	
Function / Call Stack		**CPU Time▼**
⊟ SSEHasNumber		118.714s
⊟ ↖ Solve		118.714s
⊞ ↖ Solve		118.605s
↖ GenDoWork ← main ← _tmainCRTStar		0.109s
⊟ Solve		81.888s
⊞ ↖ Solve		81.795s
↖ GenDoWork ← main ← _tmainCRTStartup		0.093s
⊞ SSESetValue		0.140s
⊞ SSEClearValue		0.093s
	Selected 0 row(s):	

FIGURE 13-14: Using Amplifier to find the generator hotspots and calling sequence

---

ACTIVITY 13-3: FINDING THE HOTSPOT IN THE GENERATOR

In this activity you build the serial version of the generator and analyze it for hotspots.

1. Build the STEP_3 configuration.

2. Run the program by pressing Ctrl+F5, and record the time taken.

3. Check for hotspots using Parallel Amplifier.

Adding Parallelism to the Generator Using OpenMP

After using intrinsics and vectorization (SSE instructions), further enhancements in speed are obtained by adding parallelism. This is accomplished by adding *OpenMP tasks* to the code high up in the calling hierarchy of the generator. In Listing 13-4, OpenMP-specific code is added to lines 5, 8, and 14. This code works in a similar manner to Listing 13-1.

Available for download on Wrox.com

LISTING 13-4: Adding OpenMP tasks to the generator

```
1: SUDOKU Puzzles[NUM_NODES];
2:
3: int Generate(SUDOKU *pPuzzle)
4: {
5:     #pragma omp parallel
6:     for(int i = 0 ; i < NUM_NODES -1; i++ )
7:     {
8:         #pragma omp single nowait
9:         {
10:            NODE Node1 = pPuzzle->Nodes[i];
11:            if(Node1.number > 0)
```

continues

LISTING 13-4 *(continued)*

```
12:                    {
13:                        memcpy(&Puzzles[i],pPuzzle,sizeof(SUDOKU));
14:                        #pragma omp task firstprivate(i)
15:                        GenDoWork(&Puzzles[i],i);
16:                    }
17:            }
18:        }
19:    return gNumCalls; //global incremented on each call to solver
20: }
```

code snippet Chapter13\13-4.cpp

Using the same architecture as the nonparallelized code, the application ran nearly 7 times faster on a machine that had 12 threads (see Table 13-2).

TABLE 13-2: Speedup with and without OpenMP

	TIME (SECONDS)	SPEEDUP
Without OpenMP	213	1
With OpenMP	32	6.7

ACTIVITY 13-4: ADDING OPENMP CODE

In this activity you build and run the parallel version of the generator.

1. Build the STEP_4 configuration.

2. Run the program by pressing Ctrl+F5, and record the time taken.

3. Calculate the speedup (and compare with Activity 13-3).

Checking Correctness in the Generator

It is essential when introducing parallelism into code to check for data races and other similar problems. Activity 13-5 involves running the Intel Parallel Inspector to search for problems that may occur when parallelizing code. The results show several data races that need to be resolved (see Figure 13-15).

ACTIVITY 13-5: CHECKING FOR PARALLELIZATION PROBLEMS

In this activity you check the newly parallelized code to see if any errors exist.

1. Build the STEP_5 configuration.

2. Check for data races using Parallel Inspector.

Problems

ID ▲		Problem	Sources	Modules	State
P1		Unhandled application exception	xutility	Sudoku_c.exe	New
P2		Data race	Generator.cpp	Sudoku_c.exe	New
P3		Data race	main.cpp	Sudoku_c.exe	New
P4		Data race	xtree	Sudoku_c.exe	New
P5		Data race	xmemory; xtree	Sudoku_c.exe	New
P6		Data race	xmemory; xtree	Sudoku_c.exe	New
P7		Data race	xmemory; xtree	Sudoku_c.exe	New
P8		Data race	xmemory; xtree	Sudoku_c.exe	New
P9		Data race	xmemory; xtree	Sudoku_c.exe	New
P10		Data race	xmemory; xtree	Sudoku_c.exe	New

FIGURE 13-15: The Inspector reveals several data races

Fixing Correctness in the Generator

The data races are caused by the following three things:

- Reading/writing the global variable `gNumSolutions` without appropriate synchronization
- Reading/writing the global variable `gNumCalls`, again without appropriate synchronization
- Calling the `std::map` functions

To solve the data races, you need to protect the access to the global variables by adding a synchronization directive. Various OpenMP directives were covered in Chapters 8 and 9. To fix the `gNumSolutions` and `gNumCalls` data races, you can use the `atomic` directive, as follows:

```
#pragma omp atomic
   gNumSolutions++;


#pragma omp atomic
   gNumCalls++;
```

To fix the data race caused by calls to `std::map` functions, wrap the call to `StoreSolution` within a critical section using the `#pragma omp critical` directive:

```
// StoreSolution returns true if solution is unique
#pragma omp critical
{
                   res = StoreSolution(pPuzzle,PuzzleIdx);
}
```

ACTIVITY 13-6: FIXING CORRECTNESS

In this activity, the data races identified in Activity 13-5 have been corrected.

1. Build the STEP_6 configuration.
2. Check for data races using Inspector XE.

Tuning Performance

After correcting errors in the parallel code, the next step is to tune the application with respect to parallelism. Typically, you need to address the following issues:

➤ Parallel overhead

➤ Load balancing

➤ Scalability

In Activity 13-7, you solve the load-balancing problem using Intel Parallel Amplifier XE (refer to Chapter 9 for more details). Using Amplifier to analyze the code shows the newly parallel code apparently performing well. Amplifier reports that all 12 logical CPUs are fully utilized (see Figure 13-16). The color of the scale indicates how good the concurrency is. The color of the scale indicates how good the concurrency is. In this case, the large histogram block in the Ideal section (colored green on your PC) shows excellent CPU usage.

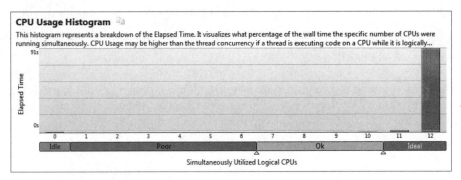

FIGURE 13-16: Apparently all the cores are being used, which hides an underlying problem

On closer examination, you can see that although the CPU usage is high, the number of simultaneous running threads is poor (see Figure 13-17).

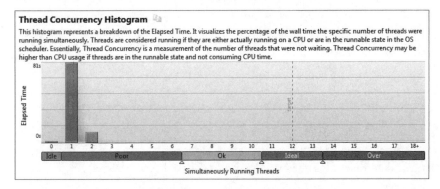

FIGURE 13-17: The program is running with very poor concurrency

Looking at the time line, you can see a lot of vertical transition lines (see Figure 13-18). A healthy program should not be dominated by these transitions.

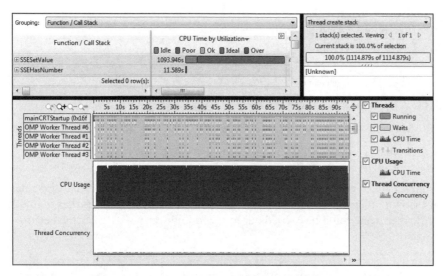

FIGURE 13-18: The timeline is dominated by vertical transition lines

Looking at the source view of the bottleneck, it is clear that an ill-placed `#pragma omp critical` directive is the cause of the problem (see Figure 13-19).

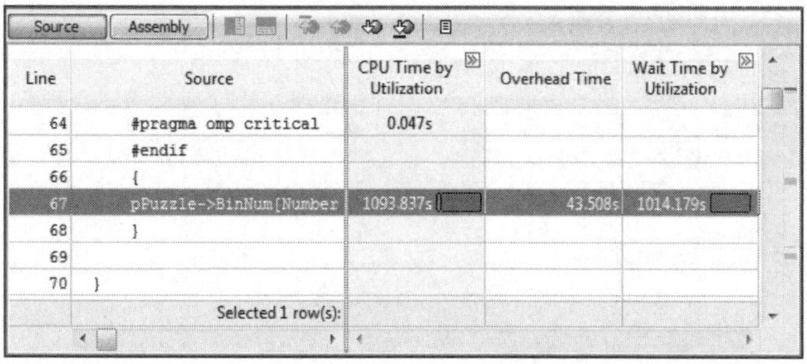

Line	Source	CPU Time by Utilization	Overhead Time	Wait Time by Utilization
64	`#pragma omp critical`	0.047s		
65	`#endif`			
66	`{`			
67	`pPuzzle->BinNum[Number`	1093.837s	43.508s	1014.179s
68	`}`			
69				
70	`}`			
	Selected 1 row(s):			

FIGURE 13-19: The reason for the poor concurrency is the critical section

Removing the `#pragma omp critical` directive leads to a better concurrency (see Figure 13-20).

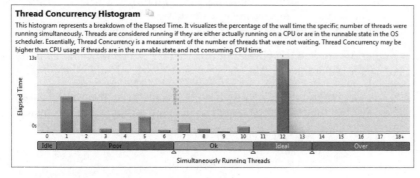

FIGURE 13-20: Removing the critical section leads to a better concurrency

---

ACTIVITY 13-7: TUNING PARALLELISM

In this activity you analyze the concurrency of the generator.

1. Build the STEP_7 configuration.

2. Check for concurrency using Amplifier XE.

3. Build the STEP_8 configuration. (This removes the critical section.)

4. Check the concurrency to see how it has improved.

Even though the program has a reasonable concurrency level, not all threads are doing the same amount of work. As shown in Figure 13-21, some threads finish their work much earlier than others. Although some further work could be carried out to try to improve the balance, the performance is quite adequate.

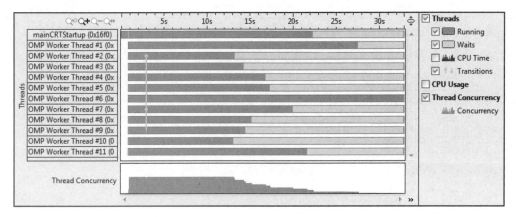

FIGURE 13-21: Not all threads are doing an equal amount of work

SUMMARY

The Sudoku puzzle case study gives a fascinating insight into how carefully crafted code using SSE intrinsics can lead to dramatic performance improvements over non-SSE code. Parallelizing using OpenMP tasks can produce well-balanced parallel applications.

The skills used to produce solutions for Sudoku puzzles in this chapter can readily be used in many applications to produce efficient and optimized code.

Chapter 14, "Nine Tips to Parallel-Programming Heaven," explores an alternative way of parallelizing using Intel Cilk Plus. The techniques learned there can likewise be applied to this Sudoku problem.

14

Nine Tips to Parallel-Programming Heaven

WHAT'S IN THIS CHAPTER?

➤ Improving the application heuristics

➤ Doing an architectural analysis

➤ Adding parallelism

This chapter is like a TV program with three interweaving plots running in parallel. It includes the following:

➤ A set of tips on how to write successful parallel programs, based on an interview with Dr. Yann Golanski of York.

➤ A description of Dr. Golanski's n-bodies research project looking at star formation.

➤ A set of hands-on exercises. Note that the code is not the same code that Dr. Golanski used, but is it written to show some of the key elements of his work.

THE CHALLENGE: SIMULATING STAR FORMATION

The original research project investigated how adding coolants to the interstellar medium (ISM) could induce the medium to collapse and thus increase the likelihood of star formation. The problem is a classic n-bodies simulation problem, where calculations are made on how particles interact with each other. As new particles are added to the model, the number of calculations required increases by N^2, where N is the number of particles in the model. Because of this N^2 relationship, the number of calculations that have to be performed on any decent-size model expands to an almost unmanageable figure.

Using brute force to calculate how the particles interact with each other is practical for small numbers of particles, but for a large collection of particles the time needed to perform all the calculations becomes too long to be useful. Dr. Golanski puts it like this:

> *The simulation works fine for 12 particles; it even works fine for 100 particles.*
> *If you try to use 1,000 particles, it takes ages; if you try to use 10,000 particles,*
> *forget it! If you try to use 100K or one million particles, then that's just a joke.*

You can employ the following strategies to overcome the "order-of-magnitude" problem:

1. Modify the algorithm of the n-bodies calculation so that the number of calculations required becomes an *N-log-N* relationship rather than N^2.

2. Use VTune Amplifier XE to analyze the code for bottlenecks.

3. Use VTune Amplifier XE to find hotspots in the code, and then parallelize them to take advantage of multi-core workstations.

The simulation code was written in C and based on the Barnes-Hut force calculation, where the whole environment to be simulated is split into a hierarchical set of boxes or cubes.

In the original research project, the development of the code was initially done on a single-core machine, the program being written in a single thread. After the model was sufficiently developed, the code was migrated to an 8-core workstation and the code was parallelized. The final step in the development was to enable the application to work on a cluster of machines. Synchronous process communication between the different nodes on the cluster handled the Message Passing Interface APIs.

The Formation of Stars

It is thought that stars are formed from the interstellar medium (ISM), an area that is populated with particles of predominantly hydrogen and helium. Within the ISM are dense clouds. These clouds are normally in equilibrium, but can be triggered by various events to collapse.

In the research work done by Dr. Golanski, the model simulates the collapse of the ISM by seeding it with coolants from a supernova — the coolants being atoms and molecules other than hydrogen (H) and helium (He), notably gaseous water (H_2O), carbon monoxide (CO), molecular oxygen (O_2), and atomic carbon (C).

The collapsing cloud, known as a *protostellar* cloud, continues to collapse until equilibrium is reached. Further contraction and fusion of the protostellar cloud takes place, resulting in the eventual formation of a star. Figure 14-1 shows a picture of an interstellar cloud taken from the Hubble telescope.

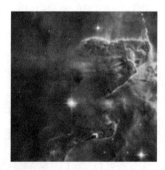

FIGURE 14-1: A cloud of cold interstellar gas

THE HANDS-ON ACTIVITIES

The n-bodies project contains the following files:

➤ `main.cpp` and `main.h` — Contain the top-level function `main()` that drives the simulation.

➤ `hash.cpp` and `hash.h` — Contain the hashed octree simulation code.

➤ `n-bodies.cpp` and `n-bodies.h` — Contain the code to initialize the array of body particles and to perform a serial simulation.

➤ `octree.cpp` and `octree.h` — Contain the octree simulation code.

➤ `Makefile` — Used to build the application. There are seven targets, `14-1` to `14-7`, which correspond to the seven hands-on activities.

➤ `print.cpp` and `print.h` — Used to print position of bodies (only for debugging purposes).

The `Makefile` is used to build the n-bodies project, which you can use in either Windows or Linux. Following are the different targets that are used for each of the hands-on activities. Notice that Step 6 uses the Debug build — to give maximum amount of information when tracking down data races. In each of the steps, all the required code changes are already included in the sources and are controlled by a series of `#defines`.

➤ `14-1` — Serial version of n-bodies application, built with optimization enabled. Use it to perform a Hotspot analysis with Amplifier XE.

➤ `14-2` — Uses octree heuristic.

➤ `14-3` — Uses hashed octree heuristic

➤ `14-4` — Same as 14-3 but with optimized division code.

➤ `14-5` — Same as 14-5 with Cilk Plus parallelism. You must use the Intel compiler for this and the following targets. This version contains data races.

➤ `14-6a` — A debug version of 14-5 but with a smaller data set. Use this version to perform a Data Race analysis with Inspector XE.

➤ `14-6b` — Same as 14-6a but with data races fixed with a `cilk::reducer_opadd` reducer.

➤ `14-7` — Same as 14-6b but with a full-size data set. This is the final version of the n-bodies.

To use the Cilk Plus part of the hands-on (Activities 14-5 to 14-7), you must build the project using the Intel compiler, because the Microsoft compiler does not support Cilk Plus at this time. You can build all the other steps with either the Intel or the Microsoft compiler (GCC on Linux).

All the screenshots and source code in this case study are taken from the hands-on activities, not the original research project.

Performance Tuning

The original project used Intel VTune Performance Analyzer to profile the application. The XE version of Intel Parallel Studio includes the latest version of VTune, referred to as Amplifier XE.

Amplifier XE works by "listening" to various performance counters while the application runs. The workflow involves the following steps:

1. Build the release version of the application.

2. Run a Hotspot analysis using Amplifier XE.

3. Examine the results, and then apply changes to the code or environment to improve the performance of the code.

4. Keep repeating steps 1–3, fixing one performance issue on each iteration.

Using the preceding steps to optimize an application, it is good practice to perform the tuning at three different scopes, or levels:

➤ **System-wide** — First, look at how the application is interacting with the system.

➤ **Application-level** — Once you have corrected any system-wide problems, try to improve any application heuristics.

➤ **Architectural-level** — Finally, having completed system-wide and application-level tuning, focus on any architectural bottlenecks.

This case study concentrates on the application heuristics and architectural bottlenecks. Once these two areas are improved, the program is then parallelized.

APPLICATION HEURISTICS

Intuitive judgment can often be used to reduce the computational effort needed to solve a problem. The brute-force approach using Newton's law of universal gravitation to calculate the forces on each particle leads to an unacceptable solution. The time needed to calculate such a solution on a reasonable number of particles may be longer than the lifetime of the programmer. Other, more experiential, methods must be applied. Many cosmologists have tried a variety of ways of reducing the computational effort, most using some sort of averaging function. This case study uses a variation on this.

Finding the Hotspots

Any optimization effort should focus on parts of the code with the most intense CPU activity. Figure 14-2 shows the results of an Amplifier XE Hotspot analysis session. The main hotspot consuming most of the CPU activity is the addAcc() function. You can try this out for yourself in Activity 14-1.

The fundamental problem of an n-bodies simulation is the number of calculations that need to be performed.

You can easily see how the number of calculations needed rapidly grows by looking at the serial version of the n-bodies code. All the bodies in the simulation are held in the array body. The size of the array BODYMAX is the same as the number of bodies you are simulating. Each element of the array body holds a BODYTYPE structure, which stores the position, velocity, acceleration, and mass of the body:

```
struct BODYTYPE {
    double pos[NUMDIMENSIONS];
    double vel[NUMDIMENSIONS];
    double acc[NUMDIMENSIONS];
    double mass;
// ...
};
BODYTYPE body[BODYMAX];
```

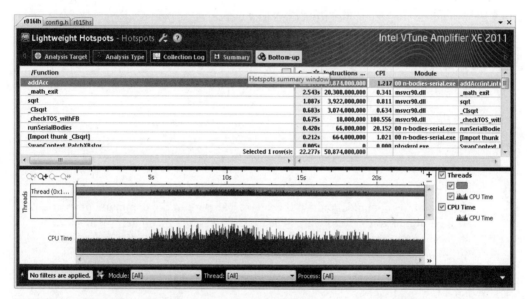

FIGURE 14-2: The Hotspot analysis shown in Amplifier XE

To perform a brute-force simulation, the interaction between every body is calculated in a triple-nested loop within the function runSerialBodies. At the innermost level of the loop, the function addAcc combines the acceleration of the two bodies. Once all the accelerations have been calculated, the function ApplyAccelerationsAndAdvanceBodies applies the new accelerations to each body in the simulation:

```
void runSerialBodies(int n)
{
  // Run the simulation over a fixed range of time steps
  for (double s = 0.; s < STEPLIMIT; s += TIMESTEP)
  {
    int i, j;
    // Compute the accelerations of the bodies
    for (i = 0; i < n - 1; ++i)
      for (j = i + 1; j < n; ++j)
        addAcc(i, j);
    // apply new accelerations
    ApplyAccelerationsAndAdvanceBodies(n);
  }
}
```

In Dr. Golanski's work, the simulation time was reduced by using a hashed tree-based n-bodies simulation using a modified Barnes-Hut algorithm.[1]

ACTIVITY 14-1: CONDUCTING A HOTSPOTS ANALYSIS

In this activity you look for the hotspots in the n-bodies application. You can run this activity on Linux or Windows.

Setting Up the Build Environment

1. Download the source files from the Wrox website.

2. Edit the `Makefile`. If you are using Linux, you will need to comment out the `include windows.inc` at the beginning of the `Makefile` and uncomment the `include linux.inc`:

```
## TODO: EDIT next set of lines according to OS

#include windows.inc
include linux.inc
```

3. Open a command prompt or shell as follows:

WINDOWS

Open an Intel compiler command prompt. The path to the command prompt will be similar to the following. (The exact names and menu items will vary, depending on which version of Parallel Studio and Visual Studio you have installed.)

Start ⇨ All Programs ⇨ Intel Parallel Studio XE 2011 ⇨ Command Prompt ⇨ Intel64 Visual Studio Mode

LINUX

Make sure the compiler variables have been sourced:

```
$ source /opt/intel/bin/compilervars.sh intel64
```

If you are running a 32-bit operating system, the parameter passed to the `compilervars.sh` file should be `ia32`.

Building and Running the Program

4. Build the application `12-1.exe` by calling `make`:

LINUX

```
make clean
make 14-1
```

---

[1]J. E. Barnes and P. Hut. 1986. A hierarchical O(N log N) force-calculation algorithm. Nature. 324, 446

WINDOWS

```
nmake clean
nmake 14-1
```

5. Run the program `14-1.exe` and record the results.

    Notice the message on the screen tells you that you are running a `Release` build of the `Serial` version with 1024 bodies. When the program runs, it first initializes the bodies with a random value and then runs the simulation. In the serial version no significant time is spent on initializing the bodies.

    ```
    Running with 1024 bodies
    Running Serial  Release version
    Body initialization took  0.0000 seconds
    Simulation took 19.218 seconds
    Number of Calculations: 524299776
    ```

Performing a Hotspot Analysis

6. Start an Amplifier XE GUI from the command line:

    ```
    amplxe-gui
    ```

7. Create a new project named `Chapter 14`.

    ➤   Select File ➪ New ➪ Project.

    ➤   In the Project Properties dialog, make sure the Application field points to your `14-1.exe` application.

8. Carry out a Hotspots analysis by selecting File ➪ New ➪ Hotspots Analysis. You should find that the main hotspot is a call to `addAcc()`.

Using a Tree-Based N-Bodies Simulation

The trick in the Barnes-Hut algorithm is to group together clusters of particles and treat them as a single body. When calculating the effect of such a group on a nearby particle, the distance of the particle to the group is first examined. If a group is greater than a certain distance away, the combined mass of the group is used rather than the mass of the individual particles within the group. Because of this grouping, the time taken to calculate the effect of particles on each other is reduced significantly.

The first stage in building up the simulation model is to create a single cube that represents the entire space of the environment. As the model is populated, this cube is partitioned into smaller cubes. Each cube can contain at most only one particle, so when two particles would occupy the same cube, the cube is split into sub-cubes so that each particle can be in its own cube. Figure 14-3 shows how this cube division takes place:

➤   The first particle is placed into the single cube. This is represented by the head node in the octree.

➤ Introducing a second particle causes the head cell to be split into eight, the two particles now being stored in the second- level of the tree.

➤ Additional particles are placed in the new leaf(s). When two particles end up being in the same cube, the cube is split into a further eight cuboids.

➤ A fully constructed tree consists of nodes and leaf(s). Only a leaf can contain a particle.

The collection of nested cubes is stored in an octree. An octree works the same way as a binary tree, except that each node has eight children rather than the usual two. The octree is traversed recursively using standard linked-list techniques. The mass and center of mass is calculated for every node in the tree.

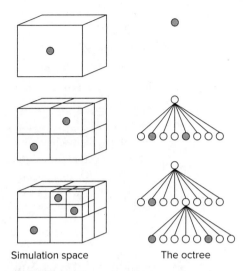

Simulation space   The octree

FIGURE 14-3: The entire environment to be simulated is represented as a set of cubes, which is stored as an octree.

The following code snippet shows the three structures that are used to store the octree — NODE, NODES, and TREE. The width of the octree is determined by TREE_WIDTH, which is defined to have the value 8.

```
struct NODE
{
        int Id;
        BODYTYPE * pCell;
        NODES *  pNodes;
        MINMAX MinMax;
        NODE * pNext; // used in linked list to all siblings
        NODE * pChild; // used in linked list to all children
        double CentreOfMass[NUMDIMENSIONS];
        double Mass;
};

struct NODES
{
        NODE Nodes[TREE_WIDTH];
};


struct TREE
{
        int NumNodes; // this includes number of leafs
        int NumLeafs;
        NODE Head;
}
```

ACTIVITY 14-2: BUILDING THE OCTREE SOLUTION

In this activity you build and run the octree version of the n-bodies simulation. You can run this activity on Linux or Windows.

1. Repeat steps 4 to 6 of Activity 14-1 but use the target 14-2 for the Makefile. The main difference between this target and the previous target is the option -DOCTREE, which is equivalent to using a #define OCTREE in the source code.

2. Run the new executable 14-2.exe. It should run much quicker than the serial version.

3. Carry out a Hotspots analysis and confirm the name of the hotspot (by repeating step 8 of Activity 14-1, but don't forget to change the name of the application to 14-2.exe in the project properties window).

4. Browse into the source code by double-clicking on the hotspot in the Bottom-up window. Find out which lines take up the most time.

5. Optional. Search for all occurrences of the preprocessor macro OCTREE in the source files and see which new sources are included in the build when this macro is defined.

Using a Hashed Octree

One way to implement the octree is to use linked lists, where each node of the linked list points to eight sub-children. Tree traversal using linked lists is expensive. Algorithms that use pointer-chasing techniques often suffer from poor performance due to inefficient use of memory. By using a hash-based algorithm rather than a linked list to store the tree, the traversal and manipulation of the tree is significantly reduced.

Dr. Golanski used a hash-based algorithm in which the *xyz* coordinates of the particle are used to construct a hash key, as described by Warren and Salmon.[2] Where the hash key is calculated to be the same for two different particles, the values are chained together under the same key. For example, in Figure 14-4(a) the bottom hash table entry has two additional entries (Bin 1 and Bin 2) that are daisy-chained to the #2249 hash.

In the n-bodies simulation code, the HASHTABLE structure is used to hold the hash table. Each entry of the hash table is stored in the Data array, with the size of the array being controlled by the MAXKEYS:

```
struct HASHTABLE
{
        unsigned int NumNodes;
```

---

[2]M. Warren and J. Salmon. 1993. A parallel hashed oct-tree N-body algorithm. Supercomputing '93 Proceedings. 12–21

```
        unsigned int NumLeafs;
        unsigned int NumChainedLeafs;
        QUEUE SortedList;

        NODE Data[MAXKEYS];

    };
```

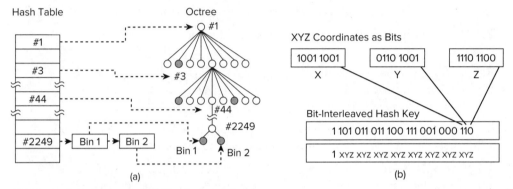

FIGURE 14-4: Tree traversal and hash generation

Implementing the simulation using a hashed octree resulted in a further improvement on the time taken for each simulation when using the same hardware. Figure 14-5 shows how the changes in the n-bodies algorithm affect the simulation time. In the traditional n-bodies solution, the time taken in the simulation rises very sharply as new bodies are introduced. The most favorable algorithm is the hashed octree, which produces a very manageable rate of rise.

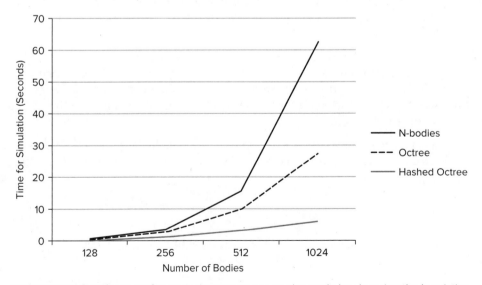

FIGURE 14-5: Significant performance improvements can be made by changing the heuristics of the application

---

ACTIVITY 14-3: BUILDING THE HASHED OCTREE SOLUTION

In this activity you build and run the hashed octree version of the n-bodies simulation. You can run this activity on Linux or Windows.

1. Build the application using the target 14-3 for the `Makefile`. The main difference between this target and the previous target is the option `-DHASHTREE`.

2. Run the new executable `14-3.exe`. It should run quicker than the octree version you ran in Activity 14-2.

3. Carry out a Hotspots analysis and confirm the name of the hotspot (by repeating step 8 of Activity 14-1, but don't forget to change the name of the application to `14-3.exe` in the project properties window).

4. Optional. Search for all occurrences of the preprocessor macro `HASHTREE` in the source files, and see which new sources are included in the build when this macro is defined.

ARCHITECTURAL TUNING

Once you have suitably tuned the heuristics of the application, it's time to turn your attention to the architectural bottlenecks. Amplifier XE is used to perform the architectural analysis. A number of predefined analysis types are available for architectural analysis, including the following event-based types, which are targeted for Intel micro-architecture (see Chapter 12, "Event-Based Analysis with VTune Amplifier XE," for more details):

➤ **Lightweight Hotspots** — Event-based sampling that captures the amount of time you spend in different parts of your code. This is different from the Hotspots analysis you have already used in Activities 14-1, 14-2, and 14-3 in that it does not collect any stack information.

➤ **General Exploration** — Event-based sampling collection that provides a wide spectrum of hardware-related performance metrics

➤ **Memory Access** — Event-based analysis that helps you understand where the memory access issues affect the performance of your application

➤ **Bandwidth** — Event-based analysis that helps you understand where the bandwidth issues affect the performance of your application

➤ **Cycles and uOps** — Event-based analysis that helps you understand where the uOp flow issues affect the performance of your application

As you become more experienced in architectural analysis, it is sometimes possible to guess what the likely bottlenecks will be. In the n-bodies code, the efficiency of the arithmetic operations, such as division, and how memory is used are at the top of the list of suspects you should investigate.

Within the identified hotspot function, there is code that contains several divisions:

```
// compute the unit vector from j to i
double ud[3];
```

```
ud[0] = dx/dist;
ud[1] = dy/dist;
ud[2] = dz/dist;
```

This code can be rewritten to use a reciprocal, resulting in the compiler generating much faster code:

```
// compute the unit vector from j to i
double ud[3];
double dd=1.0/dist;
ud[0] = dx * dd;
ud[1] = dy * dd;
ud[2] = dz * dd;
```

Table 14-1 shows the result of making such code changes on the different heuristics using the same hardware. The code was built using the Microsoft compiler. The number of particles used was 1024. Remember that it is better to look at the architectural bottlenecks *after* completing any heuristic optimization, not before. In the hashed tree solution — the code that has the most optimized heuristic — the speedup is 13 percent on a set of 1K particles and 11 percent on a set of 10K particles.

TABLE 14-1: Results of Optimizing Several Divisions

HEURISTIC	TIME (SECONDS)		
	DIVIDE	RECIPROCAL	SPEEDUP
Serial	22.56	17.28	30%
Tree	19.64	19.58	0.3%
Hashed tree (1K nodes)	2.23	1.97	13%
Hashed tree (10K nodes)	638	570	11%

You often can make code, especially mathematical number-crunching code, more efficient by looking at how the calculations are done. By simply rearranging equations you can reduce the computational effort. The preceding divisional example is one such way of reducing the effort. In this example, a temporary variable was calculated and used three times. This idea can be further developed by precalculating parts of equations and carrying the results forward. Where several equations occur, make sure you are not calculating some part of the various equations more than once; again, use temporary variables. Often, array calculations can be broken down into several parts; this also increases the chances of their successful vectorization. All these approaches can reduce time even before other methods are considered.

ACTIVITY 14-4: OPTIMIZING THE DIVISION

In this activity you build and run a version of the n-bodies simulation that has optimized division code and compare its CPI rate with and without this optimization. You can run this activity on Linux or Windows.

1. Carry out a Lightweight Hotspot analysis on the application you built in Activity 14-3:

   ➤ Select File ⇨ New ⇨ Lightweight Hotspots Analysis. Notice that we are using *lightweight* hotspots!

   ➤ In the Project Properties dialog, make sure the Application field points to your 14-3.exe application.

   ➤ Start the analysis.

2. Examine the results and make a note of the following:

   ➤ The elapsed time of the program

   ➤ The function name and CPU time of the biggest hotspot

   ➤ The CPI of the biggest hotspot (for a refresher on CPI, see Chapter 12, "Event-Based Analysis with VTune Amplifier XE")

   You should see that one hotspot has a terrible CPI (a good CPI value should be less than 1).

3. Build the new application using the target 14-4. The main difference between this target and the previous target is the option -DUSE_RECIPROCAL_DIVIDE.

4. Run a new Lightweight Hotspot analysis using 14-4.exe for the Makefile.

5. The new executable, 14-4.exe, should have a shorter elapsed time than that of 14-3.exe. Calculate the speedup using the following formula:

   speedup = new time \ old time

6. Compare the CPI rate and CPU time of the hotspot in 14-3.exe with the same source line in 14-4.exe. In the new executable the CPI should be lower, and the elapsed time shorter.

7. Optional. Search for all occurrences of the preprocessor macro USE_RECIPROCAL_DIVIDE in the source files, and see which new sources are included in the build when this macro is defined.

ADDING PARALLELISM

Once the serial version of the code is sufficiently well optimized, it's time to move on to making the code parallel. In the original research, the parallel algorithms were based on the suggestions made by Warren and Salmon. By splitting the sorted list of particles into groups, these groups can be simulated in parallel. Once the sorted particles are split into groups, a tree is created for each disjoint group — called *local trees*. Using a sorted list means that each group of particles is in spatially distinct parts of the cube. Where there is the possibility that a particle could sit in the node of an adjacent local tree, a copy of the node is held in both trees.

Identifying the Hotspot and Discovering the Calling Sequence

In the simulation, the same calculation is repeated thousands of times on the particles in the environment. Using Amplifier XE to identify the hotspots in the code shows that most of the time is spent adding the acceleration to the moving particles (refer to Figure 14-2).

Although the original research used MPI to implement parallelism, the steps that were undertaken to add parallelism are common to whatever language implementation is used.

The steps undertaken were as follows:

1. Identify the hotspot.
2. Discover the calling sequence and number of function calls.
3. Identify any dependencies.
4. Implement the parallelism.
5. Check for any errors introduced by parallelization, such as data races, and correct them.
6. Tune the parallel application.

The most significant hotspot in the code is in the `HashAdvance` function. Normally, when applying parallelism, it is usual to add the parallel construct to one of the parent functions of the hotspot. As shown in Figure 14-6, the `Step` function looks like an ideal candidate. The function controls 99.5 percent of the CPU time.

Implementing Parallelism

As previously mentioned, the original implementation was done using MPI. Intel Parallel Composer provides a number of different ways of implementing parallelism, including OpenMP, Cilk Plus, and Threading Building Blocks. Cilk Plus is ideal for this kind of problem where load balancing is of upmost importance. Cilk Plus's task-stealing scheduler does a great job at load balancing and has an intuitive programming approach. Listing 14-1 shows how Cilk Plus can be applied to the problem.

Listing 14-1 shows how a `for` loop can be easily parallelized by using the `cilk_for` keyword at line 7. The code snippet is based on the `Step()` function found in `Hash.cpp`. The only other addition to the code was to include the statement `#include <cilk/cilk.h>` at the top of the file.

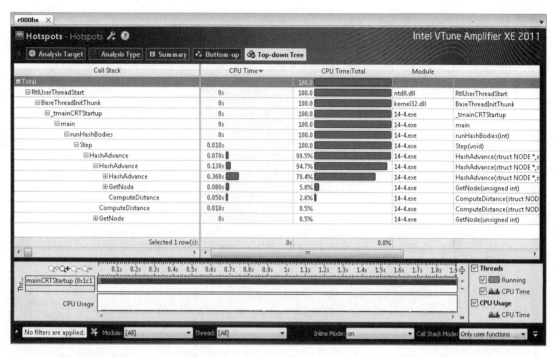

FIGURE 14-6: Identifying the hotspot and call stack

LISTING 14-1: Introducing parallelism by replacing the for loop at line 7 with a cilk_for

```
1: // This code has known data race bugs and is used as an example
2: // to explain how to detect parallelization problems.
3: unsigned int stepcount;
4: void Step()
5: {
6:   // parallelize following loop using cilk_for in place of C for
7:   cilk_for(int i = 0; i < theTable.SortedList.Cursor; i++)
8:   {
9:     // declare and set hash table value
10:    unsigned int Hash = theTable.SortedList.List[i];
11:    if(Hash != 0)
12:    {
13:      // declare pointers to first & next nodes
14:      NODE *pNode = GetNode(Hash);
15:      NODE *pChain = pNode->pNext;
16:      // advance to next node and increment stepcount
17:      HashAdvance(pNode,GetNode(0));
18:      stepcount++;
19:      // while not end of list
```

continues

LISTING 14-1 *(continued)*

```
20:     while(pChain)
21:     {
22:        // advance to next node
23:        HashAdvance(pChain, GetNode(0));
24:        pChain = pChain->pNext;
25:        stepcount++;
26:     }
27:   }
28: }
29: }
```

code snippet chapter14\14-1.cpp

ACTIVITY 14-5: PARALLELIZING THE CODE WITH CILK PLUS

In this activity you make the n-bodies program parallel using Cilk Plus. You can run this activity on Linux or Windows.

1. Build the application using the target `14-5` for the `Makefile`. The main difference between this target and the previous target is the option `-DUSE_CILK`.

2. Run the new executable `14-5.exe`, and compare the output messages with the ones that you get from running `14-4.exe`.

You should notice that the program runs faster (because it is running in parallel) but that the number of calculations reported in `14-5.exe` is different from `14-4.exe`. The differences are almost certainly caused by a data race, which you will detect and fix in Activity 14-6.

3. Optional. Search for all occurrences of the preprocessor macro `USE_CILK` in the source files, and see which new sources are included in the build when this macro is defined.

Detecting Data Races and Other Potential Errors

Once parallelism has been introduced, there is always the risk that data races or other parallel-type errors have been accidentally introduced. Access within the threaded code to any global variable will cause problems. These problems can be detected using such tools as Intel Parallel Inspector (see Chapter 8, "Checking for Errors").

A visual inspection of Listing 14-1 shows that the incrementing of the `stepcount` variable at line 18 and line 25 is likely to cause a data race. The variable is not declared with the scope of the parallelized loop, and can thus be accessed simultaneously by two or more worker threads. Using Intel Parallel Inspector XE will also show any problems.

The Intel Parallel Debug Extension (PDE) is another great way to detect data races. Figure 14-7 shows PDE detecting the data race. See Chapter 11, "Debugging Parallel Applications," for more information on how to use PDE to detect data races.

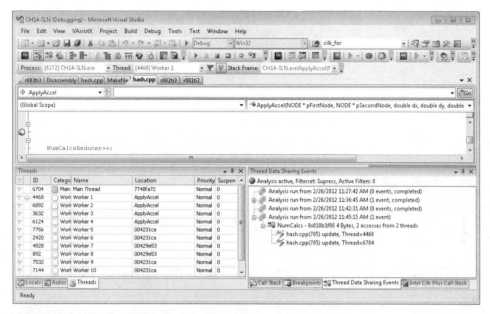

FIGURE 14-7: Using Parallel Debugging Extension to detect data races

Correcting the Data Race

Cilk Plus provides a number of different ways to fix data races. The most obvious way is to restructure the code so that global variables are not needed. If you cannot restructure the code, protect access to the variable so that only one thread can modify it at any one time. By declaring the stepcount variable to be a cilk::reducer_opadd<unsigned int>, the Cilk Plus run time automatically ensures that no data race occurs. The Cilk Plus reducer does this by creating private copies or views of the variable within the parallel region, and then adding the private copies together (reducing the result) when leaving the parallel region.

ACTIVITY 14-6: DETECTING AND FIXING DATA RACES

In this activity you use Inspector XE to look for and fix any data races in the application you built in Activity 14-5. You can run this activity on Linux or Windows.

Performing a Data Race Analysis

1. Build the application using the target 14-6a for the Makefile. The main differences between this target and the previous target are the option -DUSE_256_WORLD, which reduces the number of bodies to 256, and the inclusion of flags to build a debug version.

2. Start an Inspector XE GUI from the command line:

   ```
   inspxe-gui
   ```

continues

continued

3. Create a new project named `Chapter 14`.

➤ Select File ➪ New ➪ Project.

➤ In the Project Properties dialog, make sure the Application Field points to `14-6a.debug.exe` application.

4. Carry out a Data Race analysis by selecting File ➪ New ➪ Find Deadlocks and Data Races. You should find that there are two data races.

Fixing the Data Race

5. Build the application using the target `14-6b` for the `Makefile`. The main difference between this target and `14-6a` is the option `-DUSE_CILK_REDUCER`, which introduces two `cilk::reducer_opadd` reducers to the code.

6. Carry out a Data Race analysis, making sure that the Application field in the Project Properties dialog points to `14-6b.debug.exe`. The two data races should now be fixed.

7. Optional. Search for all occurrences of the preprocessor macro `USE_CILK_REDUCER` in the source files, and see which new sources are included in the build when this macro is defined.

Load Balancing

Once the n-bodies program is correctly running, verify that all the threads are employed usefully. The concurrency level is a measure of how parallel the program was running over its life. Figure 14-8 shows the concurrency view displayed in Parallel Amplifier XE. The application spends most of its time running all eight available cores.

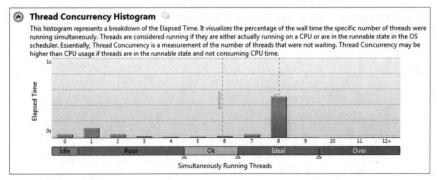

FIGURE 14-8: Parallel Amplifier XE shows that the application has ideal thread concurrency

ACTIVITY 14-7: CHECKING THE LOAD BALANCING

In this activity you run a Concurrency analysis to see if the program is load balanced. You can run this activity on Linux or Windows.

1. Build the application using the target 14-7 for the `Makefile`.

2. Run the new executable `14-7.exe`. It should run almost as quickly as `14-5.exe` and have the same output messages as `14-4.exe`.

3. Use Amplifier XE to carry out a Concurrency analysis. (Don't forget to change the Application field to `14-7.exe`.)

4. Look at the results and confirm that each thread is doing the same amount of work by observing their start and end times in the timeline view of the Bottom-up window.

The Results

The original research work showed that adding coolant to the interstellar medium could result in a medium that was good enough to begin star formation. You can find a more detailed description of the results in the paper by Golanski and Woolfson. Figure 14-9 is a snapshot of the original simulation showing how introducing a coolant leads to the formation of two protostellar clouds, which eventually form dense cold clouds — the precursor to the formation of a star. The contours represent density; the shading, temperature; and the arrows, velocity and direction.

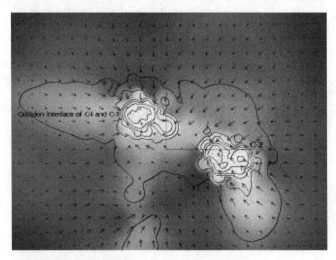

FIGURE 14-9: A snapshot of the original simulation

NINE TIPS TO PARALLEL HEAVEN

The following tips were recorded over a pleasant Thai meal in the city of York. Between the distractions of the different dishes, Dr. Golanski spoke about what advice he'd give to someone starting to parallelize an application. At the end of the meal the restaurant owner asked if the restaurant could be mentioned. Well, here goes: If you are ever in the center of York, look for the Siam House, on Goodramgate.

➤ **Buy a faster machine** — First, look at how much it will cost to make your program parallel. If it will take, say, two months of coding, consider a faster machine that will give you the speedup you want. Of course, once you reach the limits of a machine's speed, you are going to have to do some parallelization.

➤ **Start small** — Don't try to make everything parallel at once; just work on small bits of code.

➤ **Use someone else's wheel** — If you are starting from scratch, see what other people have done first. Learn from others. Don't reinvent the wheel.

➤ **Find a way of logging and/or debugging your application** — Make sure you have a way of tracing what your application is doing. If necessary, buy some software tools that will do the trick. Using `printf`s on their own will probably not help.

➤ **Look at where the code is struggling** — Examine the runtime behavior of your application. Profile the code with Intel VTune Performance Analyzer. The hotspots you find should be the ones to make parallel.

➤ **Write a parallel version of the algorithm** — Try rewriting the algorithm to be parallel-friendly.

➤ **Stop when it's good enough** — When you think it's good enough, stop! Step back and go for a pint. Have set goals — when you have achieved them, you are done.

➤ **Tread carefully** — Take care with the parallel code. Some innocent errors could blow up your program. Use a good tool to check for any data races and other parallel errors.

➤ **Get the load balancing right** — Once you've made your code parallel, make sure all the threads are doing equal amounts of work.

SUMMARY

This chapter showed how you can look at the heuristics of a program to improve its efficiency — that is, reduce time. Simply changing the code can, in many instances, bring an instant speedup.

The performance was improved further by removing, where possible, architectural bottlenecks. The Intel VTune Amplifier XE was used to help in identifying and understanding the low-level bottlenecks.

The Intel Cilk Plus method of parallelization was then used in this case study to introduce parallel execution of the application, Cilk being ideal in this case due to its ease of use and ability to produce load-balanced code.

Chapter 15, "Parallel Track Fitting in the CERN Collider," includes an example that shows how to use Intel Array Building Blocks (ArBB) to achieve parallelism on a collection of workstations. ArBB brings a flexible approach to parallelism, in which the runtime engine works alongside a just-in-time (JIT) compiler to produce optimized code, leading to software that can adapt itself to new generations of silicon as they become available.

15

Parallel Track Fitting in the CERN Collider

WHAT'S IN THIS CHAPTER?

➤ Introducing particle track fitting

➤ Introducing Intel Array Building Blocks

➤ Parallelizing programs using Intel Array Building Blocks

This chapter looks at parallelizing code that determines particle tracks within high-energy physics experiments. This represents some of the work done at the CERN GSI establishment in Darmstadt, Germany. The group is well known for its discovery of the elements bohrium, hassium, meitnerium, darmstadtium, roentgenium, and copernicium.

Intel Array Building Blocks (ArBB) is a research project, and consists of a C++ template library that provides a high-level data parallel programming solution. By using ArBB to parallelize software, you can produce thread-safe, future-proofed applications. The six hands-on activities let you try out parallelizing a serial track-fitting program using ArBB.

THE CASE STUDY

The Compressed Baryonic Matter (CBM) project is designed to explore the properties of super-dense nuclear matter by using a particle accelerator to collide charged particles against a fixed target.

The word *baryonic* in the project title refers to *baryons*, large particles made up of three quarks — a quark being an elementary particle from which all matter is made. Quarks are found neither on their own nor in isolation.

One of the aims of the CBM experiment is to search for the transition of baryons to quarks and gluons (the particles that hold together the quarks). The CBM project is carried out at GSI (center for heavy ion research) and its adjacent facility FAIR (Facility for Antiproton and Ion Research) in Darmstadt, Germany. Researchers from around the world use this facility for experiments using the unique, large-scale accelerator for heavy ions. You can find more information about CBM at www.gsi.de/forschung/fair_experiments/CBM/index_e.html.

INTERVIEW QUESTIONS

Dispersed through this chapter are several questions that the program developers were asked. Their answers are intended to tease out their experiences using ArBB.

THE STAGES OF A HIGH-ENERGY PHYSICS EXPERIMENT

Generally, a high-energy physics experiment goes through eight stages, as shown in Figure 15-1.

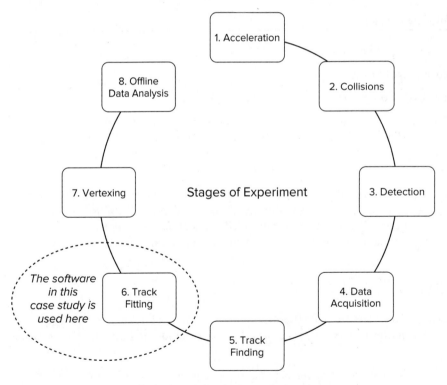

FIGURE 15-1: The stages of a high-energy physics experiment

➤   In the first two steps, *acceleration* and *collision*, particles are accelerated to almost the speed of light and then collided against a fixed target or against other accelerated particles.

➤   In the next two steps, *detection* and *data acquisition*, particles are detected as they pass through detector planes. In the case of the CBM experiment, there are seven such planes, referred to as *stations*. Each station records the position of particles passing through them — these are the particle *hits*. The collected data is then used to determine what actually happened.

➤   The *track-finding* and the *track-fitting* stages are used to reconstruct the path that the particles took. Track finding determines which hits in the various stations belong to which track. Track fitting is used to take into account the inaccuracies of the detection system. The station data and its extraction are noisy, resulting in inaccurate hit coordinates. An attempt is made to eliminate these inaccuracies and refine the particle tracks. The method involves the use of *a Kalman filter* and is the subject of this case study.

➤   At the *vertexing* stage, various constraints to the tracks are applied. For example, a particular particle may decay along its track and produce a number of other tracks, all of which must originate from the same point. This is an attempt to find correlation between tracks.

➤   Finally, the captured data is used for *offline data analysis* and the physical interpretation of events.

The Track Reconstruction Stages

The CBM experiment looks at hadrons, electrons, and photons emitted in heavy-ion collisions. Once each particle is detected, the correct path or track has to be calculated, the data then being used to help interpret what has happened.

Each event (collision) results in many thousands of potential tracks passing through the detectors. These events can be repeated many thousands of times per second, requiring extremely high data-processing rates. Modern high-energy physics experiments typically have to process terabytes of input data per second. The track-reconstruction stages are the most time-consuming parts of the analysis; therefore, the speed of any track-determination algorithms becomes very important in the total processing time.

Track determination would be trivial were it not for complications arising because of inaccuracies due to detector noise and scattering due to electric charge, energy loss, nonuniform magnetic fields, and so on.

Figure 15-2 shows a typical problem, with multiple planes positioned at different z positions across the trajectories of the particles. Each plane registers the x and y positions of the particles as they pass through (referred to as *hits*). The problem then becomes to reconstruct the paths of the various particles by using their positions on each detector.

Listing 15-1 shows the structure used to store the station information. The code is much reduced; if you want to see the original code, look in the `class.h` file from the hands-on project (see Activity 15-1). Notice that the class contains 15 different pointers (for example, `*z`). Each pointer gets allocated dynamic memory within the init method, which is called by the Stations constructor.

Notice, too, that when malloc is used in the init() function, it creates enough space for all the stations. This is true for all 15 pointers that you can see.

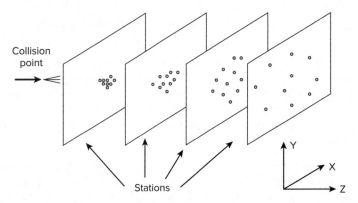

FIGURE 15-2: Typical hits at stations along trajectory

LISTING 15-1: The Stations class in the serial version of the code

```cpp
// NOTE: See class.h for complete listing.
// The listing here is not intended to be compiled.

class Stations{
public:
  int nStations;

  ftype *z, *thick, *zhit, *RL, *RadThick,*logRadThick,*Sigma,*Sigma2,*Sy;
  ftype (**mapX), (**mapY), (**mapZ); // polinom coeff.

  void initMap( int i, ftype *x, ftype *y, ftype *z){// init code }
  Stations( int ns )     {init( ns );}
  void init( int ns )
  {
    // allocate memory all 7 stations are together
    nStations = ns;
    z = (ftype*)malloc(ns*sizeof(ftype));
    // ... repeat for thick zhit RL RadThick logRadThick Sigma
    // Sigma2 Sy mapX mapY mapZ mapXPool mapYPool mapZPool
  }

  ~Stations()     {// free dynamically allocated memory}

private:
  // pointers to private pool
  ftype *mapXPool, *mapYPool, *mapZPool;
};
```

code snippet Chapter15\15-1.h

Track Finding

Track finding involves determining which hits on each of the planes were made by the same particle, therefore indicating its path through the detector. This is time-consuming and involves using the properties of a particle (spatial, velocity, mass, charge) at one plane to predict its hit position on the next plane. Once the prediction has been made, a search is made for the closest hit.

To make matters more interesting, the whole detector is embedded within a magnetic field, so any charged particles will respond accordingly (see Figure 15-3). The direction and radius of any trajectory curvature depend on the strength and polarity of the charged particle.

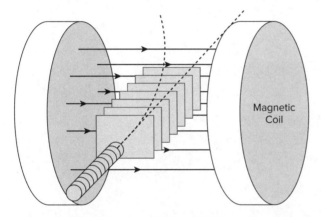

FIGURE 15-3: Detector stations embedded within a magnetic field

A lot of track finding can be related to pattern recognition, which is something humans are particularly good at, and which computers are not. Figure 15-4 shows a predicted hit on the last plane after using the two previous hits to fit a predicted curved arc. The nearest measured hit is then taken.

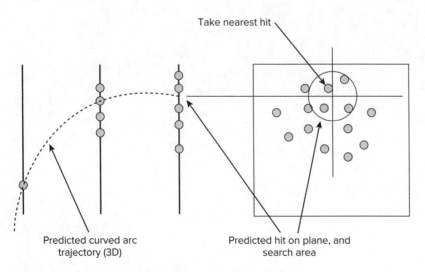

FIGURE 15-4: Using prediction to determine the next hit

Listing 15-2 shows the `Tracks` class that is used to hold all the track information. At run time more than 20,000 track details are held in the instantiation of this class. Notice, again, like the `Stations` class previously discussed, a number of pointers are used to hold dynamically allocated memory. When ArBB is added to the code, one of the first things to address is to replace the dynamically allocated structures with ArBB containers.

LISTING 15-2: The Tracks class in the serial version of the code

```
// NOTE: See class.h for complete listing.
// The listing here is not intended to be compiled.

class Tracks
{
public:
  unsigned int nStations;
  unsigned int nTracks;

  ftype *MC_x, *MC_y, *MC_z, *MC_px, *MC_py, *MC_pz, *MC_q;
  int *nHits, *NDF;
  ftype **hitsX, **hitsY;
  ftype *hitsX2, *hitsY2;
  int **hitsIsta;

  void init( int ns, int nt )
  {
    nTracks = nt;
    MC_x = ( ftype* ) malloc( sizeof( ftype ) * nt );

    // repeat for : MC_y MC_z MC_px MC_py MC_pz MC_q  nHits
    // NDF hitsX  hitsY  hitsIsta

    memXPool = ( ftype* ) malloc( sizeof( ftype ) * nt * nStations );
    // repeat for : memYPool  memIstaPool hitsX2 hitsY2
  }

  ~Tracks()      {}

  void setHits( int i, int *iSta, ftype *hx, ftype *hy )
  {
    // record hits
  }

private:
  ftype *memXPool, *memYPool;
  int *memIstaPool;
};
```

code snippet Chapter15\15-2.h

INTERVIEW Q1: WHAT WAS THE HARDEST PART OF USING ARBB IN THE TRACK-FITTING CODE?

The original code was developed without "parallel programming" in mind, and it didn't follow a particular programming model. We had various contributors along the road. When focusing on "minimal changes," the programming model of choice is obviously to augment code with pragmas or directives, to aim for SIMD vectorization, and to harvest parallelism across cores using multithreading. Using ArBB caused us to think about parallel operators and "what to do" rather than "how to do it." Instead of employing (nested) loops, we had to collect data in "dense containers" (arrays) and modify our data model. On the other hand, this helped us understand our own code better. To summarize, we had to think through the workload instead of applying hints to our existing code. We're looking forward to a more math-style formulation in order to stick with an algorithmic description of our work, and to have more descriptive/expressive code in the future because of using Intel ArBB.

Track Fitting

After determining the track by successive plane hits, track-fitting algorithms are then applied to smooth out any track irregularities due to inaccuracies along the paths. This forms the bulk of the work in this case study.

Successive station hits of a particular track may not follow a highly accurately determined track, due to noise and other inaccuracies. Track fitting is used to minimize how close the measured hits are to what they are assumed to be for a particular fit hypothesis. By using a particle's location at one station, the environment between it and the next station, together with the physical properties of the particle, a prediction can be made as to where the particle will hit the following station. A weighted average is then taken between the recorded hit position and the predicted hit position to determine the actual particle position.

Kalman Filter Overview

The Kalman filter is a mathematical method designed to filter out noise and other inaccuracies in measurements observed over time. It is used in almost all high-energy physics experiments to carry out track fitting. The Kalman filter calculates estimates of the true values of measurements recursively over time using incoming measurements and a mathematical process model.

Determining a track requires two things:

➤ A model that approximates the track's trajectory

➤ An understanding of the physical properties of the detector

The Kalman filter is very good at this because it can determine the presumed path and take all the complications of an irregular topology (both of the physical detector and nonlinear magnetic field) in its stride.

Figure 15-5 shows a Kalman filter-based track fitting. As more track hits are corrected, the confidence about the track is increased and the predicted precision becomes higher. This is shown in the illustration by the decreasing thicknesses of the prediction arrows. Various filtering effects are applied to arrive at the final track's trajectory positions.

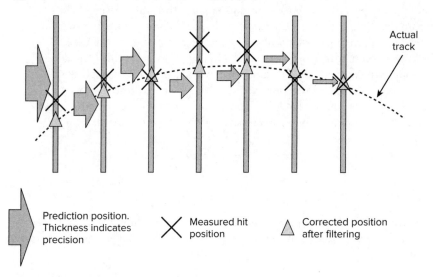

FIGURE 15-5: Using a Kalman filter to obtain an accurate path

Kalman Filter Steps

Figure 15-6 shows the steps of a Kalman filter. The symbol r is the state vector of the particle at each plane (position and velocity), and c is the covariance (confidence) matrix. The other symbols represent the magnetic field and various states of the system:

➤ The *initial approximation* step sets an approximate value of the vector r0 and the covariance matrix C0.

➤ The *prediction* step describes the deterministic changes of the vector over time to an adjacent station.

➤ The *process noise* step describes probabilistic deviations of the vector due to noise (Qk), and so on.

➤ The final step *filters* the actual values Mk, Hk, and Vk, taking into account the previous three steps.

The CBM team at GSI has implemented a fast Kalman filter for use in the track-fitting stage of their high-energy particle analysis. For each track, two arrays are maintained — one for particle state (position, velocity, and momentum), and another for the covariance values used for determining trajectory confidence. The filter is applied to each track in turn at each station along its trajectory to smooth out inaccuracies and errors, and used to derive a corrected track position.

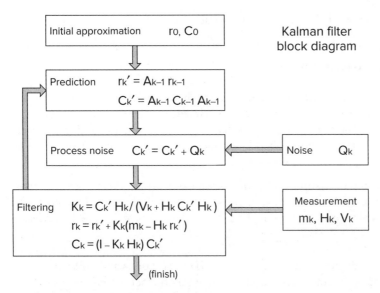

FIGURE 15-6: The Kalman filter operation

The filter has been implemented using single-precision floating-point calculations. (Traditional Kalman filters use double precision.) Additional research has been applied to ensure that working with single precision gives an accurate enough result. Using single precision over double reduces the space needed to store the data by half and results in faster calculations.

> **INTERVIEW Q2: WHAT WAS THE EASIEST PART OF USING ARBB?**
>
> Once we had stepped back from our original data design and looked at the big picture, we found that the vector-processing style of the original code and the loop-oriented code was easily modified to use the map-operator and elemental functions of ArBB. It seemed a very natural fit.

WHAT IS ARRAY BUILDING BLOCKS?

ArBB is C++ template library that provides a high-level data parallel programming solution intended to free developers from dependencies on low-level parallelism mechanisms and hardware architectures.

ArBB is designed to take advantage of multi-core processors, many-core processors, and GPUs. Under normal use, ArBB applications are automatically free of data races and deadlocks. Its main features are as follows:

➤ Has its own embedded language

➤ Uses dynamic compilation with just-in-time (JIT) compiler

➤ Provides implicit parallelism for computationally intensive maths

➤ Works across multiple cores and varying SIMD widths

➤ Provides structured data parallelism (patterns) with no data races

➤ Uses separate memory space with no pointers

➤ Does not require synchronization primitives

The essence of ArBB is *collections* (*containers*) and their associated *operators*. Collections are designed to work on arrays. The arrays can be any size and dimension, regularly or irregularly shaped. Containers either are bound to existing C/C++ data and take on the size and shape of the bound data, or they can be constructed independently without any binding. An *ArBB range* is used to transfer data from the ArBB code to the C/C++ code.

Once a set of containers is bound to existing data entities, you can work on them as though they were single variables. For example, if containers A, B, and C have been declared and bound to three separate C/C++ arrays (of any dimension), they may be processed as if normal single variables:

$$A += (B * C);$$

ArBB will produce executable code that fully utilizes any SIMD instructions and multiple cores available to carry out the operation. This is done without any further intervention by the programmer.

In general, when a container appears on both the left and right side of an expression, ArBB generates a result as if all the inputs were read before any outputs are written. In practice, you must put this expression within a function and invoke that function with a call operation.

ArBB is delivered as a library that provides data collections, operators for data processing, and an associated syntax.

As shown in Figure 15-7, the application code is written in C/C++ and looks like fairly standard nonthreaded code. You add ArBB code using a C++ API.

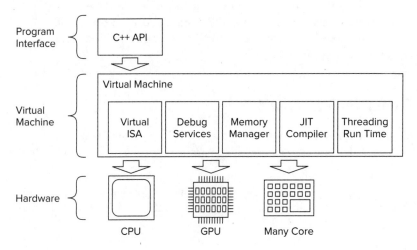

FIGURE 15-7: The ArBB platform

The ArBB runtime uses a virtual machine (VM) and employs a just-in-time (JIT) compiler. The VM works out at run time the best performance paths based on its knowledge of the hardware platform. By deferring the final compilation of the ArBB code until it resides on the target platform, the JIT compiler can produce architecture-specific optimized code.

Listing 15-3 is a program that shows a simple ArBB program. The `sum_of_differences` function will be compiled and executed at run time; the `main` function is a normal C++ function and is compiled in the usual way.

The `main` function has two dense containers, `a` and `b`, similar to the STL's `std::vector`, whose size is set to 1024.

The first time you run the application, the ArBB `call` operator causes the JIT compiler to compile `sum_of_differences`. The ArBB code is then executed. If there were further calls to the function `sum_of_differences`, it would not need to be recompiled.

LISTING 15-3: An ArBB program skeleton

```cpp
#include <arbb.hpp>
#include <cstdlib>

void sum_of_differences(dense<f32> a, dense<f32> b, f64& result)
{
  result = add_reduce((a - b) * (a - b));
}

int main()
{
  std::size_t size = 1024;
  dense<f32> a(size), b(size);
  f64 result;
  range<f32> data_a = a.read_write_range();
  range<f32> data_b = a.read_write_range();

  for (std::size_t i = 0; i != size; ++i) {
    data_a[i] = static_cast<float>(i);
    data_b[i] = static_cast<float>(i + 1);
    call(&sum_of_differences)(a, b, result);
    std::cout << "Result: " << value(result) << '\n';
  }
  return 0;
}
```

code snippet Chapter15\15-3.cpp

The big advantage of ArBB is the optimization performed by the JIT compiler. Because the ArBB code is compiled at run time, you can optimize the code to take advantage of the hardware it is running on. When you introduce the same code to a newer-generation CPU, the code will be optimized to match the new features available in the CPU.

PARALLELIZING THE TRACK-FITTING CODE

In the case study, a serial version of a track-fitting benchmark was parallelized using ArBB.

Adding Array Building Blocks to Existing Code

Figure 15-8 shows the steps to convert a serial program into a parallel ArBB program:

1. The kernel signature (that is, function prototype) of the entry point to the ArBB code is established. The code in the diagram is cut down, but you can see that the parameters to the function have new types.

2. ArBB containers and variables are defined. Some of these will need to be associated with variables and structures that exist in the coexisting C++ code. The association is done either with `arbb::bind(…)` or by employing an ArBB range.

3. A call to the kernel signature that was constructed in step 1 is inserted in the appropriate place in the source code. The kernel is called using `arbb::call(…)`.

4. The contents of the kernel are converted to ArBB.

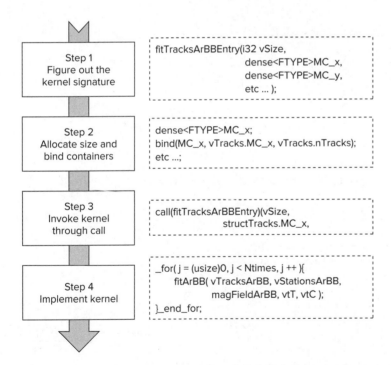

FIGURE 15-8: Converting a serial program to a parallel ArBB program

In the "Hands-On Project" section later in this chapter, you apply these steps to the filter driver code.

INTERVIEW Q3: WERE THERE ANY SPECIAL TRICKS IN THE CODE THAT YOU CONSIDER CLEVER OR WORTH EXPOUNDING?

No tricks! We learned to stick with the most natural formulation. We're looking forward to seeing robust performance independent of tricky variations.

Code Refactoring

Some of the original code required more reworking before the preceding four steps were carried out:

➤ Any references to global variables were removed so that access was by parameters passed in via the function call.

➤ A wrapper function was inserted in the call stack to help marshal the parameters and data structures.

➤ The code that was to be made parallel was changed to an inline function. This was done so that it would be easy to change the size of the data types within the code.

➤ Some local variables were moved into a higher-level function with the address being passed in.

➤ Each array of structures (AoS) was changed to a structure of arrays (SoA).

An Example of Class Change

Listing 15-4 shows a cut-down version of the `StationsArBB` class. This is the ArBB replacement for the `Stations` class shown in Listing 15-1. Note that all the variables are now dense containers and that there is no dynamic memory allocation.

Available for download on Wrox.com

LISTING 15-4: The ArBB version of the Stations class

```
/! define stations (SOA)
// NOTE: See arbb_classes.h for complete listing.
// The listing here is not intended to be compiled.

template<typename U>
class StationsArBB
{
public:
  dense<U> z, thick, zhit, RL, RadThick, logRadThick, Sigma, Sigma2, Sy;
  dense<U, 2> mapX, mapY, mapZ; // polynomial coeff.
public:
  StationsArBB(){};
  void field( const usize &i, const dense<U> &x,
  const dense<U> &y,   dense<U> H[3] )
  {
```

continues

LISTING 15-4 *(continued)*

```
    dense<U> x2 = x*x;
    // etc  ...
  }
};
```

code snippet Chapter15\15-4.h

An Example of Kernel Code Change

Listing 15-5 shows the changes that were done to the main loop in the Kalman filter. You can see how the structure of the ArBB code is similar to the original serial code:

➤ The C `for` loop is replaced by an ArBB `_for` loop.

➤ The order and names of functions called are the same.

➤ Some new ArBB types are used in place of the C types.

If you want to compare the changes for yourself, you can find the original source code for the Kalman filter in the file `serial_KF.cpp`, with the converted code being in `parallel_KF.cpp`.

LISTING 15-5: Example of loop in Kalman filter (ArBB and serial code)

```
// NOTE THIS CODE IS INCOMPLETE AND WILL NOT COMPILE!
// IT IS INCLUDED HERE FOR COMPARISON PURPOSES ONLY
```

SERIAL VERSION

```
for( --i; i>=0; i-- ){
  //    h = &t.vHits[i];
  z0 = vStations.z[i];
  dz = (z1-z0);
  vStations.field(i,T[0]-T[2]*dz,T[1]-T[3]*dz,H0);
  vStations.field(i,vTracks.hitsX[iTrack][i],vTracks.hitsY[iTrack][i], HH);
  combine( HH, h_w, H0 );
  f.set( H0, z0, H1, z1, H2, z2);

  extrapolateALight( T, C, vStations.zhit[i], qp0, f );

  addMaterial( iTrack, i, qp0, T, C );
  filter( iTrack, xInfo, vTracks.hitsX[iTrack][i], h_w, T, C );
  filter( iTrack, yInfo, vTracks.hitsY[iTrack][i], h_w, T, C );
  memcpy( H2, H1, sizeof(ftype) * 3 );
  memcpy( H1, H0, sizeof(ftype) * 3 );
  z2 = z1;
  z1 = z0;
}
```

ARBB VERSION

```
// Note 'U' is a template parameter and becomes an ArBB floating point type
_for( i -= 1, i >= 0, i-- ){
  U z0 = ss.z[i];
  dz = z1 - z0;
  ss.field( i, T[0] - T[2] * dz, T[1] - T[3] * dz, H0 );
  ss.field( i, ts.hitsX2.row( i ), ts.hitsY2.row( i ), HH );
  combineArBB<U>( HH, w, H0 );

  //! note: FieldRegionArBB f sets values here, needn't pass parameters
  f.set( H0, z0, H1, z1, H2, z2);

  extrapolateALightArBB2<U>( T, C, ss.zhit[i], qp0, f );
  addMaterialArBB( ts, ss, i, qp0, T, C );
  filterArBB( ts, ss, xInfo, ts.hitsX2.row( i ), w, T, C );
  filterArBB( ts, ss, yInfo, ts.hitsY2.row( i ), w, T, C );
  for( int j = 0; j < 3; j ++ ){
    H2[j] = H1[j];
    H1[j] = H0[j];
  }
  z2 = z1;
  z1 = z0;
}_end_for;
```

code snippet Chapter15\15-5.h

Changing to Structure of Arrays

One of the changes made in the project was how data structures are used. In the original project there were a number of places where a data structure was held as an array of structures (AoS); these were changed to structures of arrays (SoA). Actually, ArBB automatically transforms each AoS to an SoA, but relying on the automatic transformation has some associated penalties:

➤ Host pointers cannot be aliased in a relaxed safety model.

➤ De-interleaving/interleaving needs to happen ("copy-in," "copy-out") explicitly/implicitly.

➤ Explicit control for transfer and control of memory "mirror space" is often a must.

Figure 15-9 shows that by using an SoA rather than an AoS, the layout in memory of the data elements is contiguous. The user-defined type whatever_udt has two member items, m_index and m_value. If the ArBB dense container is declared using the class whatever_udt, it looks like an AoS — the dense container data being equivalent to an array, and the class whatever_udt being the structure. If you look at the layout in memory, you will see that to access a series of, say, three m_index values, the address locations are not next to each other.

To get optimal performance, it is much better to restructure the class to be like a structure of arrays.

In object-oriented programming, some programmers will naturally write their code like the first example (SoA), but the better way from a performance point of view would be to write code like the second example (AoS). The first example is not incorrect; it just carries a higher overhead.

Array of Structures (AoS)

```
// class definition
class whatever_udt {
public:
  ...
private:
  usize m_index;
  f32 m_value;
}
// object instantiation - AOS
dense<whatever_udt> data;
```

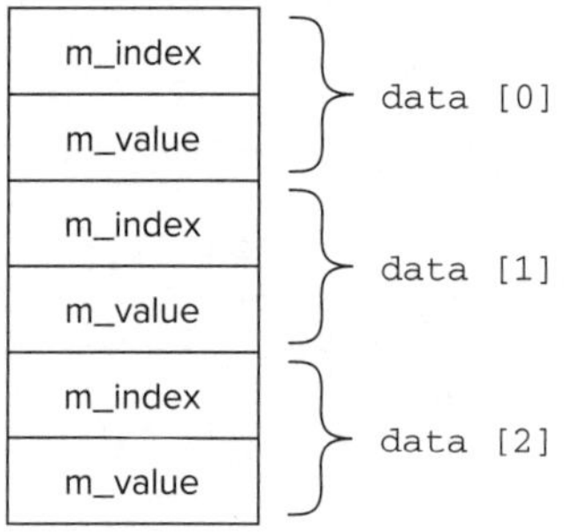

Structure of Arrays (SoA)

```
class whatever {
public:
  ...
private:
  dense<usize> m_indices;
  dense<f32> m_values;
};
// object instantiation - SOA
whatever data;
```

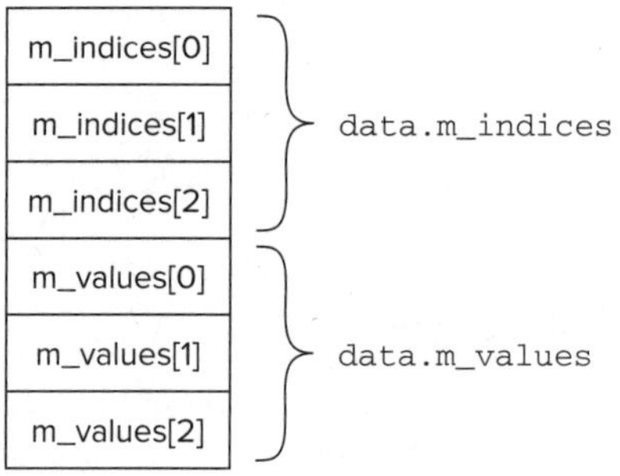

FIGURE 15-9: Using SoA helps to keep memory access contiguous

---

INTERVIEW Q4: WHAT WOULD YOU SAY IS THE BIGGEST ADVANTAGE TO USING ARBB IN THE PROJECT (AS OPPOSED TO, SAY, OPENMP)?

Using ArBB in the project is just a first try to evaluate a more operator-style (functional) formulation. Our main focus is to apply algorithmic improvements resulting from our research in the physics domain. Using ArBB gives us a more portable and forward-scaling programming language, which should protect the value of our work.

The Results

For the results of the parallel version of the track-fitting software to be of any use, the program must produce correct results and produce them fast. Let's consider the following aspects:

> ➤ Correctness
> ➤ Speedup and scalability
> ➤ Parallelism and concurrency

Correctness

A special version of the track-fitting software was written that compared the serial and parallel versions. This version first runs the serial code, obtaining the minimum time over five attempts, as before. Then the parallel version is run, again obtaining the minimum time over five attempts. The results of the parallel run are compared against the serial run to make sure that no errors exist.

Figure 15-10 shows the results of running the special version, showing no errors and a speedup factor of more than 43. The machine used has a two-socket motherboard containing two Intel Xeon X5680 (3.33GHz) processors, 12 GB of memory running Microsoft Windows 7 (64-bit). Each CPU has 6 cores and supports hyper-threading, giving a total availability of 24 hardware threads. Remember, your timings may differ.

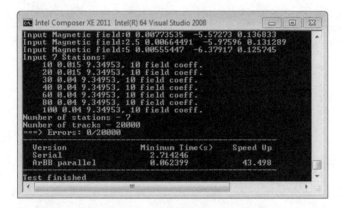

FIGURE 15-10: The results show a huge speedup with no errors

Figure 15-11 shows graphs of the residuals and pulls. Residuals show the deviation between simulated and estimated values. Pulls are a measure of the correctness of the error propagation. The *reco* and *mc* labels in the graphs refer to reconstructed values and true Monte-Carlo values, respectively.

These results are identical to the serial version (not shown), proving that the ArBB version and the original version have the same track quality.

Speedup and Scalability

Figure 15-12 shows how well the parallel program responds to different numbers of hardware threads. As you can see, there is a respectable speedup factor of almost 11 when using all 24 hardware threads available. The baseline for the speedup is the time the program takes when running one thread (not to be confused with the serial version). The speedup is calculated as follows:

$$speedup = parallel\ speed\ /\ speed\ with\ one\ thread$$

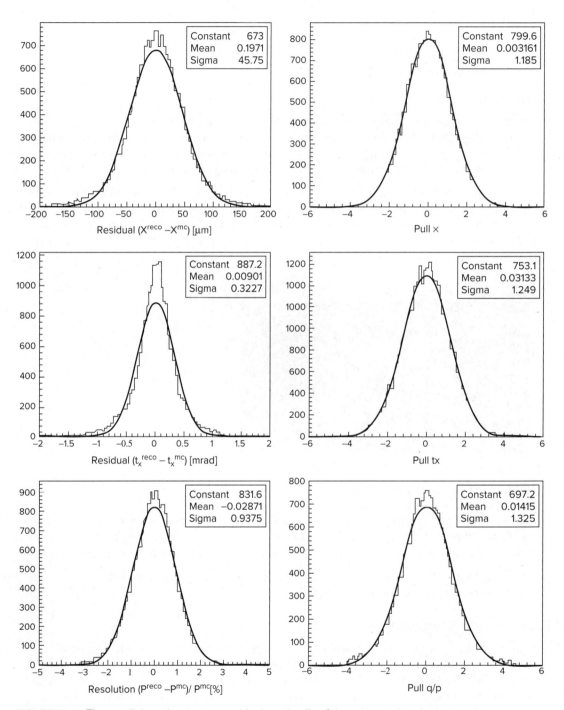

FIGURE 15-11: The parallel results showing residuals and pulls of the estimated track parameters

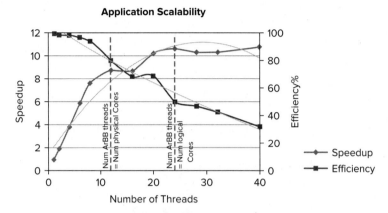

FIGURE 15-12: The scalability and efficiency of the ArBB version

Using the lower number of threads, the parallel program runs at its most efficient; as the number of threads increases, the efficiency deteriorates. The two dotted lines in the graph mark the point where the number of ArBB threads is equal to the number of physical and logical cores (that is, hardware threads), respectively. Each of the 12 physical cores supports hyper-threading, giving a total of 24 logical cores.

Once the number of ArBB threads exceeds the number of hardware threads that the test machine can support, the speedup begins to drop — this is most likely due to the extra context switching the operating system has to perform.

The efficiency figure in Figure 15-12 is a measure of how well the CPU resources are being used. If a program uses all the CPU cycles available, it is said to be 100 percent efficient. The efficiency is calculated as follows:

$$\text{efficiency} = (\text{total CPU time} / (\text{duration} * \text{num cores})) * 100$$

The number of cycles used was measured using Amplifier XE's Lightweight Hotspots analysis. To measure the scalability and efficiency of the program, two program modifications are made:

➤ Amplifier XE's Frame API is used to insert markers at the beginning and end of the measurement points in the code:

```
#include "ittnotify.h"  // to use Amplifier XE API
__itt_domain* pD = __itt_domain_create( "TrackFitter" );
pD->flags = 1; // enable domain
for(i=0; i<NUM_RUNS;i++)
{
  // create time variable
  double time;
  {
    // start ArBB scoped timer which will measure
    // time within its scoped lifetime
    // start a frame for vtune
    __itt_frame_begin_v3(pD, NULL);
```

```
        const arbb::scoped_timer timer(time);
        // call main parallel track-fitting function
        fitTracksArBB( T1, C1, nT, nS );
    }
    // scoped time ends here, var time holds its value
    // reset Timing to minimum time so far
    Timing = std::min(Timing, time);
    __itt_frame_end_v3(pD, NULL);
}
```

➤ The ArBB API is used to control the maximum number of ArBB threads the ArBB kernel
can use:

```
#include "arbb.hpp"      // to access the ArBB libraries
. . .
int main(int argc, char* argv[])
{
    ...
    int num_threads = 0;
    if(argc==2)
    {
        num_threads=atoi(argv[1]);
        arbb::num_threads(num_threads);
        printf("WARNING: Max threads set to: %d\n",num_threads);
    }
    ...
}
```

Parallelism and Concurrency

Figure 15-13 shows the screenshot of an Amplifier XE Concurrency analysis. The timeline view at
the bottom half of the screen displays two of the threads, a CPU Usage line, a Thread Concurrency
line, and a Frame Rate line.

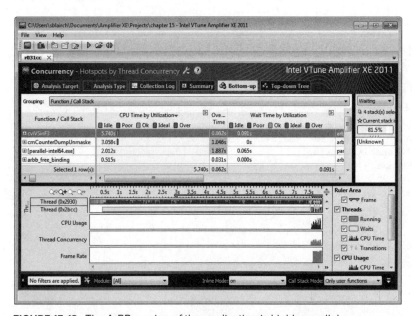

FIGURE 15-13: The ArBB version of the application is highly parallel

Notice the following:

> ➤ For most of the program, only one thread appears to be running. This is because the early part of the program was taken up with reading the data files and doing the JIT compilation.

> ➤ There is a blip of activity at the end of the program. Both the Thread Concurrency bar and the CPU Usage bar show that there is significant parallel activity. This is when the main track fitting is done.

Zooming in on a dense area of activity gives a better view of what is happening (see Figure 15-14). The timeline shows five distinct periods of activity — hence, the bumps in the CPU Usage bar.

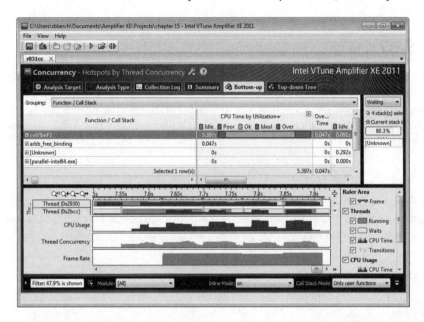

FIGURE 15-14: The CPU Usage bar confirms that all 24 hardware threads are being used

At the beginning of each area period of activity is a vertical bar. This bar is a thread transition/ synchronization point. When you hover your mouse over one of the transition lines, the gray box pops up and displays information about the synchronization object. It is a critical section in the Threading Building Blocks (TBB) scheduler. ArBB relies on its implementation of parallelism by using TBB under the hood.

In the top half of the screenshot is a bar that indicates how parallel this part of the program is — that is, the concurrency:

> ➤ The first tenth of the bar is colored red. (Sorry, you won't see the color in the printed version of the figure.) This means for 10 percent of the time the concurrency was poor.

> ➤ The next seven-tenths of the bar is colored orange, meaning that for 70 percent of the time the amount of parallelism is okay.

> ➤ The last two-tenths of the bar is colored green, meaning that for 20 percent of the time the concurrency level was perfect, with the number of the threads running being equal to the number of hardware threads the system can support.

> **INTERVIEW Q5: IF YOU WERE DOING THE PROJECT AGAIN, IS THERE ANYTHING YOU WOULD DO DIFFERENTLY?**
>
> I would have a look at the data model first (in terms of a natural/appropriate representation), and express the algorithm starting from there. The original serial code was completely decomposed in an object-oriented manner. Not that OOP is not great with ArBB, but the original decomposed code was relatively complicated because of the scattered storage model. It was a long path to find that this isn't great in terms of data parallelism (local access, alignment, and so on) in general.

THE HANDS-ON PROJECT

This section leads you through the steps to change the serial version of the track-fitting code to use ArBB. Two modules, the driver `driver.cpp` and the filter `serial_KF.cpp`, will be converted to using ArBB. This example takes one significant shortcut: the ArBB version of the filter is provided "ready-made." You still have the opportunity of going through the four steps to add ArBB, because the filter driver code has to be "ArBB-ized."

The Activities

Figure 15-15 shows the steps to perform. You start with a serial version of the code and progressively convert the program to use ArBB. The most significant parts of the hands-on are in Activity 15-3 to Activity 15-6. The steps you take here are typical of the steps you can take when adding ArBB to any project.

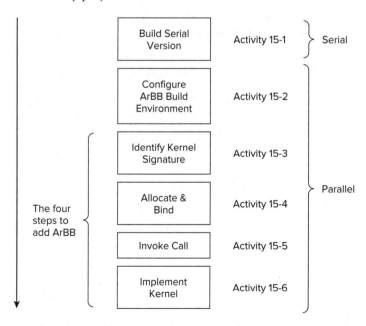

FIGURE 15-15: The steps of the hands-on activities

The Projects

The following three projects are provided with this case study:

➤ `serial_track_fit` — Contains the serial version of the track-fitting software. This is the version you will copy and modify.

➤ `ArBB_track_fit` — This is the solution. Your version should look like this once you have completed the hands-on activities.

➤ `combined_track_fit` — This version runs both the serial and parallel versions and checks their accuracy against each other and compares their run times. This version is not used in the hands-on, but it is supplied in case you are interested in looking how to validate the results. (Figure 15-10 showed an example of the output.)

Building and Running the Serial Version

Figure 15-16 shows the files included in the serial version of the track-fitting software:

➤ `main.cpp` — Contains the main function of the program.

➤ `ReadFiles.cpp` — Contains the function `readInput`, which reads two data files, `Geo.dat` and `Tracks.dat`. This function creates dynamic arrays into which it places the information. The addresses of these arrays are stored within the pointer data of the three classes defined within the header file `classes.h`.

➤ `driver.cpp` — Contains the driving function `fitTracks` of the serial Kalman filter.

➤ `serial_KF.cpp` — Contains the serial version of the Kalman filter.

➤ `classes.h` — Contains three classes, for magnetic fields, stations, and tracks. Their data consists of pointers that are loaded with the start addresses of the dynamically allocated arrays created and loaded within `ReadFiles.cpp`.

➤ `fit_util.h` — Contains a set of constant values.

The Serial Track-Fitting Code

The track-fitting code first applies the Kalman filter to all 20,000 tracks and then repeats this 100 times, obtaining a time for doing so. This is then repeated five times, with the smallest of the five results taken as the final benchmark time.

Following is the main loop at the heart of the `main` function in `main.cpp` that calls the Kalman filter driver `fitTracks` five times. The time taken for each iteration is measured and stored in the `Elapsed` variable. The iteration that records the smallest time value is accepted as the benchmark timing. On Windows, the serial version uses `timeGetTime()` to record the timestamps.

```
for(i=0; i<NUM_RUNS;i++)
{
  // set start time
  StartTime = timeGetTime();
  // call main serial track-fitting function
  fitTracks( T1, C1, nT, nS );
  // determine elapsed time
```

```
    Elapsed = (int)(timeGetTime() - StartTime);
    // get minimum time so far
    Timing = std::min(Timing, Elapsed);
}
```

main.cpp

main(...)

ReadFiles.cpp

readInput(...)

driver.cpp

fitTracks(...)

classes.h

Classes:
FieldRegion
Stations
Tracks

fit_util.h

Constants

serial_KF.cpp

fit(...)

extrapolateALight(...)

Other functions making
up the serial
Kalman filter track fitter

Serial program for benchmark test
of serial Kalman filter track fitter

FIGURE 15-16: Configuration of the serial benchmark program

The T1 parameter is a pointer to an array that holds the track information; the C1 parameter points to the covariance matrix; and the nT and nS parameters are used to store the number of tracks and stations, respectively.

Listing 15-6 shows the driver.cpp file, which contains the driver function fitTracks, which is called from main(). The Kalman filter track fitter fit(i, T[i], C[i]) is applied to each track in turn. This is then repeated 100 times to get an overall average performance. Once this has been carried out, the state and covariance data matrices for each track are extrapolated back to their start. In this hands-on, the most significant code edits will be made in driver.cpp.

LISTING 15-6: The serial version of driver.cpp

```
#include <math.h>
#include "fit_util.h"          // set of constants
#include "classes.h"           // Main Kalman filter classes

typedef float ftype;           // set ftype to be single precision data

using namespace std;

extern FieldRegion   magField;
extern Stations      vStations;
extern Tracks        vTracks;
```

```cpp
// ------------------------- Prototypes
void fit( int iTrack, ftype T[6], ftype C[15] );
void extrapolateALight( ftype T[], ftype C[], const ftype zOut, ftype qp0,
                        FieldRegion &F );

// ***** Driver of Serial Version of Kalman Filter Track Fitter *****
void fitTracks( ftype (*T)[6], ftype (*C)[15], int nT, int nS )
{
  // Repeat the Kalman filtering 100 times
  for( int times=0; times<Ntimes; times++)
  {
    // take each track in turn and process
    for( unsigned int i=0; i<nT; i++ )
    {
      // apply Kalman filter to track
      fit( i, T[i], C[i], nT, nS );
    }
  }
  // extrapolate all tracks back to start
  for( unsigned int i=0; i<nT; i++ )
  {
    extrapolateALight( T[i], C[i], vTracks.MC_z[i], T[i][4], magField );
  }
}
```

code snippet Chapter15\15-6.cpp

The Application Output

Figure 15-17 shows the output from the program. After displaying some setup information involving magnetic fields and the number of stations and tracks, the timing information is given. In this example, the time shown is just under three seconds. You need to be patient, however, because this is the best of five attempts; the actual run time is in excess of 15 seconds. You can build and run the serial version of the program for yourself in Activity 15-1.

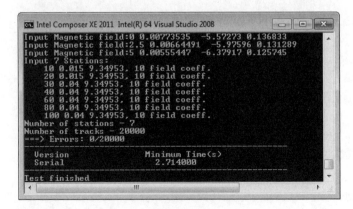

FIGURE 15-17: Results of running the serial version of track-fitting software

The machine used has a two-socket motherboard containing two Intel Xeon X5680 (3.33GHz) processors, 12 GB of memory running Microsoft Window 7 (64-bit). Each CPU has 6 cores, and supports hyper-threading, giving a total availability of 24 hardware threads. Remember, your timings may vary.

ACTIVITY 15-1: BUILDING AND RUNNING THE SERIAL VERSION

In this activity you build and run the serial version of the track-fitting program.

Building the Program

1. Unzip the `TrackFitter.zip` file to a directory for which you have read/write access.

2. Open a Parallel Studio Composer command prompt and navigate to the `serial_track_fit` folder.

3. Clean and then build the `build_serial` solution using `nmake`:

```
nmake -f Makefile-WIN32 clean
nmake -f Makefile-WIN32
```

Running the Program

4. Run the program by calling it:

```
serial-intel64.exe
```

Note that if you are building a 32-bit application, the name will be `serial-ia32`
`.exe`. Remember that the main loop in the program runs five times, so although the program may report minimum time taken of, say, five seconds, the time to run the program will be at least five times that.

Other Activities

5. Examine the makefile `Makefile-WIN32`. Which compiler was used to build the program? (Hint: Look at the variable `CPP`.)

6. Replace the CPP macro so that the Microsoft compiler is used:

```
CPP=cl
```

7. Rebuild and run the program, and then compare the time. You should find that the program built with the Intel compiler is faster.

8. Swap back to the Intel compiler by reversing the edit you did in step 6.

Parallelizing the Track-Fitting Code

As stated earlier, the Kalman filter is already provided for you with the complete ArBB code; however, you still need to modify the driver code.

Configuring the Array Building Blocks Build Environment

Some files will need to be modified, and others replaced. (You can try this for yourself in Activity 15-2.)

➤ The `main` function should call the new parallel driver `fitTracksArBB`.

➤ The ArBB-aligned functions for dynamic memory allocation and deallocation are added to the files `classes.h` and `ReadFiles.cpp`.

When binding C structures to the ArBB containers, you will get a performance improvement if the C structures are aligned. ArBB containers are aligned automatically.

In the serial code, several C constructs are dynamically allocated using `malloc`. By using the `arbb::aligned_malloc` ArBB function, the required alignment is achieved. The following code snippet gives an example of dynamically allocating and then freeing an aligned structure:

```
int lNHits = 100;
int *lIsta = (int*)arbb::aligned_malloc(lNHits*sizeof(int));
// some code to use
// etc ...
// now free the dynamic structure
arbb::aligned_free( lIsta );
```

➤ The new parallel Kalman filter `parallel_KF` replaces the serial version `serial_KF.cpp`.

The new filter is provided already built. It was developed using the same methodology as the driver — that is, identify the kernel, bind and allocate, add the call, and implement the kernel.

Figure 15-18 shows the new configuration for the parallel version. New files have a double line around them; original files that need editing have a dotted box around them; original unmodified files have a single box around them.

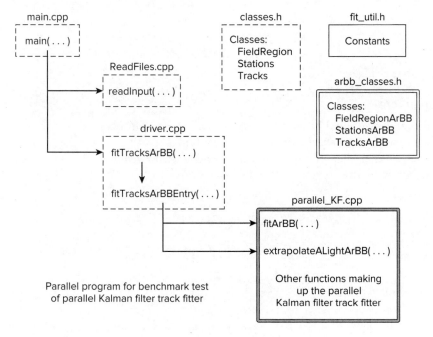

FIGURE 15-18: Configuration of the parallel benchmark program

ACTIVITY 15-2: PREPARING THE ARBB ENVIRONMENT

In this activity you prepare the parallel version of the track-fitting program.

Make sure you have installed ArBB on your computer. At the time of writing, ArBB is available as a separate product, downloadable from www.intel.com/go/arbb/.

Copying Files and Modifying the Makefile

1. Copy the contents of `serial_track_fit` into a new folder.

2. Into that new folder, copy the `arbb_classes.h` and `parallel_KF.cpp` files from the `ArBB_track_fit` folder.

3. Edit `Makefile-WIN32` (in your new folder):

➤ Add the following lines to the top of the file, making sure that the path `ARBB_ROOT` points to the place where you installed ArBB:

```
ARBB_ROOT = c:\PROGRA~2\Intel\arbb\Beta5~1
ARBB_INCS="$(ARBB_ROOT)\include"
ARBB_LIBS="$(ARBB_ROOT)\lib\$(TARGET_ARCH)"
```

➤ Change the following lines:

```
EXE=serial-$(TARGET_ARCH).exe

serial_build: driver.obj main.obj ReadFiles.obj serial_KF.obj
  $(CPP) /o $(EXE) $** winmm.lib
```
        to:
```
EXE=parallel-$(TARGET_ARCH).exe

build: driver.obj main.obj ReadFiles.obj parallel_KF.obj
  $(CPP) /o $(EXE) $** /link /LIBPATH:$(ARBB_LIBS) arbb.lib
```

➤ Save your changes.

Modifying main.cpp

The driver function name should be modified to `fitTracksArBB`. The `scoped_timer` function is used to measure the time duration within its scope — hence, the reason for the extra braces. This eliminates a pair of `includes` but requires the new `include` for the ArBB libraries.

4. Edit `main.cpp`:

➤ Add an extra `include`:

```
#include <limits>        // for data limits
#include "arbb.hpp"      // to access the ArBB libraries
#include "fit_util.h"    // a set of constants
```

➤ Comment out the following `include`:

```
// #include <mmsystem.h>  // for timeGetTime() function
```

➤ Change the name of the prototype `fitTracks` to `fitTracksArBB`:

```
void fitTracksArBB( ftype (*T)[6], ftype (*C)[15], int nT, int nS );
```

➤ Comment out the declaration of `StartTime` at the beginning of `main`:

```
int main(int /*argc*/, char* /*argv*/[])
{
    int i, nT, nS;    // loop counter, number of tracks & stations
    DWORD StartTime; // Start time
    double Timing, Elapsed;  // Timing values
```

➤ Replace the loop in `main` so that it looks like this:

```
for(i=0; i<NUM_RUNS;i++)
{
    // create time variable
    double time;
    {
        // start ArBB scoped timer which will measure
        // time within its scoped lifetime
        const arbb::scoped_timer timer(time);
        // call main parallel track-fitting function
        fitTracksArBB( T1, C1, nT, nS );
    }
    // scoped time ends here, var time holds its value
    // reset timing to minimum time so far
    Timing = std::min(Timing, time);
}
```

➤ Save your changes.

Modifying ReadFiles.cpp and classes.h

You need to modify the calls to `malloc` and `free` in `ReadFiles.cpp` and `classes.h` to use aligned ArBB calls.

5. In `ReadFiles.cpp` and `classes.h`:

➤ Replace all calls to `malloc` with `arbb::aligned_malloc`.

➤ Replace all calls to `free` with `arbb::aligned_free`.

➤ Include the header `arbb.hpp` at the top of the file:

```
#include <arbb.hpp>
```

➤ Save your changes.

Editing driver.cpp

6. In `driver.cpp`:

➤ Change the name of the `fitTracks` function to `fitTracks ArBB`:

```
void fitTracksArBB( ftype (*T)[6], ftype (*C)[15], int nT, int nS )
```

continues

continued

➤ Change the name of the `extrapolateALight` function to `extrapolateALightArBB`:

```
extrapolateALightArBB
```

➤ Save your changes.

Building the Files

7. Build the new files:

```
nmake -f Makefile-WIN32
```

You will get two linker errors complaining about unresolved external symbols. You'll deal with these errors in Activity 15-3.

Writing the Parallel Driver

Figure 15-19 shows the calling sequence of the original code and the new parallel version. To make the marshalling of parameters, you should add an extra `fitTracksArBBEntry` function to the parallel sequence.

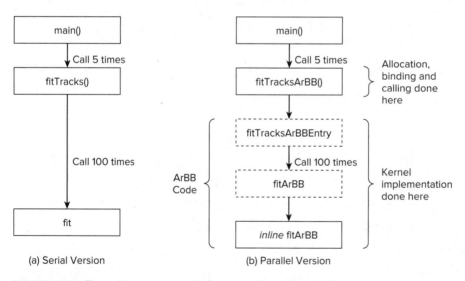

FIGURE 15-19: The calling sequence, before and after adding ArBB

The bottom box of the parallel version contains the Kalman filter and is supplied with ArBB code already implemented. You will add all the preceding blocks in Activities 15-3 to 15-6.

As described in the first part of this case study (refer to Figure 15-8 and associated text), you should apply ArBB in four steps:

1. Identify the kernel in the driver.

2. Allocate new ArBB containers and bind them to the existing data structures.

3. Invoke the kernel.

4. Implement the kernel.

 If you get confused while trying out these four steps, you can always look at the serial and parallel versions of the source code, which are in Listings 15-6 and 15-7, respectively.

Identifying the Kernel in the Driver

The kernel, which is invoked by a `call` operator, contains the entire contents of the serial driver.

New Prototype

The kernel prototype has five parameters, the first three being based on the original C code, the second two being the addresses to the newly introduced ArBB containers `vtT` and `vtC`:

```
void fitTracksArBBEntry( i32 vSize, TracksArBB<FTYPE> vTracksArBB,
                         StationsArBB<FTYPE> vStationsArBB,
                         dense< array<FTYPE, 6> > &vtT,
                         dense< array<FTYPE, 15> > &vtC     );
```

New Classes

The classes for magnetic fields, stations, and tracks defined in `classes.h` need to be replaced with ArBB equivalents. Two new classes, `StationsArBB` and `TracksArBB`, and one structure, `FieldRegionArBB`, are provided for you in `classes_arbb.h`, and have the same member items as the original classes. However, instead of being pointers, they are ArBB containers. For example, the original class `Tracks` had public members:

```
class Tracks
{
public:
    float   *MC_x, *MC_y, *MC_z, *MC_px, *MC_py, *MC_pz, *MC_q;
    int     *nHits, *NDF;
    float   **hitsX, **hitsY;
    float   *hitsX2, *hitsY2;
    int     **hitsIsta;

    Tracks(){};
```

The new class, `TracksArBB`, reflects these members as containers:

```
class TracksArBB
{
public:
    dense<f32>      MC_x, MC_y, MC_z, MC_px, MC_py, MC_pz, MC_q;
    dense<i32>      nHits, NDF;
    dense<f32, 2>   hitsX, hitsY;
    dense<f32, 2>   hitsX2, hitsY2;
    dense<i32, 2>   hitsIsta;

    TracksArBB(){};
```

Note that within all the project files, the following type definitions have been used:

```
typedef float ftype;    // set ftype to be single precision data
typedef f32   FTYPE;    // set FTYPE to be ArBB single precision data
```

ACTIVITY 15-3: IDENTIFYING THE KERNEL

In this activity you adapt the driver code to use ArBB. It is important that you have first completed Activity 15-2.

1. Open the `driver.cpp` file.

2. Rename `fitTracks` to `fitTracksArBB`.

3. Disable the contents of the new `fitTracksArBB` function with a `#if 0`:

```
void fitTracksArBBEntry(…)
{
  #if 0
…
  #endif
}
```

4. Create a new `fitTrackArBBEntry` function:

```
void fitTracksArBBEntry( i32 vSize, TracksArBB<FTYPE> vTracksArBB,
                         StationsArBB<FTYPE> vStationsArBB,
                         dense< array<FTYPE, 6> > &vtT,
                         dense< array<FTYPE, 15> > &vtC     )
{
}
```

5. Replace the function prototypes in `driver.cpp` with the function prototypes founds in lines 10–29 of Listing 15-7.

6. Move the contents of `fitTracksArBB` into `fitTracksArBBEntry` (that is, everything you disabled in step 2, including the `#if 0` … `#endif` statements).

7. Add two new header files:

```
#include "classes.h"       // Main Kalman filter classes
#include "arbb_classes.h"  // Added classes for parallel driver
#include "arbb.hpp"        // Added for ArBB namespace data
```

8. Build the project:

```
nmake -f Makefile-WIN32
```

There should be no errors. You should be able to run the executable, but it will print out only the introductory information.

Allocating and Binding

Each of the new ArBB classes now needs to be instantiating, and the original data bound to this new instantiation. This binding is carried out in `driver.cpp`, in the function `fitTracksArBB`. You can try out the allocating and binding for yourself in Activity 15-4.

Binding TracksArBB and StationArBB

An instance of the old `Tracks` class already exists within `ReadFiles.cpp`, called `vTracks`. The member items of this class contain all the track information loaded from the data files. You must now bind these member items with the containers in the new class `TracksArBB` — for example:

```
TracksArBB<FTYPE> vTracksArBB;       // create new instance of new class
                                     // bind with existing information from
                                     // instance of old class Tracks
bind(vTracksArBB.MC_x, vTracks.MC_x, nT );
bind(vTracksArBB.MC_y, vTracks.MC_y, nT );
    .   .   .   .   .  etc
```

Similarly, an instance of the new class `StationsArBB` must be created and bound with the existing information from the instance of the old `Stations` class:

```
StationsArBB<FTYPE> vStationsArBB;    // create new instance of new class
                                      // bind with existing information from
                                      // instance of old class Stations
bind(vStationsArBB.z, vStations.z, nS );
bind(vStationsArBB.thick, vStations.thick, nS );
    .   .   .   .   .  etc
```

Swapping the Order of the Track

The original track hit information is held in members `hitsX` and `hitsY`. These are two-dimensional arrays with the track number first and station number last. For ArBB parallelization, which aims to simultaneously process tracks, you should store this information in reverse order, with the track number last. To facilitate this, create two new arrays, `X2hits` and `Y2hits`, into which the hit information is transferred in the correct order. In the following example code, `nT` and `nS` are the number of tracks and stations, respectively:

```
ARBB_CPP_ALIGN(ftype * X2hits);
ARBB_CPP_ALIGN(ftype * Y2hits);
// reserve array space
X2hits = ( ftype * ) arbb::aligned_malloc( sizeof( ftype ) * nS * nT  );
Y2hits = ( ftype * ) arbb::aligned_malloc( sizeof( ftype ) * nS * nT  );
// load hit data in reverse order
for(int ix = 0; ix < nT; ix ++)
{
  for(int jx = 0; jx < nS; jx ++)
  {
    X2hits[jx * nT + ix] = vTracks.hitsX[ix][jx];
    Y2hits[jx * nT + ix] = vTracks.hitsY[ix][jx];
  }
}
```

Notice the use of ArBB alignment macros and functions. You can bind these new arrays to members of the new `TracksArBB` class instance `vTrackArBB` as follows:

```
bind(vTracksArBB.hitsX2, X2hits, nT, nS);
bind(vTracksArBB.hitsY2, Y2hits, nT, nS);
```

Swapping the Order of the State and Covariance Matrices

The order of the two-dimensional state and covariance matrices T and C also need to be swapped. These are empty arrays at this point, so no actual data needs to be transferred. However, you should create new matrices of the correct order and bind them to appropriate ArBB containers. For example, the T state matrix has a new matrix, TBuf, which is bound to the container vtT:

```
// define a state array of 6 pointers
ARBB_CPP_ALIGN(ftype *TBuf[6]);
// reserve array space for each, size number of tracks
for( int i = 0; i < 6; i ++ )
{
   TBuf[i] = ( ftype * ) arbb::aligned_malloc( sizeof( ftype ) * nT );
}
// define array of 6 dense containers for state matrix
dense< array<FTYPE, 6>  >  vtT;
// bind to state matrix
bind(vtT, nT, TBuf[0], TBuf[1], TBuf[2], TBuf[3], TBuf[4], TBuf[5]);
```

You should repeat this with the 15-component covariance matrix C, where a new matrix, CBuf, needs to be created and bound with a new container, vtC.

ACTIVITY 15-4: ALLOCATING AND BINDING

In this activity you adapt the driver code to use ArBB. It is important that you have first completed Activity 15-3.

1. In the driver.cpp file, bind the track and station variables with their ArBB equivalents by copying lines 91 to 126 of Listing 15-7 into the fitTracksArBB function.

2. To swap the order of the covariance and state matrices, copy lines 62 to 90 of Listing 15-7 into the start of fitTracksArBB function.

3. To swap the order of the track data, copy lines 40 to 61 of Listing 15-7 into the start of fitTracksArBB function.

4. Build the project:

```
nmake -f Makefile-WIN32
```

There should be no errors. You should be able to run the executable, although it will print out only the introductory information.

Invoking the Kernel

The kernel is invoked through a call operation. This new function is passed the ArBB-style data containers, as follows:

```
// set number of tracks in ArBB data type
i32 vSize = nT;
// Invoke Kalman filter track fitter by call operator
call(fitTracksArBBEntry)(vSize, vTracksArBB, vStationsArBB, vtT, vtC);
```

At this point in the code you can now invoke the kernel function through a call operation, as shown in step 3 of Activity 15-5.

Before returning from the `fitTracksArBB` function, you must store the contents of matrices `TBuf` and `CBuf` into the originally passed matrices of `T` and `C`, and release their spaces. You also need to release the space used for the `X2hits` and `Y2hits` matrices. The following snippet uses `TBuf` as an example:

```
// Store TBuf data into T matrix in desired order
for( int i = 0; i < nT; i ++ )
{
  for( int j = 0; j < 6; j ++ )
  {
    T[i][j] = TBuf[j][i];
  }
}
// Release memory of TBuf matrix
for( int i = 0; i < 6; i ++ )
{
  arbb::aligned_free( TBuf[i] );
}
```

ACTIVITY 15-5: INVOKING THE CALL

In this activity you adapt the driver code to use ArBB. It is important that you have first completed Activity 15-4.

1. In the `driver.cpp` file, invoke the call to the driver kernel by copying lines 127 to 133 of Listing 15-7 into the end of function `fitTracksArBB`.

2. Add the results back into the covariance and state matrices by copying lines 134 to 152 of Listing 15-7 into the end of the `fitTracksArBB` function.

3. Free up the dynamically allocated memory by copying lines 153 to 167 of Listing 15-7 into the end of the `fitTracksArBB` function.

4. Build the project:

   ```
   nmake -f Makefile-WIN32
   ```

There should be no errors. You should be able to run the executable, but it will print out only the introductory information.

Implementing the Kernel

Your last step in converting the program to use ArBB is to implement the contents of the `fitTracksArBBEntry` kernel function.

Calling the Parallel Kalman Filter

The new code has the same heuristics as the original serial code, applying the Kalman filter on the 20,000 tracks in a `for` loop iterating 100 times, and then extrapolating the start points of the tracks.

An ArBB-type `_for` loop is used in the first part:

```
_for( j = (usize)0, j < Ntimes, j ++ )
{
    fitArBB( vTracksArBB, vStationsArBB, magFieldArBB, vtT, vtC );
}_end_for;
```

where `usize` is an ArBB data type used for indices.

Finally, the extrapolation of the tracks requires you to use a local state and covariance matrices `T` and `C`, which you must load with the current values from the containers `vtT` and `vtC`. The following example uses the `T` state matrix:

```
// define local matrices of dense containers
dense<FTYPE> T[6];
dense<FTYPE> C[15];

// load T with contents of vtT
T[0] = vtT.get<FTYPE, 0>();
T[1] = vtT.get<FTYPE, 1>();
T[2] = vtT.get<FTYPE, 2>();
T[3] = vtT.get<FTYPE, 3>();
T[4] = vtT.get<FTYPE, 4>();
T[5] = vtT.get<FTYPE, 5>();
```

Then call the parallel version of the extrapolation function:

```
// Call extrapolation function
extrapolateALightArBB( T, C, vTracksArBB.MC_x, T[4], magFieldArBB );
```

Loading New Values Back into the C Structures

The last action is to reload the new `T` and `C` values into the containers `vtT` and `vtC`, respectively:

```
// Reload vtT with new contents of T
vtT.set<0>(T[0]);
vtT.set<1>(T[1]);
vtT.set<2>(T[2]);
vtT.set<3>(T[3]);
vtT.set<4>(T[4]);
vtT.set<5>(T[5]);
```

ACTIVITY 15-6: IMPLEMENTING THE KERNEL

In this activity you adapt the driver code to use ArBB. It is important that you have first completed Activity 15-5. Note that you are now editing the `fitTracksArBB-Entry` function.

1. In the `driver.cpp` file, add the call to the Kalman filter:

   ➤ Delete the `#if 0 … #endif` clause (and its contents) in the `fitTracks-ArBBEntry` function.

   ➤ Copy lines 174 to 187 of Listing 15-7 into the end of the `fitTracks-ArBBEntry` function.

2. Extrapolate the track starting points by copying lines 188 to 217 of Listing 15-7 into the end of the `fitTracksArBBEntry` function.

3. Load the new values back into the C structures by copying lines 218 to 244 of Listing 15-7 into the end of the `fitTracksArBBEntry` function.

4. Build the project:

   ```
   nmake -f Makefile-WIN32
   ```

There should be no errors, and everything should run. Congratulations!

You are now ready to build and run the application, which should produce the output shown in Figure 15-20.

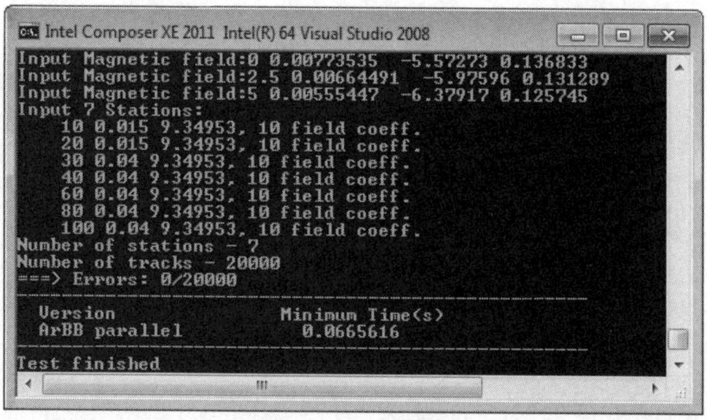

FIGURE 15-20: Results of running the ArBB version of track-fitting software

As before, after outputting some setup information involving magnetic fields and the number of stations and tracks, the timing information is given between the dashed lines. Compared to the serial timings (refer to Figure 15-17), the ArBB version is 42 times faster.

LISTING 15-7: Parallel driver for the parallel version of Kalman filter track fitter

```
1:   #include "fit_util.h"        // a set of constants
2:   #include "classes.h"         // Main Kalman filter classes
3:   #include "arbb_classes.h"    // Added classes for parallel driver
4:   #include "arbb.hpp"          // added for arbb namespace data
5:
6:   typedef float ftype;
7:   typedef f32 FTYPE;           // Added for parallel driver
8:
9:   using namespace std;
10:  using namespace arbb;        // Access to arbb
11:
12:  // -------------------------------- Prototypes
13:
14:
15:  void fitTracksArBBEntry( i32 vSize, TracksArBB<FTYPE> vTracksArBB,
16:                           StationsArBB<FTYPE> vStationsArBB,
17:                           dense< array<FTYPE, 6> > &vtT,
18:                           dense< array<FTYPE, 15> > &vtC     );
19:
20:  void fitArBB( TracksArBB<FTYPE> &ts, StationsArBB<FTYPE> &ss,
21:                FieldRegionArBB<FTYPE> &f,
22:                dense< array<FTYPE, 6> > &vtT,
23:                dense< array<FTYPE, 15> > &vtC   );
24:
25:void extrapolateALightArBB( dense<FTYPE> *T, dense<FTYPE> *C,
26:dense<FTYPE>
27:                                 &zOut,dense<FTYPE>& qp0,
28:                                 FieldRegionArBB<FTYPE> &F);
29:
30:// ----------------------- Global data, instances of classes
31:
32:extern FieldRegion    magField;
33:extern Stations       vStations;
34:extern Tracks         vTracks;
35:
36:// *** Driving ArBB Parallel Version of Kalman Filter Track Fitter ***
37:
38:void fitTracksArBB( ftype (*T)[6], ftype (*C)[15], int nT, int nS )
39:{
40:  int ix, jx;
41:
42:  // -----------------------------------------------------------------
43:  // Create new arrays to hold track hits and load with track hit data.
44:  // The new data is transposed so the last index is track number,
45:  // rather than first
46:  // Create two pointers for track hit data
47:  ARBB_CPP_ALIGN(ftype * X2hits);
48:  ARBB_CPP_ALIGN(ftype * Y2hits);
49:  // reserve array space
50:  X2hits = ( ftype * ) arbb::aligned_malloc( sizeof(ftype) * nS * nT  );
51:  Y2hits = ( ftype * ) arbb::aligned_malloc( sizeof(ftype) * nS * nT  );
52:  // load hit data in reverse order
53:  for(ix = 0; ix < nT; ix ++)
54:  {
```

```
55:    for(jx = 0; jx < nS; jx ++)
56:    {
57:      X2hits[jx * nT + ix] = vTracks.hitsX[ix][jx];
58:      Y2hits[jx * nT + ix] = vTracks.hitsY[ix][jx];
59:    }
60:  }
61:
62:  // ----------------------------------------------------------------
63:  // Create new temporary set of arrays for state
64:  // and covariance matrix data.
65:  // The passed T & C matricies are 2D in the wrong order,
66:  // with track number as the first index.
67:  // Define a state array of 6 pointers
68:  ARBB_CPP_ALIGN(ftype *TBuf[6]);
69:  // reserve array space for each, size number of tracks
70:  for( int i = 0; i < 6; i ++ )
71:  {
72:    TBuf[i] = ( ftype * ) arbb::aligned_malloc( sizeof( ftype ) * nT );
73:  }
74:  // define a covariance array of 15 pointers
75:  ARBB_CPP_ALIGN(ftype *CBuf[15]);
76:  // reserve array space for each
77:  for( int i = 0; i < 15; i ++ )
78:  {
79:    CBuf[i] = ( ftype * ) arbb::aligned_malloc( sizeof( ftype ) * nT );
80:  }
81:  // define array of 6 dense containers for state matrix
82:  dense< array<FTYPE, 6>  > vtT;
83:  // bind to state matrix
84:  bind(vtT, nT, TBuf[0], TBuf[1], TBuf[2], TBuf[3], TBuf[4], TBuf[5]);
85:  // define array of 15 dense containers for covariance matrix
86:  dense< array<FTYPE, 15> > vtC;
87:  // bind to covariance matrix
88:  bind(vtC, nT, CBuf[0], CBuf[1], CBuf[2], CBuf[3], CBuf[4], CBuf[5],
89:  CBuf[6], CBuf[7], CBuf[8], CBuf[9], CBuf[10], CBuf[11],
90:  CBuf[12], CBuf[13], CBuf[14]);
91:  // ----------------------------------------------------------------
92:  // Create and bind new instances of TrackArBB and StationArBB data
93:  // create new instance of new class
94:  TracksArBB<FTYPE> vTracksArBB;
95:  // bind with existing information from
96:  // instance of old class Tracks
97:  bind(vTracksArBB.MC_x, vTracks.MC_x, nT );
98:  bind(vTracksArBB.MC_y, vTracks.MC_y, nT );
99:  bind(vTracksArBB.MC_z, vTracks.MC_z, nT );
100: bind(vTracksArBB.MC_px, vTracks.MC_px, nT );
101: bind(vTracksArBB.MC_py, vTracks.MC_py, nT );
102: bind(vTracksArBB.MC_pz, vTracks.MC_pz, nT );
103: bind(vTracksArBB.MC_q, vTracks.MC_q, nT );
104: bind(vTracksArBB.nHits, vTracks.nHits, nT );
105: bind(vTracksArBB.NDF, vTracks.NDF, nT );
106: bind(vTracksArBB.hitsX, vTracks.hitsX[0], nS, nT );
107: bind(vTracksArBB.hitsY, vTracks.hitsY[0], nS, nT );
108: bind(vTracksArBB.hitsX2, X2hits, nT, nS);
109: bind(vTracksArBB.hitsY2, Y2hits, nT, nS);
```

continues

LISTING 15-7 *(continued)*

```
110:    bind(vTracksArBB.hitsIsta, vTracks.hitsIsta[0], nS, nT );
111:    // create new instance of new class
112:    StationsArBB<FTYPE> vStationsArBB;
113:    // bind with existing information from
114:    // instance of old class Stations
115:    bind(vStationsArBB.z, vStations.z, nS );
116:    bind(vStationsArBB.thick, vStations.thick, nS );
117:    bind(vStationsArBB.zhit, vStations.zhit, nS );
118:    bind(vStationsArBB.RL, vStations.RL, nS );
119:    bind(vStationsArBB.RadThick, vStations.RadThick, nS );
120:    bind(vStationsArBB.logRadThick, vStations.logRadThick, nS );
121:    bind(vStationsArBB.Sigma, vStations.Sigma, nS );
122:    bind(vStationsArBB.Sigma2, vStations.Sigma2, nS );
123:    bind(vStationsArBB.Sy, vStations.Sy, nS );
124:    bind(vStationsArBB.mapX, vStations.mapX[0], 10, nS );
125:    bind(vStationsArBB.mapY, vStations.mapY[0], 10, nS );
126:    bind(vStationsArBB.mapZ, vStations.mapZ[0], 10, nS );
127:    // -------------------------------------------------------------
128:    // Invoke call to track fitter by a call operation
129:    // set number of tracks in ArBB data type
130:    i32 vSize = nT;
131:    // Invoke Kalman filter track fitter by call operator
132:    call(fitTracksArBBEntry)(vSize,vTracksArBB,vStationsArBB,vtT,vtC);
133:
134:    // copy container to C buffers
135:    vtT.read_only_range();
136:    vtC.read_only_range();
137:
138:    // -------------------------------------------------------------
139:    // Pack temporary array data back into T & C arrays, transposing
140:    // order of storage back to the original with track number being the
141:    // first index
142:    for( int i = 0; i < nT; i ++ )
143:    {
144:      for( int j = 0; j < 6; j ++ )
145:      {
146:        T[i][j] = TBuf[j][i];
147:      }
148:      for( int j = 0; j < 15; j ++ )
149:      {
150:        C[i][j] = CBuf[j][i];
151:      }
152:    }
153:    // -------------------------------------------------------------
154:    // Release memory of TBuf and CBuf matrices
155:    for( int i = 0; i < 6; i ++ )
156:    {
157:      arbb::aligned_free( TBuf[i] );
158:    }
159:    for( int i = 0; i < 15; i ++ )
160:    {
161:      arbb::aligned_free( CBuf[i] );
```

```
162:    }
163:
164:    arbb::aligned_free( X2hits );
165:    arbb::aligned_free( Y2hits );
166:}
167:
168://*********************************************************************
169:void fitTracksArBBEntry( i32 vSize, TracksArBB<FTYPE> vTracksArBB,
170:                                    StationsArBB<FTYPE> vStationsArBB,
171:                                    dense< array<FTYPE, 6> > &vtT,
172:                                    dense< array<FTYPE, 15> > &vtC    )
173:{
174:    // create a FieldRegion class instance
175:    FieldRegionArBB<FTYPE> magFieldArBB(vSize);
176:    // create an ArBB index type
177:    usize j;
178:
179:    // ------------------------------------------------------------
180:    // Repeat 100 times the call to the
181:    // Kalman filter Track fitter
182:    // Using ArBB type for loop
183:    _for( j = (usize)0, j < Ntimes, j ++ )
184:    {
185:       fitArBB( vTracksArBB, vStationsArBB, magFieldArBB, vtT, vtC );
186:    }_end_for;
187:
188:    // ------------------------------------------------------------
189:    // Extrapolate to start of tracks as in serial version
190:    // define local matrices of dense containers
191:    dense<FTYPE> T[6];
192:    dense<FTYPE> C[15];
193:    // load T with contents of vtT
194:    T[0] = vtT.get<FTYPE, 0>();
195:    T[1] = vtT.get<FTYPE, 1>();
196:    T[2] = vtT.get<FTYPE, 2>();
197:    T[3] = vtT.get<FTYPE, 3>();
198:    T[4] = vtT.get<FTYPE, 4>();
199:    T[5] = vtT.get<FTYPE, 5>();
200:
201:    // load C with contents of vtC
202:    C[0] = vtC.get<FTYPE, 0>();
203:    C[1] = vtC.get<FTYPE, 1>();
204:    C[2] = vtC.get<FTYPE, 2>();
205:    C[3] = vtC.get<FTYPE, 3>();
206:    C[4] = vtC.get<FTYPE, 4>();
207:    C[5] = vtC.get<FTYPE, 5>();
208:    C[6] = vtC.get<FTYPE, 6>();
209:    C[7] = vtC.get<FTYPE, 7>();
210:    C[8] = vtC.get<FTYPE, 8>();
211:    C[9] = vtC.get<FTYPE, 9>();
212:    C[10] = vtC.get<FTYPE, 10>();
213:    C[11] = vtC.get<FTYPE, 11>();
214:    C[12] = vtC.get<FTYPE, 12>();
215:    C[13] = vtC.get<FTYPE, 13>();
216:    C[14] = vtC.get<FTYPE, 14>();
```

continues

LISTING 15-7 *(continued)*

```
217:
218:    // Call extrapolation function within the filter
219:    extrapolateALightArBB( T, C, vTracksArBB.MC_x, T[4], magFieldArBB );
220:
221:    // Reload vtT with new contents of T
222:    vtT.set<0>(T[0]);
223:    vtT.set<1>(T[1]);
224:    vtT.set<2>(T[2]);
225:    vtT.set<3>(T[3]);
226:    vtT.set<4>(T[4]);
227:    vtT.set<5>(T[5]);
228:
229:    // Reload vtC with new contents of C
230:    vtC.set<0>(C[0]);
231:    vtC.set<1>(C[1]);
232:    vtC.set<2>(C[2]);
233:    vtC.set<3>(C[3]);
234:    vtC.set<4>(C[4]);
235:    vtC.set<5>(C[5]);
236:    vtC.set<6>(C[6]);
237:    vtC.set<7>(C[7]);
238:    vtC.set<8>(C[8]);
239:    vtC.set<9>(C[9]);
240:    vtC.set<10>(C[10]);
241:    vtC.set<11>(C[11]);
242:    vtC.set<12>(C[12]);
243:    vtC.set<13>(C[13]);
244:    vtC.set<14>(C[14])
245:}
```

code snippet Chapter15\15-7.cpp

SUMMARY

This case study was used as an introduction to ArBB. Starting with a serial version of the track-fitting application, the program was altered in many steps before finally producing a parallel version.

ArBB is an excellent parallelism tool for programs that are heavily data-centric. Its containers, pseudo data objects that can be bound to existing C/C++ data, allow calculations through the use of simple mathematical operators between them. The ArBB libraries overlay complex operations between arrays and matrices (even of different sizes) as if they were single variables.

As a programmer, you are not explicitly responsible for any parallelization in ArBB. This means data races and other such problems that can occur due to parallelization are eliminated. ArBB's methods also ensure a balanced load between the threads of a parallel program.

Because of the JIT compiler, ArBB "future-proofs" your application against new CPU architectures. When an ArBB function is first called, the JIT compiler generates code tuned to its runtime environment.

Chapter 16, "Parallelizing Legacy Code," looks at some of the issues you might face when parallelizing old code. Using the Dhrystone benchmark, the code is made parallel using OpenMP and Cilk Plus.

16

Parallelizing Legacy Code

One of the biggest challenges programmers face is making existing code parallel. The older and bigger the code, the more difficult the task is. Successful parallelism should lead to improved performance and scalability without having to make wholesale changes to the code.

Legacy code represents the huge investment of time and effort that programmers have made. For most programmers, maintaining and modifying legacy code is a significant headache, because it often includes the following characteristics:

➤ Large, monolithic code base

➤ Unknown or misunderstood content

➤ Old-style programming

➤ Ubiquitous use of global variables

This case study begins by introducing the Dhrystone benchmark, and then explores adding parallelism to the code using OpenMP and Cilk Plus. The hands-on activities give you an opportunity to try out the different approaches. You explore the following ways of adding parallelism to the benchmark:

➤ Synchronizing shared variable access

➤ Duplicating global variables

➤ Wrapping the application in a C++ class

➤ Using Cilk Plus holders

Taking the original serial version of the Dhrystone benchmark, the first three attempts at parallelization use OpenMP, and the last attempt uses Cilk Plus. In all these attempts, the following questions are addressed:

➤ Will adding parallelism improve the performance of the code?

➤ Can the parallelism be added without too much programming effort?

INTRODUCING THE DHRYSTONE BENCHMARK

The Dhrystone benchmark is a typical example of code written in the 1980s, with versions available in C, Pascal, and Ada. Its intention was to reflect good programming practices of the day, and was designed to be an easy-to-use integer benchmark that could be used to compare the performance of different CPUs and compilers.

When I first attempted to make the benchmark parallel, I spent a lot of time studying the code to understand what it was doing. Thankfully, the intentions of the author are well documented in several white papers. The benchmark itself also includes five pages of notes in the source code. In this respect, the benchmark is not typical of code that you might have to work on.

The benchmark uses old-style K&R programming, with its obsolete calling convention, lack of function prototypes, and missing return types in the function definitions. K&R C is so called after the 1978 edition of *The C Programming Language*, by Brian Kernighan and Dennis Ritchie. Even though the language has been superseded by ANSI C, many compilers, including the Intel compiler, can still support K&R C code. Part of this case study involves using C++ files rather than C files, which meant much of the quirkiness of the K&R-style coding had to be attended to before the code could be compiled successfully.

The Structure of the Code

The Dhrystone benchmark code is not huge; it is split among 12 functions over two files (see Figure 16-1). The main file, dhry_1.c, consists of a number of global variables, the main() function, and a collection of test routines. The second file, dhry_2.c, has a number of test functions that are called from within the test loop of main(). Each iteration of the loop is classed as one Dhrystone. Any code executed outside of the loop does not contribute to the benchmark results.

After the benchmark runs, the results are printed to the screen. The main reason for including the print routines is *not* to verify the results — that is a secondary requirement. The real reason for adding this code is to make sure that the results of the benchmark are used. If the results were not used, there would be a danger that the optimization phase of the compiler would see the benchmark as being "unused" or "dead" code and proceed to optimize it away.

Global and Shared Variables

The benchmark has a mixture of global and local variables. Within the main() function there is a central for loop that will become the target of the parallelization effort. As shown in Figure 16-1, both global and local variables are declared outside this loop. This means that all these variables will be shared between the parallelized loop and possibly lead to data races. These shared variables will become the biggest problem to overcome.

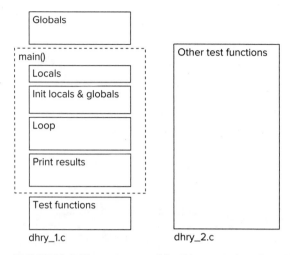

FIGURE 16-1: The structure of the Dhrystone benchmark

The /Qdiag-enable:thread Intel compiler option produces threading-related diagnostic messages, including information about global variables. The compiler reports that 12 global variables are accessed more than 50 times (see Table 16-1). Access to these variables and the shared local variables will need to be protected so that only one thread can access them at any one time.

TABLE 16-1: Global Variables Reported by /Qdiag-enable:thread

VARIABLE	NUMBER OF TIMES ACCESSED
Arr_2_Glob	2
Begin_Time	2
Bool_Glob	3
Ch_1_Glob	4
Ch_2_Glob	3
Dhrystones_Per_Second	2
End_Time	2
Int_Glob	5
Microseconds	2
Next_Ptr_Glob	7
Ptr_Glob	17
User_Time	4

THE HANDS-ON PROJECTS

Six projects are associated with this case study (see Table 16-2). You can rebuild each of these projects yourself in Activities 16-1 to 16-6. The first three activities use C, starting with the original C code, and the last three activities use C++. Each of the following sections describes the steps that were taken to implement the different approaches. At the end of each section, a hands-on activity gives instructions on how to build the new version. All the code changes are already included in the project files; all you need to do is navigate to the correct directory and follow the build instructions.

TABLE 16-2: The Different Approaches

ACTIVITY	MODEL	APPROACH	TYPE	PROJECT NAME
16-1	Serial	The original code	C	16-1-ORGFILES
16-2	OpenMP	Synchronizing shared variable access	C	16-2-OMP-C
16-3	OpenMP	Duplicating global variables	C	16-3-OMP-DUP
16-4	Serial	Converting to C++	C++	16-4-CPPFILES
16-5	OpenMP	Application wrapping	C++	16-5-WRAPEVERYTHING
16-6	Cilk Plus	Using Cilk Plus holders	C++	16-6-CILKHOLDER

Building the Projects

Within each project folder is a `Makefile`. You need to edit this file, as follows, so that the correct OS-specific `include` file is used:

```
## TODO: EDIT next set of lines according to OS

include ../CONFIG/windows.inc
#include ../CONFIG/linux.inc
```

To build a project, simply call `nmake` on Windows, or `make` on Linux.

Project Targets

The `Makefile` has a number of different targets that can be built (see Table 16-3).

After building any of the `hotspot`, `concurrency`, or `datarace` targets, you can examine the results by using Amplifier XE (for `hotspot` and `concurrency`) or Inspector XE (for `datarace`) to view the results. See the section "Viewing the Results" for more information.

TABLE 16-3: The Targets in the Makefile

TARGET	DESCRIPTION
<no target>	Builds an executable, `main.exe`. To change the name, use `TARGET` `flag` (for example, `make TARGET=test` produces a file `test.exe`).
`benchmark`	Calls the benchmark.
`hotspot`	Calls the command-line version of Amplifier XE to do a hotspot analysis.
`concurrency`	Calls the command-line version of Amplifier XE to do a concurrency analysis.
`datarace`	Calls the command-line version of Inspector XE to look for data races and deadlocks.
`clean`	Deletes objects and the .exe.

An Example Build

Always call `make clean` (for Windows, use `nmake clean`) before doing any build. Here's an example of creating and running the benchmark on a Windows platform:

```
>cd 16-1-ORGFILES
>nmake clean
>nmake benchmark
<... output from compiler here ... (deleted for brevity)>
        main.exe 100000000

Dhrystone Benchmark, Version 2.1 (Language: C)

Program compiled without 'register' attribute

Execution starts, 100000000 runs through Dhrystone
Execution ends

Final values of the variables used in the benchmark:

Int_Glob:            5
        should be:   5
Bool_Glob:           1
        should be:   1
Ch_1_Glob:           A
        should be:   A
Ch_2_Glob:           B
        should be:   B
Arr_1_Glob[8]:       7
        should be:   7
Arr_2_Glob[8][7]:    100000010
```

```
        should be:    Number_Of_Runs + 10
Ptr_Glob->
  Ptr_Comp:           5991072
        should be:    (implementation-dependent)
  Discr:              0
        should be:    0
  Enum_Comp:          2
        should be:    2
  Int_Comp:           17
        should be:    17
  Str_Comp:           DHRYSTONE PROGRAM, SOME STRING
        should be:    DHRYSTONE PROGRAM, SOME STRING
Next_Ptr_Glob->
  Ptr_Comp:           5991072
        should be:    (implementation-dependent), same as above
  Discr:              0
        should be:    0
  Enum_Comp:          1
        should be:    1
  Int_Comp:           18
        should be:    18
  Str_Comp:           DHRYSTONE PROGRAM, SOME STRING
        should be:    DHRYSTONE PROGRAM, SOME STRING
Int_1_Loc:            5
        should be:    5
Int_2_Loc:            13
        should be:    13
Int_3_Loc:            7
        should be:    7
Enum_Loc:             1
        should be:    1
Str_1_Loc:            DHRYSTONE PROGRAM, 1'ST STRING
        should be:    DHRYSTONE PROGRAM, 1'ST STRING
Str_2_Loc:            DHRYSTONE PROGRAM, 2'ND STRING
        should be:    DHRYSTONE PROGRAM, 2'ND STRING

Microseconds for one run through Dhrystone:   0.040
Dhrystones per Second:                        25000000.0
```

The call to `nmake benchmark` did two things: it built the benchmark, and then it ran the benchmark, passing in the value 100000000, which was used to control the number of iterations the benchmark ran.

After the benchmark runs, it checks that the values held in the various variables are correct, printing out messages confirming their value. The last piece of information displayed is how many Dhrystones per second was achieved.

Adding Amplifier XE APIs to Timestamp the Dhrystone Loop

To help measure the duration of the benchmark more accurately, Amplifier XE API calls have been added to the `for` loop in Activities 16-2 to 16-6. This enables Amplifier XE's data collector to record the time between the two points.

```
main()
{
// initialize Amplifier XE frame domain
```

```
    __itt_domain* pD = __itt_domain_create( "My Domain" );
    pD->flags = 1; // enable domain
  .
  .
  .
    __itt_frame_begin_v3(pD, NULL);  // record start
    for(...)
    {
      // body of loop
    }
    __itt_frame_begin_v3(pD, NULL); // record end
}
```

If you are using Windows, you will get more accurate timing results from Amplifier XE's collector if you run the application in administrator mode. To do this, open a compiler command prompt (via Start ➪ All Programs ➪ Intel Parallel Studio XE ➪ Command Prompt) in administrator mode, as shown in Figure 16-2.

FIGURE 16-2: Opening a command prompt as Administrator in Windows

Viewing the Results

To view the results of a `hotspot` or `concurrency` target, open the results file with the GUI versions of Amplifier XE. To view the results of a `datarace` target, use Inspector XE. You can also use the command-line version to give you a report. For example, to build the WRAPEVERYTHING projects and run a `concurrency` analysis:

```
>cd 16-5-WRAPEVERYTHING
>nmake concurrency
<... output from compiler here ... (deleted for brevity)>
<>
Microsoft (R) Program Maintenance Utility Version 9.00.30729.01
Copyright (C) Microsoft Corporation.  All rights reserved.

    amplxe-cl -collect concurrency -knob collect-signals=true -follow-child
```

```
-mrte-mode=auto -target-duration-type=short -no-allow-multiple-runs -no-analyze
-system  -data-limit=100 -slow-frames-threshold=40 -fast-frames-threshold=100 --
  ./main.exe 100000000 SILENT
0.9300 Elapsed Secs
Using result path `C:\dv\CH16\16-5-WRAPEVERYTHING\r000cc'
Executing actions 75 % Generating a report
Summary
-------


Average Concurrency:   12.710
Elapsed Time:          1.308
CPU Time:              15.551
Wait Time:             6.228
Executing actions 100 % done
```

Notice that the command-line collector reports which directory the results are stored in:

```
Using result path 'C:\dv\CH16\16-5-WRAPEVERYTHING\r000cc'
```

You can view the results by calling the GUI version of Amplifier XE from the command line:

```
amplxe-gui ./r000cc
```

In the bottom-up view of the results, you can read the Frame Time if you group the results by Frame Domain, Frame Type, Function, or Call Stack (which is available from the Grouping pull-down menu), as shown in Figure 16-3.

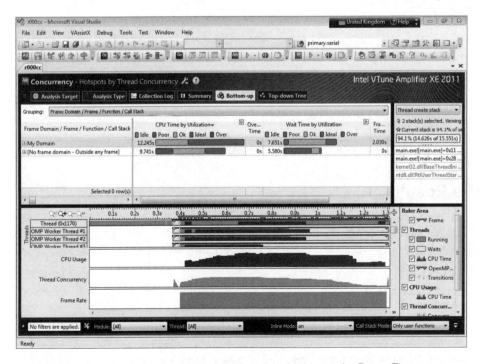

FIGURE 16-3: View the timestamp for the benchmark by looking at the Frame Time

ACTIVITY 16-1: BUILDING THE SERIAL VERSION

In this activity you perform a system-wide analysis to see how well the programs are running on your machine. You can run this activity on Linux or Windows.

Building the Project

1. If you haven't already done so, download a copy of the project files and navigate to the `16-1-ORGFILES` folder:

```
cd 16-1-ORGFILES
```

2. Edit the `Makefile` so that the correct include file is used.

WINDOWS

```
include ../CONFIG/windows.inc
```

LINUX

```
include ../CONFIG/linux.inc
```

3. Build the serial project:

WINDOWS

Open a Parallel Studio XE command prompt by selecting Start ⇨ All programs Intel Parallel Studio XE 2011 ⇨ Command Prompt ⇨ Parallel Studio XE ⇨ Command Prompt ⇨ <command prompt>. The exact location may vary, depending on which version of Parallel Studio XE you installed.

```
nmake clean
nmake
```

LINUX

```
make clean
make
```

If there is build error, edit the `*.inc` file mentioned in step 2 so that the variable VTUNEDIR is correctly pointing to your Amplifier XE installation directory.

Measuring Performance

4. Run the program and record how many Dhrystones were achieved:

WINDOWS

```
nmake benchmark
```

LINUX

```
make benchmark
```

If you see the message `Measured time too small to obtain meaningful results Please increase number of runs`, then edit the `Makefile` and increase the value assigned to the variable `LOOPCOUNT`.

PARALLELIZING THE C VERSION

In this section, the original C code of the benchmark is parallelized using OpenMP. You can build the completed versions in Activity 16-2 and 16-3. Two attempts are made at parallelizing:

➤ The first attempt looks at synchronizing all the access to shared variables.

➤ The second attempt duplicates the global variables so that each running thread has its own thread-specific copy.

Before diving into each attempt, it's a good idea to find out how many data races need to be fixed. You can do this by making the `for` loop of the benchmark parallel using the `#pragma omp parallel for` construct, and then running Inspector XE to find out how many data races exist.

Figure 16-4 shows a list of data races that are produced using this naïve parallelization step. The program has 18 data races and also an unhandled exception. It looks as though there is quite of lot of work to be done for such a small program!

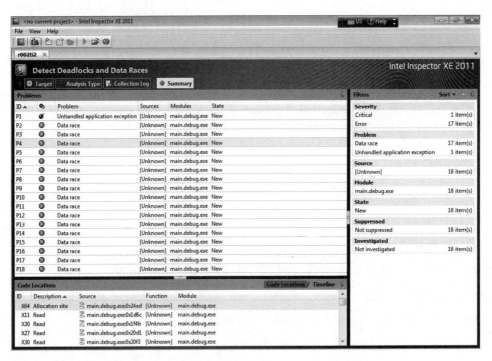

FIGURE 16-4: Inspector XE shows the data races to fix

Attempt One: Synchronizing Shared Variable Access

In the first attempt, the benchmark was made parallel in three steps, as shown in Figure 16-5. You can examine the results of these code changes in Activity 16-1.

1. The main loop is made parallel by adding a `#pragma parallel omp for` loop.

2. Each shared variable is either made `private` or, where this isn't possible, accesses are synchronized.

3. The result is displayed. Values of local variables in the threaded section are propagated back into the main part of the program by adding a `lastprivate` clause to the `for` loop.

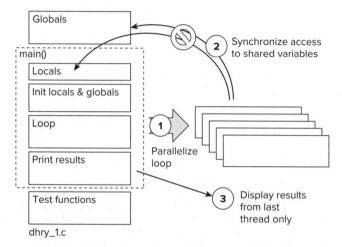

dhry_1.c

FIGURE 16-5: The steps to parallelizing with OpenMP

The following code snippet shows the OpenMP constructs used to parallelize the loop. Each variable marked as `lastprivate` has its final value copied back to the original shared variables.

```
#pragma omp parallel for lastprivate(Int_1_Loc,Int_2_Loc,Int_3_Loc, \
  Enum_Loc,Str_1_Loc,Str_2_Loc) private(Ch_Index,tmp_Glob)
for (Run_Index = 1; Run_Index <= Number_Of_Runs; ++Run_Index)
{
  .
  .
}
```

Any access to shared variables that could not be made private were declared to be a critical section. This allows only one thread to operate on the variable at any time:

```
#pragma omp critical
Int_Glob = Run_Index;
```

It was difficult and at times tedious to add these critical sections. At one stage a deadlock was accidentally introduced because of the function nesting in the benchmark. Luckily, Inspector XE detected this.

The Results

The new parallel program runs very slow, with each Dhrystone taking more than 300 microseconds to complete:

```
Microseconds for one run through Dhrystone:  300.0
Dhrystones per Second:                       3333.3
```

The Amplifier XE data collector generates so much data that it issues the following warning:

```
Warning: The result contains a lot of raw data. Finalization may take a long
time to complete.
```

Changing the loop count from 1,000,000 to 1,000 reduces the amount of data generated to a manageable size.

Figure 16-6 shows the Dhrystones per second that are achieved for different numbers of threads. The number of threads is changed using the OMP_NUM_THREADS environment variable.

Notice that the moment more than one thread is used, the Dhrystones figures dives to well under 10,000.

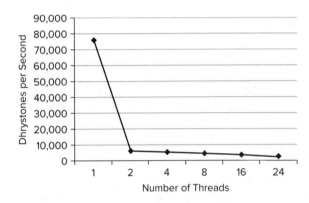

FIGURE 16-6: The performance of the OpenMP version

The summary page of the Locks and Waits analysis shows what the problem is. (The summary page opens when you first do an analysis; you can also reach it by clicking on the Summary button.) As shown in Figure 16-7, the Spin Time is excessive. Looking at the list of top waiting objects, you can see that the OMP Critical sync object is the cause if the poor performance.

Elapsed Time: 3.599s

Total Thread Count:	24
Wait Time:	70.870s
Spin Time:	62.563s

A significant portion of CPU time is spent waiting. Use this metric to c wait parameters, changing the lock implementation (for example, by

Wait Count:	120,088
CPU Time:	64.462s
Paused Time:	0s

Top Waiting Objects

This section lists the objects that spent the most time waiting in your app contended synchronizations. A significant amount of Wait time associat and, thus, reduced parallelism.

Sync Object	Wait Time	Wait Count
OMP Critical main:159 0x3e72241d	65.923s	119,990
OMP Join Barrier main:154 0x919eac2a	4.932s	23
Stream 0x9c5baeba	0.009s	62
Manual Reset Event 0x4a9f7567	0.002s	2
Multiple Objects	0.002s	2
[Others]	0.001s	9

FIGURE 16-7: Spin Time is the biggest problem

An expanded view of the time line shows that only one thread runs at once, and it spends more time waiting than running (see Figure 16-8). The dark areas on the horizontal bars are when the thread is running; the lighter areas are where the threads are waiting.

Despite having 24 threads available, this part of the code is only ever running on one thread at a time, with all the other threads in a wait condition.

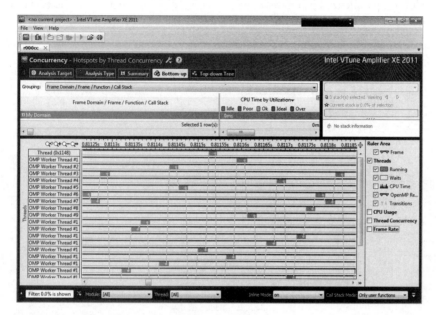

FIGURE 16-8: The expanded timeline view

Is It Successful?

In a word, no! Synchronizing the many shared variables does not seem to be a good solution. The code ends up running significantly slower than the serial version.

From an editing perspective, nearly every function of the benchmark had to be modified. It would be a painful task to replicate this effort on a larger project.

This approach does not seem too helpful. The next attempt at parallelization tries to remove the need for synchronization by duplicating the shared variables.

ACTIVITY 16-2: USING OPENMP WITH SYNCHRONIZATION

In this activity you perform a system-wide analysis to see how well the programs are running on your machine. You can run this activity on Linux or Windows.

1. Navigate to the `16-2-OMP-C` folder:

```
cd 16-2-OMP-C
```

2. Repeat steps 2 to 6 of Activity 16-1.

Attempt Two: Duplicating Global Variables

The first attempt to parallelize the code was unsuccessful, with the parallel program running much slower than the nonthreaded version. This second attempt duplicates all the global variables, so there is no need to protect access to them with a critical section. The steps are as follows (see Figure 16-9):

1. The main `for` loop is parallelized using the `#pragma omp for` construct. As in the previous attempt, the local variables are declared as `private` or `lastprivate`.

2. The global variables are duplicated in an array of structures.

3. Each reference to the global variables is edited.

4. The results are displayed from only one thread.

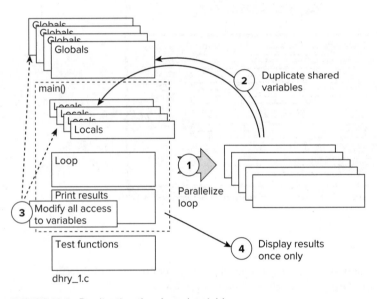

FIGURE 16-9: Duplicating the shared variables

The following code shows how the global variables are changed into a structure and placed in `dhry.h`. The highlighted part is an identical copy of the original global variables, copied from `dhry_1.c`.

```
// Structure to duplicate globals (declared in dhry.h)
typedef struct _globals
{
    Rec_Pointer     Ptr_Glob, Next_Ptr_Glob;
    int             Int_Glob;
    Boolean         Bool_Glob;
    char            Ch_1_Glob, Ch_2_Glob;
    int             Arr_1_Glob [50];
    int             Arr_2_Glob [50] [50];
} GLOB_STRUCT;
```

A new pointer, `Ptr_Glob_Arr`, is used to point to an array of the `struct _globals`. Memory is dynamically allocated using the OpenMP API calls `omp_get_max_threads()` and `omp_set_num_thread()` to make sure that the right amount of space is allocated:

```
// Allocating enough space for each thread
num_threads = omp_get_max_threads();
omp_set_num_threads(num_threads);
Ptr_Glob_Arr = malloc(sizeof(GLOB_STRUCT) * num_threads);
```

Initializing and Accessing the Global Variables

Each copy of the global variables must be initialized in every OpenMP thread (see the following highlighted code). Wherever the global variables are referenced in the source code, a new level of indirection is added so that each thread can access its own copy of the variables. The omp_get_thread_num() function is used to get the index of the current thread.

```
#pragma omp parallel private (id)
{
  // set pointer to current globals
  id = omp_get_thread_num();

  Ptr_Glob_Arr[id].Next_Ptr_Glob = (Rec_Pointer) malloc (sizeof (Rec_Type));
  Ptr_Glob_Arr[id].Ptr_Glob = (Rec_Pointer) malloc (sizeof (Rec_Type));

  #pragma omp barrier

  #pragma omp for  private(Run_Index) firstprivate(Str_1_Loc,Number_Of_Runs)
    lastprivate (Int_1_Loc,Int_2_Loc,Int_3_Loc,Ch_Index,Enum_Loc,Str_1_Loc,Str_2_Loc)
  for (Run_Index = 1; Run_Index <= Number_Of_Runs; ++Run_Index)
  {
    // other code here
  }
  .
  .
  .
} // end parallel region
```

The Results

The newly built application runs much better than the application from the first attempt, and has good scalability. The big disadvantage of this approach is the time taken to modify the files. Figure 16-10 shows the results of running the tests on a workstation that supports 24 cores.

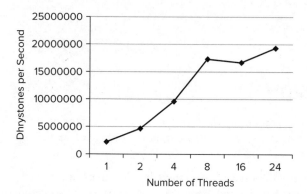

FIGURE 16-10: The performance of the duplicated variables version

Figure 16-11 shows the summary page from Amplifier XE. The number of simultaneously running threads is ideal, with between 20 and 24 threads running together most of the time, for an average concurrency of just under 18.

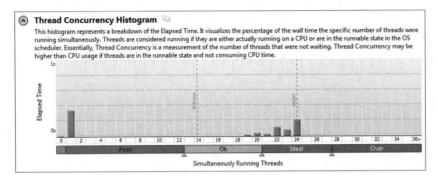

FIGURE 16-11: The concurrency of the duplicated variables version

Is It Successful?

Yes and no! Duplicating the shared variables works well and gives vast improvement when compared to attempt 1. However, from an editing perspective, not only nearly every function of the benchmark had to be modified, but also nearly every line. (A slight exaggeration, but it felt that way.) The editing task felt significantly more onerous that in attempt 1.

This approach seems more helpful than the first attempt, but the editing effort is considerable. In the next attempt at parallelization, the benchmark is converted to C++ and then encapsulated into a C++ class.

ACTIVITY 16-3: USING OPENMP WITH DUPLICATED VARIABLES

In this activity you perform a system-wide analysis to see how well the programs are running on your machine. You can run this activity on Linux or Windows.

1. Navigate to the 16-3-OMP-DUP folder:

```
cd 16-3-OMP-DUP
```

2. Repeat steps 2 to 6 of Activity 16-1.

PARALLELIZING THE C++ VERSION

The original benchmark is written using C files; renaming the files to have a C++ extension will make it easier to experiment with other threading models as well as take advantage of some C++-specific features such as classes and automatic variables.

It would be nice when changing legacy code if you only had to change the file extension to .cpp. With some legacy code, this is possible; unfortunately, the Dhrystone benchmark is not so straightforward. The benchmark uses old-style K&R programming, with its obsolete calling convention, lack of function prototypes, and missing return types in the function definitions. All of these problems have to be fixed before the code can be successfully compiled.

In the next two parallelization attempts, the C++ version of the benchmark is used, first using OpenMP and then using Cilk Plus.

ACTIVITY 16-4: BUILDING THE C++ VERSION OF DHRYSTONE

In this activity you perform a system-wide analysis to see how well the programs are running on your machine. You can run this activity on Linux or Windows.

1. Navigate to the 16-4-CPPFILES folder:

```
cd 16-4-CPPFILES
```

2. Repeat steps 2 to 6 of Activity 16-1.

Attempt Three: Wrapping the Application in a C++ Class

Moving to C++ means that it becomes relatively easy to wrap the whole Dhrystone application in a single class and then instantiate multiple instances of the class in its own thread. By doing this, fewer code changes should be needed. The steps are as follows (see Figure 16-12):

1. A class is declared in dhry_1.cpp that encapsulates the complete source code.

2. dhry_2.cpp is incorporated into dhry_1.cpp by way of an include statement.

3. A new file, driver.cpp, is written that pulls in dhry_1.cpp via an include statement.

4. Within an OpenMP for loop, multiple instances of the new class are created. The loop is designed to iterate the same amount of times as the number of threads available.

5. The dhystone::main() method is called from each iteration of the loop.

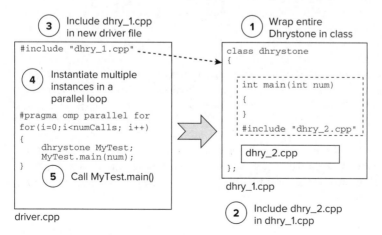

FIGURE 16-12 The steps to wrap the application

Using the #include statement to pull in the different source files is quite a nice trick, but it has one negative side effect for the benchmark. If you remember, the Dhrystone benchmark is intentionally split across two files so that inter-module access can be tested. The build instructions that come with Dhrystone say that the compiler must not do any cross-file inlining. By using the #include statements, all such inter-module access is removed, thus breaking one of the design goals of the benchmark.

Scheduling the Parallel Runs

In good parallel programming, you should not be asking how many threads you have; good parallel programs should be agnostic about the number of threads available. The following code iterates through each loop, with each loop running on a separate thread. The number of iterations can be overridden by a command-line parameter, read from argv[3]. The schedule(static,1) clause instructs the OpenMP run time to schedule each loop to a separate thread.

```
int main(int argc, char * argv[])
{
  int NumCalls = omp_get_max_threads();
  int NumDhrystoneLoops = 1000001;
  bool bSilent = false;
  .
  .
  .
  if(argc == 4)
    NumCalls = atoi(argv[3]);
  double start = wtime();
  #pragma omp parallel for schedule(static,1)
  for(int i = 1; i <= NumCalls; i++)
  {
    int num = NumDhrystoneLoops/NumCalls;
    if (i ==NumCalls)
      num += NumDhrystoneLoops % NumCalls ;
    dhrystone MyTest;
    printf("running with %d\n",num);
    MyTest.main(num,bSilent);
  }
  double stop = wtime();
  printf("%4.4f Elapsed Secs\n",stop - start);
}
```

The number of Dhrystone loops each parallel test does is calculated by dividing the number of Dhrystone tests stored in NumDhystoneLoops by the number of iterations that will be performed.

Silencing the Output

One of the consequences of wrapping the whole of the original main() function in a new class is that the code to print out the results is also run multiple times. To minimize the clutter on the output, an extra Boolean flag is added to the code to control whether the results are printed to the screen:

```
class
{
  void main (int num,__itt_event & Event,bool bSilent)
  {
  .
  .
  .
  // compiler will not optimize this away, because it cannot know at compiler time
  // what the value of bSilent will be.
  if(!bSilent)
  {
    printf ("etc\n");
  }
  .
  .
  .
  }
}
```

If you remember, one of the reasons for having the output printed to the screen is to stop any optimizing compiler from removing what it considers to be unused code. Without the printfs, the compiler will see that some of the results of the benchmark are not used and optimize away most of the code. By using a Boolean variable that is initialized at run time using a scanf, the compiler will not strip away most of the code, because it cannot know at compile time whether or not the printfs are being used.

The Results

Figure 16-13 shows the results running with different threads on a 24-core machine. There is still a measure of scalability, but the performance is poorer than the previous attempt. The spike at 16 threads is probably an anomaly. Running the tests several times gave results that varied by more than 20 percent.

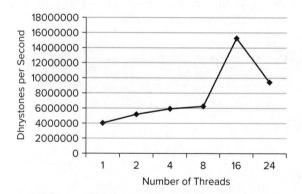

FIGURE 16-13: The results of the wrapped application

Figure 16-14 is a timeline view of the application. If you look at the thread concurrency bar (the one next to the bottom bar), you will notice that concurrency is not uniform. In the first and last quarters of the time period, concurrency is low. It looks like many of the threads do not start straight-away or finish together.

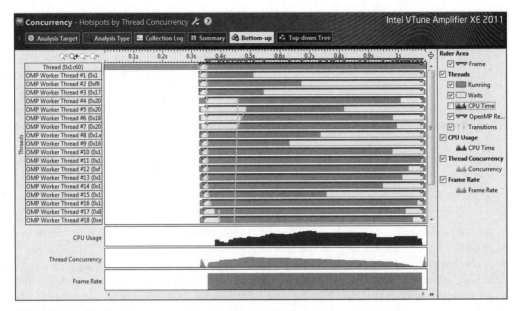

FIGURE 16-14: The time-line view of the wrapped application

Is It Successful?

Well, sort of. The application displayed scalability, but the rate of change is much poorer than the previous attempt. And the editing effort required was moderate and required less effort than the previous two attempts.

Some more work needs to be done on this project. If the threading can be tuned so that it has a much punchier start and finish, the performance would improve.

> **ACTIVITY 16-5: WRAPPING THE APPLICATION IN A C++ CLASS**
>
> In this activity you perform a system-wide analysis to see how well the programs are running on your machine. You can run this activity on Linux or Windows.
>
> **1.** Navigate to the `16-5-WRAPEVERYTHING` folder:
>
> ```
> cd 16-5-WRAPEVERYTHING
> ```
>
> **2.** Repeat steps 2 to 6 of Activity 16-1.

Attempt Four: Using Cilk Plus Holders

One of the main concerns when adding a new feature to a piece of code is the amount of time it takes and the extent of the code changes. The less code has to be changed, the less likely the risk of introducing errors.

The Cilk Plus parallelization of the Dhrystone benchmark is a good example of where the simplicity of Cilk Plus can be combined with the powerfulness of the C++ language (such as templates and overloading) to add parallelism to legacy code with very few changes required in the original code.

The steps to introduce Cilk Plus holders into the benchmark are as follows (see Figure 16-15):

1. The main loop is parallelized using the keyword `cilk_for`.

2. A set of wrapper classes is written that act as the interface between a `cilk::holder` and the shared variables.

3. Each shared variable is declared to be one of the new `myholder` wrappers.

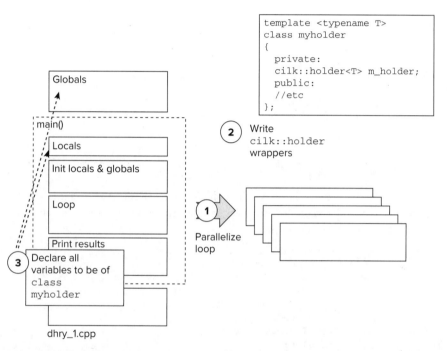

```
template <typename T>
class myholder
{
    private:
    cilk::holder<T> m_holder;
    public:
    //etc
};
```

FIGURE 16-15: The steps to introduce Cilk Plus holders into the application

Developing the Wrappers

In the three previous examples of parallelizing the benchmark, the shared variables were either reduced in scope, their access locked, or the variables duplicated. For the purpose of the benchmark, duplicating the variables is a legitimate approach and has proved to be the best performing solution.

Cilk Plus Hyperobjects

Cilk Plus's hyperobjects are designed to help fix data race problems associated with shared variables. In the case of the Dhrystone benchmark, the `cilk::holder` objects can be used to provide local variables for each worker (that is, each thread). Holders are discussed in Chapter 6, "Where to Parallelize."

Listing 16-1 shows how a wrapper can be placed around a `cilk::holder` object to provide almost transparent local storage. It is transparent in the sense that very little of the legacy code needs to be changed to use the wrapper class.

Without these wrappers, every access to the global variables would have to be modified to call the function operator. As you can see, however, the use of the function operator is hidden in the overloaded operators of the class `myholder`. For example, `operator->` calls the `m_holder()` function operator in the implementation code.

LISTING 16-1: Wrapper code for the Cilk Plus holder

```cpp
#include <cilk/holder.h>
#include "dhry.h"
template <typename T>
class myholder
{
  private:
    cilk::holder<T> m_holder;
  public:
    T & operator->(){return m_holder();}
    myholder<T> & operator=(const T &rhs ){m_holder()=rhs;return *this;}
    myholder<T> & operator +=(const T &rhs ){m_holder()+=rhs;return *this;}
    T * operator &(){return &(m_holder());}
    operator T (){return m_holder();}
    void operator ++(){m_holder()++;}
};
```

code snippet Chapter16\16-1.cpp

In the benchmark code, the only changes that have to be made are to change the declaration of the shared variables. For example, in the following code snippet, the original global variables are replaced with holder wrappers of the same name:

```cpp
#if 0                        // original globals
Rec_Pointer                  Ptr_Glob, Next_Ptr_Glob;
int                          Int_Glob;
Boolean                      Bool_Glob;
char                         Ch_1_Glob, Ch_2_Glob;
#else                        // new code
myholder<Rec_Pointer>        Ptr_Glob,Next_Ptr_Glob;
myholder<int>                Int_Glob;
myholder<Boolean>            Bool_Glob;
myholder<char>               Ch_1_Glob, Ch_2_Glob;
#endif
```

Arrays require slightly more complicated treatment, because you cannot return an array in C/C++. Some of the derived classes in the `cilk::holder` class expect to return objects, so arrays need to be encapsulated.

Listing 16-2 shows how single-dimensional arrays are handled. A similar holder will also need to be constructed for two-dimensional arrays (see `holder.h` in the example project).

LISTING 16-2: An array holder

```cpp
template <typename T, int SZ>
struct CArrayOneDimension
{
  T Data[SZ];
```

```
};

template <typename T, int SZ>
class array_holder
{
  private:
    cilk::holder<CArrayOneDimension<T,SZ>> m_holder;
  public:
    operator T* (){return m_holder().Data;}
};
```

Listing 16-3 shows the declaration of the original global variable `Arr_1_Glob` with the new holder version underneath:

LISTING 16-3: A two-dimensional array holder

```
// int                 Arr_1_Glob [50];
array_holder<int,50> Arr_1_Glob;


template <typename T, int SZ1, int SZ2>
struct CArrayTwoDimension
{
  T Data[SZ1][SZ2];
};


template <typename T, int SZ1,int SZ2>
class array_2_holder
{
  private:
    cilk::holder<CArrayTwoDimension<T,SZ1,SZ2>> m_holder;
  public:
    operator Arr_2_Dim &(){return m_holder().Data;}
    T* operator[](const T x){return m_holder().Data[x];}
};
```

Initializing the Global Variables

The original initialization code for the global variables sits outside the main `for` loop. To make the initialization be on a per-thread basis, the code is moved to sit inside the new parallel loop (see the following code snippet). One new holder variable, `myholder<bool> bInitialized`, is introduced outside the loop. On instantiation all the different worker views of the variable will be automatically initialized to false. As each new Cilk Plus worker enters the loop for the first time, it will see that bInitialized is false, and therefore execute the initialization code. On subsequent iterations of the loop by the same worker, the initialization code will not be run because its view of bInitialized will have been set to true.

In the same code snippet, you can see that the local variables are moved from the top of the main() function to be within the cilk_for loop. This has the desired effect of making the variables thread-specific.

```
myholder<bool> bInitialized;
cilk_for(int Run_Index = 1; Run_Index < Number_Of_Runs+1; ++Run_Index)
{
    // locals moved from beginning of main
    One_Fifty        Int_1_Loc;
    REG   One_Fifty Int_2_Loc;
    //... etc
    // move initialization into loop
    if(!bInitialized)
    {
        Next_Ptr_Glob = (Rec_Pointer) malloc (sizeof (Rec_Type));
        Ptr_Glob = (Rec_Pointer) malloc (sizeof (Rec_Type));
        // ... etc
        bInitialized = true;
    }
    // ... rest of for loop
}
```

The Results

Figure 16-16 shows the results of the Cilk Plus version. The performance dips, because the number of threads is the same as the number of cores available on the workstation that was used.

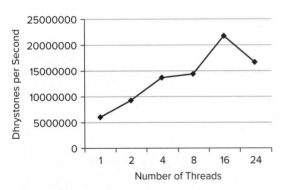

FIGURE 16-16: The performance using Cilk Plus

Is It Successful?

In one word, yes (well, almost yes). The performance is still less than the serial version, but the programming is scalable, with a decent rate of change; the editing effort on the original source files is minor; and the fact that the shared variable references stay exactly as they are (you only change the declarations of the variables) makes this solution extremely attractive.

OVERVIEW OF THE RESULTS

The main interest in the results of the different parallelization efforts is performance and editing effort. Ideally, there should be a performance improvement without having to completely rewrite the original source code.

Performance

You can use two metrics — speedup and scalability — to measure an application's performance. The speedup metric is expressed by the number of Dhrystones executed in one second. Scalability can be observed by plotting a graph of the improved speed as the number of threads is increased.

Figure 16-17 shows how many Dhrystones per second were executed in the main `for` loop of the benchmark program; the bigger the figure, the better the performance. You can see the following:

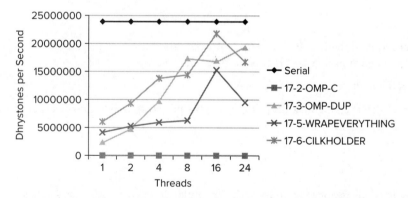

FIGURE 16-17: The Dhrystone results of the parallelized benchmark

➤   The serial version (the top line on the graph) runs better than any of the parallel versions. The root cause of this is the lack of sufficient work being executed in the Dhrystone tests, combined with the excessive use of shared variables.

➤   The best performing parallel version is the one using Cilk Plus holders.

➤ The two most scalable solutions are the Cilk Plus holders and the OpenMP duplicated variables.

➤ The OpenMP version using synchronization does not scale and has terrible performance.

Editing Effort

One of the goals of this exercise was to keep any code changes to a minimum. The benchmark is quite small, so the total coding effort is quite small. Table 16-4 shows the number of words that were changed in adding the parallelism. Because the main measure should be how much the original code has been changed, the new files that have been added have not been included in Changes column.

TABLE 16-4: Editing Effort

BUILD	WORDS	CHANGES	NEW FILE
ORG	4800	0	0
HOLDER*	4934	105	149
WRAPEVERYTHING*	4979	112	159
OMP	4894	114	0
CPP	4871	171	0
OMP-DUP	4938	302	0

*Compared to CPP file

You can see the following:

➤ The solution that required the fewest changes to the original legacy code (if you ignore the effort of making the benchmark a C++ file) is the HOLDER project.

➤ The OMP-DUP has the highest number of changes.

➤ If you consider the cost of changing a project to C++, the projects needing the fewest changes are WRAPEVERYTHING and OMP.

SUMMARY

Adding parallelism to legacy code is not easy; indeed, the examples you saw in this case study show how hard it can be. Given a sufficient workload, it should be possible to incrementally parallelize your old code, using tools such as Amplifier XE and Inspector XE to help verify that the parallelism is correct and optimal. Cilk Plus holders stand out as an interesting way of dealing with global variables without demanding many changes to the original source code.

The case study in the next chapter shows you how to parallelize a program for finding duplicate code blocks using Intel Parallel Advisor XE.

INDEX